Global Perspectives on Youth Language Practices

Contributions to the Sociology of Language

Edited by
Ofelia García
Francis M. Hult

Founding editor
Joshua A. Fishman

Volume 119

Global Perspectives on Youth Language Practices

Edited by
Cynthia Groff, Andrea Hollington, Ellen Hurst-Harosh,
Nico Nassenstein, Jacomine Nortier, Helma Pasch
and Nurenzia Yannuar

DE GRUYTER
MOUTON

ISBN 978-1-5015-2222-2
e-ISBN (PDF) 978-1-5015-1468-5
e-ISBN (EPUB) 978-1-5015-1477-7
ISSN 1861-0676

Library of Congress Control Number: 2021952137

Bibliographic information published by the Deutsche Nationalbibliothek
The Deutsche Nationalbibliothek lists this publication in the Deutsche Nationalbibliografie;
detailed bibliographic data are available on the Internet at http://dnb.dnb.de.

© 2023 Walter de Gruyter Inc., Boston/Berlin
This volume is text- and page-identical with the hardback published in 2022.
Cover image: sculpies/shutterstock
Typesetting: Integra Software Services Pvt. Ltd.
Printing and binding: CPI books GmbH, Leck

www.degruyter.com

Foreword

Youth languages are important. They reveal, often simultaneously, how language works and how young people express themselves. One may perceive a youth language as a pressure cooker of high-speed renewal, perfectly equipped to help us understand language change more broadly. Couched in the dominant language of its city or region of origin, the expanded, modified, and substituted lexicon of a youth language can become so abundant that its grammatical skeleton is hidden like a tree overgrown by ivy. To study youth languages is to study the linguistic norms of tomorrow. They show us what speakers can and cannot do when they take control over language. The choices they make, consciously or semiconsciously, are charged with meaning and express how young people position themselves in society through their conversation. It is not surprising, then, that efforts to study youth language have become global, hosting multiple approaches. One particularly popular theme is how youth languages can spread beyond the street, beyond the subcultures of the urban youth, and how they enter mainstream language use. Sheng of Kenya, for example, has expanded its domains of usage so widely that it nearly functions as a full-fledged language. Such processes reveal how new languages can emerge from existing ones – not through the pidgin-creole route, and not through a slow linguistic differentiation out of variation, but akin to a caterpillar becoming a butterfly.

The differences and commonalities in youth language phenomena across the world thus offer a rewarding area of research, to which this edited volume has allowed us to contribute. Its chapters came, to a large extent, out of the *8th International Conference on Youth Languages*, held on May 24 to 26, 2019, at Leiden University. In comparison to previous events, the conference had an emphasis on the youth languages of Africa and Asia, in addition to those of Europe. This regional focus is well motivated by the richness of youth languages in these parts of the world. If we can be forgiven for generalizing, the speakers from the African and Asian settings highlighted in this volume have taken language play and linguistic appropriation to a whole new level, supported in their efforts by a much larger part of society compared to, say, youth language speakers in Europe. On average, cities in Africa and southern Asia have a higher social media penetration and lower median age than elsewhere. Youth languages can be heard ubiquitously: at university campuses, in shopping malls, on screen, in popular songs, in the countryside, in the diaspora, and online. Arguably, some have now become native tongues.

Research on youth languages has seen a number of interesting developments. In the past decade, the field experienced a remarkable boost accompanied by dedicated conferences and edited volumes.¹ Particularly in the context of Africa, it gained momentum with a series of conferences held in Cologne (2012), Cape Town (2013), Nairobi (2015), and Ivory Coast (2017).² Yet the academic study of youth language in Africa has older roots.³ Initially the main focus was on reporting the existence of the phenomenon in a particular city. Kießling & Mous (2004) made a first attempt at comparing the youth languages of a number of different cities in Africa and noted the commonalities in formation and function. A lot of discussion in the early literature focused on the best linguistic label: pidgin, creole, slang, etc. Later studies addressed sociolinguistic aspects and the development of youth languages beyond the city and beyond the conventional domain of rebellious youth. Youth languages indeed entered the mainstream media – including advertisements, radio and television – and researchers reported on that. The spread of youth languages through music and poetry has also become a popular theme of study. Whereas the social aspects of youth language use have for some time been central in studies on the European situation – using terminology such as *crossing* and *translanguaging* – they received less attention in the contexts of Africa and Asia. This research gap has recently started to improve for several African settings. The effect of youth language on the educational system has also become a matter of concern and debate (Hurst-Harosh 2020b).

Cumulatively, these developments underline the importance and centrality of Africa – and presumably parts of Asia as well – in understanding the phenomenon of youth language in its full diversity. In the near future, we hope and expect that more methodologies will be developed in these regions, rather than solely in the confines of Global North universities. The greatest challenge at present is a lack of empirical data. From the beginning of youth language studies in Africa, data have often been anecdotal. Much of the collected data have furthermore been numerical – on language use, attitude and knowledge – but only rarely included the rich, annotated, video-taped data of natural conversations required to arrive at a fuller understanding of the phenomenon being researched. A logical next step would be to compile more corpora and make them available for research.

The recent burgeoning of conferences and edited volumes have furthermore made it clear that youth languages are not restricted to a number of cities in Africa but exist all over the continent and are used in rural areas as well. A similar situation

---

1 For example, Nortier and Svendsen (2015), Jørgensen (2010), and Drummond (2018).
2 These events have yielded numerous edited volumes (Hurst-Harosh and Kanana Erastus 2018, Atindogbé and Ebongue 2019, Nassenstein and Hollington 2015). Additional recent publications include Ebongue and Hurst (2017), Hurst-Harosh (2020a, 2020b), Hollington and Nassenstein (2017), Brookes (2014, 2019), and Barasa and Mous (2017).
3 Ebongue and Atindogbé (2019) provide a detailed overview of African youth languages.

has been reported for parts of Asia (Djenar 2015). Typologically, the youth languages of Asia and Africa seem to have a lot in common and less so with those of Europe, where ethnicity and class exhibit rather different social functions. Interestingly, the kinds of playful, deviant youth languages of Africa and some parts of southern Asia – most of which have their own name – have not been reported to the same degree in Latin America, North America, the Pacific, and large parts of Asia. Perhaps this chiefly reveals a lack of academic interest in documenting such phenomena. Alternatively, one might speculate that the social situations in those parts of the world differ to such an extent that they leave no fertile ground for youth codes to emerge.

Instead of regional generalizations, perhaps a focus on socio-demographic specificities might provide more fruitful ways to understand youth language as a broader linguistic phenomenon. The most obvious factor is, of course, age. In the realm of gender, the more streetwise and abusive-laden speech tends to be associated with performative masculinity. Female youth languages do exist but deserve far greater attention than they have received so far. Migration, both within a country and internationally, is clearly important too. Examples of youth languages popularized by people with migrant backgrounds abound in the literature and indeed in this volume. These are not always confined to a single ethnicity. In fact, as we see worldwide, youth languages invariably draw from multiple languages in contact. Economic differences play a role too. In Nairobi, for example, Sheng originated in the poor urban neighborhoods, whereas Engsh is spoken by more affluent communities. In Indonesia, the correlation between university cities, such as Jakarta, Malang, and Yogyakarta, and the development of youth languages is hard to miss. While English and – in some parts of the world – French continue to influence youth languages worldwide, we also see local centers of cultural orientation emerge, such as Abidjan, Jakarta, and Nairobi.

Lastly, we must stress that those who were able to attend the *8th ICYL* only reflect a fragment of all the interest we received and abstracts we accepted. Regrettably, the usual hurdles prevented many colleagues from outside Europe from making their way to Leiden: visa struggles, financial uncertainty, excessive paperwork, and last-minute rejections from their department. Nevertheless, it is palpably manifest how their studies and perspectives have enriched the field and will continue to do so in the future. We feel that our colleagues working in Africa and southern Asia, if given the same chances, are better situated to study the phenomena discussed in this volume, including beyond their own regional contexts. For this reason, it would only be appropriate that academic theorization around youth language practices will increasingly originate from the Global South.

Tom Hoogervorst and Maarten Mous
Leiden University

References

Atindogbé, Gratien Gualbert and Augustin Emmanuel Ebongue (eds.). 2019. *Perspectives linguistiques et sociolinguistiques des pratiques linguistiques jeunes en Afrique : Codes et écritures identitaires = Linguistic and sociolinguistic perspectives of youth language practices in Africa: Codes and identity writings*. Mankon, Bamenda: Langaa Research & Publishing CIG.

Barasa, Sandra N. and Maarten Mous. 2017. Engsh, a Kenyan middle class youth language parallel to Sheng. *Journal of Pidgin and Creole Languages* 32 (1). 48–74.

Brookes, Heather. 2014. Urban youth languages in South Africa: A case study of Tsotsitaal in a South African township. *Anthropological Linguistics* 56. 356–388.

Brookes, Heather. 2019. Youth language in South Africa: the role of English in South African tsotsitaals. In Raymond Hickey (ed.), *English in multilingual South Africa*, 176–195. Cambridge: Cambridge University Press.

Djenar, Dwi Noverini. 2015. *Youth language in Indonesia and Malaysia*. Jakarta: PKBB, Atma Jaya Catholic University of Indonesia.

Drummond, Rob. 2018. *Researching urban youth language and identity*. Cham: Palgrave Macmillan.

Ebongue, Augustin Emmanuel and Gratien Gualbert Atindogbé. 2019. Introduction: La linguistique et sociolinguistique des parlers jeunes / Linguistic and sociolinguistic description of youth languages. In Gratien Gualbert Atindogbé and Augustin Emmanuel Ebongue (eds.), *Perspectives linguistiques et sociolinguistiques des pratiques linguistiques jeunes en Afrique : Codes et écritures identitaires = Linguistic and sociolinguistic perspectives of youth language practices in Africa: Codes and identity writings*, ix–xxviii. Mankon: Langaa Research & Publishing CIG.

Ebongue, Augustin Emmanuel and Ellen Hurst (eds.). 2017. *Sociolinguistics in African contexts: Perspectives and challenges*. Cham: Springer.

Githiora, Chege 2018a. *Sheng: Rise of a Kenyan Swahili vernacular*. Woodbridge: James Currey.

Githiora, Chege 2018b. Sheng: The expanding domains of an urban youth vernacular. *Journal of African Cultural Studies* 30 (2). 105–120.

Hollington, Andrea and Nico Nassenstein. 2017. From the hood to public discourse: The social spread of African youth languages. *Anthropological Linguistics* 59 (4). 390–413.

Hurst-Harosh, Ellen 2020a. *Tsotsitaal in South Africa: Style and metaphor in youth language practices*. Cologne: Rüdiger Köppe.

Hurst-Harosh, Ellen 2020b. They even speak Tsotsitaal with their teachers at school: The use (and abuse) of African urban youth languages in educational contexts. *Africa Education Review* 17 (1). 35–50.

Hurst-Harosh, Ellen and Fridah Erastus Kanana (eds.). 2018. *African youth languages: New media, performing arts and sociolinguistic development*. Cham: Palgrave Macmillan.

Jørgensen, Jens Normann, 2010. *Love ya hate ya: The sociolinguistic study of youth language and youth identities*. Newcastle upon Tyne: Cambridge Scholars.

Kießling, Roland and Maarten Mous 2004. Urban youth languages in Africa. *Anthropological Linguistics* 46 (3). 303–341.

Nassenstein, Nico and Andrea Hollington 2016. Global repertoires and urban fluidity: Youth languages in Africa. *International Journal of the Sociology of Language* 242. 171–193.

Nassenstein, Nico and Andrea Hollington (eds.). 2015. *Youth language practices in Africa and beyond*. Berlin: De Gruyter Mouton.

Nortier, Jacomine and Bente Svendsen (eds.). 2015. *Language, youth and identity in the 21st century: Linguistic practices across urban spaces*. Cambridge: Cambridge University Press.

Contents

Foreword —— V

Nurenzia Yannuar, Helma Pasch, Jacomine Nortier, Nico Nassenstein,
Ellen Hurst-Harosh, Andrea Hollington and Cynthia Groff
1 Youth language research: Changing perspectives, international trends and emerging themes —— 1

Part I: Words and patterns

Chantal Tropea
2 The emergence of Bahasa Gaul: A comparative study of Yogyakarta and Jakarta youth —— 31

Janika Kunzmann
3 Diverging verb derivational strategies in the youth language Yanké (DR Congo) —— 49

José Antonio Sánchez Fajardo
4 Exploring euphemistic initialisms in teenage computer-mediated communication —— 67

Ignacio M. Palacios Martínez and Paloma Núñez Pertejo
5 Teenagers and social networking. Twitter as a data source for the study of the language of London teenagers and young adults —— 85

Thabo Ditsele
6 Locating Sepitori in relation to South Africa's youth language practices: An overview —— 105

Alexandra Y. Aikhenvald
7 Innovation and change in a multilingual context: The Innovative Tariana language in northwest Amazonia —— 121

Part II: Specific purposes

Ellen Hurst-Harosh and Nico Nassenstein
8 On conversational humour in South African and Congolese youth's interactions: A pragmatic approach to youth language —— 141

Andrea Hollington and Dennis Gengomoi Akena
9 Youth language manipulation as decolonial practice in Uganda —— 165

Eyo O. Mensah
10 "Whenever I smoke, I see myself in Paradise": The discourse of tobacco consumption among rural youth in Nigeria —— 179

Christoph Holz
11 Notes on children's secret language games in New Ireland, Papua New Guinea —— 203

Anna-Brita Stenström
12 Three "bad" favourites in Spanish-speaking teenagers' conversation —— 225

Part III: Ideologies and belonging

Florian Busch and Maria Grazia Sindoni
13 Metapragmatics of mode-switching: Young people's awareness of multimodal meaning making in digital interaction —— 245

Nico Nassenstein and Helma Pasch
14 Whose way of speaking? Youth's self-reflexive voices and language ideologies in Uganda and Central African Republic —— 265

Yusnita Febrianti and Nurenzia Yannuar
15 The youth linguistic index: Narrative persuasion and sense of belonging in a movie trailer —— 293

Jill Vaughan and Abigail Carter
16 "We mix it up": Indigenous youth language practices in Arnhem Land —— 315

Anne Storch
17 Youth language before youth language —— 337

Subject Index —— 351

Nurenzia Yannuar, Helma Pasch, Jacomine Nortier,
Nico Nassenstein, Ellen Hurst-Harosh, Andrea Hollington
and Cynthia Groff

1 Youth language research: Changing perspectives, international trends and emerging themes

In this introduction, we present our approach to "global perspectives on youth language" and provide an orientation to the study of youth's language practices worldwide, based on current debates and developments in the field. The introduction intends to embrace the diverse and divergent perspectives that are available in studies on youth language. It firstly addresses terminological issues around youth language, notably "youth" and "language" (which will enable readers to reflect on the terminological choices made by authors); secondly, it considers the affordances of a global or international perspective alongside the importance of the local in youth language research; and it then turns to emerging themes in youth language research, specifically, linguistic manipulation, identity and ideology. The final section of this introduction will present the chapters in this volume. The chapter seeks to identify core topics in scholarly work and pave the way to a more global approach toward youth linguistic practices. In the study of youth language practices, especially on a global scale, investigation from diverse angles and through manifold perspectives in terms of theory and methods remains imperative, as these practices are not homogenous.

1 Introduction

A volume on youth language research assumes some common understanding of what is meant by "youth" and "language". However, when we look at these con-

---

Nurenzia Yannuar, Universitas Negeri Malang, e-mail: nurenzia.yannuar.fs@um.ac.id
Helma Pasch, University of Cologne, e-mail: ama14@uni-koeln.de
Jacomine Nortier, Universiteit Utrecht, e-mail: J.M.Nortier@uu.nl
Nico Nassenstein, Johannes Gutenberg-Universität Mainz, e-mail: nassenstein@uni-mainz.de
Ellen Hurst-Harosh, University of Cape Town, e-mail: ellen.hurst@uct.ac.za
Andrea Hollington, University of Cologne, e-mail: andrea.hollington@yahoo.de
Cynthia Groff, Leiden University, e-mail: c.d.groff@luc.leidenuniv.nl

https://doi.org/10.1515/9781501514685-001

cepts in various places all over the earth, we learn that "youth" is defined differently across cultures, and that "youth language" is understood and manifests differently in different contexts. Identifying commonalities in youth language practices, therefore, necessarily involves attention to differences. This volume brings together research from a global perspective that sheds further light on some of these terminological and contextual challenges alongside the commonalities by presenting empirical research on the linguistic practices of youth from various contexts. The volume has partly emerged from the *9th International Conference on Youth Languages*, which was held on May 23–25, 2019 at Leiden University in The Netherlands.[1] A variety of interesting questions were raised for discussion during the closing roundtable at this conference. The topics on the table ranged from methodological issues, including the size of corpora and the opportunities of digital spaces; to contextual issues, such as urban versus rural dimensions and similarities and differences in youth languages across continents; to terminological issues, such as slang versus youth language; to motivational and ideological issues such as the value of youth languages in different social groups, anti-languages versus mainstream languages, degree of conventionalization versus improvisation, and the degree of conscious awareness of divergent speech forms; and of course, to linguistic issues, such as common properties of those linguistic manipulations and the potential for dialect formation from specific youth languages.

Clearly a range of topics remain open for discussion and fruitful research in this still-emerging field. These topics are to a great extent reflected in the sections of the volume. The chapter authors deal with linguistic, lexical, methodological and terminological issues in the section "Words and Patterns" (Part One); contextual and motivational issues related to identity in "Specific Purposes" (Part Two); and awareness and ideological issues in "Ideologies and Belonging" (Part Three), with some obvious overlap.

Our concern in this introduction therefore is to set the scene for the chapters in as useful a way as possible. The aspects covered here are those we think need most clarification – namely, the challenges of terminology (which will enable readers to reflect on the terminological choices made by authors); the affordances of a global or international perspective (which provides the motivation for this volume); and the emerging themes in youth language research (which to an extent explains the organization of the volume). The final section of this introduction presents the chapters in this volume, which in turn speak back to many of the topics in this introductory chapter.

---

[1] The present authors acknowledge inspiring ideas that were generously contributed by numerous participants and warmly thank all participants for their intellectual input as well as the organizational committee for their work and efforts.

2 Terminology in the study of youth (and) language: Rethinking labels

Terminological debates are intrinsic to the study of youth languages and have been under discussion from the outset. The very words "youth" and "language" are contested in relation to actual practices in social contexts, and these issues have been raised widely in publications on the topic (see, among others, de Féral 2012, Makoni and Pennycook 2007). For example, the question of whether "language" is always a good description of the non-standard linguistic varieties used by youth has led to a reconsideration of terminology and to labels such as "(urban) youth speech styles" (UYSSs) (Dorleijn, Mous and Nortier 2015), "youth language practices" (Nassenstein and Hollington 2015), "style" as an agentive force of youth (Coupland 2007, Eckert 2012), "stylects" (Hurst and Mesthrie 2013), "dialects/sociolects" (Ndlovu 2018, among others), "slang" (Davie 2018), "slanguage" (Wong Man Tat 2006, Mensah and Nkamigbo 2016), "codes" (Atindogbé and Ebongue 2019), "ways of speaking" (de Féral 2012) or, more generally, the "linguistic outcomes of emerging youth identities" (Vaughan and Carter, this volume).

Some other terms that have been discussed with regard to youth language include pidgins, creoles and mixed languages (Hurst-Harosh forthcoming), mostly based on the fact that linguistic varieties and/or youth languages referred to under these labels have in common that they make use of multilingual resources and that they deviate from a perceived or socially constructed "standard" or "national" language (see also Nortier and Dorleijn 2013 for a discussion of contact varieties). Important to highlight, however, is the fact that these terms are themselves not unproblematic with regard to the ways in which they delimit our concepts of language and fail to illuminate the fluid nature of actual communicative practices (see Ansaldo and Matthews 2007, Kouwenberg and Singler 2008: 9).

This terminological negotiation is also reflected in the various terms used in contributions in the present volume, some highlighting the fluid nature of the investigated and described practices, and others focusing on contexts of (relative) stability. Some contexts, e.g., Vaughan and Carter (this volume), invoke terms such as "stable variety", "mixed variety", and "code".[2] Many practice-based approaches (e.g., Hurst-Harosh and Nassenstein this volume, Nassenstein and

---

[2] The term "variety" itself is often used in labeling the language of youth yet is rarely explained in terms of its actual meaning. As the most general of terms, "linguistic variety" or type is often simply used to avoid more contested and value-laden labels such as "language" or "dialect". A specific form of language usage can be described as it exists, as a way of speaking existing in the

Hollington 2015) focus on the linguistic realities rather than attempting categorization of the linguistic performances. This perspective is in line with current developments in sociolinguistics that seek to look at the spoken and performed realities of language rather than analyzing language as a system.

While many descriptions of youth language are still reliant on the assumption of languages as whole, bounded entities, youth practices themselves, and the vernaculars on which they are often based, tend to involve creative means of drawing upon multilingual and translingual resources. This has led to descriptive labels such as, among others, "multilingua franca" (Makoni and Pennycook 2012: 447). There are also crossovers here with terminology for urban varieties such as those described by Rampton (2011) in his shift from "multi-ethnic adolescent heteroglossia" to "contemporary urban vernaculars", and by Kerswill and Wiese (forthcoming), who label these phenomena "urban contact dialects" (UCD). Meanwhile some studies more strongly differentiate the urban varieties from youth language practices, which are considered "registers", "styles" (Mesthrie and Hurst 2013, Mesthrie, Hurst-Harosh and Brookes 2021), or "ways of speaking" (de Féral 2012, Bose 2019, Nassenstein and Pasch, this volume), based on Hymes' (1974) framework and on the ethnography of communication/speaking in the linguistic anthropological tradition. However, overlaps remain between the urban varieties and youth language in actual usage (see Ditsele, this volume). For example, Sheng was initially used mostly by urban youth in Nairobi, Kenya, but the age-range of Sheng speakers is now much broader than youth only. The variety still marks urban youth identity but at the same time also Kenyan citizenship and modernity for a wider group of speakers (Dorleijn, Mous and Nortier 2015: 283).

This highlights the problematic nature of the term "youth" and the category "age" in this field. An emphasis on the identity work of youth, involving the frequent linking of language practices to social styles that have currency, implies that it is only youth who are involved in this kind of identity work, yet if so, why would this be the case? Scholars such as Brookes (2014), and to some extent also Kießling and Mous (2004), have argued that the youth phase marks a period of intense peer sociality and the development of individual and group identities, which become stable later in life. Yet, youth itself is a slippery concept that can describe a wide and often culturally specific age-range (Hurst-Harosh and Mensah 2021), rooted in cultural concepts and complicated by definitions of "biological age" (i.e., being considered a child or an adult, counting the years since one's birth) vs. "social age" (e.g., the age of marriage, founding a family,

---

world, without necessarily claiming a substantial distinctness from other ways of speaking or from its roots in a(nother) specific language.

being economically independent, or taking on one's responsibilities and duties within society).³ Eckert (1997) differentiates between three different age categories, namely "chronological age" (years), "biological age" (physical maturity) and "social age" (legal status, marriage, etc,). The younger generation of speakers of an endangered language such as Tariana may not themselves be young (Aikhenvald, this volume). Furthermore, what we refer to as youth language may also be used by older people, as also emphasized by Rampton (2011) in his labeling of "contemporary urban vernaculars", as pointed out in studies on urban language (McLaughlin 2009), and as shown in, for example, the DR Congo (Nassenstein 2014), Kenya (Githiora 2018), and Central African Republic (Landi and Pasch 2015). When people tend to consider Sango Godobé the language of the Godobé, street children, we have a clearly definable group, but people of other age groups use Sango Godobé as well (see Nassenstein and Pasch, this volume).

We may thus ask ourselves whether a so-called "youth language" when transferred from one generation to the next – as is the case with Sheng in Kenya and in Germany or with Camfranglais in Italy (Machetti and Siebetcheu 2013) – is then still to be considered a youth language. Such a "transfer" would be subject to the so-called "youth" language becoming accessible beyond the youth in-group, and the new youthful generation would likely produce new innovations in their language practices, to which older generations would not be privy. It is important to recognize, therefore, that youth practices are not static across generations. In some contexts, specifying and narrowing down the age of speakers is rather unproblematic, e.g., for relatively young users of (Swahili-based) Yabacrâne in Eastern DR Congo and (Acholi-based) Leb pa Bulu in Northern Uganda, whereas in other contexts this is impossible: the urban language Sheng in Kenya allows no such specification, nor does Camfranglais in Cameroon, Langila in Congolese communities, or Dakar Wolof in Senegal. Moreover, the problematic category of "age" also reflects researchers' heterogenous ways of studying this social variable among speakers: Studies of youth language practices are mostly based on synchronic "apparent-time" measurements, whereas diachronic "real-time" studies would offer more valuable and comprehensive insights into how language evolves and changes across the lifespan. "Real-time" studies re-assess the same community several times over a longer timespan and are longitudinal, while "apparent-time" approaches assess a community's speech once, with age-strati-

---

3 Social age in numerous contexts in the Global South may depend upon factors such as (accomplished) initiation rites into society, events such as marriage, or public prestige. Also specific professions may ascribe status and social recognition to a person, and thus turn a "child" into a "woman" or "man". In these contexts, determining whether somebody is "young" or "old" seems like a very complex task. Turner's (1969) *rites de passage* are a useful application here.

fied variation understood as the specific language of an age group ("children" vs. "youth" vs. "old people", etc.). The latter method is often criticized as being less efficient in representing ongoing language change or in terms of the changing speech habits of individuals (e.g., Chambers 1998, Labov 1963).[4]

We have highlighted the intrinsic messiness of youth language and the research and labeling thereof. De Féral (2012) who has worked extensively on Camfranglais (Cameroon) and discusses the different labels given to youth languages and their indexicalities as well as researchers' subjectivity in these processes, asks in the title of a paper: "'Youth languages': A useful invention?". Even as we present a volume on youth languages, we echo this question, leaving it deliberation open to the researcher and the reader.

3 Youth languages in different global and local settings

The use of various labels and definitions discussed in the previous section are influenced by different regional contexts and cultural assumptions. As we consider what exactly we mean by youth language, the importance of a global perspective becomes evident, a perspective that carefully considers the local settings and ideologies involved in the development and use (and study) of youth languages. Much current research on youth languages shows interesting characteristic features that might be similar or different from the European-centered literature on the topic (see, for instance, Kerswill and Wiese forthcoming). This section describes how local contexts influence the development of youth languages in different parts of the world (Nortier 2018, Ziegler 2018) and considers the affordances of a global perspective and some of the comparative points that benefit from an international approach such as the one taken in this volume.

An important characteristic of youth languages globally is the fact that they are used to express a shared identity (Kießling and Mous 2006, Nassenstein 2014, Nassenstein and Hollington 2015). Identity has thus emerged as a central concept in the study of youth languages, and it is important to note that identity work can connect both with the local and the global. Youth use language to start accepting and shaping their identities; i.e., they become more aware of who they are

---

[4] Moreover, the resulting data depends upon the different kinds of study: Is a panel study or a trend study intended? Do researchers deal with age-specific approaches or generation-specific approaches? How is the complexity of age-grading met in the researcher's approach? We will not go into detail here but would like to raise awareness for the complexity of the topic.

and through language they choose the identities they wish to present. A youth language in Zimbabwe, for example, helps speakers highlight their identities as different from those who are not residing in the urban area (Hollington and Makwabarara 2015). Hoogervorst (2014) shows how in East Java, Indonesia, youth languages can be used to demonstrate closeness with a group of friends; such cultivation of an "in-group identity" is often cited as a function of youth language. A local language in Indonesia, Malangan Javanese, is used in a movie with a local setting and theme but is able to attract a national audience, thus promoting pride and diversity within national identity (Febrianti and Yannuar, this volume). On the other hand, youth draw on global discourses and cultural forms to construct their social and personal identities (Kanana and Hurst-Harosh 2020), as for example, in the broad impact of hip hop and reggae on youth identities and youth language globally (see Isiaka 2018, Tomei and Hollington 2020).

Youth languages often carry more prestige than stigma when they are used for affinity and access to the urban population, with ties to modernity. This prestige can be seen as a form of empowerment or social mobility within specific local contexts. For example, the use of Bahasa Gaul in Indonesia serves to strengthen traditional ethnic and linguistic identities before the speaker is allowed to be part of the urban community in the capital (Tropea, this volume). African youth languages such as Sheng, Langila, Tsotsitaal, and Sango Godobé make people from the village appear more urban, helping them avoid the stigma attached to peasants. The status of Sango Godobé is also raised when it is used by politicians as a way to integrate users of so-called youth languages into the society or at least get their votes. In using this variety, politicians present themselves as persons from among the people and members of Central African society as a whole. Upward social mobility may also involve group membership, which is facilitated by the use of youth language. In Nigeria, a certain youth language is used by both students and teachers for belonging to the educated part of the community (see also Storch, this volume, regarding *Burschensprache* 'students' speech' in Germany). Yet interpretations of youth language play out differently depending on the social and class structures encountered in a particular context. The notion of upward social mobility commonly involves economic advancement and a well-paid job, which usually requires mastery of a more or less standard variety of the dominant language, rather than a youth or urban variety.

Looking at youth languages globally also brings attention to different historical contexts. African youth languages are not only linked to the colonial history of a specific African country and the dominance of colonial languages as official languages, but they also exist in opposition to, or alongside, the national de jure official language (e.g., Sango in CAR, Swahili in Tanzania) or the de facto official language (e.g., Swahili in Kenya). The emergence of Sango Godobé and Congolese youth languages came partly as a reaction to urbanization (Nassenstein and Pasch, this volume, Kunzmann, this volume), an urbanization that introduced scarcely-used, school-enforced standard varieties of local languages. Such reactions against standard varieties, which are not accessible for all, are also reactions against the middle-class, who defend the standard variety, enjoying access to school education and living economically comfortable lives. Bahasa Gaul in Indonesia can also be seen as a reaction to the standardization of the lingua franca Bahasa Indonesia by the government. The youth create their youth language as a way to express themselves and respond to this imposition of an overly standardized variety.

In Russia, on the other hand, youth language is a reaction to oppressive government, and Namyalo (2017) gives several reasons for the emergence of Ugandan Luyaaye, including political factors among which are the human rights abuses of the 1970s and resultant political repression, which necessitated a secret code. Hurst-Harosh (2019) argues that youth language can be considered a decolonial practice because of the ways practices often emerge from economically and politically disenfranchised populations as a response to suppression and for solidarity and power – for example, youth styles amongst African Americans, youth languages in European migrant populations, and youth language in economically disadvantaged townships or ghettos in, e.g., South Africa and Kenya.

As this discussion has suggested, a global perspective on youth practices presents the opportunity to compare and contrast, to find commonalities that can lead to a clearer understanding of the roles, strategies, and implications of youth language practices, leading to further theoretical development of the field. At the same time, it can add texture and depth to the study of youth language by highlighting the importance of a wide range of social and contextual factors on specific youth language practices and data. The following section will turn to some of the main themes that have emerged as common across youth language research globally.

4 Core topics in youth language research

Some of the main developments in the field of youth language research are reflected in the chapters in this volume. The organization of the sections broadly reflects researchers' preoccupation with: linguistic manipulation of lexicon and forms; identity as negotiated in specific contexts; and ideology in relation to youth language practices. In a way, this follows Silverstein's (1985) 'total linguistic fact' framework, which proposes that cultural ideology can mediate meaningful sign forms that are mutually interacting when used in certain contexts and situations (Silverstein 1985: 220). A holistic look at the lexicon and forms, its practices and ideology are thus necessary to completely describe a language. This section expands on these core themes in youth language research and also considers the impact of digital contexts on youth language practices and the field of youth language research.

4.1 Linguistic manipulations

A much-cited characteristic of youth language practices worldwide are linguistic manipulations, with a specific focus on phonological, morphological and semantic manipulations. Numerous studies follow Kießling and Mous' (2004) analysis of a set of manipulations in African languages, while in the study of German youth language the focus was directed to syntactic changes (see, for instance, Androutsopoulos 1998, Lenzhofer 2017, Siegel 2018). Interestingly, linguistic manipulations are often set apart and considered to be more conscious processes than other processes of linguistic change. However, studies on innovation and change have shown that "the invisible hand" in language (Keller 1994) works regardless of how conscious some speakers are of linguistic change (as a collective consequence of speakers' deliberate and non-deliberate, or unconscious, actions). For youth language practices, however, Dimmendaal (2011: 249) assumes that "[i]n all these register-like languages, conscious language engineering appears to be involved, i.e. speakers are controlling the language". Labeling adolescent speakers "engineers" due to their creative minds reflects common perceptions of youth as creative and often also anti-mainstream. Yet, youth languages have often been shown to enter a stage in which they become more mainstream and more socially accepted (Kießling and Mous 2004, Milani, Jonsson and Mhlambi 2015, Nassenstein and Hollington 2016). Hence these languages may be comprehensible to non-members of the community and lose their exclusive character (Beck 2015, Pasch and Landi 2018: 126). This has been reported for several contexts worldwide. Among Lingala ya Bayankee-speaking youth in the Congo (Nassenstein 2014), in-group community members often come up with relexicalized forms and semantic manipulations to keep up the concealing character of youth language and make it more exclusive and less intelligible to the mainstream public. In other contexts, speakers seem to embrace the increasing status of their spoken variety (e.g., Febrianti and Yannuar, this volume).

In linguistic approaches to youth language, linguists often separate "base language", i.e., the underlying grammatical structure, from multilingual influences, seen either as conscious "linguistic manipulations" (mainly lexical, phonological, morphological, semantic, and less often, syntactic) or as processes of "linguistic change". Initially concerned with code-switching explanations, more recent studies have turned away from language contact approaches toward theory that describes fluid language practices. This work draws from theory that has reshaped and redefined sociolinguistics over the past decade, namely theoretical approaches such as translanguaging (see, among many other works, García 2009, Li Wei 2010, Creese and Blackledge 2010, García and Li Wei 2014), metrolingualism (Pennycook and Otsuji 2015), polylanguaging (Jørgensen 2008, etc.), translingual practice (Canagarajah 2013) and bricolage (Galliker 2014), just to name the most influential directions in the "(trans)languaging turn" (for an overview, see Pennycook 2016, Nassenstein and Hollington 2016). Surely the most widely applied of these new and fluid approaches to conceptualizations of the resources of bi- or multilingual speakers is translanguaging, having emerged in the context of classroom learning and pedagogy. In youth language research, this serves as an analytical and theoretical frame in a number of studies, including Kolu (2018) on Finnish youth, Nassenstein (2020) on Swahili-speaking youth from the Congo, and Dovchin, Sultana and Pennycook (2015) on youth from Mongolia and Bangladesh. What all these different theoretical approaches have in common is their attempt to describe linguistic practices that are sometimes hard to pin down.

Still, the features of the languages of youth that are most often described, even using these more sophisticated theoretical tools, are lexical features, manifesting in lexical difference, play and innovation, and semantic change. For example, one phenomenon of great interest in youth language practices is that of play language (or ludlings, language games), in which mostly young speakers deliberately manipulate language, often based on the syllable structure, to conceal their communicative practices (see also Holz, this volume). An example is Smibanese, a form of Straattaal in the Netherlands in which words are reversed (see also Storch 2011, Botne and Davis 2000, and Sherzer 1976, 2002). In many parts of the world, these playful acts work together with other youth language practices as well as with urban or other contemporary ways of speaking as youth draw on their full repertoire or range of language resources (see, e.g., Hollington 2019, Febrianti and Yannuar, this volume, and Tropea, this volume). The paradigm shift in sociolinguistics that moved the focus from structure to actual language practices in all their messiness (see Jones 2018) has enabled a new perspective that allows us to consider the multilayeredness of language use – in youth language and beyond. However, a challenge remains of how to represent the complex, entangled, multimodal and diverse ways of speaking that we encounter among youth and others in changing sociolinguistic scenarios. One promising approach is the direction towards the pragmatics of youth language, i.e., studying the context of language use in interaction (Hurst-Harosh and Nassenstein, this volume, as suggested by Hollington and Nassenstein 2015).

4.2 Identity

The purposes for which youth vary their linguistic practices have often been tied to identity, as also described by Jørgensen (2010) in his work on youth identity and youth culture. These practices have been theorized in terms of enregisterment (Agha 2007), indexicality, and metapragmatic stereotypes (Bucholtz 2009, Eckert 2008), with youth linguistic practices understood as indexical of particular social identities within specific contexts of use. For example, Brookes' (2021) work on Tsotsitaal and similar or related youth language practices in South Africa suggests that they constitute performative styles which function as part of male sociality. This "male, in-group, street-aligned, youth language practice" (Mesthrie, Hurst-Harosh and Brookes 2021) involves linguistic choices which index attitudes, stances, and identities, such as the mainstream, educated *softies*, the disrespectable *pantsulas*, or the streetwise *clevas* in Brookes' fieldwork setting. These indexical alignments create social distinction in local social situations.

In terms of identity construction and affiliations, gender is a frequent topic in youth language studies: Youth languages have often been described as used predominantly by male speakers (Kießling and Mous 2004). In some African youth language practices, both genders use youth language but more taboo words are used by the male speakers (Nassenstein and Hollington 2015). Female speakers of Yarada K'wank'wa in Addis Ababa, for example, would not use some strong/vulgar words in their youth language even though they understand them (Hollington 2015). Boso Walikan Malangan in Indonesia (Yannuar 2019) is used by both male and female speakers. However, the men are more confident in acknowledging their fluency, and words that are considered taboo in the society are avoided by female speakers. In other words, the youth language is spoken by female speakers as well, but they use it more restrictively. In Teheran, more men use the youth language than women (Soohani 2019). The same is said with regard to Camfranglais (Cameroon), Sheng (Kenya), Sango Godobé (Central African Republic), and Tsotsitaal (South Africa), but further research is required to find out whether and to what degree this hypothesis is valid and generalizable. Girls may also have their own linguistic strategies; for example, girls may use different kinds of Sheng (Kenya) or Langila (DR Congo), make use of different ludlings or employ other strategies to conceal their language. Strenström (this volume) clearly shows that the use of so-called "bad words" by female and male university students in Santiago, Buenos Aires and Madrid differs considerably. She shows that girls tend to use the so-called "bad" words with different intentions than boys. On the other hand, Nortier (2019) shows that youth languages indexing upward social mobility and a cosmopolitan orientation are used and considered acceptable by both men and women. Examples of such youth languages were found in Asia (Hong

Kong: Sau-Ling 2005, Wong Man Tat 2006; Indonesia: Smith-Hefner 2007, Yannuar 2019), North Africa (Algeria: Becetti 2011), and South Africa (Bembe and Beukes 2007). Most youth languages studied in Europe that are used to express a non-conformist, anti-mainstream orientation are considered inappropriate for women by both men and women. Practices that go beyond the male-female dichotomy are especially interesting, such as work on homosexual communities' linguistic practices in South Africa, labeled isiNgqumo (Rudwick 2008) and in Russia (Chernenko 2019). Of course, more work needs to be done on this issue, but the relation between gender identities and types of youth languages is worth noting.

Youth languages are often described as being anti-mainstream (cf. above) and having an anti-language element, or as having developed from an anti-language (Halliday 1976). Linguistic manipulation in youth languages can make them unintelligible to others (Kießling and Mous 2004), and this can be linked to the definition of an anti-language, developed and used by a stigmatized community of speakers, or an anti-society which sets itself up in opposition to mainstream society (ibid.). Nouchi in Abidjan, Sheng in Kenya and Boso Walikan Malangan in Indonesia are examples of youth languages that were developed from an anti-language. The use of youth language in Congolese music is not only a way of demonstrating resistance, but it is also a means to achieve economic success, at least for the musicians, the music industry and bars, restaurants, and discotheques where this music is played. As such, youth language can relate to professional identities as well as social and individual identities in use.

4.3 Ideology

Regarding ideologies about, and attitudes towards, the use of youth language, youth language is often maligned and marginalized in educational contexts due to the social stigma oftentimes attached to non-standard language practices. This can manifest, for example, when teachers claim to not understand a so-called youth language because of its low status, although they do in practice. Examples are Straattaal in the Netherlands, the use of which within school is rejected by 75% of the population.[5] Multilingual London English (MLE) has been considered "incompatible with, or even a threat to, the education system" (Kerswill n.d.). Youth language practices offer potential with regard to educational use, as do all diverse multilingual and translingual practices (García 2009, García and Li Wei 2014).

---

5 See [https://www.volkskrant.nl/nieuws-achtergrond/vlekkeloos-abn~be1a0fbf/] (accessed 30 January 2021).

However, monolingual ideologies tend to prevail in educational contexts, with a strong emphasis on standard varieties and official media of education. Rejection of youth language practices is not only a reaction against the use of youth languages in schools but against any spoken or common variety. In fact, youth may get the blame for not upholding language standards, when in actuality the urban vernacular or even language contact and resultant borrowings may have introduced the non-standard practices, such as in some African contexts where urban vernaculars commonly borrow from colonial languages (Hurst-Harosh 2020, Pasch 2020). Standard varieties may contain only a few loanwords from European languages, as in the case of Sango (in the short period that it was used as a school language), Lingala (Congo), Sepedi and other languages in South Africa, although these varieties may never actually be used in their standard form.

Another recent development in the field is in relation to ideologies surrounding youth language research itself. Despite the extensive academic studies of youth language in many regions of the world that testify to the fluidity, boundlessness and fuzziness of the language practices, "youth language" persists as a conceptual phenomenon, both in academic and public discourse. In recent times, more critical studies have dealt with youth language notably using decolonial/postcolonial approaches, highlighting the colonial backgrounds and contexts from which youth's linguistic practices emerged. While Storch (2018) looks at youth language and ruination in Nigeria, a concept rooted in Laura Ann Stoler's postcolonial framework, Hurst-Harosh (2019) has worked on youth language and decoloniality, applying Mignolo's framework of a "decolonial option" to South African youth language (see also Hollington and Akena, this volume). In a somewhat related way, Storch (this volume) challenges the field of youth language research, not only through her bold choice of directing the attention to a controversial and troubling topic, namely youth language and fascism, but also through her approach and writing style: She breaks with established norms of academic writing in terms of linearity and genre boundaries and thus presents a thought-provoking perspective on youth language.[6] Taking an explicitly critical approach to youth language research, Nassenstein, Hollington and Storch (2018) argue that approaches that single out the linguistic practices of youth involve the exoticization of practices that are in fact common to all language use. Contributions in the Nassenstein, Hollington and Storch (2018) volume show that the linguistic category "youth language" can easily be deconstructed once the actual practices are compared with other linguistic phenomena that people

---

[6] Her piece, which is intentionally placed as a final outlook and as the last contribution to the present volume, can be read as personal commentary and as attempt to open up established formats.

produce in their daily interactions in various environments. What may have contributed to the increased academic interest in youth language in recent years is the fact that some youth practices are named, e.g., Sheng, Tsotsitaal, Nouchi, and other "African youth languages" (see Ditsele this volume), as well as Kiezdeutsch (Wiese 2012), Rinkebysvenska (Kotsinas 1996), and Straattaal (Appel and Schoonen 2005) in Europe, and Hong Kong Slanguage (Wong Man Tat 2006) and Boso Walikan Malangan (Yannuar 2019) in Asia. Cornips, Jaspers and De Rooij (2015), meanwhile, discuss the complex task of labeling youth languages.

In drawing attention to certain linguistic practices, commodification plays an important role, when youth language is used for advertisements, media and public discourse, such as is the case with Sheng in Nairobi (Kenya) and Lingala ya Bayankee in Kinshasa (DR Congo). Such public use of youth languages creates the impression that youth languages are special varieties with their own special status rather than stigmatized, highly non-standard varieties. Similarly, when politicians make use of the youth language in order to show that they understand the people and their problems, as is the case with Sango Godobé (Nassenstein and Pasch, this volume), they are in effect commodifying youth language, using it to connect to the people. In the Netherlands, the municipality of Lelystad used Straattaal in an attempt to reach young people living there, although in this case it was not appreciated. According to the young people, Straattaal should not be used by "old" mainstream municipality workers (De Jong 2017). In other words, decontextualization changes the in-group character of youth languages, which is not always a welcome change. The examples above show that there is no strict universal way in which youth languages are perceived and used. Ideologies, practices and local factors need to be taken into consideration.

Although such doubt has been cast on the uniqueness of youth language practices, and on the reification of them in much research, youth are undoubtedly drivers of linguistic change (the "movers and shakers", see Kerswill 1996, Eckert 1997) and are involved in (named and unnamed) innovative practices, which have been investigated over the past few decades as part of "third wave variation studies" (Eckert 2012). The study of their language use is certainly of value. In youth language practices, language is being played with, including the use of humor and linguistic puns. More recently, memes and other strategies in social media are being developed, and links are being made to styles and cultural waves such as isikhotane in South Africa, where young people dress extravagantly and burn clothes and other consumer goods to demonstrate their wealth. Examples like these lead people to differentiate youth language and to mark out the linguistic skills of youth. This persistent attention to youth language is an acknowledgment that young people within their social contexts and peer groups engage in language variation and lead in linguistic change (Eckert 2003).

4.4 Digital contexts

More people than ever before are in touch with each other, and the form of these contacts has changed dramatically. The introduction of social media in large parts of the world has far-reaching consequences for the development and spread of youth languages beyond the original users. They are now widely accessible, which may lead to changes in the meaning of youth languages and, for example, in their in-group character. Moreover, outsiders can participate in online discussions when they know the linguistic rules and change their nicknames or avatars accordingly. Participants can change identities, which is easier online than in real life. They do not necessarily see each other, which is unavoidable in real life communication. In real life, age, gender, ethnicity, and speech are observable, but online there is only the written text and the nickname or avatar, as chosen by the individual participants (Dorleijn and Nortier 2009). Spontaneity also differs on the Internet as compared to real life. In oral communication, once an utterance is produced, it cannot easily be corrected or revoked. Computer-mediated communication (CMC) is less spontaneous in the sense that there is more time to reflect before an utterance is produced. However, more informal forms of CMC such as chatbox, Facebook or Instagram are more approximate to oral communication in terms of spontaneity and monitoring (see also "mode-switching" in Busch and Sindoni, this volume).

In several chapters in this volume we see how the digital world is complementary to (not replacing) the real world (see Palacios and Nuñez, Busch and Sindoni, Febrianti and Yannuar, this volume). What will the linguistic consequences be when the use of youth languages spreads beyond the groups who used to practice it for oral communication? The role of CMC will increase, and the increase of CMC has far-reaching consequences for the methodologies used in youth language research.

In order to collect youth language data, researchers used to observe, participate and record at street corners and school yards with a cassette recorder or more advanced equipment. As CMC has to some extent replaced oral communication, new ways of data collection have emerged, making use of Internet sources. e.g., based on numerous digital or virtual ethnographies in in the fields of anthropology, sociology and linguistics, participant observation in digital communities of practice, and many more. Time and effort are saved, with no appointments to be made and technical issues concerning recording equipment made obsolete. Moreover, the data appears in transcribed form. An example is the chapter by Palacios and Nuñez (this volume) in their search for the degree to which data from Twitter can be used in the study of the language of London teenagers and young adults.

Of course, as mentioned above, CMC cannot replace oral data, but it should take an increasingly prominent place in the study of youth languages, reflecting the reality of the communities of practice (and particularly in light of recent intensification of these modes of communication as a result of Covid-19 lockdowns globally). It must be taken into account, however, that in countries where access to communication technology and education are more limited, the use of CMC plays a minor role. For example, no digital forums have been observed where Sango Godobé plays a role. Again, different methodological and theoretical perspectives are essential to take into account the different realities of particular contexts, even in relation to the digital world. While digital technologies are in a sense removed from social and geographical restrictions, their users are not.

5 Overview of the chapters in this volume

The chapters in this volume reflect the diversity of labels and contexts discussed above, presenting new angles and in some ways pressing the borders of this fuzzy category called "youth language". As described above, the volume is divided into three sections, under the purposefully loose headings of "Words and Patterns", "Specific Purposes" and "Ideologies and Belonging". Some of the chapters fit more comfortably in one than another section, and there are many crossovers.

First of all, the section "Words and Patterns" presents a series of empirical studies that demonstrate different perspectives on lexicon and morphology. *Chantal Tropea* investigates the linguistic practices of Indonesian students in two major university cities, Jakarta and Yogyakarta. She shows that the youth language *Bahasa Gaul*, which emerged in 1998 as a reaction to the Bahasa Indonesia policy developed quite differently in the two cities. While syntax and morphology of *Bahasa Gaul* is based on that of standard Indonesian, there is strong influence from the local languages. In Yogyakarta, young people maintain Javanese to show their identity, and in Jakarta it is primarily Betawi language. But *Bahasa Gaul* in Jakarta is also characterized by a considerable amount of loanwords from English, which indicates that the youth identify with the cosmopolitan reality and take part in the internationalization process of the metropolis. These different interferences make the two varieties of *Bahasa Gaul* clearly distinct.

Janika Kunzmann focuses on the verb morphology of the African youth language Yanké (or, Lingala ya Bayankee, see above) spoken by young people in Congo's capital, Kinshasa. Unlike existing sociolinguistic studies on the Lingala-based youth language, her study offers an empirical overview of verb derivational strategies, with specific focus on applicative, causative, reciprocal and passive constructions, explaining more and less common morphosyntactic structures. The solid theoretical foundation of the chapter, distinguishing morphological and periphrastic constructions, makes this study interesting in terms of processes of linguistic change in youth languages.

José Antonio Sánchez Fajardo discusses word formation trends and patterns that characterize a compound-initialism hybrid (henceforth CIH) in teen slang in contemporary American English. Examples are *b-day, f-word, b-girl,* and *a-hole*. So far, little attention has been paid to these word formation mechanisms and motivations. Some preliminary data suggest that their complexity lies in their similar construction and different semantic/stylistic value. Whereas *a-hole* and *h-bomb* are structurally similar, the former is more sociolectally restricted, which explains its higher euphemistic motive. Colloquial CIHs seem to be highly compliant with the notions of mitigation and secrecy within the contextualizing effects of teenage slang. The data for this study consist of both already-attested CIHs and a corpus based on online teen magazines. Special attention is given to the scalarity of pejoration and amelioration in the expression of euphemism and dysphemism.

Ignacio M. Palacios Martínez and *Paloma Núñez Pertejo* discuss Twitter as a data source for the study of the language of young Londoners. They investigate the material extracted from the Twitter accounts of three rappers directly connected with Multicultural London English (MLE) and argue that such data can enable researchers to describe and get deeper into youth language practices in use. They look at the grammar and lexis of the examples in their corpus, and suggest that the combination of more traditional corpora, such as sociolinguistic interviews with data from social networks such as Twitter, may enhance findings overall. In conclusion, they propose that Twitter constitutes a rich source of data, one that can provide new highlights and additional information in the study of language variation and change.

Thabo Ditsele focuses on Sepitori in South Africa and aims to outline the difference between this variety and tsotsitaal, arguing that, while the latter is a youth practice, Sepitori itself acts as the urban vernacular in greater Pretoria. He outlines three major phases in Sepitori research, each of which have looked at crossovers between Sepitori and tsotsitaal. He then provides examples from a 2018 feature film called *Matwetwe,* which was popularized by its exclusive use of Sepitori, and from an ongoing television soap opera called *The River,* which features actors who speak Sepitori. His examples demonstrate the inclusion of "commonly known tsotsitaal lexical items" within Sepitori. His analysis highlights the links between youth language and urban vernacular, and how lexical innovations from youth may enter into broader usage.

Alexandra Y. Aikhenvald investigates processes of language change among speakers of the Amazonian language Tariana, focusing on Innovative Tariana, the language of the younger generations in an indigenous South American speech community. While Innovative Tariana is not necessarily a "youth language" when compared to often stylized European or African youth registers, it displays internally motivated linguistic changes due to major impact of Tucano and Portuguese in a context of both multilingualism and language endangerment. Yet, similar to practices of change and mediatiziation in other contexts worldwide, Innovative Tariana is increasingly used in emergent literary genres, including stories, letters and anecdotes shared on WhatsApp, Facebook and other social media platforms. This chapter offers valuable insights into age- and generation-related matters of youth language and language change and is among the few studies for indigenous contexts in the Americas.

Part Two moves to topics relating to the specific purposes of youth language practices, starting with *Hurst-Harosh* and *Nassenstein's* chapter, which analyzes humor in African youth languages. Their analysis aims to further our understanding of "everyday language use" amongst youth by looking at interactions during conversational storytelling narratives in South Africa (focusing on Tsotsitaal/isiTsotsi speakers), and at humorous anecdotes as a practice of joint reminiscing in DR Congo (by speakers of Lingala ya Bayankee/Yanké). The chapter presents humor as a new and relevant field of study in youth language research. The authors furthermore suggest a "pragmatic turn" in the study of African youth languages. Their analysis of the conversational storytelling narratives highlights the numerous ways in which pragmatic approaches can contribute to an understanding of youth language practices, such as through interactional stylistics, conversation analysis, and approaches that consider indexicality.

In their chapter on youth language as decolonial practice in sports education, *Andrea Hollington* and *Dennis Gengomoi Akena* illustrate how youth language and language manipulation has formed part of the institutional and historical processes in the Ugandan education system, as well as forming part of everyday practices and rituals in school assemblies, classes, sports and school ceremonies. Using the linguistic examples of students' sports anthems, they demonstrate how the youth manipulate colonial, national and school rituals as a tool of resistance and as a decolonial practice. They show the ways in which youth language practices and music have been playing and continue to play a significant role in the context of education and politics in Uganda.

Eyo O. Mensah reports on a study among rural male youth in Southern Cross River State, southeastern Nigeria, where smoking behavior is an important form of sociability that signals "self-liberation" and proper manhood in their social universe. In this chapter, the social and cultural aspects of the smoking ritual among youth are examined. The study is rooted in the community of practice framework, focusing on participant observation, focus groups, semi-structured interviews and metalinguistic conversations. The results show that young men utilize smoking culture and its accompanying linguistic codes as forms of style that enable them to articulate other male-centered subcultural capital in their rural space and to connect with urban identity and modernity.

Christoph Holz has studied youth language practices in New Ireland (Papua New Guinea) intensively and compared practices across the several locations of the island. His chapter focuses on secret language practices used by school girls. Interestingly, the manipulative linguistic strategies that the young female speakers employ to make their speech unintelligible can be applied to several languages spoken on the island, namely Tok Pisin, English as well as local indigenous languages. The author analyzes and compares the language game, its rules, practices and contexts, and thus offers innovative insights into play and secret languages of youth in a little-studied area.

Anna-Brita Stenström discusses the "bad" words *gilipollas, huevón/a* and *boludo/a* used by male and female youth in Madrid, Santiago and Buenos Aires, respectively. The use of *huevón/a* in Santiago and *boludo/a* in Buenos Aires as address terms is far more common than that of *gilipollas* in Madrid, which tends to be substituted by a neutral term like *tío/a*. Another difference is the greater versatility of *gilipollas*, which is used not only with reference to foolish, stupid persons but also with reference to stupid actions. While *huevón/a, boludo/a* and *gilipollas* have similar etymologies and serve as "bad" terms when talking about others, they are mainly used as friendly address terms and as a phatic device, helping to keep the conversation going. This shows that a general qualification as "bad" is no longer valid. Boys and girls use the terms in different ways, and even the masculine and feminine forms of *huevón/a* and *boludo/a* are used differently by boys and girls.

Part Three gathers chapters together around the themes of ideologies and belonging. First, *Florian Busch* and *Maria Grazia Sindoni* investigate the multimodality of youth language practices in digital forms of communication. In particular, they analyze live conversations on Skype as well as text-based communicative practices on WhatsApp. By employing the concept of mode-switching, the authors shed light on young communicators' metapragmatic awareness. In particular, the chapter focuses on media ideologies and on the ways young people use different semiotic and multimodal resources in collaborative interactions in digital spaces. Their comparative account sheds light on similiarities and differences in the communicative behavior and metapragmatic awareness of young people in different digital interactive scenarios.

Yusnita Febrianti and *Nurenzia Yannuar* analyze a movie trailer to show how several Indonesian varieties are used for persuasion and how they index identities and sociolinguistic contexts. The selected trailer is *Yowis Ben* (Javanese for 'yes, let it be'), a movie released in 2018 that centers its storyline on the making of a band and the drama among the band members. Unlike most Indonesian movies, which use Indonesian, the country's national language, the characters of Yowis Ben speak in a local language, Malangan Javanese, and they make use of the local youth variety Boso Walikan Malangan. The findings show that the movie trailer's narrative persuasion is constructed by the local language, supplemented by the trailer's visual and sound elements. Furthermore, the use of a local language succeeds in making the movie characters' local linguistic practice appealing to a national audience.

Next, *Jill Vaughan* and *Abigail Carter* describe a diverse linguistic ecology in their chapter titled "'We mix it up': Indigenous youth language practices in Arnhem Land". In a coastal Australian context where linguistic diversity is the norm, youth use their linguistic resources to express both their allegiance to traditional cultural life and their connection to an emergent urban subculture. The chapter describes the creative multilingual practices of Maningrida youth, which express agency and resistance, and highlights local Indigenous perspectives on those practices, drawing on a variety of data sources in their collaborative, community-driven research.

Nico Nassenstein and *Helma Pasch* present three concise case studies from Uganda and Central African Republic that focus on youth who conceptualize their speech as non-deviant but conformist "everyday speech", and who reveal blurry in-group/out-group boundaries with regard to the innovative character of their language. The authors address young speakers' self-reflexive utterances about their language use against a background of language ideologies, a prominent topic in linguistic anthropology. This includes speakers' beliefs and thoughts about their social positioning and their language practice, and it raises the questions how and why youth language could potentially be understood as "ways of speaking". The chapter focuses on metalinguistic reference to youth language and recommends a turn toward local and "southern" epistemologies in the study of youth's speech.

Anne Storch investigates the topic of youth language in Germany in the first half of the 21st century with strong reference to her grandfather's generation. She reflects upon students' speech (*Burschensprache*), which was not an anti-language but part of mainstream elitist practices and training for future membership in the elite, hence interspersed with French and Latin words, which indicated learnedness. Secondly, she bases her study on books, the German school novel and adventure tales in particular, and films that were produced for young men, which were allegedly educational but finally aimed at implanting ideologies like heroism, traditionalism, and nationalism, Othering the peoples in the colonies. Youth language in those days had much to do with class performance. Storch's innovative and unconventional approach to youth language, combining personal reflection and reminiscence with media and literary works can be understood as an open invitation to scholars to engage in new formats in the study of youth language practices worldwide.

References

Agha, Asif. 2007. *Language and social relations*. Cambridge: Cambridge University Press.
Androutsopoulos, Jannis. 1998. *Deutsche Jugendsprache. Untersuchungen zu ihren Strukturen und Funktionen*. Frankfurt am Main: Peter Lang.
Ansaldo, Umberto and Stephen Matthews. 2007. Deconstructing creole: The rationale. In Umberto Ansaldo, Stephen Matthews and Lisa Lim (eds.), *Deconstructing creole*, 1–18. Amsterdam: Benjamins.
Appel, René and Rob Schoonen. 2005. Street language: A multilingual youth register in the Netherlands. *Journal of Multilingual and Multicultural Development* 26. 85–117.
Atindogbé, Gratien Gualbert and Augustin Emmanuel Ebongue (eds.). 2019. *Linguistic and sociolinguistic perspectives of youth language practices in Africa: Codes and identity writings*. Mankon, Bamenda: Langaa RPCIG.
Becetti, Abdelali. 2011. Parlers de jeunes lycéens à Alger: Pratiques plurilingues et tendances alteritaires. *Revue Le Français en Afrique* 25. 153–164.
Beck, Rose Marie. 2015. Sheng: an urban variety of Swahili in Kenya. In Nico Nassenstein and Andrea Hollington (eds.), *Youth language practices in Africa and beyond*, 51–79. Berlin: De Gruyter Mouton.
Bembe, Magdeline Princess and Anne-Marie Beukes. 2007. The use of slang by black youth in Gauteng. *Southern African Linguistics and Applied Language Studies* 25 (4). 463–472.
Bose, Paulin Baraka. 2019. Analyzing ways of speaking Kivu Swahili: Variation and ethnic belonging. *Swahili Forum* 26. 258–276.
Botne, Robert and Stuart Davis. 2000. Language games, segment imposition and the syllable. *Studies in Language* 24 (2). 319–344.
Brookes. Heather. 2014. Urban youth languages in South Africa: A case study of Tsotsitaal in a South African township. *Anthropological Linguistics* 56 (3–4). 356–388.
Brookes, Heather. 2021. Rethinking youth language practices in South Africa: An interactional sociocultural perspective. In Rajend Mesthrie, Ellen Hurst-Harosh and Heather Brookes (eds.), *Youth language practices and urban language contact in Africa*. Cambridge: Cambridge University Press.
Bucholtz, Mary. 2009. From stance to style: Gender, interaction, and indexicality in Mexican immigrant youth slang. In Alexandra Jaffe (ed.), *Stance: Sociolinguistic perspectives*, 146–170. Cambridge: Cambridge University Press.
Chambers, J.K. 1998. Social embedding of changes in progress. *Journal of English Linguistics* 26 (1). 5–36.
Canagarajah, Suresh. 2013. *Translingual practice: Global Englishes and cosmopolitan relations*. London and New York: Routledge.
Chernenko, Julia. 2019. Multilingualism of young Runet users as a tool of identity. Paper presented at the 9th International Conference on Youth Languages, Leiden University, 23–25 May.

Cornips, Leonie, Jürgen Jaspers and Vincent de Rooij. 2015. The politics of labelling youth vernaculars in the Netherlands and Belgium. In Jacomine Nortier and Bente Ailin Svendsen (eds.), *Language, youth and identity in the 21st Century*, 45–70. Cambridge: Cambridge University Press.

Coupland, Nikolas. 2007. *Style. Language variation and identity*. Cambridge: Cambridge University Press.

Creese, Angela and Adrian Blackledge. 2010. Translanguaging in the bilingual classroom: A pedagogy for learning and teaching? *Modern Language Journal* 9. 103–115.

Davie, Jim. 2018. *Slang across societies: Motivations and constructions*. London and New York: Routledge.

de Féral, Carole. 2012. "Parlers jeunes": une utile invention? / "Youth languages": a useful invention? *Langage et Société* 3 (141). 21–46.

De Jong, Barbara. 2017. Lelystad slaat plank mis met denigrerende straattaalfolder [Lelystad misses the point with denigrating brochure in Straattaal] In *AD*, 17 August. [https://www.ad.nl/binnenland/lelystad-slaat-plank-mis-met-denigrerende-straattaalfolder~acaff4c9/] (accessed 28 January 2021).

Dimmendaal, Gerrit J. 2011. *Historical linguistics and the comparative study of African languages*. Amsterdam/Philadelphia: John Benjamins.

Dorleijn, Margreet, Maarten Mous and Jacomine Nortier. 2015. Urban youth speech styles in Kenya and the Netherlands. In Jacomine Nortier and Bente Ailin Svendsen (eds.), *Language, youth and identity in the 21st Century*, 270–289. Cambridge: Cambridge University Press.

Dorleijn, Margreet and Jacomine Nortier. 2009. Code-switching and the internet. In Barbara Bullock and Jacqueline Almeida Toribio (eds.), *The Cambridge handbook of linguistic code-switching*, 127–141. Cambridge: Cambridge University Press.

Dovchin, Sender, Shaila Sultana and Alastair Pennycook. 2015. Relocalizing the translingual practices of young adults in Mongolia. *Translation and Translanguaging in Multilingual Contexts* 1. 4–26.

Eckert, Penelope. 1997. Age as a sociolinguistic variable. In Florian Coulmas (ed.), *The handbook of sociolinguistics*, 151–167. Oxford: Blackwell.

Eckert, Penelope. 2003. Language and adolescent peer groups. *Journal of Language and Social Psychology* 22 (1). 112–118.

Eckert, Penelope. 2008. Variation and the indexical field. *Journal of Sociolinguistics* 12 (4). 453–476.

Eckert. Penelope. 2012. Three waves of variation study: The emergence of meaning in the study of sociolinguistic variation. *Annual Review of Anthropology* 41 (1). 87–100.

Galliker, Esther. 2014. *Bricolage. Ein kommunikatives Genre im Sprachgebrauch Jugendlicher aus der Deutschschweiz*. Frankfurt: Peter Lang.

García, Ofelia. 2009. Education, multilingualism and translanguaging in the 21st century. In Ajit K. Mohanty, Minati Panda, Robert Phillipson and Tove Skutnabb-Kangas (eds.), *Multilingual Education for social justice: Globalising the local*, 128–145. New Delhi: Orient Blackswan.

García, Ofelia and Li Wei. 2014. *Translanguaging. Language, bilingualism and education*. New York: Palgrave Macmillan.

Githiora. Chege. 2018. Sheng: The Expanding Domains of an Urban Youth Vernacular. *Journal of African Cultural Studies* 30 (2): 105–20.

Halliday, Michael. 1976. Anti-languages. *American Anthropologist* 78 (3). 570–584.

Hoogervorst, Tom. 2014. Youth culture and urban pride: The sociolinguistics of East Javanese slang. *Wacana* 15 (1). 104–130.
Hollington, Andrea. 2015. Yarada K'wank'wa and urban youth identity in Addis Ababa. In Nico Nassenstein and Andrea Hollington (eds.), *Youth language practices in Africa and beyond*, 149–168. Berlin: De Gruyter Mouton.
Hollington, Andrea. 2019. Chibende – Linguistic creativity and play in Zimbabwe. *International Journal of Language and Culture* 6 (1). 29–44.
Hollington, Andrea and Nico Nassenstein. 2015. Conclusion and outlook: Taking new directions in the study of youth language practices. In Nico Nassenstein and Andrea Hollington (eds.), *Youth language practices in Africa and beyond*, 345–356. Berlin: De Gruyter Mouton.
Hollington, Andrea and Tafadzwa Makwabarara. 2015. Youth language practices in Zimbabwe. In Nico Nassenstein and Andrea Hollington (eds.), *Youth language practices in Africa and beyond*, 257–269. Berlin: De Gruyter Mouton.
Hurst, Ellen and Rajend Mesthrie. 2013. "When you hang out with the guys they keep you in style": The case for considering style in descriptions of South African Tsotsitaals. *Language Matters* 44 (1). 3–20.
Hurst-Harosh, Ellen. 2019. Tsotsitaal and decoloniality. *African Studies* 78 (1). 112–125.
Hurst-Harosh, Ellen. 2020a. "They even speak Tsotsitaal with their teachers at school": The use (and abuse) of African Urban Youth Languages in educational contexts. *Africa Education Review* 17 (1). 35–50.
Hurst-Harosh, Ellen. 2020b. New identities and flexible languages: youth and urban varieties. In Umberto Ansaldo and Miriam Meyerhoff (eds.), *Routledge handbook of pidgin and creole languages*, 302–321. London and New York: Routledge.
Hurst-Harosh, Ellen and Eyo Mensah. 2021. Authenticity and the object of analysis: Methods of youth language data collection. In Rajend Mesthrie, Ellen Hurst-Harosh & Heather Brookes (eds.), *Youth language practices and urban language contact in Africa*. Cambridge: Cambridge University Press.
Hurst-Harosh, Ellen. forthcoming. South Africa: Tsotsitaal and urban vernacular forms of South African languages. In: Paul Kerswill and Heike Weise (eds.). *Urban contact dialects and language change: insights from the Global North and South*. London: Routledge.
Hymes, Dell. 1974. Ways of speaking. In Richard Bauman and Joel Sherzer (eds.), *Explorations in the ethnography of speaking*, 433–452. Cambridge: Cambridge University Press.
Isiaka, Adeiza Lasisi. 2018. Plurality, translingual splinters and music-modality in Nigerian youth languages. In Ellen Hurst-Harosh and Fridah Erastus Kanana (eds.), *African youth languages: New media, performing arts and sociolinguistic development*, 161–180. Cham: Palgrave Macmillan.
Jones, Rodney. 2018. Messy creativity. *Language Sciences* 65. 82–86.
Jørgensen, Jens Normann. 2008. Poly-lingual languaging around and among children and adolescents. *International Journal of Multilingualism* 5. 161–176.
Jørgensen, Jens Normann (ed.). 2010. *Love ya hate ya: The sociolinguistic study of youth language and youth identities*. Cambridge: Cambridge Scholars.
Kanana, Fridah Erastus and Ellen Hurst-Harosh. 2020. Global and local hybridity in African youth language practices. *Africa Development: CODESRIA* Volume XLV (3). 13–32.
Keller, Rudi. 1994. *On language change: The invisible hand in language*. London/New York: Routledge.

Kerswill, Paul. 1996. Children, adolescents and language change. *Language Variation and Change* 8. 177–202.
Kerswill, Paul. No date. Case study: Multicultural London English in schools. [https://www.futurelearn.com/info/courses/accents-attitudes-and-identity-an-introduction-to-sociolinguistics/0/steps/64584] (accessed 15 January 2021).
Kerswill, Paul and Heike Wiese (eds.). forthcoming. *Urban contact dialects and language change: insights from the Global North and South*. London: Routledge.
Kießling, Roland and Maarten Mous. 2004. Urban youth languages in Africa. *Anthropological Linguistics* 46 (3). 303–341.
Kießling, Roland and Maarten Mous. 2006. Vous nous avez donné le francais, mais nous sommes pas obligés de l'utiliser comme vous le voulez: Youth languages in Africa. In Christa Dürscheid and Jürgen Spitzmüller (eds.), *Perspektiven der Jugendsprachforschung/Trends and developments in youth language research*, 385–401. Frankfurt am Main: Peter Lang.
Kolu, Jaana. 2018. Translanguaging as a multilingual practice. The negotiation of meaning in bilingual adolescents' conversations in Haparanda and Helsinki. In Arne Ziegler (ed.), *Jugendsprachen/Youth languages*, 575–598. Berlin: De Gruyter Mouton.
Kotsinas, Ulla-Britt. 1996. Rinkebysvenska – ett ungdomsspråk. [Rinkeby Swedish – a youth language]. In Åke Daun and Barbro Klein (eds.), *Alla vi svenskar*, 125–148. Stockholm: Nordiska Muséet.
Kouwenberg, Silvia and John Victor Singler. 2008. Introduction. In Silvia Kouwenberg and John V. Singler (eds.), *The handbook of pidgin and creole studies*, 1–16. Oxford: Blackwell.
Labov, William. 1963. The social motivation of a sound change. *Word* 19 (3). 273–309.
Landi, Germain and Helma Pasch. 2015. Sango Godobé: The urban youth language of Bangui (CAR). In Nico Nassenstein and Andrea Hollington (eds.), *Youth language practices in Africa and beyond*, 207–226. Berlin: De Gruyter Mouton.
Lenzhofer, Melanie. 2017. *Jugendkommunikation und Dialekt. Syntax gesprochener Sprache bei Jugendlichen in Osttirol*. Berlin: De Gruyter Mouton.
Li Wei. 2010. Moment analyses and translanguaging space: Discursive construction of identities by multilingual Chinese youth in Britain. *Journal of Pragmatics* 4. 1222–1235.
Lüpke, Friederike and Anne Storch. 2013. *Repertoires and choices in African languages*. Berlin: De Gruyter Mouton.
Makoni, Sinfree and Alastair Pennycook (eds.) 2007. *Disinventing and reconstituting languages*. Bristol: Multilingual Matters.
Makoni, Sinfree and Alastair Pennycook. 2012. Disinventing multilingualism: From monological multilingualism to multilingua francas. In Marilyn Martin-Jones, Adrian Blackledge and Angela Creese (eds.), *The Routledge handbook of multilingualism*, 451–465. London: Routledge.
Machetti, Sabrina and Raymond Siebetcheu. 2013. The use of Camfranglais in the Italian migration context. *Tilburg Papers in Cultural Studies* 55. [https://www.tilburguniversity.edu/research/institutes-and-research-groups/babylon/tpcs] (accessed 28 January 2021).
McLaughlin, Fiona. 2009. Introduction to the languages of urban Africa. In Fiona McLaughlin (ed.), *The languages of urban Africa*, 1–18. London/New York: Continuum.
Mensah, Eyo and Linda Nkamigbo. 2016. All I want is your waist: Sexual metaphors as youth slanguage in Nigeria. *Sociolinguistic Studies* 10 (1). 177–198.

Mesthrie, Rajend and Ellen Hurst. 2013. Slang registers, code-switching and restructured urban varieties in South Africa: An analytic overview of Tsotsitaals with special reference to the Cape Town variety. *Journal of Pidgin and Creole Languages* 28 (1). 103–130.

Mesthrie, Rajend, Ellen Hurst-Harosh and Heather Brookes (eds). 2021. *Youth language practices and urban language contact in Africa*. Cambridge: Cambridge University Press.

Milani, Tommaso M., Rickard Jonsson and Innocentia J. Mhlambi. 2015. Shooting the subversive: When non-normative linguistic practices go mainstream in the media. In Jacomine Nortier and Bente A. Svendsen (eds.), *Language, youth and identity in the 21st century: Linguistic practices across urban spaces*, 119–138. Cambridge: Cambridge University Press.

Namyalo, Saudah. 2017. The sociolinguistic profile and functions of Luyaaye within its community of practice. In Augustin Emmanuel Ebongué and Ellen Hurst (eds.), *Sociolinguistics in African contexts: Perspectives and challenges*, 225–246. Cham: Springer.

Nassenstein, Nico. 2014. *A grammatical study of the youth language Yanké*. Munich: LINCOM.

Nassenstein, Nico 2020. Translanguaging in Yabacrâne: On youth's fluid linguistic strategies in Eastern DR Congo. *Working Papers of the Department of Anthropology and African Studies* 190. [https://www.ifeas.uni-mainz.de/files/2020/01/AP-190.pdf] (accessed 15 January 2021).

Nassenstein, Nico and Andrea Hollington (eds.). 2015. *Youth language practices in Africa and beyond*. Berlin: De Gruyter Mouton.

Nassenstein, Nico and Andrea Hollington. 2016. Global repertoires and urban fluidity: Youth languages in Africa. *International Journal of the Sociology of Language* 242. 171–193.

Nassenstein, Nico, Andrea Hollington and Anne Storch. 2018. Disinventing and demystifying youth language: Critical perspectives. *The Mouth* 3. 9–27.

Ndlovu, Sambulo. 2018. Characterisation and social impact of urban youth languages on urban toponymy: S'ncamtho toponomastics in Bulawayo. *Literator* 39 (1), a1373. [https://doi.org/10.4102/lit.v39i1.1373] (accessed 30 January 2021).

Nortier, Jacomine. 2018. Youth languages. In Arne Ziegler (ed.), *Jugendsprachen – Youth languages: Aktuelle Perspektiven internationaler Forschung – Current perspectives of international research*, 3–25. Berlin: De Gruyter Mouton.

Nortier, Jacomine. 2019. Gender-related online metalinguistic comments on Straattaal and Moroccan flavored Dutch in the Moroccan heritage community in the Netherlands. *Applied Linguistics Review* 10 (3). 341–366.

Nortier, Jacomine and Margreet Dorleijn. 2013. Multi-ethnolects: Kebabnorsk, Perkerdansk, Verlan, Kanakensprache, Straattaal, etc. In Peter Bakker and Yaron Matras (eds.), *Contact languages: A comprehensive guide*, 229–271. Berlin: De Gruyter Mouton.

Pasch, Helma. 2020. Sango, a homogenous language with religiolectal and sociolectal varieties. *Sociolinguistic Studies* 14 (3). 277–298.

Pasch, Helma and Germain Landi. 2018. How to get information on Sango Godobé and the Godobé of Bangui: A dialogue between Helma Pasch and Germain Landi. *The Mouth* 3. 126–137.

Pennycook, Alastair and Emi Otsuji. 2015. *Metrolingualism. Language in the city*. London and New York: Routledge.

Pennycook, Alastair. 2016. Mobile times, mobile terms: The trans-super-poly-metro movement. In Nicholas Coupland (ed.), *Sociolinguistics: Theoretical debates*, 201–216. Cambridge: Cambridge University Press.

Pfurtscheller, Lisa Marie. 2013. *Soziolinguistische Aspekte des Nouchi, einer Mischsprache der Côte d'Ivoire*. Vienna: Universität Wien Diploma thesis.

Rampton, Ben. 2011. From 'multi-ethnic adolescent heteroglossia' to 'contemporary urban vernaculars'. *Language & Communication* 31 (4). 276–294.

Rudwick, Stephanie. 2008. IsiNgqumo – introducing a gay Black South African linguistic variety. *Southern African Linguistics and Applied Language Studies* 26 (4). 445–456.

Samper, David Arthur. 2002. *Talking Sheng: The role of a hybrid language in the construction of identity and youth culture in Nairobi, Kenya*. Philadelphia: University of Pennsylvania dissertation.

Sau-Ling, Luk. 2005. *The use of Cantonese slang by teenagers in Hong Kong*. Hong Kong: The Chinese University of Hong Kong MA thesis.

Sherzer, Joel. 1976. Play languages: Implications for (socio)linguistics. In Barbara Kirshenblatt-Gimblett (ed.), *Speech play*, 19–26. Philadelphia: University of Pennsylvania Press.

Sherzer, Joel. 2002. *Speech play and verbal art*. Austin: University of Texas Press.

Siegel, Vanessa. 2018. *Multiethnolektale Syntax. Artikel, Präpositionen und Pronomen in der Jugendsprache*. Heidelberg: Universitätsverlag Winter.

Silverstein, Michael. 1985. Language and the culture of gender. In Elizabeth Mertz and Richard J. Parmentier (eds.), *Semiotic mediation*, 219–259. New York: Academic Press.

Smith-Hefner, Nancy. 2007. Youth language, Gaul, sociability, and the new Indonesian middle class. *Journal of Linguistic Anthropology* 17 (2). 184–203.

Soohani, Babareh. 2019. Linguistic manipulations in urban youth language in Tehran. Paper presented at the 9th International Conference on Youth Languages, Leiden University, 23–25 May.

Storch, Anne. 2011. *Secret manipulations. Language and context in Africa*. Oxford: Oxford University Press.

Storch, Anne. 2018. Silencing youth. In Nico Nassenstein, Anne Storch and Andrea Hollington (eds.), *Critical studies in youth languages. The Mouth* 3. 65–84.

Tomei, Renato and Andrea Hollington. 2020. Transatlantic linguistic ties: The impact of Jamaican on African youth language practices. *Linguistics Vanguard* 6 (s4).20190048. DOI: [10.1515/lingvan-2019-0048] (accessed 31 January 2021).

Wiese, Heike. 2012. *Kiezdeutsch: Ein neuer Dialekt entsteht*. Munich: C. H. Beck.

Wong Man Tat, Parco. 2006. *A sociolinguistic study of youth Slanguage of Hong Kong adolescents*. Hong Kong: University of Hong Kong MA thesis.

Yannuar, Nurenzia. 2019. *Bòsò Walikan Malangan: Structure and development of a Javanese reversed language*. Leiden: Leiden University dissertation.

Ziegler, Arne (ed.). 2018. *Jugendsprachen – Youth languages: Aktuelle Perspektiven internationaler Forschung*. Berlin: De Gruyter Mouton.

Part I: **Words and patterns**

This thematic section represents one of the core themes in youth language studies as it focuses on linguistic strategies and practices employed in youth languages. The ways in which speakers manipulate 'standardized' or 'established' linguistic conventions, words and patterns can take manifold forms as the chapters in this section testify. Speakers of youth language make use of creative and versatile strategies to establish new meanings by drawing on large repertoires of linguistic and other semiotic resources. The present volume describe a broad variety of youth language phenomena from a multitude of angles. Very few – if any – of the chapters concentrate on one angle exclusively, though each has its own focus. In a chapter about linguistic forms, for example, practices and ideologies are not ignored, as evidenced in this section. Although the main focus is on linguistic phenomena, other aspects are considered without which we cannot understand Silverstein's (1985: 220) 'total linguistic fact': the "mutual interaction of meaningful sign forms contextualized to situations of interested human use, mediated by the fact of cultural ideology". In practice, this means that a full understanding of language encompasses not only lexicon and grammar, but also practices and ideologies. While each can be studied in isolation, only together do they form a complete perspective that is more than the sum of the parts. We believe that this contextualized study of words and patterns is important to arrive at a deeper and more comprehensive understanding of the actual linguistic practices.

An analysis of lexical and grammatical characteristics of youth language practices can be employed to shed light on the ways in which the youth variety expresses identity as well as a cosmopolitan orientation, for instance through the use of loanwords (see Tropea on Bahasa Gaul). Moreover, the investigation of linguistic structure in youth language practices, combined with sociolinguistic findings, can constitute a more holistic perspective on actual youth language practices, their linguistic strategies as well as issues such as linguistic variation and change (Kunzmann). The interplay of strategies, structure and pragmatics can also be observed in a description of specific linguistic strategies such as compound-initialism hybrids, shedding light on the possible relations between form and function in such word formation processes (Sanchez).

As youth language practices change and evolve at rapid rates, youth language studies are important for a broader understanding of linguistic variation and change (Kunzmann, Palacios and Nuñez, Aikhenvald). While the primary focus is on the form of the respective youth language practices, these chapters show that a thorough analysis provides insights into aspects of diversity and change, innovation and new contexts of usage, such as digital domains. Another relevant aspect of the study of youth language practices and structure is the comparative perspective. Looking at two or more youth language varieties and comparing them in terms of their manipulations, semantic and morphosyntactic strategies and their grammatical patterns allows us to gain yet another perspective on differences and commonalities in lexicon, form and function (Ditsele).

Altogether, this first section looks at words and patterns, form and structure from diverse angles and sheds light on various domains from the digital to the local and the global, from language change to linguistic ideologies and from pragmatics and sociolinguistics to comparative linguistics, demonstrating various ways in which an analysis of linguistic form in different contexts of our discipline can contribute to our understanding of the "total linguistic fact" (Silverstein 1985).

Reference

Silverstein, Michael. 1985. Language and the culture of gender. In Elizabeth Mertz and Richard Jay Parmentier (eds.), *Semiotic mediation*, 219–259. New York: Academic Press.

Chantal Tropea
2 The emergence of Bahasa Gaul: A comparative study of Yogyakarta and Jakarta youth

The patrons of "youth language" are youth, who distinguish themselves from "others" in a given anthropo-social space (i.e., neighborhood, city, region, country) by their particular way of speaking (de Féral 2012). Indonesia, home to over 718 local languages (*bahasa daerah*), offers numerous case studies. Youth linguistic registers share specific linguistic processes, such as phonetic manipulation, semantic reversal, morphological reduction and borrowing. Most of these characteristics are found in Indonesia's generic youth language, known as Bahasa Gaul, literally 'the language of socializing' or 'the social language' (from *bergaul* 'to socialize'). From the late 1990s, a new Indonesian youth language emerged. Its syntax and morphology follow that of standard Indonesian, with strong influence from the Betawi language of Jakarta, Javanese, and linguistic registers such as Prokem (the language of Jakartan gangsters), Bahasa Walikan (inverted language) and Bahasa Waria (transgender language). This study traces the emergence of this language register and its spread in Indonesia, highlighting the linguistic practices of young Indonesian students in two major university cities, Jakarta and Yogyakarta. It reveals highly personal ways of youth interaction and socializing linked to the exploration of personal identity. These identities exhibit different linguistic expressions in the two cities. Naturalistic data obtained through informal conversations in university contexts and questionnaires for the general understanding of the linguistic background of the informants form this study's backbone. It compares conversations between young students from the university cities of Yogyakarta, Depok and South Jakarta. Taking into consideration the influence of local vernaculars, this study demonstrates how students manage to express their culture linguistically. Data were collected during two fieldwork periods, sponsored by the University of Naples "L'Orientale", in the academic years 2017–2018 in the city of Yogyakarta and 2018–2019 in Jakarta. Bahasa Gaul allows young people to build a social identity by distinguishing themselves from older generations.

Chantal Tropea, University of Naples "L'Orientale", e-mail: chantix.ct@gmail.com

https://doi.org/10.1515/9781501514685-003

1 Introduction

Indonesia's size and ethnic diversity has made national identity a challenge. Throughout the twentieth century standard Indonesian was designed to unify the nation in the shortest possible time amidst a constantly evolving modernity (Heryanto 2007). During the Suharto era (1966–1998), the government considered the standardization and modernization of Indonesian a driver of economic development and a national responsibility, promoting the use of *Bahasa Indonesia yang baik dan benar* ('correct and appropriate Indonesian language') (Djenar 2018: 4). Many people were alienated from this "high form" and had no incentive to participate actively in language development (Heryanto 1995: 50). In the last decade of the Suharto era, the young people sparked some of the loudest criticism against the government, triggering the president's resignation in May 1998 (Bodden 2005). The post-Suharto era heralded a period of transition known as *Reformasi,* characterized by significant socio-political reforms and a more open environment. This democratization process included free elections, press freedom and "one of the most radical decentralization programs attempted anywhere in the world" (Aspinall and Fealy 2003: 9). Previously the standard variety had been prioritized, but afterwards the focus shifted to preserving local languages. In addition to social changes, Indonesia's young middle classes thus also acquired linguistic freedom. Local vernaculars began to foster artistic and individual expression, whereas Bahasa Gaul became a means to articulate freedom. The Bahasa Gaul of Indonesia's youth expresses familiarity and solidarity between youth from different regional and linguistic backgrounds, as shown below.[1]

(1) a. A:
    Jadi **piye?** *Mau buka puasa* **dimane** *nih kita?*
    so how? want open fasting where PRTCL 1PL
    'So how? Where do we want to open the fast?'
  b. B:
    Terserah, **gue** *ikut lo aja sih!*
    up_to_you 1SG follow 2SG just PRTCL
    'It's up to you, I'll just follow you.'

The above conversation demonstrates how utterances indicate familiarity and solidarity through code-switching. Students based in Yogyakarta and Jakarta (who

---

[1] All forms that are not marked bold are also used in standard Indonesian. Capital letters indicate Speaker A and B, respectively.

were informants for this research) come from everywhere around the archipelago, and tend to adapt to the local Bahasa Gaul to express, both, a localized and a cosmopolitan identity. In (1a) the Javanese word *piye* 'how' indicates the student's ethnic identity, and the Betawi words *gue* 'I' (1b) and *dimane* 'where'(1a) his wish to belong to the cosmopolitan identity of the capital. This Colloquial Jakartan Indonesian (Sneddon 2003) emerged among the capital's young middle classes, where regional linguistic differences and standard Indonesian have blended into a new linguistic register commonly known today as Bahasa Gaul. Highly popular in university contexts, it expresses an increasingly cosmopolitan Indonesian youth culture. Today, young people living in big cities are a particularly salient group in Indonesian society for demonstrating the reinvention of their identity after the fall of the New Order, with a new identity characterized by mobility and outward-looking aspirations (Smith-Hefner 2007). Sneddon (2003) has never applied the term Bahasa Gaul to youth language, but Djenar, Ewing and Manns (2018), and Hefner (2012), agree that Bahasa Gaul constitutes a new youthful colloquial register expressing a shared social identity and a sense of belonging among its speakers. According to their definition, the function of Bahasa Gaul is to build a solidarity-based social identity through the register of young speakers, actively rejecting the previous generation and its orientation towards patriarchy, formality and fixed social hierarchies.

2 The social language

The term *gaul*, as a social phenomenon, emerged at the end of the twentieth century and was initially linked to the language of Jakarta's young middle classes. The Gaul identity shows regional, ethnic and religious differences. Those associated with the Gaul identity are connected by a departure from the conventions of the previous generations, with their emphasis on hierarchy and uniformity, towards new ways of connection within the intersubjective space (Djenar 2018: 28). The informal "social language" is considered the successor of Bahasa Prokem 'the gangster and criminal slang' that became Jakarta's youth slang in the 1980s (Hoogervorst 2014: 105). It makes extensive use of loanwords from Bahasa Walikan 'the inverted language' (known also as Bahasa Kilab from Malang and Yogyakarta city), Bahasa Alay, literally 'the language of the kite runner kids', Bahasa Binan and Waria, 'the languages of homosexuals and transgender', and from local languages such as Betawi and Javanese. It rejects standardization, and embodies aspirations toward a new modernity, expressed through Indonesia's enormous linguistic melting pot. Of particular interest for the present research are the distinctive elements in the Bahasa Gaul of two major university cities, Jakarta and Yogyakarta.

Through code-switching, the speaker simultaneously marks a proud sense of local rootedness through the use of colloquial language, but also internationalization through borrowings from English, as shown in the example (2).

(2) a. A:
Next time *ber-kata-lah* *jujur,* *ya?*
next time AV-talk-PRTCL honestly INTJ
'Next time talk honestly, ok?'
    b. B:
Maksud *kowe* *opo,* *sis?*
meaning 2SG what sister
'Sister, what do you mean?'

The example above shows a situational code-switching type. In (2a) a student from Jakarta uses the English words 'next time' and in (2b) his interlocutor the form 'sis' as the abbreviation of 'sister', a common friendly appellative. He also uses the Javanese pronoun *kowe* 'you' and the interrogative *opo* 'what'. This type of almost unconscious code-switching among students marks affinity to a cosmopolitan society where English words are used as part of the Indonesian language, as well as regional belonging through Javanese.

3 Method and materials

This study uses a qualitative sociolinguistic approach with a focus on participant observation – for a relatively long period of time – in the social life of the group whose language I studied. This granted me not only naturalistic data but also the opportunity to develop a vision from the "inside". For me as a student it was not difficult to immerse myself in the Gaul world and to collect data from student groups based in Yogyakarta and Jakarta for two semesters (from August 2017 to February 2018 in Yogyakarta and from September 2018 to February 2019 in Jakarta). The *budaya nongkrong* ('hangout culture') allowed me to spend time with young informants (Yogyakarta and Jakarta-based and aged 18 to 28). For the follow-up research, I chose 25 informants based in Yogyakarta and 25 in Jakarta, from different linguistic backgrounds (Central Java, Sunda, Jakarta, Padang, Sumatera Selatan). Questionnaires were used to gain a general understanding of their linguistic backgrounds. The choice of informants developed organically, without a clear preference for men or women. I ended up working with easily approachable students who had lived in the university cities for a minimum of two years. Age was relatively important to their selection as 19 to 29 is still considered young: no longer adolescent but not yet adult. This is the age in which my consultants – to varying degrees – experimented, broke away from normative behavior, formed social groups, undertook adventures, and engaged with taboo topics (sex and drugs), all of which express through the language of socializing.

Opportunities for social interaction and a comparison between the two university cities were created in a completely informal way. As I became a part of these groups, collecting naturalistic data became not only simpler, but also fun, breaking down the walls of seriousness and discipline imposed by questionnaires and preprinted word lists, and giving space to the spontaneity and creativity so important to the Gaul identity. The 100 brief conversations considered most important were analyzed and 1926 terms belonging to the Bahasa Gaul were extrapolated. Informants were not only students from the various faculties of the University of Indonesia (UI) in Jakarta (where I was an exchange student), but also from the well-known Jakarta Institute of Arts (IKJ), Studio Hanafi, Yogyakarta State University (UNY), and Gadjah Mada University (UGM) in Yogyakarta. Important sites of research were the *tempat nongkrong* 'hangout places' of the *anak jaksel*[2] 'youth from South Jakarta', the street kiosks (*warung*), and the main bars in the southern area of Yogyakarta city. Students in Indonesia usually gather at the *kantin* 'university food court' after class to, as the idiom goes, *ngopi sambil nongki* 'enjoy a coffee and hangout playing music, drinking and smoking together'. Data extrapolated from about three and a half hours of recordings of natural conversations were transcribed and analyzed using the linguistic documentation tool ELAN (Eudico linguistic annotator).

4 The main sources of Bahasa Gaul

The initial manifestations of colloquial languages from Indonesia (such as Bahasa Prokem, Walikan and Banci) can be defined as anti-languages or argots, whose function was cryptic and restricted to small communities to strengthen the cohesion of their group. Together with English loanwords and borrowings from local languages, Bahasa Prokem became one of the main sources for the formation of new vocabulary in Bahasa Gaul. The environment of its users is different, however: Bahasa Gaul is used to some degree by all young educated people and has spread broadly (among youth who want to appear cool, on social media and

---

[2] Abbreviation of Jakarta Selatan 'South Jakarta'.

in teen literature), while Bahasa Prokem is limited to criminals, gangsters and street kids. The street kids using Bahasa Prokem can be considered the intermediates who transferred their language from the criminal realm to the students who, thanks to their education, began to pay attention to the linguistic processes of words formation (Chambert-Loir 1984: 17).[3]

The main element that characterizes Prokem-derived words is the addition of the infix -ok- and the loss of the final rhyme of the syllable, as shown in example (3) (now addressing me).

(3) a. A:
Di Italy **rokum** mbak-nya dimana sih?
in Italy house Miss-DET where PRTCL
'Where do you live in Italy?'

In the example above, the word for 'home' *rumah* becomes *rokum* through the infixation -ok- and apocope (eliminating the final rhyme -ah). The phonetic changes found in Prokem words seem to follow coherent phonological processes. Table 2.1 below summarizes the various phonetic changes that occur in the formation of Prokem words adopted in Bahasa Gaul.

Table 2.1: Linguistic study of Bahasa Gaul terms from Prokem derivation.

Processes	Word transformation	Meaning
Prothesis + metathesis	kaos → wakos	't-shirt'
	kain → wakin	'fabric'
	gaun → wagun	'formal dress'
infix -ok- + apocope	rumah → rokum	'house'
	jelek → jokel	'ugly'
	minum → mokin	'to drink'
	bapak → bokap	'father'
	preman → prokem	'criminal'
	duit → doku	'money'
Epenthesis + syncope	jual → jokul	'to sell'
	keluar → kelokur	'go out'
Epenthesis + syncope + metathesis	berdua → bedokau	'in two'
	ngopi → nokip	'drink coffee'

---

[3] In the late 1960s, Bahasa Prokem was already used by criminals and drug dealers, but only after 1975 did the language began to spread widely among young people in the capital city evolving and influencing much of the vocabulary of the current Bahasa Gaul (Chambert-Loir 1984: 117).

Other secret linguistic registers used as lexical sources for Bahasa Gaul are Boso Walikan Malang 'the inverted language' from the city of Malang, Boso Walikan Jogja, an inverted language based on the Javanese syllabic alphabet (see Hoogervorst 2014: 106–107), Bahasa Alay 'the kids' language' famous for its abbreviations used with alphanumeric codes in text and social media, Bahasa Binan and Waria 'the homosexuals' and transgender languages', and Bahasa Senang, associated with streetwise youth from Yogyakarta (Stodulka 2017).

Speakers of Boso Walikan ('the inverted language') as currently spoken in the city of Yogyakarta, invert syllables of the Javanese syllabic alphabet, using these words as part of their slang. Many words have thus been assimilated within this register of socializing, which is unique to Yogyakarta. Yogyakarta's Boso Walikan is based on an inversion in the Javanese syllabic alphabet, which consists of four rows of five characters (*aksara*) in a fixed order. The characters of line 1 and 3 are replaced with their odd correspondents, and 2 and 4 with their even ones:

- Row 1: *ha-na-ca-ra-ka*
- Row 2: *da-ta-sa-wa-la*
- Row 3: *pa-dha-ja-ya-nya*
- Row 4: *ma-ga-ba-tha-nga*

For example, *nyothe boho* in (4a) is the Boso Walikan inversion of Javanese *kowe sopo*, 'who are you?', where the syllable *ko* has been replaced by its counterpart *nyo*, while the second row character *we* has been replaced by its counterpart *the*, becoming *nyothe* 'you'. The same process took place for the Javanese word *sopo* 'who', which became *boho*. Similarly, *pinyi* in (4b) is the inversion of the Javanese word *(h)iki* 'this', *dhewe* 'we' has become *methe*, *dab* is the inversion of *mas* 'older brother', *ngombe* 'to drink' has been reversed as *lodse*, and *rokok* 'smoking' as *nyonyon* (4c).

(4) a. A:
       Nyothe boho?
       2SG   who
       'Who are you?'
  b. B:
       Pinyi jape methe, dab
       this friend 1PL mas
       'He's our friend, bro!'
  c. A:
       Sinilah,   **lodse** *sambil* **nyonyon.**
       sini-lah lodse sambil nyonyon
       here-PRTCL drink while rokok
       'Come here, let's drink and smoke.'

d. B:
    | *Yo* | **wis,** | *dia* | *jadi* | **mumet** | *ngomongnya* | *baja* | please! |
    | yo | wis | dia | jadi | mumet | ngomong-nya | baja | please |
    | INTJ | enough | 3SG | become | confused | talk-DET | normal | please |
    'Hey, enough! You are confusing him. Talk normal, please!'

Through this language, young speakers in Yogyakarta proudly demonstrate their sense of cultural and traditional belonging, using Boso Walikan in daily interactions.

4.1 The influence of the local languages: Javanese and Betawi

The influence of local languages in the two university cities (Javanese in Yogyakarta and Betawi in Jakarta) brings local culture into Bahasa Gaul. Considering the complex ethno-linguistic situation in Indonesia most people's first language is a local one. Yogyakarta is promoted as the most culturally proud Javanese city (which was named the ASEAN city of culture 2018–2019). Javanese is the native language of more than 98 million people in Indonesia (more than 42% of the total population). Spoken in Yogyakarta, Central and East Java, as well as West Java and Banten, it has a rich written and oral literary tradition with a strong influence on the political and socio-economic life in the country. Javanese influence is also evident in the contemporary Bahasa Gaul spoken by youth in Yogyakarta.

In the conversations analyzed among Indonesian youth, the influence of local languages is reflected differently in the two cities. In Yogyakarta, the influence of tradition, which young people want to proudly maintain and use to show their identity, is often evident in interactions in Bahasa Gaul through the code-switching with the use of Javanese terms and forms. The prevalent type of code-switching that takes place between the young students in the two university cities is situational switching, that is, switching that signifies belonging to a specific ethnic or social group, thus becoming a marker of ethnic and social identity (Holmes 2001: 37). The example below shows a brief conversation between two university students in Jakarta who both have roots in Java.

(5) a. A:
    | *Lo* | *kelihatan* | *capek* | *banget.* |
    | lo | ke-an- lihat | capek | banget |
    | 2SG | INV.UV-see | tired | very |
    'You look so tired.'

b. B:
Literally *gue beneran pusing banget* sama UAS   Pak Untung
literally gue bener-an pusing banget sama UAS   Pak Untung
literally 1SG right-EMPH dizzy   very   with final_exams P. U.
'I am literally dizzy because of Pak Untung final exams...'

c. which is *dikumpulin   minggu depan.*
which is di-kumpul-in   minggu depan
which is UV-collected-APP week   next
'...which are to be handed over next week.'

d. *Tolong, piye iki   ngerjainnya?*
tolong piye iki   Ng-(k)erja-in-nya
help   how this AV-carry_out-APP-3SG
'Help, how to carry out with it?'

e. A:
Mangats bebski   gokill!
mangat-s beb-ski   go-kill
luck-PL   baby- EMPH go-kill
'Good luck, babe!'

This brief conversation shows an example of code-switching that includes both English and local languages. In fact, *piye iki* used in (5d) is Javanese and literally means 'how [to do] this'. The second personal pronoun *lo*, is a Betawi word (used in Jakarta); the English expressions "literally" and "which is" used in (5b) and (5c) have become part of the vocabulary of daily Indonesian interactions in Bahasa Gaul; *mangats* is from *mangat* 'good luck' with the English pluralization -*s*-; *bebski* (from 'baby') with the addition of the suffix -*ski* marking emphasis; *gokill*[4] used in (5e) is typical of the Gaul language, ('go get'em') and used to wish someone 'good luck'. The speakers, coming from Yogyakarta but settled in the capital city, switching between Bahasa Gaul, English and Javanese, use their speech to show an international identity, but at the same time they proudly preserve their origins through the use of Javanese.

Students in Yogyakarta, meanwhile, often use abbreviations from Javanese words, while code-switching with Javanese shows a sense of belonging to one's ethnic origin, as evident in example (6).

---

4 In Bahasa Prokem this word means 'crazy' (with the infix -*ok*- to the original word *gila* 'crazy').

(6) a. *Boleh   ngak   aku   dijodohin   sama   temannya   mbak?*
    boleh   ngak   aku   di-jodoh-in   sama   teman-nya   mbak
    can   NEG   1SG   UV-match-APP   with   friend-DET Miss
    'Can I be your friend's soulmate?'
  b. *tapi   aku   **pecelele**,   dong!*
    tapi   aku   pecelele   dong
    but   1SG   lover_of_fat_girls   PRTCL
    'But I'm a fat girls' lover! You know it!'

The word *pecelele* used in (6b) is an abbreviation of the Javanese phrase *pecinta cewek lemu lemu*, or 'fat girls' lover'. A large number of Bahasa Gaul words are formed on the basis of new meanings attributed to existing signifiers for which abbreviated forms are created. Numerous conversations in Bahasa Gaul among youth in Yogyakarta demonstrated this use of abbreviations from Javanese, reproducing words that actually exist in the language but which have been given new meanings. The most frequent ones are listed in Table 2.2.

Table 2.2: Javanese abbreviations in Bahasa Gaul of Yogyakarta.

Abbreviation	Original meaning	Meaning in Bahasa Gaul
mendes (menthel ndeso)	'village girl'	'rube'
pede (pokok dhewe)	*pd (percaya diri)* ('believe in yourself')	'stupid'
pecelele (pecinta cewek lemuk-lemuk)	fish dish	'lover of fat girls'
bimoli (bibir monyung lima senti)	oil brand	'surly' ('mouth protruding five centimeters')
bojonegoro (bojo nesu nergo aku goro)	city name	'angry wife' ('my wife got angry about my lies')
cangkih (cangkeme nggah-nggih)	'sophisticated'	'nod without understanding' ('mouth yes yes')
cengklu (boceng telu)	–	'ride a bike in three'
cabe-cabean	'chili'	'eccentric girls'
klaten (kelalen yes wes manten)	province of central Java	'eager to please' ('forget to be married')
lugu (lucu tur guoblok)	'sincere'	'stupid' ('funny but stupid')
pahpoh	'dodgy'	'klutz'
setu legi (setengah tuek lemu gini-gini)	*satu lagi* ('another one')	'fatty but adorable'
kacang (kakean cangkem)	'nut'	'chatty' ('big mouth')

Table 2.2 (continued)

Abbreviation	Original meaning	Meaning in Bahasa Gaul
kentang (kena tanggung)	'potatoes'	'to be responsable'
randek (randa keren)	–	'cool widow'
hamsyong (hampa kosong)	–	'loneliness' ('empty soul')
macan tutul (manis cantik turunan Bantul)	a type of feline	'beautiful girl from Bantul city'
mantul (mantap betul)	–	'wonderful' ('really good')
jablay (jarang dibelai)	–	'prostitute' ('rarely protected')
mukrit (munyuk kriting)	–	'curly hair'

The Bahasa Gaul used in the capital city, Jakarta, is strongly influenced by the local language Betawi. The Betawi language is the variety of Malay spoken in Jakarta (also known as Jakartan Indonesian, Jakarta Malay and Betawi Malay), a creole language based on low Malay and the only variety of Malay spoken on the north coast of Java Island. In the conversation shown in example (7), there are many terms of the Bahasa Gaul vocabulary influenced by Betawi.

(7) a. A:
   Kadang **lu** *enggak* **danta**.
   sometimes 2SG NEG clear
   'Sometimes you are not clear.'

b. **Gimane** *mau dia dekatin* **lu** *kalo manyun trus?*
   gimane mau dia dekat-in lu kalo manyun trus
   how want 3SG approach-BEN 2SG if surly keep_on
   'How do you want her to approach you if you continue to be grumpy?'

c. B:
   Bener *bet.*
   bener bet
   right very
   'She's right!'

d. *Jika kamu coba senyum certainly enggak akan di-pikir-in*
   If 2SG try smile certainly NEG FUT UV-think-BEN
   songong!
   arrogant
   'If you try to smile, certainly you'll not be seen as arrogant.'

e. C:
Eeh, bagen aje, **gue** bubar elu berdua jangan **ngejeplak** trus!
eeh bagen aje gue bubar elu berdua jangan Ng-jeplak trus
INTJ let just 1SG go 2PL NEG AV-nonsense keep_on
'Hey, forget it, I'm leaving. You don't keep talking in vain.'

f. A:
Kenape dia oi? Dongo, di-tambah bete banget.
why 3SG INTJ delayed UV-add bad_temperament very
'Why? He's very stupid and surly.'

All of the words used in this brief conversation are of Betawi origin. In (7a) *enggak* is the negation used in the capital city, *danta* is the Betawi term for 'clear', *gimane* is the distortion with the vowel change from /a/ to /e/ from the standard word *gimana* 'as', a distortion that is also evident in *bener* (7c) from *benar* 'right' and *kenape* (7f) from *kenapa* 'why'. *Songong* in (7d) is the distortion of the word *sombong* 'arrogant', in which the sounds /mb/ have been replaced by /ng/. In (7e) *bubar* is the intransitive verb 'to leave' in the colloquial register, and *dongo* in (7f) is an insult that can be translated as 'retarded'. *Elu berdua* is the second plural personal pronoun 'you' of Betawi origin. The word *ngejeplak* derives from *njiplak* 'to fake something' used in the Bahasa Gaul of Jakarta to say 'speak in vain' or 'say something fake'. Interesting is the case of the word *manyun*, a term of Sundanese origin spread in the capital city with the meaning 'grumpy'.

Quite common in Bahasa Gaul is the use of metaphors, opposite metaphors, euphemisms and word games hidden behind the frequent use of acronyms, forming new words especially for insults (see Table 2.3) and taboo elements, such us drug and sex terms (Table 2.4). My data from informal conversations contains many words used by informants as insults and swear words. A selection can be seen in Table 2.3.

Table 2.3: Differences in insults between Yogyakarta and Jakarta.

Yogyakarta	Jakarta	Meaning
asu	anjing, buset	'bastard'
goblok, bego, pede (pokok dhewe) dhegleg, congok, pekok	tolol, kunyuk bodoh	'stupid'
mendes (menthes ndeso)	kampungan, udik	'rube'
ndasmu njebluk	pale lu peang	'crazy' (out of your mind)
kopet	taik	'piece of shit'
modyar	mampus	'die, asshole'

Table 2.3 (continued)

Yogyakarta	Jakarta	Meaning
ribet	rempung	'annoying'
dagamu	manyun	'surly'
gombrek	kulkas pintu ('fridge door')	'fat man'
pah-poh	dudul, lambat/lola ('loading lama')	'bumbling'
uedan	gokil	'crazy'

Numerous differences have been found in Gaul terms regarding the *dugem* world, an abbreviation for *dunia gemerlap* 'the shining world', used when talking about sex and drugs.

Table 2.4: Differences in taboo words between Yogyakarta and Jakarta.

Yogyakarta	Jakarta	Meaning
dasuny, mendem	teler	'high' (by drug)
semok	bohay	'sexy'
dhaid	ML (making love)	'to have sex'
ngocong peli	coly	'to masturbate'
fundamental	pantat	'butt'
susu ('milk')	toket	'boobs'
pee pee	seminar	'to ejaculate'
lonte, pelacur, kupu-kupu malam ('night butterfly'), mami, muncikari	ayam kampung ('village chicken'), pecun, lonte, bitch, keple, pereks, jablay	'prostitute'
sangek (sakau ngewek)	sangek, horney	'horny'
intil, memek	parji; pussy	'vagina'

Knowledge of the use of these terms and many others relating to sex and drugs (a fundamental domain for the development of the Gaul vocabulary), and their variants between the two university cities is important in order not to be, as the youth say, *kudet*, abbreviation of *kurang update*, or 'backward'.

4.2 The influence of the English language in Bahasa Gaul

Intentional code-switching with the language, a feature that is found especially in the capital city, shows a feeling of belonging to a social group that consciously takes part in the internationalization process, indicating a cosmopolitan identity.

Like borrowings from Javanese and Betawi languages, Bahasa Gaul uses numerous acronyms and abbreviations also from English, to which new meanings are given (Table 2.5). Frequent in Bahasa Gaul is the use of English-sounding terms that are actually abbreviated forms of Indonesian words.

Table 2.5: English sounding words used as abbreviations in Bahasa Gaul.

English sounding words used in Bahasa Gaul	Indonesian abbreviations of the English-sounding words	Meaning in Bahasa Gaul
brownies	*brondong manis*	'handsome guy'
gazebo	*gak jelas bro*	'it's not clear, bro'
modus	*modal dusta*	'to cheat'
gamon	*gagal* + move on	'to fail to move on'/'to be nostalgic/reminiscent about love'
primus	*pria mushola*	'man praying in mushola'
netting	negative thinking	–
darting	*darah tinggi*	'high blood pressure'
jones	*jomblo ngenes*	'sad single'
ilfil	*ilang* + feeling	'losing interest'
intel	*indomie pakai telor*	'noodles with eggs'
baper	*bawa perasaan*	'sentimental'
jilboobs	*jilbab* + boobs	'sexy Muslim girl'
jaim	*jaga* + image	'preserving someone's image'
missqueen	*miskin*	'poor'
she book cari do it	*sibuk cari duit*	'busy to find money'

Missqueen is the distortion of the word *miskin* 'poor' with the use of the English words *miss* and *queen* spoken with the Indonesian pronunciation; the expression *she book cari do it* takes on a new meaning if it is spoken using the Indonesian phonetic system *sibuk cari duit*, or 'busy to find money'. These word games show the fascinating processes of word formation in Bahasa Gaul, with the young speakers' attempts to represent their youth language through English.

Many English loanwords are abbreviations of whole sentences or expressions, which are not necessarily used in English but have become part of Bahasa Gaul as abbreviations and acronyms, as shown in the following Tables 2.6 and 2.7.

In addition to acronyms, there are numerous English loans that have undergone phonological assimilation and have been adapted to the pronunciation of the Indonesian language, such as *klebing* from Engl. 'clubbing', *chekidot* from 'check it out', *enjoi* from 'enjoy', *saiko* from 'psycho'. Other English terms have been adapted to Indonesian morphophonological characteristics. This is the case of

Table 2.6: Abbreviations from English.

Abbreviations	Literal meaning	Meaning in Bahasa Gaul
kepo	'knowing every particular object'	'too curious'
lola	'loading' + *lama*	'long loading'/'delayed'
oretz	'all right'	–
tal	'thanks a lot'	–
tfr	'thanks for ride'	–
beib	'baby'	–
bohay	body haduhai	'sexy'
menfess	menyebut dan confess	'anonymous message'
bece	'because'	–
bete	'bad temperament'	'surly'
tempra	'temperamental'	–
sensi	'sensitive'	–

Table 2.7: Acronyms from English.

Acronyms	Fully spelled	Meaning in Bahasa Gaul
CMIIW	correct me if I wrong	–
CYA	see you again	–
BRB	be right back	–
MBA	married because accident	'unwanted pregnancy'
FYI	for your information	–
NSFW	not safe for work	'violent elements/porno'
TGIF	thank God it's Friday	–
IMHO	in my humble opinion	–
IYKWIM	if you know what I mean	–
LMAO	laugh me my ass off	–
ROTFL	rolling on floor laughing	'laughing too much'
BF	blue film	'porn film'
ML	making love	'have sex'

verbal forms that have been made transitive in active voice by adding the Indonesian prefix *meN-* such as *ngedance* 'to dance', *ngejam* 'jamming', *ngeprank* 'to prank'.[5]

5 Concluding remarks

The present study was conducted with the aim of analyzing Bahasa Gaul, Indonesia's latest youth linguistic register, developed by the new generations of the archipelago. The first anti-languages born in Indonesia (Bahasa Prokem, Walikan and Waria) together with English and local languages constitute the base for the creation of this modern linguistic melting-pot. In Indonesia, as a multilingual nation, the concept of diglossia often reflects what Berruto (1995: 242–250) calls *dilalìa*, in which there is the continuum between the "high" and the "low" varieties of speech. The emergence of different linguistic registers, with similar but different ways of speaking, became a distinctive sign of belonging to a certain community. This colloquial language, born out of historical-political motivations emerging in the Reformasi period, gave young people a new youth identity. Language, in its different and changing forms of expression, has become a fundamental tool to express new group identities. The identity-formation of Bahasa Gaul speakers has become an integral part of modern society. A prerogative of the young metropolitan middle classes, it emphasizes the individual needs and desires of new generations, keeping the hierarchies and formalities of the previous generations at bay. For Indonesian young people, not speaking Gaul is not being cool, not being fashionable, not being sociable and not belonging to the new cosmopolitan identity. In Yogyakarta, young speakers deliberately (and proudly) link their cultural identity to traditional values of what is considered Indonesia's cultural capital city. Through their variety of Bahasa Gaul, its youth manage to combine their local culture with needs related to internationalization, through the powerful medium of interactional language. In Jakarta, despite the strong Betawi influence, the frequent code-switching and sometimes the excessive use of loanwords from English, underline a more cosmopolitan reality, reflecting the international orientation of one of the most influential metropolitan cities of Southeast Asia. Although it is not easy to determine the extent to which code-switching is spon-

---

5 In standard Indonesian the transitive verbs in active voice take the prefix *meN-*, where the *N* symbolizes a nasal that is assimilated by the first sound verb base. In Bahasa Gaul verbs tend to take only the *N-* of the prefix *meN-* or the most common prefix in Bahasa Gaul *Nge-* (with verbs beginning with *b, d, j, g, l, r, h y*, preceding a vowel or with foreign loans).

taneous, the modern interactions and linguistic socializing highlighted in this chapter reflect the dynamics of changing times and the desire among youth to belong to a society in which *gaul* has become synonymous with 'modern'.

Abbreviations

1SG	first-person singular
2SG	second-person singular
3SG	third-person singular
1PL	first-person plural
2PL	second-person plural
3PL	third-person plural
ADJ	adjective
APP	applicative
AV	actor voice
BEN	benefactive
CAUS	causative
DET	determiner
FUT	future
INV	involuntary
NEG	negation/negative
PRTCL	particle
UV	undergoer voice

References

Aspinall, Edward and Greg Fealy. 2003. *Local power and politics in Indonesia: Decentralization and democratization*. Singapore: ISEAS.

Berruto, Gaetano. 1995. *Fondamenti di sociolinguistica*. Roma: La Terza.

Bodden, Michael. 2005. Rap in Indonesian youth music of the 1990s: Globalization, outlaw genres, and social protest. *Asian Music* 36. 1–26.

Chambert Loir, Henri. 1984. Those who speak prokem. In Henri Chambert Loir and James Collins (eds.), *Indonesia* 37. 105–117.

de Féral, Carole. 2012. "Youth languages": A useful invention? *Langage et Société* 141 (3). 21–46.

Drummond, Rob. 2018. *Researching urban youth languages and identity*. Basingstoke: Palgrave Macmillan.

Djenar, Dewi Noverini, Michael Ewing and Howard Manns. 2018. *Style and intersubjectivity in youth interaction*. Berlin: De Gruyter Mouton.

Hefner, Nancy J. Smith. 2012. Youth language, gaul sociability, and the new Indonesian middle class. *Jurnal Studi Pemuda* 1 (1). 61–78.

Heryanto, Ariel. 1995. *Language development and development of language* [Pacific Linguistics 86]. Canberra: The Australian National University.
Heryanto, Ariel. 2007. Then there were languages: Bahasa Indonesia was one among many. In Alastair Pennycook and Sinfree Makoni (eds.), *Disinventing and reconstituting languages,* 42–61. Clevedon: Multilingual Matters.
Holmes, Janet. 2001. *An Introduction to sociolinguistics*. London: Longman.
Hoogervorst, Tom. G. 2014. Youth culture and urban pride. The sociolinguistics of East Javanese slang. *Wacana: Journal of the Humanities of Indonesia* 15 (1). 104–131.
Sneddon, James. 2006. *Colloquial Jakartan Indonesian*. Canberra: Pacific Linguistics ANU Press.
Stodulka, Thomas. 2017. *Coming on age on the streets of Java: Coping with marginality, stigma and illness*. Bielefeld: Transcript.

Janika Kunzmann
3 Diverging verb derivational strategies in the youth language Yanké (DR Congo)

It has been argued that African (urban) youth languages share many features not only regarding their functions, but also in terms of the linguistic strategies that are applied (Kießling and Mous 2004: 303). In this context, youth languages are not only an interesting field of study from a sociolinguistic perspective, but also regarding morphosyntactic deviations. This paper uses morphosyntactic data to gain insights into the linguistic strategies that are applied to express applicative, causative, reciprocal, reflexive and passive in the youth language Yanké (or Lingala ya Bayankee). As the youth language is based on the Bantu language Lingala, it is expected that it will diverge from the Bantu typical verbal extensions which are commonly used to express derivative concepts. It is assumed that Yanké speakers will draw on alternative constructions in order to set themselves apart from Lingala. Based on the supposition that in adolescents' linguistic practices the complexity of verb morphology decreases, it is expected that periphrastic constructions will be preferred over verbal extensions in the youth language. An analysis of Yanké derivative strategies and a comparison to the base language will reveal that in both varieties, speakers make use of almost the same derivative strategies, involving borrowing and calquing from French. Although developing in the same direction, this linguistic change seems to be taking place faster in Yanké than in Lingala, as more alternative constructions occur in Yanké than have been attested for Lingala. Since most of the alternative structures found in Yanké can be identified as a product of language contact with French, it cannot be confirmed that Yanké speakers make use of periphrastic constructions in their aim of reducing the complexity of verbal morphology in the youth language, but rather, the borrowing and calquing techniques inherently evoke analytic structures.

1 Introduction

African youth languages are mainly examined from a sociolinguistic perspective, since their main function and motivation lies in the marking of a group identity, together with the aim of distancing the adolescent group of speakers from non-

---
Janika Kunzmann, Goethe University Frankfurt, e-mail: janikakunzmann@gmail.com

https://doi.org/10.1515/9781501514685-004

group members. These aspects and many others make African youth languages an interesting field of study, but not only from a sociolinguistic perspective: the linguistic divergence between African youth languages and other prevailing languages is generated deliberately, using creative linguistic strategies in order to distance the group from "the others" (Kießling and Mous 2004: 303, Hollington and Nassenstein 2015: 1). Especially against this background, the study of African youth languages offers exceptional insights into their deviant morphosyntax. As Kießling and Mous (2004: 303) argue, African (urban) youth languages share many features, not only regarding their function but also in terms of the linguistic strategies that are applied by youth language speakers. This approach aims to contribute to the recent study of youth language practices in Africa by focusing on morphosyntactic issues, here, verb-to-verb derivational strategies in the youth language Yanké.[1] Yanké is spoken in Kinshasa, the capital of the Democratic Republic of the Congo, and is based on the Kinshasa variety of the widely used Bantu language Lingala (classified as C30b [see Maho 2009]). A typical feature of Bantu languages is the use of verbal extensions to mark derivational processes on the verb. In this work it is assumed that Yanké, as a youth language, will deviate from the properties of its base language[2] by making use of periphrastic constructions instead. This is based on the supposition that in adolescents' linguistic practices the complexity of verb morphology decreases. Therefore, periphrastic constructions would be the preferred choice of construction, since they allow the grammatical and lexical information to be spread over more than one lexeme.

This work[3] is based on *A grammatical study of the youth language Yanké* by Nassenstein (2014a) and on unpublished elicited data.[4] The existing data on

---

[1] In this work, the name "Yanké" will be used, which, according to Nassenstein (2014a: 4), is perceived as adequate by the speakers. Another commonly used term is "Lingala ya Bayankee".
[2] The term "base language" is intended to emphasize that the grammatical properties of the language constitute the grammatical base of the youth language. However, this grammatical base is not used without deviations. In this work, "base language" is preferred over the term "matrix language", since the latter is primarily used in the context of codeswitching, which, according to Kießling and Mous (2004: 304), is not sufficient to describe the phenomenon of youth languages in the African context.
[3] This study is a completely reworked, adapted and translated part of my thesis, submitted at Johannes Gutenberg University Mainz.
[4] I want to express my gratitude to Nico Nassenstein, who kindly made available the linguistic data he collected during multiple fieldwork stays in Kinshasa, without which this work would not have been possible. I would also like to take this opportunity to express my appreciation to Nico Nassenstein and Svenja Völkel for their valuable guidance and support throughout this work. Furthermore, I want to thank the anonymous reviewers for their comments and thoughts, as well as Mary Chambers for proofreading.

Yanké will be examined regarding the verb derivative strategies used to express applicative, causative, reflexive, reciprocal and passive meanings. This first step will reveal which derivative strategies are used in the youth language. In the second step, the results will be contrasted with data on Lingala, based on Nassenstein (2012, 2014b) and Meeuwis (1998, 2010, 2013). This comparison will show which of the strategies found in Yanké are particularly characteristic of the youth language.

First, in Section 2, the reader will be introduced to the historical and social context of Yanké. In Section 3, general insights will be given into Bantu verbal morphology, followed by the analysis of verb derivative techniques in the youth language. The results will be analyzed and compared to findings on Lingala in Section 4.

2 The African youth language Yanké

The youth language Yanké is based on the Lingala[5] variety that is spoken in Kinshasa (see also Hurst-Harosh and Nassenstein, this volume). Following its earliest predecessors in the 1950s, Yanké arose in the 1970s and is still spoken today by young adolescents, who belong to a youth movement called *Yankisme*, *Bayanké(e)* or *les Yankées*. The movement embraces a collective identity with certain norms, social practices, style and ideology. Yanké speakers are mainly male adolescents between the ages of 5 and 25. Usually they live on the streets of Kinshasa or are members of (former) so called *Kolúna* gangs that used to rule Kinshasa's streets for many years. Hardly any girls or women can be found who speak Yanké or are able to understand it. In contrast to age and gender, the social background and ethnicity of the speakers seem to play only a minor role for the street children. Many of them are forced to live on the streets because they have been banished from their families due to accusations of practicing witchcraft. Thus, many have rather loose connections to their families (Nassenstein 2014a: 15–24). Generally, the status of the group is considered to be more important than that of the individual. Criteria such as job, education or salary are less important than

---

5 Lingala evolved in the late 19th century in the northwestern province of the DR Congo. It is one of the national languages of the DR Congo and the Republic of Congo. In the capitals, Lingala is usually spoken as a mother tongue, whereas in rural areas it is used more often as a lingua franca. Lingala is spoken by approximately 20–25 million speakers (Meeuwis 2010: 11, Nassenstein 2014b: 13).

the social rank of the speaker, which is based more on values like "'toughness', 'masculinity', 'callousness' and being a 'trendsetter'" (Nassenstein 2014a: 29).[6]

Shared linguistic practices serve to mark in-group identity amongst the adolescents and exclude non-group members. Yanké speakers draw on Kinshasa Lingala as their base language. However, this grammatical base is not used without deviations. As is characteristic of African youth languages, Yanké differs from Lingala to such a degree that it is almost incomprehensible to Lingala speakers (Kießling and Mous 2004: 303). Regarding verbal morphology, these deviations include the development of the grammatical future marker *ké-*, the shortening of the Lingala progressive marker *zó-* to *ó-*, and the loss of two past tense markers (Nassenstein 2014a: 60–61). Deviations in derivative verbal morphology will be examined in the following sections, giving general insights into the verbal morphology of Bantu languages, followed by the analysis of the derivative categories applicative, causative, reflexive, reciprocal and passive in the youth language Yanké.

3 Verbal derivation techniques in Yanké

Languages of the Bantu family share some characteristic structural properties. These include a strongly agglutinating character and a complex verbal morphology, whereby the verb carries multiple affixes. Subject and object markers carrying information on e.g. person and number, as well as inflectional categories such as tense or aspect, are predominantly prefixed (Schadeberg 2003: 71). In contrast to inflectional categories, derivational categories are predominantly suffixed in Bantu languages. Derivative processes on the verb are largely realized by verbal extensions, which usually occur in the form -VC-. Their main function is to modify the verb root semantically and/or syntactically. Verbal extensions may also occur in other functions, such as expressing emphasis, but generally they serve to increase or decrease the valency of a verb. Suffixed to a verb root, and sometimes involving morphophonological processes, extensions form a new (extended) verb stem with modified meaning. A special feature of verbal extensions in Lingala is that they are tonally neutral. They receive their tone by assimilation from the subsequent morpheme (Meeuwis 2013: 29). In Lingala, the productive verbal extensions are the applicative morpheme *-el*, the causative morpheme *-is*, *-an*

---

[6] However, Yanké is not solely spoken by this subgroup of male adolescents involved in the criminal scene. As Nassenstein and Pasch (this volume) argue, varieties usually labeled as youth languages are found to be used by speakers of all ages and beyond the typically presumed urban context.

for neuter or reciprocal, the passive morpheme *-am* and the less productive morpheme *-w*, which marks separative or reversive (Meeuwis 2010: 147).

Verbal extensions facilitate the expression of derivative and lexical information in a single lexeme, whereas periphrastic constructions require the speaker to spread the grammatical and lexical information over two or more lexemes. Splitting grammatical and lexical information as well as not requiring the same morphophonological processes, periphrastic constructions are here assumed to be somewhat less complex and are thus expected to be preferred in youth language practices. Therefore, it is assumed that Yanké will make use of alternative periphrastic constructions instead of synthetic verbal extensions, as is common in Bantu languages, to reduce morphological complexity in the verbal phrase. In the following, strategies used to express applicative, causative, reflexive, reciprocal and passive concepts in the youth language Yanké will be examined.

3.1 Applicative

The applicative is a valency increasing category that allows the promotion of a participant from an adjunct position to the position of the direct object. In other words, the S argument takes on the function of the A argument and a peripheral noun phrase is introduced as a new core argument in the position of the O argument (Dixon 2010: 169). This newly introduced argument most commonly specifies the goal towards which the action of the verb is directed (Glück 2000: 52). The semantic role of the new argument is usually that of the beneficiary. In Yanké, the applicative can be formed morphologically, using the verbal extension *-el*. Example (1) shows the extension in its prototypical function of naming a beneficiary in the position of a core argument:

(1) *A-tak-él-é*[7] *móro nayé bouteille*[8] *mó ya bóki.*
SM$_1$-steal-APPL-FV mother POSS$_{3SG}$ bottle one CON beer
'He stole a bottle of beer for his mother.'

The verbal extension is inserted between the verb root and (the TAM suffix and/ or) the final vowel. The beneficiary holds the position of the direct object. In addition to the function of promoting adjuncts with benefactive semantic roles,

---

[7] The final *-é* is labelled as "FV". However, it should be noted that it inherently denotes the present tense, which is not overtly marked in the interlinear gloss. The final vowel *-é* appears in verbs derived from French or English, such as *-bayé* 'smoke', *-také* 'steal' or *-damé* 'eat'.
[8] Lexemes derived from French will follow French orthography.

the verbal extension -*el* can also be used to express instrumental and directional concepts (Nassenstein 2014a: 62). Another function is illustrated in example (2):

(2) *Centr-él-é   nga   tál-á   kâ!*
    get.closer-APPL.EMPH-FV:IMP 1SGO look-FV:IMP only
    'Push me closer/introduce me, come on!'[9]
    (Nassenstein 2014a: 62)

Here, the verbal extension emphasizes the action denoted by the verb (Ngonyani 1995: 1, in Nassenstein 2014a: 62). It is not used to introduce a new object and has no influence on the valency of the verb. Even though the extension is productive in Yanké, there are several examples showing the applicative morpheme lexicalized. Example (3) shows its lexicalization in the verb -*yébela*:

(3) *Na-yéb-él-í   petit   wâná   lóbí.*
    SM$_{1SG}$-know-APPL-PRS girl DEM   yesterday
    'I had sex with that girl yesterday.'
    (Nassenstein 2014a: 62)

In this case the verbal extension has no applicative function but is lexicalized with the verb -*yéba* 'know' to become the new verb stem -*yébela*, which has the meaning 'keep up to date' or 'have sex' (Nassenstein 2014a: 62). Besides morphological constructions using the verbal extension -*el*, the applicative can also be formed analytically, as illustrated in example (4):

(4) *Ba-tak-an-ak-a   pó na ba-momí ya   Victoire ó*
    SM$_2$-steal-RECP-HAB-FV for LOC CL2-girl CON place   DEM
    ba-seng-ak-a   peng   belé.
    SM$_2$-demand-HAB-FV   money much
    'They steal from each other for the girls around Victoire Square, who ask a lot of money.'

Here, the beneficiary is introduced by the preposition *pó na*, which directly follows the verb. The verb is not extended by the applicative extension but carries a combination of the reciprocal extension -*an*, which indicates the mutuality of the action, and the prefinal -*ak*, which indicates that the action is habitual.

---

[9] The original interlinear glosses of cited examples have been partly modified for reasons of uniformity.

3.2 Causative

Like the applicative, the causative derivation allows the valency of the verb to be increased and another object added as a core argument. The S argument of the previously intransitive sentence takes on the function of the O argument and a new argument is introduced in position of the A argument (Dixon 2012: 239–240). The new argument usually introduces a participant that causes the action denoted by the verb (Glück 2000: 338). In Yanké, the causative can be formed morphologically by the verbal extension -*is*:

(5) *Na-ko-dam-ís-é   yó   tí   na   dix-sept heures, bôngó*
    SM$_{1SG}$-FUT-eat-CAUS-FV 2SGO tea LOC 17   o'clock then
    ó-kend-e.
    SM$_{2SG}$.SBJV-go-FV
    'I will let you eat until 5 o'clock, then you (may) go!'

The verbal extension adds the causative meaning to the verb. The argument denoting the causer is in subject position as the subject marker *na-*. The direct object, which was previously in subject position, follows the verb in first position. The extension -*is* has the allomorph -*es*, as shown in example (6):

(6) *O-bul-és-ákí   pásta wâná té   pó   na   níni?*
    SM$_{2SG}$-think-CAUS-PST priest DEM   NEG   for LOC ITRG
    'Why didn't you make the priest think?'

In this example, the allomorph -*es* is probably used to create a higher phonetic similarity to the underlying form -*bulé* 'think' (Nassenstein 2014a: 46). Like the applicative extension, the causative extension is lexicalized in some verbs, such as -*kótisa* 'sell' from -*kóta* 'enter' or -*bimisa* 'buy' from -*bima* 'go out/outside'. In addition to the morphological causative construction, Yanké reveals two types of periphrastic constructions (Nassenstein 2014a: 61–62). One is a typical syntactic construction, as illustrated in example (7):

(7) *Sókí o-súndol-í   nga   na-bay-é   nwa   póro*
    if   SM$_{2SG}$-cause-PRS 1SGO SM$_{1SG}$-smoke-FV marijuana father
    a-o-bót-é   nga.
    SM$_1$-FUT-beat-FV 1SGO
    'If you make me smoke marijuana, father will beat me up.'
    (Nassenstein 2014a: 61)

The example shows a biclausal periphrastic construction. The causative meaning is conveyed by the verb *-súndola*, which can be translated as 'cause'. The causer is marked on the verb as the subject. The first person singular *nga* follows the verb, denoting the grammatical information of a direct object, and is followed by the verb denoting the lexical information, here *-bayé* 'smoke', marked in the subjunctive mood. The second type of periphrastic construction in Yanké is based on a calque borrowed from French, as illustrated in example (8):

(8) Ó   wâná   e-sál-ak-a   ná-lí-a   butú   mobimba.
     DEM   DEM   SM$_{INAN}$-do-HAB-FV   SM$_{1SG}$.SBJV-eat-FV   night   whole
     'This causes me to eat all night long.'
     (Nassenstein 2014a: 62)

Here, the causative meaning is conveyed by the verb *-sála*, which can be translated as 'do'. It follows the verb carrying the lexical information 'eat'. The lexical verb is marked in the subjunctive mood, as is typical in periphrastic constructions (Nassenstein 2014a: 62).

3.3 Reflexive

The reflexive derivation usually indicates that two arguments of a transitive verb, the A and O arguments, have the same reference (Dixon 2010: 175). In contrast to the applicative and causative derivations, the valency of the verb decreases. In Lingala, reflexivity can be conveyed using the prefix *mi-*. In Yanké, however, the reflexive prefix is only rarely used, but still occurs lexicalized (Nassenstein 2014a: 63):

(9) Petit   ya   quartier   a-mi-kóm-ís-í   na   place
     boy   CON   neighborhood   SM$_1$-REFL-arrive-CAUS-PRS   LOC   place
     ya   mawa.
     CON   sadness
     'A boy of the neighborhood committed suicide.'
     (Nassenstein 2014a: 64)

The reflexive marker is prefixed to the verb 'arrive', which is extended by a causative extension. The verb obtains the altered meaning 'commit suicide'. Besides this, the prefix can also be used to express a certain notion of group membership. This use of the reflexive morpheme is not freely applicable but is restricted to certain verbs (Nassenstein 2014a: 63–64).

The common strategy for expressing reflexivity in Yanké is the use of reflexive verb forms borrowed from French, such as *s'expliquer* 'explain yourself' or *s'excuser* 'excuse yourself'. In Yanké, these are realized as *s'expliquer* [sɛksplike:] and *s'excuser* [sɛkskize:], whereby the French reflexive third person singular pronoun *s'* is lexicalized as a part of the verb stem. Example (10) shows the reflexive use of the borrowed verb *-kipé ya/na*, which comes from the French verb *s'occuper* and can be translated as 'take care of someone' (Nassenstein 2014a: 64):

(10) Yó,   s-o-kip-é   na   Kimbangu!
     2SGS   REFL-SM$_{2SG}$-take.care-IMP   COM   Kimbangu
     'You, take care of Kimbangu!'
     (Nassenstein 2014a: 64)

What is special about this example is that the *s-* is prefixed to the subject marker instead of being lexicalized with the verb stem, as is the case with other borrowed verbs. The *s-* is only prefixed if the subject marker denotes the second person singular *o-*. This is due to the phonetic resemblance to the underlying French verb *s'occuper* (Nassenstein 2014a: 64).

3.4 Reciprocal

The reciprocal derivation is a valency decreasing process, indicating that two or more arguments of the verb are interrelated (Glück 2000: 579). Generally, it causes a transitive verb to change to an intransitive verb with reciprocal meaning. This reciprocal verb requires an S argument that coordinates the arguments in A and O functions (Dixon 2010: 176). In Yanké, the reciprocal can be realized using the verbal extension *-an*, as illustrated in example (11):

(11) Pó   ba-dam-án-é   móko   síma   móko,   na   forêt équatoriale
     for   SM$_2$-eat-RECP-FV   one   after   one   LOC   rainforest
     mo-to   móko   té   a-tíkal-í.
     CL1-person   one   NEG   SM$_1$-remain-PRS
     'Since they ate each other, there are hardly any people left in the jungle.'

The extension causes the action to be understood as mutual. The verb refers twice to the subject marker *ba-* and no other actor is mentioned in object position. In addition to the morphological construction, reciprocal concepts can be expressed periphrastically using the reflexive prefix *mi-*, as shown in example (12):

(12) *Ba-zó-mi-tík-a   bá-bay-é   nwa   móko síma móko.*
     SM₂-PROG-REFL-let-FV SM₂.SBJV-smoke-FV   marijuana   one   after one
     'They let/make each other smoke marijuana one after another.'
     (Nassenstein 2014a: 62)

The reflexive morpheme is prefixed to the causative verb *-tíka*, which is a French calque going back to the verb *laisser* 'let' (Nassenstein 2014a: 62). It is followed by the lexical verb 'smoke' marked in the subjunctive mood. Both verbs carry the subject marker *ba-*, denoting the third person plural. The given example could indicate that the reflexive marker can be used to express reciprocal concepts when combined with a subject marker in its plural form.

3.5 Passive

As is the case in reflexive and reciprocal derivation, the passive reduces the valency of the verb by one argument. The prototypical passive applies to a transitive verb, causing the O argument to become the S argument of the passive sentence. The A argument moves to a peripheral position or is omitted. As a consequence, the new S argument comes to the fore (Dixon 2010: 166). This is usually accompanied by a formal marking on the verb that indicates the change in the semantic roles of agent and patient in their grammatical positions. In Yanké, the morphologically marked passive has almost become obsolete. Instead of verbal extensions, various alternative strategies are used to convey passive meaning. For example, the subject marker of the third person plural *ba-* can be used for an impersonal construction, as illustrated in example (13) (Nassenstein 2014a: 62):

(13) *Lóbí   ba-lón-ákí   yé   na   cimetière.*
     yesterday SM₂-bury-PST   3SGO   LOC   cemetery
     'Yesterday he was buried at the cemetery.'
     (Nassenstein 2014a: 63)

The unspecific subject marker is prefixed to the verb, allowing the speaker not to mention the agent of the action. The patient, the third person singular *yé*, follows in the position of the direct object. If the agent is to be named, it can be mentioned in a prepositional phrase, as illustrated in example (14):

(14) Lóbí   ba-káng-ákí   nga   epá   na   ba-mbíla
     yesterday SM₂-arrest-PST   1SGO   at/with LOC   CL2-policeman
     pó   na-bénd-ákí   ordinateur.
     because   SM₁ₛ𝒢-pull-PST   computer
     'Yesterday I got arrested by the police for stealing a computer.'

The agent is in adjunct position, introduced by the preposition *epá(i) na*. The patient, here the first person singular *nga*, follows the verb as a direct object. Another periphrastic strategy to convey passive meaning is calquing from French. In French, the passive can be formed using the auxiliary 'be' and a main verb in the past participle (Nassenstein 2014a: 63). This strategy has been taken on by Yanké speakers, as illustrated in example (15):

(15) Na-gnal-é [naɲaleː]   mo-to   wâná   yó   o-zal-ákí   boloké
     SM₁ₛ𝒢-inform-FV   CL1-person   DEM   2SGS 2SGS-be-PST   arrest
     na   lapolice.
     COM   police
     'I told that man that you were (had been) arrested by the police.'
     (Nassenstein 2014a: 63)

The verb *-zala* 'be' in its inflected form serves as an auxiliary. The lexical information is conveyed by the verb *-boloké* 'arrest', which goes back to the French verb *bloqué* in its past participle form.[10] This alternative form of passivation is not freely applicable but is restricted to a specific group of verbs (Nassenstein 2014a: 63). Another method of expressing passive meaning is the borrowing of French participles, as shown in example (16):

(16) Rolex   trop   porté   ya   b(a)-ásí...
     luxurious.watches   too.much   worn   CON   CL2-woman
     'Luxurious watches are pretty much worn by women (nowadays)...'
     (Nassenstein 2014a: 63)

---

10 As suggested by an anonymous reviewer, example (15) could also be analyzed as a copular sentence with a borrowed adjective in its participle form, whereby the construction does not need to be analyzed as a case of "calquing".

This impersonal construction makes use of the participle verb *porté*, which cannot be inflected and does not carry any further affixes, such as a subject marker. In this way, naming the agent of the action can be avoided (Nassenstein 2014a: 63).[11]

4 Tendencies of morphological and periphrastic constructions

To summarize the preceding analysis of derivative constructions occurring in Yanké, it can be concluded that constructions based on verbal extensions as well as alternative periphrastic strategies can be found in almost every derivative category. The occurrence of morphological constructions (relying on verbal extensions) and periphrastic constructions (relying on prepositions, calquing, borrowing and other strategies) found in Yanké are summarized in Table 4.1. In order to reveal which types of construction are particularly used in the youth language, the findings will be contrasted with derivative constructions in Lingala. Since the method used in this study does not allow any statement on the frequency of the derivative strategies, frequency will be roughly taken into account by drawing on statements from the literature (Meeuwis 1998, 2010, Nassenstein 2014a, 2014b). This information is incorporated into Table 3.1 by pointing out seldom used constructions in square brackets ([yes]).

Table 3.1: Occurrences of morphological and periphrastic constructions in the derivative categories applicative, causative, reflexive, reciprocal and passive in Yanké and Lingala.

	Yanké		Lingala	
	morphological	periphrastic	morphological	periphrastic
applicative	yes	yes	yes	yes
causative	yes	yes	yes	yes
reflexive	[yes]	yes	[yes]	yes
reciprocal	yes	yes	yes	no
passive	[yes]	yes	[yes]	yes

---

11 The reviewer also pointed out the lack of a copula (or rather any verb) in example (16). Further research can be carried out to investigate copula-dropping in spoken Lingala. Other examples are: *Wápi yó?* 'Where (are) you?' or *Yé ndeko na nga.* 'He (is) my brother.'.

4.1 Morphological constructions

It becomes apparent that morphological constructions expressed by verbal extensions are found in Yanké as well as in Lingala in almost every derivative category examined. However, the use of some verbal extensions seems to be declining, as the reflexive and passive extensions are reported to be used only rarely in both Yanké and in Lingala. Conversely, reciprocals, which are likewise a valency decreasing category, can only be realized morphologically in Lingala, whereas a periphrastic alternative construction occurs in Yanké. Regarding the form of the verbal extensions, there is no deviation observable between Yanké and Lingala.

4.2 Periphrastic constructions

In both varieties, constructions alternatively used for verbal extensions occur in all derivative categories, except for the reciprocal in Lingala. The majority is formed periphrastically. However, not only the term "alternative" is inaccurate, but also the term "periphrastic" covers a range of different kinds of constructions. Table 3.2 displays the variety of forms occurring in Yanké and Lingala:

Table 3.2: Constructions alternatively used for verbal extensions in the derivative categories applicative, causative, reflexive, reciprocal and passive in Yanké and Lingala.

	Yanké	Lingala
applicative	preposition: *pó na*	preposition: *pó na*
causative	calquing (French): *-sála* 'do' + lexical verb	calquing (French): *-sála* 'do' + *que* + lexical verb
	syntactic construction: *-súndola* 'cause' + lexical verb	
reflexive	reflexive verbs (French): *-kipé ya/na* 'take care of someone' (*s'occuper*)	reflexive verbs (French): *-kipé ya/na* 'take care of someone' (*s'occuper*)
reciprocal	reflexive marker: *mi-* + calque (French)	no construction
passive	impersonal construction: *ba-*	impersonal construction: *ba-*
	calquing (French): auxiliary + past participle	
	borrowing of participles (French)	

Comparing the youth language and its base language it becomes apparent that the periphrastic constructions found in Lingala do also occur in Yanké. However, there are periphrastic constructions in Yanké that do not occur in Lingala according to my data, such as the syntactic causative construction using the verb *-súndola*.

In both varieties, there is only one alternative construction for the productive applicative extension realized by the preposition *pó na*, whereas causative concepts can be expressed using biclausal constructions.[12] Also notable is the use of the reflexive marker to express reciprocal concepts in Yanké. As for the passive, multiple periphrastic constructions occur, offering alternatives to the less frequently used verbal extension. It is especially noticeable that all occurrences of calquing and borrowing stem from French, the official language in the Democratic Republic of the Congo.

5 Conclusion

When beginning to work on Yanké it was assumed that the youth language would tend to make use of periphrastic constructions over morphological constructions. This was based on the assumption that verbal morphology tends to be less complex in youth language practices than in their base language counterparts. Thus, in the case of Yanké, youth language speakers would prefer periphrastic constructions, which could be defined as less complex than typical Bantu verbal derivations, since lexical and grammatical information can be spread over more than one lexeme. The analysis of Yanké derivative strategies and the comparison to Lingala has shown that in Yanké more types of periphrastic strategies occur to convey verb derivational concepts than in Lingala. However, Yanké does not rely on periphrastic constructions alone, but also makes use of verbal extensions, which are productive to varying degrees. It does not seem to be the case that the reduction of complexity is the driving factor for the use of periphrastic constructions in the youth language. The distribution of grammatical and lexical information over more than one lexeme rather seems to be the result of language contact with French. Periphrastic constructions are not freely invented, but rather, speakers draw on existing constructions from French. Newly invented alternative constructions such as French calques are inherently periphrastic. In other words, the borrowing and calquing of French verbs comes with a periphrastic type of construction. Thus, a decreasing complexity in youth languages cannot be confirmed. Rather it can be stated that Yanké has developed away from Bantu properties, as speakers deliberately borrow lexically or structurally from French in order to deviate from Lingala. However, this is not only the case for Yanké. Lingala too

---

12 This is not surprising as Dixon (2010: 169) states that a significant difference between the categories is that the applicative is "normally marked by a morphological process to the verb, whereas causative is often shown periphrastically".

seems not to solely rely on typical Bantu constructions. This is not surprising given the fact that Kinshasa Lingala emerged from the pidgin language Bangala,[13] which at some point lost all its verbal extensions due to pidginization (Meeuwis 2019: 1, 28–29). The contact situation, involving several languages throughout the 20th century, has seemingly led to the reintroduction of verbal extensions in Lingala, but also of (new) periphrastic constructions. Besides the influence from French, it also must be considered that linguistic innovations from Yanké might find their way into Lingala, even though the youth language speakers are trying to avoid it (Nassenstein 2015: 86). It seems likely that Yanké is developing from morphological to periphrastic constructions, though this is occurring in some derivative categories more than in others. Therefore, it falls back on French on the lexical and structural level. Although implementing almost the same derivational strategies as Lingala, Yanké reveals more constructions based on calquing and borrowing from French. This might be due to the small number of Yanké speakers and the geographic limitations of the city, but also to the incentive for linguistic innovation in (African) youth languages.

6 Outlook

Examining African youth languages from a descriptive point of view is a little explored field that needs to be studied further. The comparative approach provides insights into the linguistic strategies applied by speakers on a structural level. As Kießling and Mous (2004: 303) state, urban youth languages (in the African context) share common properties not only in their function, but also in the linguistic strategies that are applied. It would be especially interesting to compare Yanké with other African (Bantu) youth languages to be able to determine whether morphosyntactic parallels exist, for example in the case of verbal derivations. A comparison between youth languages or between them and their base languages would lead to a better structural understanding. In future studies, the frequency and distribution of morphological and periphrastic derivations could be investigated. If more than one construction exists, what factors trigger the choice between a morphological or a periphrastic construction? The choice seems to be partially determined by social triggers, such as using constructions based on French "in order to convey 'coolness' and 'creativity'" (Nassenstein 2014a: 40).

---

[13] The pidgin language Bangala as described by Meeuwis (2019) can be seen as a predecessor to today's Lingala and to Northeastern Bangala (classified as C30a [see Maho 2009]), which is spoken until today in the northeastern parts of the DR Congo.

However, linguistic triggers must also be considered. Are different shades of meaning expressed by the proximity of the object to the verb in morphological constructions, in contrast to periphrastic constructions, in which the object is in an adjunct position? As the use of periphrastic constructions increases in some categories or even replaces the use of verbal extensions in others, such as the passive construction in Yanké, taking a closer look at semantic aspects would be valuable (Nassenstein 2014a: 62). Further examining morphosyntactic deviations in African youth languages will not only help us to gain a better understanding of the structural properties of youth languages in general but will also give further insights into the negotiation of linguistic practices in a multilingual and postcolonial context.

Abbreviations

1	first person
2	second person
3	third person
APPL	applicative
CAUS	causative
CL	noun class
COM	comitative
CON	connective
DEM	demonstrative
EMPH	emphasis
FUT	future
FV	final vowel
HAB	habitual
IMP	imperative
INAN	inanimate
ITRG	interrogative
LOC	locative
NEG	negation
O	object
PL	plural
POSS	possessive
PROG	progressive
PRS	present
PST	past tense
RECP	reciprocal
REFL	reflexive
S	subject
SBJV	subjunctive

SG   singular
SM₁   subject marker/class 1
SM₂   subject marker/class 2

References

Dixon, R. M. W. 2010. *Basic linguistic theory. Volume 1: Methodology*. Oxford: Oxford University Press.
Dixon, R. M. W. 2012. *Basic linguistic theory. Volume 3: Further grammatical topics*. Oxford: Oxford University Press.
Glück, Helmut. 2000. *Metzler Lexikon Sprache*, 2nd edn. Stuttgart and Weimar: J. B. Metzler.
Hollington, Andrea and Nico Nassenstein. 2015. Youth language practices in Africa as creative manifestations of fluid repertoire and markers of speakers' social identity. In Nico Nassenstein and Andrea Hollington (eds.), *Youth language practices in Africa and beyond*, 1–22. Berlin: De Gruyter Mouton.
Kießling, Roland & Maarten Mous. 2004. Urban youth languages in Africa. *Anthropological Linguistics* 46 (3). 303–341.
Maho, Jouni Filip. 2009. NUGL Online. The online version of the new updated Guthrie list, a referential classification of the Bantu languages. [https://brill.com/fileasset/downloads_products/35125_Bantu-New-updated-Guthrie-List.pdf] (accessed 22 March 2020).
Meeuwis, Michael. 1998. *Lingala*. Munich: LINCOM.
Meeuwis, Michael. 2010. *A grammatical overview of Lingála*. Munich: LINCOM.
Meeuwis, Michael. 2013. Lingala. In Susanne Maria Michaelis, Philippe Maurer, Martin Haspelmath and Magnus Huber (eds.), *The survey of pidgin and creole languages. Volume 3: Contact languages based on languages from Africa, Asia, Australia, and the Americas*, 25–33. Oxford: Oxford University Press.
Meeuwis, Michael. 2019. The linguistic features of Bangala before Lingala: The pidginization of Bobangi in the 1880s and 1890s. *Afrikanistik Aegyptologie Online* 2019 (1). [https://www.afrikanistik-aegyptologie-online.de/archiv/2019/5012] (accessed 28 April 2020).
Nassenstein, Nico. 2012. Directionality in Lingala. In Ulrike Claudi and Angelika Mietzner (eds.), *Directionality in grammar and discourse*, 189–203. Cologne: Rüdiger Köppe.
Nassenstein, Nico. 2014a. *A grammatical study of the youth language Yanké*. Munich: LINCOM.
Nassenstein, Nico. 2014b. *Kurzgrammatik Lingala: Eine Beschreibung der Sprache von Kinshasa und Brazzaville*. Aachen: Shaker Media.
Nassenstein, Nico. 2015. The emergence of Langila in Kinshasa (DR Congo). In Nico Nassenstein and Andrea Hollington (eds.), *Youth language practices in Africa and beyond*, 81–98. Berlin: De Gruyter Mouton.
Ngonyani, Deo. 1995. Towards a typology of applicatives in Bantu. Paper presented at the Annual Conference on African Linguistics, University of California, 23–25 March.
Schadeberg, Thilo. 2003. Derivation. In Derek Nurse and Gérard Philippson (eds.), *The Bantu languages*, 71–89. London: Routledge.

José Antonio Sánchez Fajardo
4 Exploring euphemistic initialisms in teenage computer-mediated communication

This study is intended to explore the morphosemantic and pragmatic features of euphemistic initialisms in teenage computer-mediated communication (CMC), particularly in chat rooms and forums (*Reddit r/teenagers* and *Teen line online*). The initialisms were extracted from the *Teenage Chat Rooms Corpus* (TCRC), and they were examined quantitatively and qualitatively to see if there was a recurring morphological pattern in the use of euphemisms. Findings show that, contrary to popular belief, initialed constructions are not frequent in teenage chat rooms, and that the vast majority of euphemistic forms are pragmatic markers. On the morpohological plane, multiple initialisms (*gtfo* < *get the fuck out*) are more common than single (*f* < *fuck*) or hybrid (*a off* < *ass off*) ones. Close attention has also been paid to the case of compound hybrids (CHs), e.g. *a-hole, n-word*, whose morphosemantic variability is dependent on etymons and sociological constraints.

1 Introduction

Word formation patterns are not limited to standard vocabulary. Colloquial youth language, for instance, shows that peripheral word-building is far from arbitrary, and that words can become means of community cohesiveness, in which a sense of togetherness is expressed through the exclusion of "unwished" members. This dimension of slang is based on the premises of solidarity and acceptance (Eble 1996: 11, Mattiello 2005: 13), through which participants are expected to become aware of linguistic norms and shared notions. The use of lexis as a bonding strategy has an impact on the processes of lexicalization and lexical creativity (Adger, Wolfram and Christian 2007: 27).

Euphemisms are a linguistic expression of said creativity, and teenagers especially use them to conceal tabooing in language. Of the various types of euphemistic formulas, this paper is particularly interested in the use of the so-called

José Antonio Sánchez Fajardo, University of Alicante, e-mail: jasanchez@ua.es

https://doi.org/10.1515/9781501514685-005

initialisms,[1] either pure (*f* < *fuck*, *fo* < *fuck off*) or hybrid (*a-hole* < *asshole*, *n-word* < *nigger*).[2] Although a number of initialisms have been documented by descriptive dictionaries in English (e.g. OED3, MWD11), far less attention has been paid to the morphological and euphemistic properties of such abbreviated constructions. Thus, this study is aimed at exploring the morphosemantic traits and pragmatic functions of euphemistic, initialism-based words in teenage computer-mediated communication (CMC), in contemporary English. The reduction (or shortening) of taboo words has been recognized as a well-established mechanism of euphemistic expression, making such words be felt less offensive (Jamet 2018: 12). There are manifold ways of disguising the offensiveness of words: the use of dingbats accompanying the initial letter (*f*$#*), the use of asterisks (sometimes only one is preferred) accompanying the initial and the final letters (*f**k*), just the initial letter (*f*), letter alteration (*fukc*), or lexical substitution (*fax*). These examples show the downgrading effects of letter/sound omission in certain euphemisms. The use of CMC as a source of linguistic data, as suggested by Palacios and Núñez (this volume), shows that young users embrace an array of syntactic and morphological conventions. The use of initialed constructions corresponds to one of these sources or conventions, and it is hypothesized that it might be currently used by English-speaking teenagers in the creation of euphemistic constructions in CMC, particularly in chat rooms and forums.

Through the study of euphemism-referencing initialisms in English, this chapter offers an interesting insight into the global nature of youth linguistic strategies, which are not necessarily restricted by language origins and families. Colloquial youngspeak never ceases to change, and the appropriation of word formation mechanisms, such as initialism or acronymy, is an expression of how language reflects common codes and current global trends. A case study such as the one being discussed here contributes to a better understanding of how teenagers' communicative practices are not realistically envisaged by adult speakers.

---

1 This process has been previously described as a type of "distortion" by Burridge (2012), as either "an earmark of professional '-eses' such as Bureaucratese and Medicalese" (e.g. *OAPs* < *Old Age Persons and Pensioners*) or a form of verbal disguise in which the speakers just keep the first letter of the taboo word (75).
2 All the initialisms used throughout the study are written in an uncapitalized form to keep exemplars more orthographically coherent.

2 Limiting the scope of study

2.1 Types of initialism

Initialisms and acronyms are generally excluded from major morphological volumes, e.g. *The Oxford reference guide to English morphology* (Bauer et al. 2015), owing to their orthographic and phonological properties. However, an initialism might also be considered a morphological device in which the "initial letters of words are used as an abbreviation for a name or an expression, usually pronounced separately" (Hamawand 2011: 11), which are "used in place of words or phrases that otherwise might be considered harsh or unpleasant" (Annan-Prah 2015: n.p.). The fact that these constructions have been linked to their etymons shows that their morphological constituency is not as superficial as hinted. Whilst acronyms are found to show a more visible lexicalization process (e.g. *laser* < *light amplification by stimulated emission of radiation*), initialisms seem to fail on the phonological level, resulting in an apparently more conventionalized unit in writing (e.g. *UN* < *United Nations*), with lesser chances of being used in oral discourse.

The present analysis is based on the notion that initialisms are lexicalized constructions that comply with the principles of economy of language and semantic compositionality. Some authors differentiate the types of initialism in terms of lexical sourcing, and on some occasions units such as *A-line* and *D-Day* are left out because either *A* does not stand for any lexical item or *D* is a redundancy of the base *day* used in the complex word (Cannon 1989: 106). The discrepancies on what is to be considered initialism are not really dependent on the actual nature of the process, but on the analytical criteria used in the study.

Figure 4.1 provides an overview of two global models of euphemistic initialisms that are based on their morphological constituency: (i) pure initialism (PI), which can be single (S-PI) as in *f* < *fuck*, or multiple (M-PI) as in *wtf* < *what the fuck*; and (ii) hybrid initialism (HI), which can be either a phrase hybrid (PhrH) or a compound hybrid (CH).

A phrase hybrid, as in *a off* (< *ass off*) or *f you* (< *fuck you*), is a syntactic combination of full words and at least one initialism. Alternatively, a compound hybrid, is a morphologically complex unit that involves the process of compounding, in which one of the bases is an initialism (only the initial letter is used) and the other one is a full word, e.g. *a-hole* < *asshole*, *n-word* < *nigger* + *word*, *b-girl* < *bar* + *girl*. Figure 4.2 shows a construction-based template of a compound hybrid, in which the leftmost base is generally an initial, and the rightmost base, a full word.

Prior studies on the use of initialisms and acronyms in instant messaging or computer-mediated communication demonstrate that initialisms are not as frequent as lower case typing and slang words (Tagliamonte and Denis 2008, Varnha-

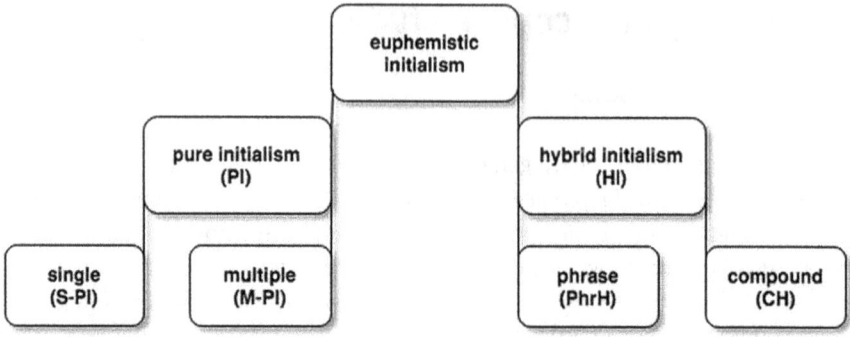

Figure 4.1: A morphological typology of euphemistic initialisms in English.

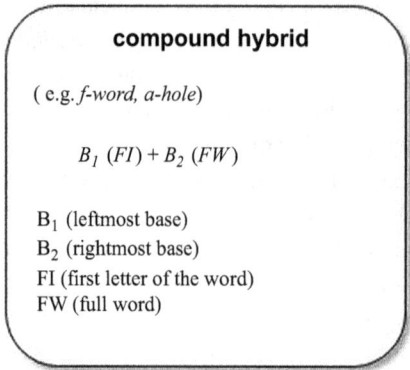

Figure 4.2: A construction-based template of compound hybrids in English.

gen et al. 2009, Baron 2011). Some of them did find, however, that various types of highly frequent abbreviations, such as *omg* and *lol*, were characterized by a pragmatic transition from the expression of surprise or laughter to the status of phatic fillers, "used by the participants in the flow of conversation as a signal of interlocutor involvement, just as one might say *mm-hm* in the course of a conversation" (Tagliamonte and Denis 2008: 11). In other words, *omg* and *lol*, might have lost their primary communicative goal, and are currently used as linguistically "vague" units to keep a conversation going. This kind of pragmatic transition is not exclusive to English: Stenström (this volume) has found that the rudeness of three Spanish vocatives is fading, and the semantic values of their original meaning are not retained at present. Euphemistic units are meant to neutralize occurrences of dispreferred language in face-to-face communication. However, teenage online speech is also found to be "emblematic of nonconformity to established social norms of appropriate behavior," and hence to be "generated in the social milieu that most consistently defies those norms" (Labov 2001: 501). Accordingly, euphemisms can be expressed by the use of initialisms but not all initialisms refer to a euphemistic motivation.

In short, one of the inherent features of initialisms is their pragmatic and semantic ephemerality, particularly in netspeak. The ever-growing immediacy of messages has made initialisms even more prolific, and somehow more cryptic. Abbreviated forms such as initialisms and acronyms are the utmost representations of CMC-based cryptolect, as they are orthographically restricted in the formation of words. Initialisms have traditionally been part of slang word-stock, and slang has managed to nest in writing "in the glow of a handheld or laptop or desktop screen", in which users "create ties that bind users in a group" (Dalzell and Victor 2012: xii–xiii).

2.2 Euphemism in teenage slang

The theory of euphemism has generally been linked to that of faces and politeness as "[a] euphemism is used as an alternative to a dispreferred expression, in order to avoid possible loss of face: either one's own face or, through giving offense, that of the audience, or of some third party" (Allan and Burridge 1991: 11). Therefore, a euphemistic expression is a context-driven choice that is available to speakers to mitigate linguistic taboos, for it is associated with an individual's desire "to be positively regarded in social context" (Crespo-Fernández 2015: 45). When speaker A chooses *freaking* (and not *fucking*) as an intensifier in an utterance, A is aware that *freaking* complies with the social norm, and the speech act of disapproval (or anger) is understood by speaker B. The innate conflicting emotions of individuals towards the concept of taboo result in multiple ways of euphemistic expression (Casas Gómez 2012: 44). However, this study is not meant to explore the axiological categorization of euphemisms but rather to focus on the morphosemantic changes undergone by dispreferred words in specific contexts.

The motivations underlying the euphemistic constructs are more palpable by members of such a community, particularly because "[s]hared taboos and the rites and rituals that accompany our euphemistic behavior increase group identity through feelings of distinctiveness; they strengthen the social fabric" (Burridge 2012: 70). From a sociolinguistic perspective, teenage slang is characterized by numerous "rituals" that are meant to reinforce the cohesiveness of the group. This responds to the anthropological urges of teenagers to restrict their speech community (Eble 1996, Allen 1998, Smith 2011); as well as to the natural acquisition by children and teenagers of taboo topics such as death or sex (Carter 2016: 99–100).

An important part of this language construction or cryptolect (cf. Davie 2019) is taboo representation in everyday language, chiefly due to the immanent realization of what aspects of a cultural frame are more taboo than others. In their process of unraveling taboo domains (and dispreferred terms to designate them), a number of formulas are identified, which might replicate standard word formation strategies in English.

From a psychological point of view, it has been suggested that teenagers discuss their real-life problems online, and some everyday taboo topics (e.g. sexuality) are more comfortably explored through computer-mediated communication (Huffaker and Calvert 2005) rather than face-to-face communication. This is expected to show some quantitative and qualitative results on the use of online euphemisms that differ from everyday speech, since teenage users are responsible for creating both these online communities and the adapted language used in them.

3 Methodology

All the data was gathered from two teenage chat rooms (*Reddit r/teenager*, *Teen line online*) from July to December 2019, in the form of a linguistic corpus: *Teen Chat Room Corpus* (TCRC). The TCRC is naturally the backbone of the present analysis as this paper seeks to explore the speech produced by teenagers, and not necessarily for teenagers. The corpus-based analysis of the data consists of two stages: (a) manual annotation of initialism-based euphemistic units, and (b) examination of morphosemantic and syntactic constructions. In the case of (a), a preliminary search was intended to log the units that fit both of the following parameters: (a.1) an initialism is identified as one of their bases; (a.2) at least one of their etymons is seen as offensive or taboo (*fuck*, *God*). Acronyms (e.g. *milf*, *yolo*) are left out as they do not fit the conceptual properties of initialisms on the level of morphology.

Using *AntConc*, a freeware toolkit available online for the compilation and processing of data, it was possible to identify the frequency of previously annotated units, and to isolate text strings to examine their pragmatic functions and morphosemantic paradigms (stage b). These paradigms are established through the classification criteria introduced in Section 2.1: (i) pure initialism and (ii) hybrid initialism. Findings are expected to show which type of euphemistic initialism and dispreferred topic is more frequent in the chat rooms. Due to the volume of data (approx. 820,000 words in the TCRC corpus), two annotators have participated in the disambiguation process, one of whom acting as an expert annotator or superannotator. The inter-annotator agreement (or IAA) shows high figures of recall: 97.5% for Part of Speech (POS) and 90% for word senses.

4 Findings and discussion

4.1 Euphemistic initialisms: Pragmatic motivations and frequency

In the process of data-gathering, all the initialism-based units were annotated (see a full list of initialisms in the Appendix), and those which are euphemistically motivated were also isolated for further analysis (see Table 4.1). As commented above, the euphemistic units collected in Table 4.1 are made up of at least one initialism-type base, which represents a dispreferred etymon.

Table 4.1: Euphemistic initialisms taken from the TCRC corpus.

Initialism	Dispreferred etymon
af	as fuck
a-hole	asshole
ak	ass kisser
a off	ass off
asf	as fuck
bs	bullshit
f	fuck
f-bomb	fuck
fs	fuck's sake
f-word	fuck, fat
fy	fuck yeah
gtfo	get the fuck out
hs	holy shit
jfk	just fucking kidding
mf	motherfucker
nnn	no nut November
n-word	nigger
og	oh God
omfg	oh my fucking God
omg	oh my God

Table 4.1 (continued)

Initialism	Dispreferred etymon
oml	oh my Lord
owo	oral without
thot	that hoe over there
tf	the fuck
wtf	what the fuck

The total number of initialisms (word tokens) in the TCRC corpus is 1,952,470 of which (24,1%) are initialism-based euphemisms. The number of initialisms in the corpus accounts for 0,24% of the total number of word tokens. This figure corroborates previous studies on the low use of abbreviations or shortenings in CMC-based texts (Baron 2004, Tagliamonte and Denis 2008), in which the use of these forms by teenagers is "much rarer than the media has led us to believe" (Tagliamonte 2016: 2019). This is also reflected in the use of full "dispreferred" etymons. For example, the word forms *fucked, fuck, fucks, fucking, fucker* appear 1,081 times in the TCRC, approximately accounting for four times the number of initialed *fuck* forms (266). As suggested by Huffaker and Calvert (2005) in their analysis of teenage computer-mediated communication, this is owing to their feeling of disinhibition and their online (fictional) representation of self. Hence, the use of disparaging language and euphemistic devices in chat rooms and forums cannot be used as a reliable illustration of teenage everyday speech. Findings on the recurrent morphosemantic and syntactic patterns can help understand which formulaic constructions are generally preferred by teenage users.

With regard to the correlation between *fuck* forms and their corresponding initialisms (e.g. *gtfo* < *get the fuck out, af* < *as fuck, fy* < *fuck yeah*), the most striking result to emerge from the data shows that initialism-based constructions are mostly discourse or pragmatic markers. Interestingly, the verb or noun *fuck*, with its literal informal meaning, is rarely attested as an initialism type; yet it is by far the most common etymon of initialed bases: *f, af, gtfo, fs, fy*. This indicates that some pragmatic functions are more prone to being euphemistically motivated than others. Table 4.1 also shows that 15 out of the 25 euphemistic initialisms are pragmatic markers,[3] particularly those with expressive or phatic functions. The

---

[3] The concept of pragmatic marker (sometimes also called "discourse marker" or "discourse-pragmatic marker") that is used here is based on four basic features: (a) the truth conditions of utterances are not modified; (b) the propositional content of utterances also remains intact; (c) the markers are related to speech situations, not situations themselves; and (d) their emotive

categorization of pragmatic markers is relevant here as various units, such as *f* (< *fuck*) or *gtfo* (< *get the fuck out*), might be used as phrases expressing surprise or disgust, rather than the (primary) denotative meaning of their constituents. Some of these units conform to standard initialisms that can only accept initialed graphemes: *just kidding* > *jk*, *just (fucking) kidding* > *jfk*. A plausible explanation for this is that some traditional pragmatic markers, not necessarily phatic fillers, are used as initialisms in CMC-based texts, e.g. *btw*, *wtf*, *tmi*, *fyi*, etc., and hence they can trigger new analogical constructions.

The preference of some pragmatic functions also confirms prior examination of computer-mediated and face-to-face types of communication in youngspeak. For instance, it has been suggested that CMC, as opposed to face-to-face communication, is characterized by higher levels of irony (Aguert et al. 2016), lesser semantic opacity in the case of sexual-identity commitment (Bond and Figueroa-Caballero 2016), and stronger speech-community cohesiveness and higher levels of linguistic variability (Greiffestern 2010). This shows that social or anthropological variables in teenage CMC are relevant traits, for teenage users find in their social groups the adequate channels to express "nonconformity" (Labov 2001) towards standard linguistic norms. Whereas initialisms seem to be restricted to some pragmatic forces (e.g. phatic filler), full (and dispreferred) etymons convey denotative or referential function in their sentences, and they are hence used dysphemistically. Therefore, the dichotomy of initialism/full etymon constitutes a linguistic variable, and its essential function can be ascribed to marking group membership (Chambers 2004: 349).

Besides being linked through their initialism-related constituency, all the euphemistic units compiled might share common pragmatic motivations. Their choice obviously depends on a given contextual situation, in which language economy plays no leading role. In examples (1) and (2), the forms *n-word* and *f-bomb* respectively are both used to attenuate the expression of a referent or reality. What distinguishes (1) from (2) is that the former is more dependent on the speaker's face as they attempt to convey a negative attitude towards racism. The *-word* construct accentuates the attitudinal perspective of the speaker in a communicative situation. The latter, alternatively, denotes a clear-cut perlocutive act which is, on the linguistic plane, intended to expressively neutralize a given forbidden reality (Casas Gómez 2012: 56–57), but on the pragmatic one, it can evocatively reinforce the feelings towards a subject matter through a visual guise of dispreferred lexis.

(1) Boomer is as offensive as the *n-word*.
     (Nov. 30, 2019, *Reddit*)

---

or expressive functions are more important than their referential or denotative ones (Jucker and Ziv 1998: 3).

(2) So you can drop *F-bombs* constantly but they will fine you if the title and/or thumbnail don't stick out as 'not for kids'.
(Nov. 26, 2019, *Reddit*)

(3) Idk how *tf* this works, leaving just seemed more logical.
(Nov. 30, 2019, *Reddit*)

Readers are able to interpret the communicative effect of *tf* in (3) as they are aware of the formulaic strategies that are used to (a) enhance social "incorrectness" and (b) express an illocutionary force, such as disapproval, disparagement, condemnation, etc. These strategies are repurposed by adult writers, particularly in magazines aimed at teenagers, who replicate these constructs while addressing certain taboo issues such as weight and eating disorders. In example (4), the author uses the *-word* pattern to convey their disapproval of the notion *fat* and all the social reality that has been built around the controversial issue of weight standards.

(4) The *F-word* is a series celebrating what it means to be fat – from destigmatizing the word to taking stock of the discrimination fat people face.
(Aug. 26, 2019, *teenvogue*)

As commented above, various forms such as *omfg* and *jfk* have been listed in Table 4.1 as euphemistic initialisms since one of their bases originates from a dispreferred etymon (i.e. *f* < *fucking*). However, these forms are different from "authentic" initialism-based euphemisms, namely *a-hole* and *hs*, because they are used within conventionalized patterns in English (*omg* and *jk*), which are primarily motivated by language economy and lexical innovation. This guarantees that speakers can signal group membership, but shows no intentionality of disguising an unwished word or concept. In other words, the euphemistic representation of dispreferred etymons is mediated through existing initialisms. The case of *tf* (< *the fuck*) is an interesting case as it is an initialed phatic filler being used within a standard, non-initialed utterance. Examples (5) and (6) show two extracts from the corpus in which *tf*, although conveying the intention of intensifying a communicative act, is used in two different syntactic frames. The truth is that although *tf* has been recorded in Table 4.1 as a euphemistic unit, it is never seen in isolation, as it necessarily combines with other complementary units which might be initialed or not.

(5) Yeah and honestly who *tf* is afraid of houses? What a bunch of pussies.
(Dec. 12, 2019, *Reddit*)

(6) 90% of people that think they have anxiety don't even know what *tf* it is.
(Dec. 17, 2019, *Reddit*)

4.2 Euphemistic initialisms: Morphosemantic traits

From a morphological perspective, the type of PI (20 items) is more frequent than that of HI (5 items) in the TCRC. M-PIs (e.g. *gtfo, tf*) are more prevalent than single ones (e.g. *f*), whereas CHs are scarce. Only 4 occurrences of CH have been attested in the TCRC corpus: *a-hole, n-word, f-word, f-bomb*. Interestingly, the *-word* constructs show that the unit is prone to polysemy as the leftmost base might be used to convey a dispreferred etymon. Although *n-word* has been rather conventionalized, the *-word* frame seems to be more "flexible" in the case of *f-word*.[4] The justification for this different pragmatic perception rests on the gradable aspect of taboo, and on how it is felt by proficient speakers of English: the domain of racism (*n-word*) is perceived as more politically incorrect (or "dispreferred") than the use of conversational expletives (*f-word*). Polysemy in this case is a clear reflection of both connotational input and sociological constraint. As seen in examples (4), (7), (8), (9) and (10), all extracted from the NOW Corpus, the initialed base *f-* stands for different etymons: *fat, future, faggot, fake, feminist*, respectively. These examples demonstrate that *-word*, besides gaining a combinatorial property, is also imbued with some appreciative traits that lead interlocutors to identify the guise of depreciation (or condemnation) within the frame itself. The base *-word* is not exclusive to teenage communication, but it has been imported, or appropriated, by young users to disguise dispreferred etymons.

(7) My sleeping schedule was off, and every time I heard, saw, or even thought of the dreaded *f-word* (future), I broke out in a cold sweat.
(May 31, 2019, *universitytimes.ie*)

(8) We spoke about straight people using the *f-word* ("faggot") and decided it wasn't okay but another listener is wondering.
(Jul. 19, 2019, *thestranger.com*)

---

4 Whilst the NOW Corpus shows 4,917 matching strings for *n-word*, in all of which *n* stands for *nigger*, the strings for *f-word* is 2,182, in which a number of 32 senses (including *fuck*) have been attested: *fat, future, fake, family*, to name a few.

(9) Fake news: Stunning how popular the new four letter *F-word* – FAKE! – has become.
(Jan. 19, 2007, *capebretonpost.com*)

(10) And Combs especially took issue with the fact that the new iteration of the beloved show was being described as a "fierce, funny, feminist reboot of the original series," mostly that final *F-word*: feminist.
(Oct. 18, 2012, *eonline.com*)

The nature of CH constructions (see Figure 4.2) in English also shows that B_2 (rightmost base) does not always have the same degree of frequency in the system. The (apparent) base -*hole* has only one lemma, i.e. *a-hole*, whereas the base -*word* has 6 attestations in the OED3 (see Table 4.2). Therefore, what seems to be a commonality among all these formations is the frame: $B_1(FI) + B_2(FW)$, but they are obviously induced by the morphological and semantic integration of the bases in the full etymon. The word *asshole* exists as a full word in English but *fuck-word* does not. The latter construct is built upon (a) the existing morphological paradigmaticity of CH schema and (b) the lack of semantic compositionality between the bases *fuck-* and -*word*. These two aspects lead to a high level of combinability of the base -*word* (as opposed to -*hole*, for instance), and perhaps its productivity.

Table 4.2: -*word* CH extracted from the OED3.

-*word* CH	Senses
c-word₁	The word *cunt*, usually euphemism with reference to its taboo status. Chiefly with *the*.
c-word₂	Any of various words having c as their initial letter, which are regarded in a particular context as contentious or taboo; specifically the word *cancer*. Chiefly with *the*.
f-word	Used as a euphemism for the word *fuck* because of the latter's taboo status.
l-word	Used in place of the word *liberal* in a political context where this word is regarded as having negative connotations.
n-word	Used instead of or in reference to the word "*nigger*" because of its taboo nature.
y-word	From offensive *Yid* 'Jew'.

A preliminary corpus-based analysis shows that *f* is highly frequent in the TCRC corpus, but further examination shows that the degree of frequency is linked to its morphological structure and pragmatic functions. *f* < *fuck*, an S-PI, is occasionally used as a pragmatic marker expressing surprise or disgust, and other similar M-PIs, such as *fs* < *fuck's sake*, are less frequent. However, the use of *f* here should not be confused with the popular form of showing respects by pressing the 'F' key. This function was appropriated from the videogame *Call of Duty: Advanced Warfare*, in which gamers were asked to pay respects by pressing 'F' on their keyboards after the funeral of one of their deceased comrades. This *F* in particular is not an initialism, so it is left out of our analysis. However, because of its homonymic nature, all the instances of *f* (367) were manually disambiguated to determine in which cases *f* (< *fuck*) was used as an initialism expressing surprise/disgust (57) to quantify its lexical load within the corpus. One effective means of disambiguating this unit is to examine the syntactic frame where it is used: *f* ('paying respects') is usually used alone and capitalized, without punctuation marks. Expletive *f*, on the other hand, is generally accompanied with syntactic collocates as in *Oh f* and *f yeah*.

This brief examination of morphosemantic traits of initialisms proves that CMC-based youngspeak imports standard mechanisms such as CH (e.g. *f-word*) and multiple-base constructions (e.g. *gtfo*). The assimilation of standardized formulas shows that certain units might be more favored than others, and this is related to slang language, group membership and ephemerality. However, further research should be undertaken to explore how teenage slang in general permeates into the word stock of standard English, particularly in computer-mediated communication.

5 Conclusion

The results of this investigation show that the frequency of initialism-based units is remarkably low in teenage chat rooms, which strengthens the premise on the use of abbreviations and acronyms in teenage CMC (Baron 2004, Tagliamonte and Denis 2008). The media, biased by appropriated standard forms (e.g. *wtf, btw, fyi*, etc.), is prone to stereotyping teenage talk as a type of speech that is fraught with initialisms and abbreviations. Contrary to expectations, the vast majority of the euphemistically motivated initialisms compiled are pragmatic markers. Full forms (e.g. *fuck, ass, fucking, fag*) are preferred when they are syntactically recognized as verbs or nouns (not as pragmatic markers), and their perlocutive force is perceived as dysphemistic. A possible explanation for this might be the correlation between euphemisms and chat rooms. Chat rooms are characterized by spontaneous, dialogic speech stretches in which interlocutors are not socially exposed, so the possible loss of face is not necessarily compensated through an alternative word or phrase, i.e. euphemism, to a dispreferred one. This, alongside with the sense of group membership and cohesiveness, has significant implications on the role played by morphological analogy in the creation of initialisms. The process of analogy dictates which forms, or syntactic functions, are more liable to be used as euphemistic expressions.

The quantitative analysis of the data suggests that PIs are predominant, while multiple constructs (*gtfo*) are more common than single ones (*f*). The examination of HIs, particularly CHs, undertaken here has extended our knowledge of the euphemistic value of this type of initialed compound in youngspeak. While not common in teenage chat rooms, the case study of -*word* units, particularly *f-word*, has shown that its leftmost initialed base might be open to homonymy (as in *f-word* < *fat, feminist, faggot, fake*, etc.), but some other forms (e.g. *n-word*) are more restricted owing to sociocultural constraints. Also, although *f-word* and *a-hole* are morphologically similar, the former only exists as a euphemistic unit whereas the latter has a full etymon (< *asshole*).

Appendix: Initialism-based units, and their frequencies, extracted from the TCRC corpus (in alphabetical order)

Initialism	Etymon	Frequency
add	Attention Deficit Disorder	8
adhd	Attention Deficit Hyperactivity Disorder	27
af	as fuck	42
a-hole	asshole	2
ak	ass kisser	6
aka	also known as	3
ama	American Music Awards	6
a off	ass off	4
asap	as soon as possible	4
asf	as fuck	8
bf	best friend	17
bs	bullshit	15
btw	by the way	31
ceo	Chief Executive Officer	3
did	Dissociative Identity Disorder	3
dnd	Dungeons and Dragons	4
dm	direct message	58
f	fuck	57
f-bomb	fuck	4
ffa	free for all	5
ffo	for fans of	2
fgs	for God's sake	3
fs	fuck's sake	6
ftm trans	female to male	1

(continued)

Initialism	Etymon	Frequency
fr	for real	24
f-word	fuck	2
fy	fuck yeah	18
gad	Generalized Anxiety Disorder	9
gd	goddamn	4
gf	girlfriend	76
gfs	girlfriends	54
gid	Gender Identity Disorder	6
gl	good luck	19
gm	good morning	3
gpu	Graphics Processing Unit	6
gtfo	get the fuck out	21
hp	Harry Potter	3
hpd	Histrionic Personality Disorder	6
hs	holy shit	8
hw	homework	2
idc	I don't care	11
idk	I don't know	97
ied	improvised explosive device	1
ig	I guess	18
ik	I know	26
jk	just kidding	56
jfk	just fucking kidding	24
imo	in my opinion	11
irl	in real life	23
la	Los Angeles	7
larp	live action role-playing	1
lgtb(q)	lesbian, gay, transsexual, bisexual, queer	2
lsd	lysergic acid diethylamide	7
mf	motherfucker	8
mtf trans	male to female	1
ngl	not gonna lie	57
nnn	no nut November	38
np	no problem	27
nsfw	not safe for work	8
nvm	nevermind	9

(continued)

Initialism	Etymon	Frequency
n-word	nigger	6
nz	New Zealand	1
ocd	Obsessive Compulsive Disorder	6
ocpd	Obsessive Compulsive Personality Disorder	2
ofc	of course	34
og	oh God	18
op	original poster	126
omfg	oh my fucking God	9
omg	oh my God	67
oml	oh my Lord	7
owo	oral without	10
pe	physical education	4
pm	private message	37
psn	Playstation Network	2
ptsd	Posttraumatic Stress Disorder	13
qb	quarterback	5
rn	right now	32
rotc	Reserve Officers' Training Corps	1
sat	Scholastic Assessment Test	6
sh	same here	11
shs	sitting here stoned/smiling	23
sjw	Social Justice Warrior	3
smh	shaking my head	28
sour d	sour diesel (marijuana)	1
sro	School Resource Officer	2
t	totally	33
tbf	to be fair	18
tbh	to be honest	67
thot	that hoe over there	28
tf	the fuck	38
wtf	what the fuck	54
wu	what's up	7
yk	you know	8
yt	youtube	72
		1,952

References

Adger, Carolyn T., Walt Wolfram and Donna Christian. 2007. *Dialects in schools and communities*. New Jersey and London: Lawrence Erlbaum Associates.
Aguert, Nadia, Virgine Laval, Nadia Gauducheau, Hassan Atifi and Michel Marcoccia. 2016. Producing irony in adolescence: a comparison between face-to-face and computer-mediated communication. *Psychology of Language and Communication* 20 (3). 199–218.
Allan, Keith and Kate Burridge. 1991. *Euphemism & dysphemism: Language used as shield and weapon*. New York and Oxford: Oxford University Press.
Allen, Irving L. 1998. Slang: sociology. In Jacob L. Mey and Ronald E. Asher (eds.), *Concise encyclopedia of pragmatics*, 878–883. Amsterdam: Elsevier.
Annan-Prah, Elizabeth C. 2015. *Basic business and administrative communication*. Bloomington: Xlibris.
Bauer, Laurie, Rochelle Lieber and Ingo Plag. 2015. *The Oxford reference guide to English morphology*. Oxford: Oxford University Press.
Baron, Naomi S. 2004. See you online: Gender issues in college student use of instant messaging. *Journal of Language and Social Psychology* 23. 397–423.
Baron, Naomi S. 2011. Assessing the internet's impact on language. In Mia Consalvo and Charles Ess (eds.), *The handbook of internet studies*, 117–137. Oxford: Wiley-Blackwell.
Burridge, Kate. 2012. Euphemism and language change: the sixth and seventh ages. *Lexis* 7. 65–91.
Bond, Bradley J. and Andrea Figueroa-Caballero. 2016. Exploring the relationship between computer-mediated communication, sexual identity commitment, and well-being among lesbian, gay, and bisexual adolescents. *Communication Research Reports* 33 (4). 288–294.
Cannon, Garland. 1989. Abbreviations and acronyms in English word formation. *American Speech* 64 (2). 99–127.
Carter, Marian. 2016. *Helping children and adolescents think about death, dying and bereavement*. London and Philadelphia: Jessica Kingsley Publishers.
Casas Gómez, Miguel. 2012. The expressive creativity of euphemism and dysphemism. *Lexis* 7. (accessed 15 September 2019).
Chambers, J. K. 2004. Patterns of variation including change. In J. K. Chambers, Peter Trudgill and Natalie Schilling-Estes (eds.), *The handbook of language variation and change*, 349–372. Oxford: Blackwell.
Crespo-Fernández, Eliecer. 2015. *Sex in language: euphemistic and dysphemistic metaphors in internet forums*. London: Bloomsbury Publishing.
Dalzell, Tom and Terry Victor. 2012. *The new Partridge dictionary of slang and unconventioanl English* (2nd edn.). London and New York: Routledge.
Davie, Jim. 2019. *Slang across societies: Motivations and construction*. New York: Routledge.
Eble, Connie. 1996. *Slang and sociability*. Chapel Hill: The University of North Carolina Press.
Hamawand, Zeki. 2011. *Morphology in English: Word formation in cognitive grammar*. London and New York: Continuum.
Greiffestern, Sandra. 2010. *The influence of computers, the internet and computer-mediated communication on everyday English*. Berlin: Logos.
Huffaker, David A. and Sandra L. Calvert. 2005. Gender, identity, and language use in teenage blogs. *Journal of Computer-Mediated Communication* 10 (2). [https://doi.org/10.1111/j.1083-6101.2005.tb00238.x] (accessed 15 August 2019).

Jamet, Danis. 2018. The neological functions of disease euphemisms in English and French: verbal hygiene or speech pathology? *Lexis* 12. 1–26.
Jucker, Andreas and Yael Ziv. 1998. Discourse markers: Introduction. In Andreas Jucker, A. and Yael Ziv (eds.), *Discourse markers*, 1–12. Amsterdam and Philadelphia: John Benjamins.
Labov, William. 2001. *Principles of linguistic change*. Malden and Oxford: Blackwell.
Mattiello, Elisa. 2005. The pervasiveness of slang in standard and non-standard English. *Mots Palabras Words* 6. 7–41.
MWD11: *Merriam-Webster dictionary online*, 11th edn., Merriam-Webster, Inc. [http://www.merriam-webster.com] (accessed 10 September 2019).
NOW: Davies, Mark. 2013. *Corpus of News on the Web*: 3+ billion words from 20 countries, updated every day. [http://corpus.byu.edu/now/] (accessed 30 September 2019).
OED3: *Oxford English dictionary online*. 2000–, 3rd ed. Oxford: Oxford University Press. [http://www.oed.com] (accessed 30 November 2019).
Smith, Rachel. 2011. Urban dictionary: Youth slanguage and the redefining of definition. What's up with meep and other words in the Urban dictionary. *English Today* 27 (4). 43–48.
Tagliamonte, Sali and Derek Denis. 2008. Linguistic ruin? LOL! Instant messaging and teen language. *American Speech* 83 (1). 3–34.
Tagliamonte, Sali. 2016. *Teen talk: The language of adolescents*. Cambridge: Cambridge University Press.
Varnhagen, Connie, G. Peggy McFall, Nicole Pugh, Lisa Routledge, Heather Sumida-MacDonald and Trudy E. Kwong. 2009. LOL: New language and spelling in instant messaging. *Reading & Writing* 23 (6). 719–733.

Ignacio M. Palacios Martínez and Paloma Núñez Pertejo
5 Teenagers and social networking. Twitter as a data source for the study of the language of London teenagers and young adults

The role of computer-mediated communication (CMC), through its many formats and genres, e.g. forums, chats, blogs, instant messaging, emails and social networks like Twitter or Instagram, has been studied extensively (cf. Herring 2001, Androutsopoulos and Beisswenger 2008, Zappavigna 2012, Squires 2016, Cutler and Røyneland 2018). However, little research has been conducted so as to determine the extent to which these media can serve as a data source for teen (and young adult) talk. The present paper focuses on how data from Twitter can be used to study the language of London adolescents and young adults, especially if compared with other methods or research tools, such as corpora and sociolinguistic interviews. To this end, a sample of more than 2,000 tweets, extracted between July 2018 and April 2020, were selected from the Twitter accounts of three well-known London rappers, all associated with Multicultural London English (cf. Cheshire et al. 2011). The analysis shows that the material examined is linguistically very rich and offers a great deal of insightful information, mainly from the point of view of grammar and lexis. In addition, a number of features characteristic of the language used in Twitter were taken into consideration. The paper concludes with some reflections on the possible contributions of Twitter for (teen and young adult) language research, especially in terms of the spontaneity, genuineness and freshness of the material, while some potential drawbacks in terms of quantitative analysis are also discussed.

Ignacio M. Palacios Martínez, University of Santiago de Compostela,
e-mail: ignacio.palacios@usc.es
Paloma Núñez Pertejo, University of Santiago de Compostela, e-mail: pnunez.pertejo@usc.es

https://doi.org/10.1515/9781501514685-006

1 Introduction

The main purpose of this chapter is to show how material extracted from the Twitter accounts of three rappers directly connected with Multicultural London English (MLE) provide interesting data that can serve us to describe and get deeper into the language used by London teenagers and young adults.[1] To this aim, we start by describing the concept of "Internet slang" or "netspeak" and by later delving into the area of computer-mediated communication (CMC) with particular reference to Twitter (Section 2). Section 3 follows with a brief review of the main literature on the field. Section 4 summarises the main aims of the study and the method employed for the gathering and analysis of the data. Section 5 describes the main findings, organised under two main categories: grammar and lexis. The chapter concludes with a summary of the most outstanding results and with a number of reflections in light of the previous issues.

2 The importance of information and communication technologies (ICTs) and the emergence of computed-mediated communication (CMC) genres

Technologies clearly play an important role in contemporary life, particularly for teenagers, who can be regarded as "cyberkids", the "net generation", or the "digital generation" (McKay, Thurlow and Zimmerman 2005, Cutler and Røyneland 2018). In this respect, the following figures are revealing: At the beginning of the 21st century, European teenagers represented at least 12% of the total online world population, and in the UK 75% of all 7-to-16-year-old boys and girls were already Internet users (McKay et al. 2005).

Technologies have changed not only our way of living but also how we socialise and even communicate; this may explain why scholars such as Crystal have coined the term "netspeak", a hybrid of spoken and written language where the use of slang and acronyms, clipped words and graphical icons is very common (2001: 31). As a result of this new mode of expression, new CMC or digital genres have

---

[1] For generous financial support, we are grateful to the Spanish Ministry of Science and Education (grants PGC2018-093622-B-100 and PID2020-114604GB-100), the European Regional Development Fund, the University of Santiago and the Regional Government of Galicia (grants EDB431 2020/01 and EDB431 2021/02).

emerged. These include all kinds of interpersonal communication carried out on the Internet (Herring 2001, Androutsopoulos and Beisswenger 2008, Thurlow and Mroczek 2011, Squires 2016), in most cases being multimodal in nature (Herring 2001, 2019).

Twitter as a network was launched in 2006, and can be defined as a microblogging service. It is characterised by its immediacy since it reflects what is happening in the world right now. It is multimodal, in that we can find not only words, but also visuals. Twitter posts are notable for their directness, since it is possible to initiate, join or respond to a conversation at any time. Retweeting is very easy, and hence messages can reach a very high number of people in a short period of time. Hashtags function as leitmotifs and connect tweets that deal with the same topic. Users are forced to summarise their ideas, since only 280 characters are allowed in a single tweet.

3 Brief literature review

A full review of the very extensive literature on Twitter would not be feasible here, so in what follows we will mention some of the main studies which have used material from Twitter as their basis for research. Thus, Puschman (2015) is concerned with quoting and information sharing in social media services, while Gruber (2017) concentrates not only on quoting but also on retweeting. Kytölä and Westinen (2015) explore the ways in which features of "gangsta" English are deployed, evaluated and adopted in web forums and on Twitter; meanwhile, Atifi and Marcoccia (2017) focus on political-social TV, van der Bom et al. (2018) look at the instantaneity of Twitter as a communicative medium and Scott (2018) explores the pragmatic functions of hashtags.

Bohmann (2016), in turn, analyses innovative uses of *because* on Twitter, while Coats (2016) considers both Twitter-specific discourse and part-of-speech features in English tweets in Finland. Data on CMC have also been used in the study of particular varieties of English. Thus, Mair (2011), Hinrichs and White-Sustaíta (2011) and Hinrichs (2018) have focused on cyber Jamaican and Jamaican blog and email writing, respectively. Recently, Grieve and his colleagues (2019) published the findings of a survey on lexical variation in British English conducted with the aid of a dataset of 180 million tweets. Corpus-based approaches have also been adopted in corpus compilation, including the HERMES Twitter corpus, a 100-million-word randomised database originally collected in 2009. This corpus has been used in the studies by Zappavigna (2012) on Twitter as a mode of expression. There is, however, a serious problem with the compilation of material extracted from Twitter, in that the platform itself has discouraged since 2013 the use of publicly available data. Apart from this, there are also some technical and legal shortcomings.

4 Purpose and method

As mentioned above, our main objective here is to see the extent to which material from Twitter can be used to study the language used by British teenagers and young adults, specifically Londoners, as well as to explore its potential contribution to language research, with particular attention to variation, and especially in comparison to other research methods or tools, such as corpora and sociolinguistic interviews. Our previous work on MLE thus far has been based mainly on data from widely available corpora, including the *Linguistic Innovators Corpus* and the *Multicultural London English Corpus* (Cheshire et al. 2011), and also from sources such as magazines, comics, songs and video clips directly associated with MLE. However, we came to perceive the need for additional and updated data, in the sense that this variety is multicultural in nature and is in continuous evolution, given that the language of teenagers and young adults can change very quickly, especially at the lexical level.

Our analysis includes a sample of about 2,200 Twitter posts extracted between July 2018 and April 2020 from the accounts of three well-known rappers who are generally identified with MLE (Cheshire et al. 2011). The period covered comprises almost two years and, even though the sample selected is not very large, we deem it enough for our main purposes, since frequencies, concordances and collocations are not our main interest and no extralinguistic variables are considered. MLE can be defined as a "multiethnolect" (Clyne 2000)[2] which has been formed by a feature pool derived from local varieties (namely Cockney), plus other UK dialects of English, standard English and the expression of an array of second language speakers from different backgrounds: Caribbean, African-American, Indian, North African and Asian. Many of these MLE speakers are young, which makes this sociolect particularly interesting, since teenagers and youths are generally regarded as precursors of language innovation and change

---

[2] A multiethnolect is, according to Clyne (2000: 87), an ethnolect where members of the dominant group, particularly young age speakers, share it with other ethnic minorities in a language-crossing situation. This notion has also been referred to in the literature with other terms, such as "contemporary urban vernaculars" (Rampton 2015), "urban vernacular" and "urban youth speech style" (Wiese 2009, Nortier and Svendsen 2015, Cheshire, Nortier and Adger 2015).

(cf. Tagliamonte 2016). The rappers selected for the study are The Dappy, Wiley and Dizzee Rascal.[3] The accounts of these three artists were closely studied because they emerged in the East End of London and they overtly make a public use of this sociolect in their everyday communication and in their exchanges with their fans. The three of them have received Caribbean influence in their tunes and expression, although this is especially so in the case of Wiley, because of his Trinidadian and Antiguan descent. The Dappy in contrast, is of Greek origin, while Dizzee Rascal combines both Nigerian and Ghanaian heritage. In the analysis, not only were the tweets posted by these three rappers considered, but also the responses and retweets of the other participants. All this material was manually examined and filtered out, and special attention was paid to those grammar, lexical and discourse features which pertained to MLE and youth language. While it is true that these three rappers cannot be regarded as teenagers since two of them, The Dappy and Dizzee Rascal, are in their early thirties and Wiley is 41, most of their fans are definitely young and this also applies to the language they use. In addition, there are some tweets where several posters portray Dizzee Rascal as a "teenager with tendencies for young children", or refer to this rapper performing at the City Hall in front of "excited teenagers". The same applies to The Dappy who is regarded by some of his fans as a "role model to teenagers" and "inspirational to teenagers". Furthermore, back in May 2014, the language used by Dizzee Rascal was included as part of a new English A level, since educational administrators considered it deserved close study by secondary school students as it reflected contemporary uses of English. Finally, some scholars such as Drummond (2017, 2018) have noted that many teenagers try to imitate the accents of these singers and artists to the extent that the latter can also be regarded as genuine agents of language innovation.

5 Findings

Findings have been grouped into the following two categories: (i) Grammar (address terms, verb paradigm, negatives, intensification, noun system) and (ii) vocabulary (new terms, changes in meaning, word formation processes, loans from other languages).

---

3 Further information about these three rappers can be found at: [https://en.wikipedia.org/wiki/Dappy], [https://dizzeerascal.co.uk] and [https://wileyofficial.com], respectively.

5.1 Grammar

5.1.1 Address terms, vocatives and familiarisers

Vocatives can be defined principally as nouns of address which are not fully integrated into the clause and which generally refer to other participants in the discourse (Braun 1988, Leech 1999). Within the wide range of these address terms (Biber et al. 1999), we have focused on the category of "familiarisers", which generally denote a close relationship between speaker and interlocutors, since they occur frequently in participants' posts in this social network. The material collected shows a wide range of such address terms, these totalling 42. Table 5.1 contains a selection:

Table 5.1: Nominal vocatives recorded in the Twitter material analysed.

Form	Example	Source
akh (brother)	I always tell you fam stop worrying about everyone and just do youuuuuu *akh*	Wiley (19/11/2019)[4]
angel	Congrats *angel*	Rascal (18/10/2018)
boy	he mentioned pizza *boy* but I still don't understand why he did it 😂😂😂	Wiley (22/12/2018)
bitch(hh)	do you know what guilty pleasure means you little *bitch*???	Dappy (17/04/2020)
brother, bro, bru(h), bruv, brudda(h), blad, blud	Keep being u *bruv* cuz you're amazing as u are	Rascal (06/12/2018)
champ	Nah I rate that bro, love for the feedback *champ*	Dappy (10/03/2020)
chile	Whew *chile*	Dappy (26/11/2018)
crew	What's the plan for today quarantine *crew*	Dappy (21/03/2020)
cuz/cousin	Do a track with me *cuz*	Dappy (22/8/2019)
don(ny)	Big up Wiley you *don*	Dappy (03/11/2018)
dosser	lazy person big stiff *dosser*	Wiley (04/12/2018)
family, fam	You was right *fam* Merry Xmas *family*	Rascal (20/04/2020) Wiley (25/12/2018)

---

[4] The information provided after each of the examples makes reference to the Twitter account from where they were extracted, that is, the accounts of Dizzee Rascal, The Dappy and Wiley. However, this does not necessarily mean that they were all actually posted by one of these three rappers since, in our analysis, we also studied the posts of the other participants in the exchanges, i.e. mainly fans and supporters.

Table 5.1 (continued)

Form	Example	Source
fella	I agree *fella*	Wiley (11/6/2019)
g	Congrats my *g.*, you did it	Rascal (09/3/2018)
geezer	LOOL. Don't be jealous, *geezer*	Wiley (21/12/2018)
girl	Teel me something *girl*, Are you happy in this modern 🌍	Wiley (22/12/2018)
hack	The fucking judge isn't allowed to take a piss break in between counts, you fucking *hack*	Wiley (05/12/2018)
hunty	YOU LOOK AMAZING YASSSSSS *HUNTY* ❤️💯	Dappy (09/8/2018)
lad(s)	Get your haggis out again *lad* 🍆 Cheers *lads*	Dappy (04/12//2018) Dappy (24/09/2019)
pagan	answer my text you *pagan*	Dappy (10/02/2019)
peep(s)	Go grab that *peeps*	Dappy (09/8/2018)
playa	Talk to em it's just us against da world *playa*	Rascal (19/1/2019)
queen	Get it *Queen*	Dappy (09/8/2018)
(young) sir	you are a different class, *Sir*?	Dappy (24/1/2019)
sis	Waiting impatiently *sis*	Dappy (21/12/2018)
sweetheart/sweetie	Congratulations *sweetheart*	Dappy (20/9/2019)
wanker, wanka	Mi bredda respect fi life yuh *wanka* yuh diss di brothas pan media an yuh support a sick abusing *wanka* ak	Wiley (06/12/2018)

The large number of address terms and their extensive use by almost all the participants lead us to conclude that the way communicative exchanges in Twitter take place may favour the use of these expressions, in that contributors to exchanges address and interact with one another frequently.

Brother and its variants are the most common of all, with the reduced forms clearly prevailing over the full one. At times *bro* occurs preceded by the possessive *my*, that is, *my bro*. This also applies to *guy* (i.e. *how are you my guy?*), *don* and *g*. The second familiariser in terms of frequency is *mate(s)*, followed by *man*, *guys*, *pals* and *fam*. Although these address terms mainly occur in statements, they can also be found in questions (1) and in imperatives (2):

(1) People still listening to you *dude*?
    (Dappy 18/12/2018)

(2) Get it *Queen*.
    (Dappy 09/08/2018)

Some forms, such as *wanker, brother, man, don* and *king*, may be preceded by *you*, to identify and single out a particular referent, and possibly in line with some general plural terms of address, such as *you guys*, which is becoming increasingly popular, not only in American English, but also in British English (Heyd 2010):

(3) *You brudda* if you get time have a scan through this.
(Wiley 22/01/2019)

It is important to note that the position of these address terms in the clause makes a difference in terms of their pragmatic meaning (Leech 1999, Clancy 2015). Although they can occur in initial, medial and final position, the latter is most common in English speech, followed by initial position (Leech 1999, Palacios 2018). However, in Twitter, address terms in initial position seem to be more common than in spontaneous speech. These address terms may thus convey different pragmatic functions; when in initial position, they usually serve to call the addressee's attention (4), expressing a wish or request, disagreeing or contradicting the previous participant in the interaction (5), or adding a new perspective or highlighting what is being discussed (6):

(4) *Guys* ALLWEKNOW will be on spotify.
(Dappy 03/10/2018)

(5) *Geezer* it's not murder.
(Wiley 21/12/2018)

(6) *Kids*, this is why doing drugs is badd.
(Wiley 01/12/2018)

However, in final position they are very often added by the fans of those rappers to express their solidarity and full agreement (7), gratefulness (8), encouragement (9), or praise (10):

(7) Keep being u *bruv* cuz you're amazing as u are.
(Rascal 06/12/2018)

(8) Thank you so much *King*.
(Rascal 18/10/2018)

(9) Big up Wiley *you don*.
(Dappy 03/11/2018)

(10)   ur music has helped me ur a legend *bro*
       (Dappy 18/08/2019)

Some of these vocatives are undergoing grammaticalisation processes; such is the case of *man* (Cheshire 2013, Palacios 2018), which has evolved from being a common noun to an address term, functioning very often as a pragmatic marker, and then becoming a pronoun (Cheshire 2013). Consider the following:

(11)   Yess, @JMBBK you are back.
       Man never left [*he never left*]
       (Wiley 24/12/2018)

5.1.2 Verb system

Some tendencies are found in the use of verbs which do not necessarily follow the standard. Thus, *BE* presents some particular features with *was/were* variation in both positive and negative polarity contexts, as in the following:

(12)   You *wasn't* lying when you said listen to Don't Gass me on some proper speakers
       (Rascal 14/09/2018)

This is quite pervasive in other varieties of English (Kortmann and Lunkenheimer 2013, feature 163) and was already attested in MLE by Cheshire and Fox (2009), where they identified differences between inner and outer London. It is also quite common to find the past participle form of *DO*, that is, *done*, instead of the simple past form *did*:

(13)   True dat, gal act like they *done* their nine and now it's your turn
       (Wiley 13/12/2018)

Also quite frequently found is the levelling of past tense/past participle verb forms, that is, regularisation of irregular verb paradigms. This means that the *-ed* form is used for all verbs, irrespectively of whether they are regular or not, as in (14):

(14)   my sister tells me she's *payed* for us to meet and greet at players...
       (Wiley 21/02/2018)

5.1.3 Negation

The system of negative polarity also shows a high frequency of negative vernacular forms such as *nope* as a variant of *no* (in response to a statement), *ain't*, plus third person singular *don't* and negative concord structures. *Ain't* may function as equivalent to *are not, am not, is not, haven't (got)*, and even as auxiliary for the perfect, and also occurs in question tags (15):

(15)   It's a asap rocky song *ain't it*
       (Wiley 05/11/2018)

Examples with third person singular *don't* are also frequent (16), especially when a noun phrase (rather than a personal pronoun) fills the subject position, thus confirming findings of previous studies (cf. Palacios 2016):

(16)   Hahahahhaa Dizzee *don't* want it.
       (Rascal 01/04/2020)

Negative concord or double negative structures are also found quite often, particularly with *ain't* as the first negator and *no* as the second:

(17)   This *aint no* Fekir
       (Wiley 08/08/2018)

5.1.4 Intensification

So is the most common adjective intensifier, while *really* is attested very infrequently, and *very* not at all. Instead of *very* and *really*, the participants in these posts make use of a wide range of adjectives of positive semantic prosody which function as intensifiers: *true, real, legal, massive, brilliant, dope* (cool), *great, pure, absolute, ligit* (legitimate, true for real), *favourite*:

(18)   *true* talent
       (Dappy 09/12/2018)

As expected, *fucking* is also quite common as an intensifier. In contrast, very few cases are recorded of *bloody* with this function. We also find some cases of *truly* and *proper* as adjective intensifiers:

(19) My favourite track on this album has to be 'imagine' *proper* deep tune
(Rascal 14/09/2018)

Prefixes functioning as lexical words here such as *super, ultra* and *mega* also serve to express intensification, as do *beyond* and *way*:

(20) we have a *MEGA* end of year SALE on atm! *super* excited
(Wiley 29/10/2018)

Innit as an invariant tag is quite multifunctional (Palacios 2015) and typically conveys an intensifying value in many of these interactions:

(21) Fam I thought youtube is a platform too *innit*!
(Rascal 20/09/2018)

5.1.5 Noun system

As regards the noun system, the most interesting feature is the formation of the plural with the suffix *-dem*, which is most commonly attached to animate nouns or to those referring to a group of individuals, namely *mandem, peopledem, galdem/ gyaldem*, etc. This can be considered a typical feature from Jamaican English (cf. Sebba 1993) and shows the influence of this sociolect in the expression of many of these speakers:

(22) Artists *dem*, don't let these end of year lists draw you out. . .
(Wiley 08/12/2018)

(23) ust tryna deliver bangers for the people *dem*
(Dappy 11/01/2020)

In (22) above, the use of *dem* added to the already plural form *artists* could also be interpreted as a switch of Wiley to Jamaican patois due to his Caribbean background.

5.2 Vocabulary

5.2.1 Innovative features at the lexical level

The presence of traces of Jamaican English can also be perceived in certain lexical items and expressions found in these Twitter exchanges. Examples include *bludclart* (a Jamaican swear word, equivalent to *bloody* in British English), *yardman/ yardie* (a local person), *ends* (local area), *bumbaclat* (an expression of surprise), *allow it* (to forget about something), *batti* (a homosexual) and *yute* (a young person or child):

(24) Petitions to save *bludclaart* greasy chicken cooked in a dirty kitchen by two Indian man[5] that cuss u in they're own language under their breath. Kmttt!! (Wiley 06/12/2018)

As expected, words connected with music are also attested, since this topic is central to these artists and indeed is very often the focus of discussion: *bars* (sentences in lyrical hip hop songs), *crew* (group of rappers, breakdancers or graffiti artists), *banger* (an awesome song/video), *stem* (multitracks of songs), *bootleg* (a recording made and distributed illegally), *mc'ing* (rapping), *bubblin'* (feeling the vibe), *to clash* (to have an MC battle with rhymes and songs), *jam* (a musical event where artists improvise and play solos), *spit bars*:

(25) Jack will ain't heard all the low voice yardman *bars* yet. (Wiley 04/12/2018)

Words undergoing semantic change from the expression of something negative to the opposite, that is, something positive, are also commonly reported. Thus, *wicked, sick, shit, insane, heavy, raw, baddest, hard, cold/coldest* are most often associated with positive qualities, experiences, circumstances or behaviour, as in the following:

(26) The Dappy was *insane* last night. (Dappy 07/11/2018)

---

[5] Notice here the use of *man* as a plural form instead of the standard form *men*. This was also previously attested by Cheshire (2013).

(27) The Dappy is too *sick*
(Dappy 15/01/2020)

At times common words also shift their meaning to some extent. Therefore, *decent*, as in *a decent song*, seems to denote a generally good song (*decent* here does not seem to imply any obvious nuance of lacklustre approval, as in the more traditional sense of something *half-decent*), and the adjective *hard* is also equivalent to something good. Moreover, a high number of lexical items with a pejorative meaning are also recorded. Examples include *mental* (crazy), *pagan* (good for nothing), *wack* (full of oneself), *wasteman*, *hoe* (girl who only cares about herself), *roadman*, *rent boy* and *dosser* (lazy):

(28) Migos (American hip hop trio) are *wack*.
(Wiley 06/12/2018)

The same is true for terms connected with drugs and some marginal sectors of society: *plug* and *shotter* (drug dealer), *cats* (people that buy drugs), *food* (drugs), different terms to refer to marijuana (*draw*, *benner*(s), *ganja*, *jax*, *score*, *tens*, *spliff*), and to be under the effects of drugs (*zoned, mashed*).

We also find lexical items associated with technology and video games, such as *Play Station 4*, *Wizzie* for the game *Wizard*, *Grand Theft Auto*, which teenagers and members of the younger generations are so fond of, as well as a high number of euphemistic forms of lexical items that may be regarded as taboo or inappropriate, although they also belong to basic informal English, e.g. *shxt*, *Jeez*, *gee*, *oh my (flipping) gosh*, *(flipping) heck*.

5.2.2 Clippings

These forms are very frequent. In all the items listed in Table 5.2 below, with the exception of *hood*, the ending of the words has been shortened. Some of these clippings are frequent in spontaneous and informal speech, especially among young speakers, and they are not necessarily exclusive to this London variety. The following are the most common, in which both upper- and lower-case forms can be used.

Table 5.2: Most common clippings found in the Twitter material analysed.

Clipped term	Full form	Example
certi	certified (referred to something good, cool)	sing, rap and play instruments your *certi* BUY you need an album soon. (Dappy 31/5/2018)
collab	collaborate/ collaboration	Whoever made this *collab* happen thank you. (Dappy 28/06/2019)
divo	divorce	Cardi B announces she's DONE with Offset and They will be getting a *DIVO*... (Wiley 06/12/2018)
G	great man/ gangster	Wiley Updates is a *g* abd real grime mc. (Wiley 23/12/2018)
gen	generation	You've done the most for grime but this mission is for the new *gen*. (Wiley 05/12/2018)
govt	government	I think news feature was about how previous labour *govt* imposed max sentence. (Wiley 21/12/2018)
hood	neighbourhood	I'm in the *hood* mate. (Wiley 21/12/2018)
mofo	motherfucker	That *mofo* compared 80 m to 1 dollar (Wiley 24/03/2019)
OG'S	originals	No proof he was ever talking about dizzee in that bar tho, it could just as easily been about Wiley or any other of the grime *OG's*. (Wiley 01/11/2018)
pedo	pedophile	The kids a *pedo* (Wiley 07/12/2018)
reps	represents	Proud to say he *reps* UK. (Dappy 27/06/2019)
ridic	ridicule	find it *ridic* that Dizzie Rascal was to be kicked out of school (Rascal 05/10/2019)

5.2.3 Abbreviations

Abbreviations of different types are common to all digital genres, and as such are a characteristic feature of Twitter posts. Some are related to the communication process involved when responding to other posts, as a means of indicating agreement, disagreement, surprise, laughter, incredibility, etc., and include forms such as *DW, kmt, lol* and *lmao*. In other cases, they are everyday expressions that have been shortened for practical purposes to make the communication swift and more fluid. Examples include *cya, btw, N* and *pl* (see Table 5.3).

Table 5.3: Main abbreviations used in the Twitter material analysed.

Abbreviation	Full term	Example
acc	actually	Dappy is *acc* too hard (Dappy 13/06/2019)
asf	and so forth	I am glad *asf*. (Wiley 12/11/2018)
ATM/atm	at the moment	Pretty broke *atm* (Dappy 24/05/2018)
bbk	Boy Better Know	Just pure ramble about fuck *bbk* and skepta and dizz saying they pagens and that (Rascal 17/10/2018)
BD/bd	birthday	plz say *bd* to my daughter, she has overcome a lot (Dappy 09/04/2014)
bs	bullshit	Looool you gotta ask them now because that is *bs*. (Rascal 17/11/2019)
btw	by the way	Hiya Joy it was the one near the Screaming Monkey pub, the corn tortillas were delicious *btw*, is it a new recipe? X (Wiley 25/11/2018)
DW	don't worry	*DW* by tko i think bro, who you got? (Wiley 17/12/2018)
dxx	double kiss	*Dxx* (Wiley 27/1/2019)
EP	extended play record	Liven up your Friday witi this amazing *EP* from your boy (Rascal 26/10/2018).
FFS	for fuck's sake	Joshua is going to get out of the fight now *ffs* loool (Wiley 5/12/2018)
fr	for real	*fr* no short cuts (Wiley 20/11/2019)
frm	from	Man been on this grsft *frm* early. (Wiley 21/11/2019)
FT	follow-up tweet	"Not today" by the Plug *ft* (Dappy 10/07/2019)
GG	good game	This goes hard *GG*. (Rascal 18/01/2019)
gd	good	*Gd* to see u friday bro hope you & yours have a *gd* christmas & all the best for 2019 (Wiley 20/12/2018)
GOAT	greatest of all time	*GOAT* 🔥🔥 (Dappy 03/01/2019)
GRODT/ GRoDT	get rich or die trying	*GRODT* Hip Hop Classic. (Rascal 18/11/2018)
IDGAF	I don't give a fuck	*IDGAF* Wiley has done so much for the UK scene that Charli Sloth can't say shit to him. (Wiley 07/07/2013)
IMO	in my opinion	The whole album is underrated *imo* (Rascal 03/02/2019)
kmt	kiss my teeth (expression to show disapproval)	I knew it was staged *kmt* (Wiley 12/04/2019)
L	lose/loss	If that's your girl, then that's your *L*. (Dappy 1/12/2018)
lm(f)ao	laughing my (fucking) ass off	here Wiley give me wot youre atm creased is not the word *lmao* xxx. (Wiley 23/11/2018)

Table 5.3 (continued)

Abbreviation	Full term	Example
lol	laugh out loud, lots of laughs	Reallol priceless *lol* (Dappy 1/12/2018)
Mc	Master of Ceremonies	@MaxwellD1 Is actually the godfather of us all. First *Mc* with a record deal and first *Mc* with Mercedes C180. (Wiley 29/11/2019)
ngl	not gonna lie so now you know	*ngl* was wondering who the fuck you were talking about yesterday 😂😂 (Wiley 05/12/2018)
nmp	not my problem	Big things fam *nmp* (Dappy 03/03/2018)
OG	Original Gangster or real OG	This week's Slacker Podcast was with *OG* @ Dizzee Rascal (Rascal 27/10/2018)
OHMY	Oh hear me	Look I'ma ride for ya, can't spend all my time with ya But if you ever need a shoulder to cry on I got two for you This is the cutest part *OHMY*. (Dappy 19/06/2018)
omfg	Oh my fucking God	*omfg* banger. (Dappy 01/01/2019)
omg	Oh my God	*Omg* I been waiting on some juice grime juices. (Rascal 17/10/2018)
pfft	people for fair trade (used to signify sarcasm or disagreement)	*Pfft* . . . honestly. 🍎🍏🍇 (Wiley 20/12/2018)
RMX	Remix	DJs if you haven't got the *RMX* yet give @Gabby Buttaci a shout she will look you up. (Dappy 05/12/2018)
RN	right now	Dappy's new song is soooo good *rn* (Dappy 22/05/2018)
SMH	shake my head (to show disapproval)	Why would that even be a bad thing let ppl make what they want *SMH*. (Wiley 21/11/2018)
TBF	to be fair	That tracksuit was a fashion statement *tbf*. (Wiley 24/12/2018)
tbh	to be honest	*tbh* "not that deep" sounds like the title of a porn film. (Wiley 23/12/2018)
tko	technical knock out	DW by *tko* i think bro, who you got? (Wiley 17/12/2018)
tsks	(sound of annoyance)	Stop promoting these companies *tsks* (Wiley 21/11/2019)
UKG	UK garage music	Woi let's do some *UKG* please (Wiley 13/06/2019)
UWAT	ultimate waste of time	*Uwat*? (Wiley 17/10/2018)
WTF	What the fuck!	The Dappy is actually toooo talented *Wtf* (Dappy 31/07/2019)
XDD	(form of laughter, such as *lol*)	Hasn't this been on YT for a while now *xdd* (Rascal 18/10/2018)

5.2.4 Loans from other languages

Loans, despite not being frequent in number, attracted our attention because of their high expressive force and because they serve to reinforce the assumption that teenagers and young speakers are more open to words from other languages and varieties (Drange 2007), even though they may not always be aware of that in their everyday use. That is the case with *Que* . . . borrowed from Spanish and meaning 'I don't get', 'I don't understand'; *akh*, a short form for 'brother' from Arabic; *bandana* from Hindi meaning 'a large coloured handkerchief'; *chav* from Romani, referring to a young person with brash and loutish behaviour; *holla* and *en route* from Spanish and French, being equivalent to 'hello' and 'on the way', respectively, although several of these examples are not exclusive to the London variety (e.g. *chav, bandana, en route*).

6 Conclusions

This study has shown how Twitter can be used to investigate language variation. The data have helped us to describe and characterise different grammatical and lexical features of MLE, taking as reference material the accounts of three East London rappers who can be regarded as representative of this sociolect. Evidence has also been provided to account for the special jargon used by many teenagers and young people in this social network, in which spontaneity, directness, language play and creativity acquire their fullest expression through emoticons and other graphic conventions, including the use of a non-standard orthography. The element of multimodality, which we have not here discussed for limitations of space, also helps to achieve these aims, the combination of the printed form with different types of visuals serving to attract the attention of participants and having a direct impact on the reception of the message. All these features clearly indicate that we are dealing with a new kind of expression.

Twitter data do not specially favour quantitative and frequency-based studies, since the figures for particular linguistic phenomena may not be large enough to come to definitive conclusions. However, in the last few years, different tools and applications have been designed so as to obtain more information about the posters and to process the data in such a way that it may allow language research and analysis to be conducted more smoothly (cf. Hiltunen et al. 2017). In contrast, qualitative research can indeed be undertaken here, in that Twitter users do not behave randomly, but follow, be it consciously or unconsciously, a number of conventions that seem to have been previously agreed upon by that community of practice or small social network formed by the rappers with their respective fans and followers, one which is characterised by a mutual engagement, a jointly negotiated enterprise and a shared repertoire (cf. Meyerhoff 2006). This indeed applies not only to Twitter but also to most other forms of digital genres which are, again, not so well-suited to frequency-based and quantitative methods (cf. Cutler and Røyneland 2018) as corpora and databases.

More traditional sources, unlike Twitter, make it fairly easy to investigate the role of different sociolinguistic variables, such as a speaker's age, gender, social background or ethnic group. With regard to Twitter, it is sometimes possible to garner certain details about participants, but not reliably so, since users are not always required to give their real names, gender or age, and these personal details therefore remain uncontrolled. In addition, ethical matters are also an issue here, making the use of such variables difficult, if not impossible.

Sociolinguistic interviews are very useful at gathering useful and interesting material, but it is not always easy for the field worker or the interviewer to remain neutral without having an influence on the answers obtained from the respondents. However, the combination of corpora with data from social networks such as Twitter, may help researchers to conduct studies that otherwise could not be carried out, thus enhancing findings overall. Twitter constitutes a rich source of data, one that can provide new highlights and additional information in the study of language variation and change.

References

Androutsopoulos, Jannis and Michael Beisswenger. 2008. Introduction: Data methods in computer-mediated discourse analysis. *Language@Internet* 5. [https://www.languageatinternet.org/articles/2008/1609/introduction.pdf] (accessed 25 April 2020).

Atifi, Hassan and Michel Marcoccia. 2017. Exploring the role of viewers' tweets in French political programs: Social TV as a new agora? *Discourse, Context and Media* 19. 31–38.

Biber, Douglas, Stig Johansson, Geoffrey Leech, Susan Conrad and Edward Finegan. 1999. *Longman grammar of spoken and written English*. London: Longman.

Bohman, Axel. 2016. Language change because Twitter? Factors motivating innovative uses of *because* across the English-speaking Twittersphere: Variation, representation, and change. In Lauren Squires (ed.), *English in computer-mediated communication. Variation, representation, and change*, 149–178. Berlin: De Gruyter Mouton.

Braun, Friederike. 1988. *Terms of address*. Berlin/New York/Amsterdam: De Gruyter.

Cheshire, Jenny. 2013. Grammaticalisation in social context: The emergence of a new English pronoun. *Journal of Sociolinguistics* 17 (5). 608–633.

Cheshire, Jenny and Sue Fox. 2009. *Was/were* variation. A perspective from London. *Language Variation and Change* 21 (1). 1–38.

Cheshire, Jenny, Paul Kerswill, Susan Fox and Eivind Torgersen. 2011. Contact, the feature pool and the speech community: The emergence of Multicultural London English. *Journal of Sociolinguistics* 15 (2). 151–196.

Cheshire, Jenny, Jacomine Nortier and David Adger. 2015. Emerging multiethnolects in Europe. Queen Mary's OPAL #33 *Occasional Papers Advancing Linguistics* 33. 1–27.

Clancy, Brian. 2015. "Hurry up baby son all the boys is finished their breakfast". Examining the use of vocatives as pragmatic markers in Irish traveller and settled family discourse. In Carolina P. Amador-Moreno, Kevin McCafferty and Elaine Vaughan (eds.), *Pragmatic markers in Irish English*, 229–247. Amsterdam and Philadelphia: John Benjamins.

Clyne, Michael. 2000. Lingua franca and ethnolects in Europe and beyond. *Sociolinguistica* 14. 83–89.

Coats, Steven. 2016. Grammatical feature frequencies of English on Twitter in Finland. In Lauren Squires (ed.), *English in computer-mediated communication: Variation, representation, and change*, 179–210. Berlin: De Gruyter Mouton.

Crystal, David. 2001. *Language and the internet.* Cambridge: Cambridge University Press.

Cutler, Cecelia and Unn Røyneland (eds.). 2018. *Multilingual youth practices in computer mediated communication.* Cambridge: Cambridge University Press.

Drange, Eli-Marie. 2007. Anglicisms in Norwegian and Chilean adolescent language. *New voices in linguistics.* Newcastle: Cambridge Scholars Publishing.

Drummond, Rob. 2017. (Mis)interpreting urban youth language: White kids sounding black? *Journal of Youth Studies* 20 (5). 640–660.

Drummond, Rob. 2018. Maybe it's a grime [t]ing. TH-stopping in urban British youth. *Language in Society* 47 (2). 171–196.

Grieve, Jack, Chris Montgomery, Andrea Nini, Akira Murakami and Diansheng Guo. 2019. Mapping lexical dialect variation in British English using Twitter. *Frontiers in Artificial Intelligence* 2. [https:// doi: 10.3389/frai.2019.00011].

Gruber, Helmut. 2017. Quoting and retweeting as communicative practices in computer-mediated discourse. *Discourse, Context and Media* 20. 1–9.

Herring, Susan C. 2001. Computer-mediated discourse. In Deborah Schiffrin, Deborah Tannen and Heidi Hamilton (eds.), *Handbook of discourse analysis.* 612–634. Oxford: Blackwell.

Herring, Susan C. 2019. The coevolution of computer-mediated communication and computer mediated discourse analysis. In Patricia Bou-Franch and Pilar Garcés-Conejos Blitvich (eds.), *Analyzing digital discourse.* 25–67. Cham: Palgrave Macmillan.

Heyd, Theresa. 2010. "How you guys doin?" Staged orality and emerging plural address in the television series *Friends. American Speech* 85 (1). 33–66.

Hiltunen, Turo, Joe McVeigh and Tanja Säily (eds.). 2017. *Studies in variation, contacts and change in English 19. Big and rich data in English corpus linguistics.* Helsinki: VARIENG, University of Helsinki.

Hinrichs, Lars. 2018. The language of diasporic blogs: A framework for the study of rhetoricity in written online code-switching. In Cecelia Cutler and Unn Røyneland (eds.), *Multilingual youth practices in computer mediated communication.* 186–204. Cambridge: Cambridge University Press.

Hinrichs, Lars and Jessica White-Sustaíta. 2011. Global Englishes and the sociolinguistics of spelling: A study of Jamaican blog and email writing. *English World-Wide* 32 (1). 36–73.

Kortmann, Bernd and Kerstin Lunkenheimer (eds.). 2013. *The electronic world atlas of varieties of English* [eWAVE]. Leipzig: Max Planck Institute for Evolutionary Anthropology. [http://www.ewave-atlas.org/] (accessed 23 April 2020).

Kytölä, Samu and Elina Westinen. 2015. "I be da reel gansta" – A Finnish footballer's Twitter writing and metapragmatic evaluations of authenticity. *Discourse, Context & Media* 8. 6–19.

Leech, Geoffrey. 1999. The distribution and function of vocatives in American and British English. In Hilde Hasselgård and Signe Oksefjell (eds.), *Out of corpora: Studies in honour of Stig Johansson*. 107–120. Amsterdam: Rodopi.

Mair, Christian. 2011. Using the 'Corpus of Cyber-Jamaican' to explore research perspectives for the future. In Fanny Meunier, Sylvie De Cock, Gaëtanelle Gilquin and Magali Paquot (eds.), *A taste for corpora: In honour of Sylviane Granger*, 209–236. Amsterdam and Philadelphia: John Benjamins.

McKay, Susan B., Crispin Thurlow and Heather Toomey Zimmerman. 2005. Wired whizzes or techno-slaves? Young people and their emergent communication technologies. In Angie Williams and Crispin Thurlow (eds.), *Talking adolescence: Perspectives on communication in the teenage years*, 185–203. New York: Peter Lang.

Meyerhoff, Miriam. 2006. *Introducing sociolinguistics*. London and New York: Routledge.

Nortier, Jacomine and Bente A. Svendsen (eds.). 2015. *Language, youth and identity in the 21st Century. Linguistic practices across urban spaces*. Cambridge: Cambridge University Press.

Palacios, Ignacio. 2015. Variation, development and pragmatic uses of *innit* in the language of British adults and teenagers. *English Language and Linguistics* 19 (3). 383–405.

Palacios, Ignacio. 2016. *He don't like football, does he?* A corpus-based study of third person singular *don't* in the language of British teenagers. In Elena Seoane and Cristina Suárez-Gómez (eds.), *World Englishes: New theoretical and methodological considerations*, 61–84. Amsterdam and Philadelphia: John Benjamins.

Palacios, Ignacio. 2018. "Help me move to that, blood." A corpus-based study of the syntax and pragmatics of vocatives in the language of British teenagers. *Journal of Pragmatics* 130. 33–50.

Puschman, Cornelius. 2015. The form and function of quoting in digital media. *Discourse, Context and Media* 7. 28–36.

Rampton, Ben. 2015. Contemporary urban vernaculars. In Jacomine Nortier and Bente A. Svendsen, (eds.), *Language, youth and identity in the 21st Century*, 24–44. Cambridge: Cambridge University Press.

Scott, Kate. 2018. "Hashtags work everywhere": The pragmatic functions of spoken hashtags. *Discourse, Context and Media* 22. 57–64.

Sebba, Mark. 1993. *London Jamaican: Language systems in interaction*. London: Longman.

Squires, Lauren. 2016. *English in computer-mediated communication: Variation, representation, and change*. Berlin: De Gruyter Mouton.

Tagliamonte, Sali. 2016. *Teen talk: The language of adolescents*. Cambridge: Cambridge University Press.

Thurlow, Crispin and Kristine Mroczek (eds.). 2011. *Digital discourse: Language in the new media*. Oxford and New York: Oxford University Press.

van der Bom, Isabelle, Laura L. Paterson, David Peplow and Karen Grainger. 2018. 'It's not the fact they claim benefits but their useless, lazy, drug taking lifestyles we despise': Analysing audience responses to *Benefits Street* using live tweets. *Discourse, Context & Media* 21. 36–45.

Wiese, Heike. 2009. Grammatical innovation in multiethnic urban Europe: New linguistic practices among adolescents. *Lingua* 119. 782–806.

Zappavigna, Michele (ed.). 2012. *Discourse of Twitter and social media: How we use language to create affiliation on the web*. New York: Continuum.

Thabo Ditsele
6 Locating Sepitori in relation to South Africa's youth language practices: An overview

A major research study which explored the youth language (YL) spoken in greater Pretoria (or Tshwane) in South Africa was done by Schuring (1985), albeit within a larger scope of research on Sepitori (or Pretoria Sotho). This near-40-year-old study separated Sepitori, a Black Urban Vernacular (BUV), from a YL which he termed "Slang Sotho". Since that time, while less research on Sepitori has been forthcoming, research on tsotsitaal (a name for YLs spoken in South Africa) has been undertaken on a regular basis. This development has led to uncertainty about YL practices in greater Tshwane, and perhaps explains the assumption that Sepitori is a YL spoken in Tshwane. The aim of this chapter is to review the literature on Sepitori with a view to locate this BUV within Africa's YL practices in general, and South Africa in particular. As a result of this review, I propose three phases in which research on Sepitori should be classified. I conclude that Sepitori is in the same category as Town Bemba of Zambia and Dakar Wolof of Dakar in that they are BUVs which the youth manipulate to create YLs. In the absence of a specific name for the YL spoken in greater Pretoria, an impression was created that Sepitori is itself the name of that YL, when the evidence shows that is not the case.

1 Introduction

The literature on "youth languages" (YLs) spoken in Africa (e.g. Kießling and Mous 2004) acknowledges tsotsitaal[1] as a YL spoken in South Africa. Ditsele (2014: 218) submits that tsotsitaal is the most studied non-standard variety in South Africa, a view which is supported by Hurst (2019: 8) who remarks that it

---

[1] Mesthrie (2008: 96) submits that a lower case tsotsitaal refers to the overarching phenomenon while the upper case Tsotsitaal and alternative names (e.g. Flaaitaal) denote specific varieties previously described in the literature (see Hurst and Mesthrie 2013: 18). This study follows this naming convention.

Thabo Ditsele, Tshwane University of Technology, e-mail: ProfDitsele@outlook.com

"has received a significant amount of attention in academic literature, and its features, including its linguistic structure, history, functions, and reception have been dealt with in depth".

On the other hand, the term Black Urban Vernacular (BUV) was coined by Calteaux (1994: 191) who defines it as "the variety of speech commonly found in Black urban areas, which is used by most members of the urban speech community in varying degrees, to facilitate communication between speakers of different mother tongues, and which usually contains elements from more than one language" (for further reading, see Calteaux 1996: 51–63). These phenomena are elsewhere referred to as the urban vernacular (Hurst-Harosh forthcoming, Mesthrie, Hurst-Harosh and Brookes forthcoming). The distinction between the BUV and the YL in particular communities has often been unclear. For example, Makalela (2013: 112) suggested that all references for YLs spoken in South Africa (e.g. tsotsitaal, Flaaitaal, Iscamtho, etc.) should be collapsed into one reference, kasi-taal, in order to account for weakening boundaries between Sotho-Tswana,[2] Nguni, Afrikaans and English language forms. However, his description of kasi-taal implied the BUV rather than the YL. In contrast, there is a strong argument (Hurst and Buthelezi 2014, Mesthrie, Hurst-Harosh and Brookes forthcoming) that BUVs should be distinguished from the stylistic practice and lexicon which is the main characteristic of a tsotsitaal, which Hurst (2008) describes as a "stylect" or style-related lexicon embedded in other languages which act as base languages.

In their seminal work on youth language in Africa, Kießling and Mous (2004) describe YLs spoken in Africa as varieties spoken by the youth at several urban centres[3] in the continent and suggest that the youth create such varieties in order to set themselves apart from the older generation, through the use of certain types of conscious language manipulation. Through these varieties, the youth create a powerful statement of identity. Hurst (2019) suggests that they are often characterised by extreme multilingualism, featuring lexical items from numerous African languages, as well as colonial languages and influences from popular culture such as hip hop music.

While Kießling and Mous (2004: 3) and Mous (2009: 216) stated that many YLs spoken in Africa have a clear name by which they are known to their speak-

---

[2] In contemporary literature, "Sotho-Tswana" is used to refer to three mutually intelligible languages (viz. Northern Sotho, Setswana and Southern Sotho) to avoid possible confusion with the latter.

[3] There is no dispute that YLs spoken in Africa developed within urban centres, and as such, "African urban youth languages" (AUYLs) is used in earlier literature. The reality of contemporary Africa is that these languages have spread to rural areas, thus it is reasonable to refer to them as YLs as this acknowledges the reality of the time.

ers, Hurst (2015: 169) states that while they are sometimes "named" (a particular phenomenon may explicitly receive a name in a specific national context), equally, some of the examples are just referred to as "street language" or "youth language". Some of the YLs spoken in Africa which have been given names and studied include: Camfranglais in Cameroon (e.g. by Kouega 2003, Schröder 2007); Sheng in Kenya (e.g. by Githinji 2006, Kioko 2015); tsotsitaal in South Africa (e.g. by Brookes 2004, who elsewhere critiques the use of tsotsitaal as a naming convention peculiar to linguists, see Brookes 2014, Deumert 2018), Chibrazi in Malawi (e.g. by Kamanga 2015); Langila in DR Congo (e.g. by Nassenstein 2015); Luyaaye in Uganda (e.g. by Namyalo 2017); and S'ncamtho in Zimbabwe (e.g. by Ndlovu 2018).

One feature of YLs (whether spoken in Africa or elsewhere) is that they use the grammatical base of an existing language, usually the lingua franca or urban vernacular (Kießling and Mous 2004: 3, Mous 2009: 218, Mesthrie and Hurst 2013). This is then supplemented by lexical items borrowed from other languages (Gunnink 2012: 9). In the case of tsotsitaal, Ntshangase (1993) notes that such lexical items are drawn from all 11 official languages of South Africa.

Hurst (2015: 169) states that there are different varieties of tsotsitaal which utilise a range of base languages (or matrix languages, as noted by Deumert 2018). This means that each official language in South Africa has a corresponding tsotsitaal style. As such, varieties of tsotsitaal which have been studied include those based on: isiXhosa[4] (e.g. Hurst 2008, Mesthrie and Hurst 2013), isiZulu (e.g. Aycard 2014, Mfusi 1990), Setswana (e.g. Cook 2009, Ditsele and Hurst 2016), Tshivenda (e.g. Mulaudzi and Poulos 2001); and English (e.g. Mesthrie 2014).

The use of a particular base language for a tsotsitaal variety is geographically determined by the dominant language of the region, for instance, isiZulu-based tsotsitaal would be predominantly spoken across the province of KwaZulu-Natal, and parts of the provinces of Mpumalanga (e.g. Ermelo, Standerton, etc.) and Gauteng (mainly Johannesburg and Ekurhuleni). A mixed base language might be used in parts of Johannesburg such as Soweto where people speak a mixed BUV drawn from Sesotho and isiZulu. As such, tsotsitaal can be based on the BUV (see also Mesthrie and Hurst 2013). For example, in Soweto (located southwest of central Johannesburg), Gunnink (2012) distinguishes between Sowetan Zulu and Sowetan Tsotsitaal; the latter uses the former as its grammatical base. Johannesburg being the place where tsotsitaal developed in the 1940s (Hurst and Mesthrie 2013: 5), early

---

[4] Ordinarily, Bantu languages are written with prefixes (e.g. *isi-*, *Se-*, *Chi-*, etc.) as it is the case in the Constitution of South Africa. However, these prefixes may be dropped if desired (e.g. Xhosa, Tswana, Venda, etc.).

research on tsotsitaal was concentrated in that city and particularly the variety based on isiZulu (e.g. Ntshangase 1993). Since then, research has been conducted on other tsotsitaals, for example in KwaZulu-Natal (Rudwick 2005), Cape Town (Hurst 2008), alongside further research on Johannesburg tsotsitaals (Aycard 2014).

In contrast, as far as the author could ascertain, the last research study on tsotsitaal spoken in greater Pretoria (or Tshwane) was done by Gerard Schuring in the late 1970s to the mid-1980s – nearly 40 years ago (in his study he refers to tsotsitaal as Flaaitaal – an early term for the YL). Due to language fluidity, there is the potential that tsotsitaal spoken in greater Pretoria might have gone through significant changes, which has not been described in more contemporary research. Furthermore, attention is needed regarding how to place or characterise greater Pretoria's lingua franca of Black residents in relation both to tsotsitaal and the bigger field of YL research. This lingua franca is known as Sepitori or the "language of Pretoria" (Ditsele and Mann 2014: 159). Schuring (1985: x) defines Sepitori (also known as Pretoria Sotho) as the once-dominant Setswana dialect (called Sekgatla) of Hammanskraal with additional lexicon mainly from Northern Sotho (also known as Sepedi), Afrikaans and English (also see Ditsele and Mann [2014: 220] and Malimabe [1990: 12]).

The aim of this chapter is therefore to address this gap in research by locating Sepitori in relation to Africa's YL practices in general, and South Africa in particular. The chapter makes the argument that Sepitori is the BUV rather than the YL in greater Pretoria. This chapter comes at a point where, in recent years, Sepitori has been gaining momentum far beyond the limits of greater Pretoria and has been used prominently in film and television in South Africa. Examples are drawn from these media to illustrate the relations between Sepitori and tsotsitaal (see Section 4).

2 Uncertainty about Sepitori in relation to YL

As indicated in the previous section, nearly 40 years has passed since research was conducted on tsotsitaal spoken in greater Pretoria, an area in northern Gauteng which in geopolitical terms is known as the City of Tshwane Metropolitan Municipality. In popular perception in South Africa, the BUV is often incorrectly conflated with tsotsitaal, likely because the BUV often draws on tsotsitaal-originating lexical elements; and also due to the fact that tsotsitaal receives disproportionate attention from researchers and media practitioners (viz. newspapers and television reporters), relative to BUVs (e.g. Sepitori, Jozi Sotho, etc.).

The gap in research on tsotsitaal in greater Pretoria was recently highlighted in June 2017 when a Twitter user (or 'twitterati') urged others to post Sepitori material under #LearnPitori. This hashtag was overwhelmed with submissions to a point where it caught the attention of the South African media (i.e. local and national newspapers, and national television networks). These submissions were not peer checked as was noted by Ditsele (2019: 1):

> As social media platforms, such as *Twitter,* accept contributions from all members of the public regardless of how informed or knowledgeable they are about the subject matter at hand, there was a need to establish, from speakers of Sepitori, whether they would equally regard submissions to *#LearnPitori* as Sepitori.

Ditsele (2018, 2019) analysed lexical items from the data he gathered from this hashtag. His work shows the uncertainty about the place of Sepitori in relation to South Africa's YL practices, as many contributors were unable to distinguish between tsotsitaal lexical items and the Sepitori BUV. A study by Álvarez-Mosquera, Bornman and Ditsele (2018) also shows the need to conduct research on tsotsitaal in greater Pretoria as their participants could not agree whether Sepitori was a version of tsotsitaal (or not). In order to locate Sepitori in relation to South Africa's YL practices, there is a need to do an overview of what is known about this BUV thus far.

3 An overview of research on Sepitori

I propose three phases in which research on Sepitori can be classified, that is, "before 1990", "between 1990 and 2010" and "after 2010", respectively. The split among the three phases is based on focus areas:
1. Before 1990 – determining whether (or not) Sepitori was a lingua franca or a koiné language;
2. From 1990 to 2010 – the influence of Sepitori in education; and
3. After 2010 – going beyond the previous tradition of a sociolinguistic focus by spreading to other sub-fields (viz. psycholinguistics and linguistic anthropology).

As Section 3.3 will show, there was a relatively sharp increase in the number of research studies in the third phase, relative to the first and second phases. In all three phases, the question of the relationship between Sepitori and YL/tsotsitaal is highlighted.

3.1 First phase (before 1990)

Following two early studies (Cronjé 1955 and Ziervogel 1969) which considered the lingua franca status of early forms of Sepitori (Malimabe 1990: ii), a seminal research study on Sepitori was conducted in the mid-1980s by Schuring (1985). His study built on the earlier work, and he sought to establish whether Sepitori showed the characteristics of a koiné language, which as Ditsele and Mann (2014: 161) explain, is a language which develops out of contact between languages which are mutually intelligible. Schuring's data were gathered at two Black townships, that is, Mamelodi and Atteridgeville. Schuring (1985: x) concluded that Sepitori is a koiné language like Koiné Greek, and such conclusion is based on the hypotheses he tested and proved to hold. Ditsele and Mann (2014: 161) present a succinct summary of Schuring's hypotheses, which were as follows: that Sepitori (a) is a colloquial language; (b) is a dynamic language; (c) is a mixed language, consisting of a base language to which familiar elements of other languages are added; (d) may have regional varieties; (e) is a lingua franca; (f) is a cosmopolitan language; and, (g) is an autonomous popular language with a lower status than that of the related standard language or languages. Ditsele and Mann (2014: 161) furthermore note:

> Of all the hypotheses, only the fourth [i.e. may have regional varieties] did not hold, because his respondents could not distinguish between varieties spoken in two of the Pretoria townships – Mamelodi, which is one on the eastern side, and Atteridgeville, which is on the western side. However, Schuring argues that regional varieties are not a necessary distinguishing feature of a koiné.

Whereas Schuring's (1985) primary focus was on establishing whether Sepitori is a koiné language or not, he could not ignore the presence of tsotsitaal (which he referred to as 'Slang Sotho'). He notes the following about Sepitori and tsotsitaal (Schuring 1985: 132, my own translation from Afrikaans):

> The question of whether the speaker is a tsotsi[5] or not a tsotsi is an important question in this investigation. One of the major problems when studying Pretoria Sotho is to distinguish between Pretoria Sotho and Slang Sotho. At first, the distinction between Pretoria Sotho and slang languages of the youth seemed to lie in the fact that Pretoria Sotho is basically a Sotho language, while slang languages are basically Afrikaans. However, it soon became clear that slang languages with a Sotho language as a base also exist.

While he acknowledges that it is not easy to distinguish between Sepitori (Pretoria Sotho) and a YL spoken in greater Pretoria (Slang Sotho), the two are not the

---

[5] Brookes (2014: 385) states that the word *tsotsi* means 'crook, gangster, criminal' (most likely from the Southern Sotho word *tsoha* 'wake up, be alert').

same. The former is a Sotho-Tswana variety, while "the base of the Slang Sotho spoken in Pretoria is Pretoria Sotho" (Schuring 1981: 128). This is in keeping with the work of researchers such as Gunnink (2012) and Mesthrie and Hurst (2013) who have distinguished between an urban variety, and tsotsitaal which uses the urban variety as its grammatical base. Furthermore, Schuring (1985: 137, my own translation from Afrikaans) submits that:

> A slang language like Pretoria's Slang Sotho is even more mixed than Pretoria Sotho. Although language mixing often occurs in slang languages, language mixing is not a necessary feature of the origin of slang languages. A slang language is meant to be exclusive and different, and to achieve this, it is convenient to use familiar words from other languages.

The work of Schuring supports the perspective that while the YL tsotsitaal is about manipulation, the BUV (in this case, Pretoria Sotho or Sepitori) arises from contact (between e.g. Northern Sotho and Setswana) in the urban environment.

3.2 Second phase (from 1990 to 2010)

Five years after Schuring's seminal work on Sepitori, Malimabe (1990) conducted the next research study on Sepitori, albeit indirectly. Her study sought to determine the degree to which the learning of standard Setswana (as a Home Language) was influenced by other languages. She gathered data at schools in Mamelodi, Atteridgeville, Soshanguve and Ga-Rankuwa (all located in greater Pretoria). Sepitori emerged as the language with the most influence on participants' learning and use of standard Setswana.

She notes that relative to standard varieties of Southern Bantu[6] languages, Sepitori is a prestigious language.[7] People who relocated to greater Pretoria learned to speak the variety so as to avoid being associated with rural areas[8] and regarded as country bumpkins, and many Northern Sotho and Tsonga people

---

6 "Bantu" refers to a group of languages spoken in Sub-Saharan Africa. However, in a geopolitical context of pre-democratic South Africa, it was used as a derogatory term for Black Africans. This chapter is located in the field of Linguistics, thus "Bantu" here has been used in a linguistic context (and not a geopolitical one).
7 Calteaux (1994: 200) similarly found that the non-standard variety spoken in Tembisa (a Black township very close to greater Pretoria) carries its own prestige and marks a person who speaks it as a "city-wise" urbanite.
8 Bornman, Álvarez-Mosquera and Seti (2018: 30), note that some analysts (e.g. Ditsele 2014, Kone 2010, Webb 2010) believe that standard varieties of Southern Bantu languages are increasingly becoming symbols of traditionalism, and are thus rejected by many urban youth, and urban varieties – in addition to English – are believed to have been gaining in social prestige.

even changed their surnames to adopt Afrikaans, Setswana and isiZulu ones because they were too ashamed to acknowledge their ethnic affiliations (Malimabe 1990: 13). Sepitori's social prestige extends beyond the limits of greater Pretoria, as Malimabe (1990: 12) notes:

> When one overhears a Black Pretorian speak at any place outside Pretoria, one automatically knows that the person hails from Pretoria because his speech betrays him. It automatically characterises him/her as a Pretorian urban person.

She also established that there was a difference between Sepitori and tsotsitaal by asking participants to speak what they understood to be tsotsitaal. While all participants could speak Sepitori, female participants said that they could not speak tsotsitaal, instead they suggested the names of boys whom they regarded as being good in tsotsitaal. Male participants had no problem speaking what they understood to be tsotsitaal, and used specific lexical items such as *zwakala* ('come here'), and *O a jaja?* ('Do you understand?'). She discovered that in their speech, male participants were prone to invent exaggerated expressions when in mixed company so as to impress women with their familiarity with urban life (Malimabe 1990: 15).

Nearly 20 years after Malimabe's work, Nkosi (2008) conducted the next research on Sepitori. Like Malimabe, her study was not directly about Sepitori because she sought to investigate the effects of the interference of other languages on standard Northern Sotho (as a Home Language), following poor educational performance in the language over a number of years. Her data were gathered at a high school in Soshanguve (located northwest of central Pretoria). She established that participants used terminologies from their township, such being drawn from Sepitori and tsotsitaal.

She asked the participants to state which languages they spoke with their friends, and they selected Northern Sotho, Southern Sotho, isiZulu, Sepitori and tsotsitaal (Nkosi 2008: 53–64). To gather the lexical items which they used, she asked participants to write an essay in Northern Sotho based on any picture they desired and found that female and male participants used different lexical items (Nkosi 2008: 70–73) as shown in Table 6.1.

The lexical items used by female participants were those used in standard varieties of the three Sotho-Tswana languages (viz. *borotho* and *robala*) or in standard varieties of Setswana and Southern Sotho only (viz. *dumelang* and *tsamaya*); the latter are commonly used in Sepitori. With regards to *mama* and *papa*, Black communities use them colloquially throughout South Africa.

The lexical items used by male participants were those used in different varieties of tsotsitaal, and have been cited in several sources, for example, *dough*

Table 6.1: Lexical items used by participants.

Lexical items used by females	Lexical items used by males	Northern Sotho	English
borotho	dough	borotho	'bread'
robala	gidla	robala	'to sleep'
dumelang	heita	thobela	'hello'
tsamaya	vaya	sepela	'to go'
mama	ou lady (oledi)	mma	'mother'
papa	thaema/tayima	tate	'father'

(Ditsele 2019: 21 also as *ndolish*), *gidla* (Msimang 1987: 86), *heita* (Bembe and Beukes 2007: 469), *ou lady/oledi* and *thaema/tayima* (Molamu 2003: 77), and *vaya* (Brookes and Lekgoro 2014: 155). Nkosi (2008: 75) also presented a number of utterances from male participants such as the following examples (1) and (2).

(1) **Authi** ela ga e na **verstaan**.   tsotsitaal
    Mošimane ola ha a nyake ho **tlhalohanya**.   Sepitori
    '**That guy** does not want to understand/is **difficult**.'
    (examples 1–6: my own translation).

This example comprises tsotsitaal lexical items which are used in different varieties of tsotsitaal, and have been cited in several sources, for example *authi* (Brookes 2014: 364) and *verstaan* (Ditsele and Hurst 2016: 5). The utterance's grammatical base is Sepitori.

(2) *My bra, jy moenie so maak nie.*   tsotsitaal
    Abut'a ka, o ska ira byao.   Sepitori
    'My brother, don't do that.'

The clause *jy moenie so maak nie* is Afrikaans, and when combined with *my bra* (Mulaudzi and Poulos 2001: 6) completes the statement to be tsotsitaal with an Afrikaans grammatical base.

This research demonstrates the ways in which tsotsitaal and Sepitori are sometimes conflated by participants as well as researchers. But there is a clear distinction between the language use by males and females in these research studies, and tsotsitaal can be distinguished from the BUV as a male youth style (Mesthrie, Hurst-Harosh and Brookes forthcoming).

3.3 Third phase (after 2010)

The third phase in Sepitori research started with presentations by Ditsele (2012, 2013a, 2013b). These presentations were translated into the following two publications: Ditsele and Mann (2014); and Ditsele (2014). One of the main objectives of Ditsele and Mann's (2014) largely theoretical paper was to call for more research on Sepitori because it is a BUV that is not institutionally recognised and promoted, while Ditsele (2014) presented arguments for using Sepitori vocabularies to enrich those of Setswana and Northern Sotho.

Following these two publications, research on Sepitori was conducted more frequently than before, with an average of at least one study every two years. Three such studies were Master's degree projects and they were conducted within a three-year period, that is, 2016 to 2019. The first, by Ntuli (2016), was a psycholinguistic study whereby she tested speakers of Southern Sotho from Vosloorus (located southeast of central Johannesburg) and of "Mamelodi Lingo" from Mamelodi (located east of central Pretoria), regarding how they related back a speechless short cartoon. She notes that "Mamelodi Lingo" is a variety of Sepitori spoken in Mamelodi (Ntuli 2016: 20), thus slightly different from varieties spoken at other townships. Participants from both townships (i.e. Vosloorus and Mamelodi) used well known tsotsitaal lexical items (e.g. *spana, vaya,* etc.) in their compositions.

The second, by Wagner (2018), sought to determine the degree to which the learning of standard Setswana (as a Home Language) was influenced by Sepitori in Ga-Rankuwa, Mabopane and Soshanguve (located northwest of central Pretoria). In many respects, Wagner's (2018) study and findings were similar to that of Malimabe (1990); both of them found evidence of the influence of Sepitori on work produced by learners who studied Setswana as a Home Language. The third, by Madingwaneng (2019), focused on the linguistic contributions (particularly lexicon) of Northern Sotho to Sepitori. She gathered her data from Northern Sotho home language speakers who were brought up at different areas of greater Pretoria. She found that Northern Sotho and Setswana shared many lexical items, which were transferred to and settled as Sepitori lexical items. These studies tended to treat Sepitori as a BUV rather than a YL, although they acknowledged the inclusion of tsotsitaal lexical items in Sepitori.

Two further research studies focused on "language and identity" in greater Pretoria that is, how participants viewed Sepitori and the people who speak it. The first, by Bornman, Álvarez-Mosquera and Seti (2018), surveyed participants who lived in greater Pretoria (regardless of where they grew up). Like Malimabe (1990), they stated that the ability to speak Sepitori portrayed a speaker as urbanised, and also separated them from people from rural areas. However, they stressed the importance of being able to communicate in Southern Bantu languages associated with their heritages, because such ability meant taking pride in who they were as Africans. This study did not explore tsotsitaal at all. The second study, by Álvarez-Mosquera et al. (2018), surveyed insiders (people who grew up in greater Pretoria) and outsiders (people who grew outside greater Pretoria). The former group were of the view that Sepitori was not a tsotsitaal variety, but a language with home language speakers, while the latter were adamant that Sepitori was a tsotsitaal variety spoken in greater Pretoria and could not have home language speakers. Outsiders also believed that people who speak Sepitori had a particular style of clothing, movement and speech, all of which recall typical behaviours of tsotsitaal speakers (Hurst 2008). This reflects the popular tendency to conflate the two phenomena.

The most recent research study on Sepitori was done by Ditsele (2019). He selected statements from the Twitter hashtag *#LearnPitori*, then asked participants who grew up speaking Sepitori in greater Pretoria to classify the statements along the Sepitori/tsotsitaal continuum. Consistent with the literature on tsotsitaal regarding sex as a variable (Hurst 2015), male participants overwhelmingly regarded known tsotsitaal lexical items as part of their regular speech (part of Sepitori, rather than tsotsitaal-specific) relative to their female counterparts. The study also confirmed the significance of "ethnic affiliation" in the use of home languages, which was previously noted by Bornman et al. (2018).

The research conducted thus far on Sepitori therefore highlights on the one hand that there is crossover in lexicon between Sepitori and tsotsitaal, but also that, from a research perspective, the two phenomena cannot be conflated, as Sepitori functions as the BUV, used by a majority of residents of greater Pretoria, while tsotsitaal is predominantly a male youth style.

4 Sepitori/tsotsitaal dynamic in the entertainment industry

As an illustration of Sepitori, this section presents a number of examples drawn from its common usage in film and television in South Africa, notably productions with storylines which are attractive to the youth. The examples demonstrate the use of tsotsitaal lexical items in Sepitori, but these are all commonly known and used tsotsitaal items, which can be seen to have moved into the BUV. Alternative Sepitori versions are provided to show the impact of tsotsitaal lexicon on Sepitori. Examples (3) and (4) are utterances extracted from a 2018 feature film called *Matwetwe*, which was popularised by its exclusive use of

Sepitori, and examples (5) and (6) were extracted from an ongoing television soap opera called *The River*, which comprises a significant number of actors who speak Sepitori.

(3) *O bua ka lepona **my bra** nkare o **gidla** mo dim'a lona; o tsoha mo* tsotsitaal
dim'a lona.
*O bolela ka lepona **monna** nkare o **robala** mo dim'a lona; o tsoha* Sepitori
mo dim'a lona.
'You talk about a naked body **my brother** like you **sleep** and wake up on it.'

Example (3) comprises *my bra* and *gidla*, which are commonly known tsotsitaal lexical items. In Sepitori, *bolela* ('to speak/talk' in Northern Sotho) is more commonly used than *bua* ('to speak' in Setswana and Southern Sotho).

(4) *Tlohela ho tshwara **daai goetes** ka matsogo **bra**!* tsotsitaal
*Tlohela ho tshwara **dilo tseo** ka matsogo **monna**!* Sepitori
'Stop touching **that stuff** with your bare hands **man**!'

Including *bra* (already discussed), example (4) comprises tsotsitaal lexical items *daai* (an Afrikaans colloquial form of *daardie*) and *goetes* ('goods/stuff' in Afrikaans).

(5) *He o re wa lebella le wena, o **verloora spane** sa hao, wang* tsotsitaal
***verstana**?*
*He o re wa lebella le wena, o **latlhehelwa ke mmereko** wa hao,* Sepitori
*wang **ntlhalohanya**?*
'When you look at it yourself, you **lose your job**, do you **understand** me?'

Including *verstana* (already discussed), example 5 comprises tsotsitaal lexical items *verloor* ('to lose' in Afrikaans) and *spane* ('work/job', Aycard 2014: 80).

(6) *Re ka ho **griza** ka **nyuku** e nngwe **azanga** wa e bona **in jou lewe**.* tsotsitaal
*Re ka ho **tshwarisa chelete** e nngwe **e iseng** w'e bone **mo boph-*** Sepitori
***elong ba hao**.*
'We could **give you a bribe of an amount of money** you've never seen **in your life**.'

Example (6) comprises *griza* ('to grease'), *nyuku* ('money', Mfusi 1990: 5–6 spelled as *nyoko*), *azanga* ('never' in Nguni languages), and *in jou lewe* (as is in Afrikaans), which are commonly known tsotsitaal lexical items.

5 Conclusion

This overview of research on Sepitori demonstrates that it is a BUV similar to Sowetan Zulu (Gunnink 2012), Town Bemba, which is spoken at urban centres in central Zambia (Spitulnik 1998) and Dakar Wolof in greater Dakar in Senegal (Mc Laughlin 2001). Kießling and Mous (2004: 2) note that Town Bemba and Dakar Wolof are urban varieties, which the youth manipulate further to set themselves apart from older generation. Like Town Bemba and Dakar Wolof, the youth of greater Tshwane also manipulate Sepitori mainly by embedding tsotsitaal lexical items in it.

The examples above highlight the crossovers between tsotsitaal and Sepitori particularly at the lexical level, but it is important to reiterate that the tsotsitaal lexical items are commonly known and therefore can be understood to have moved into the BUV – they are no longer innovations exclusive to the youth. This highlights the distinction again between a male youth language style which seeks to manipulate and differentiate, and a BUV which acts as a common lingua franca in the multilingual space of greater Pretoria.

References

Álvarez-Mosquera, Pedro, Elirea Bornman and Thabo Ditsele. 2018. Residents' perceptions on Sepitori, a mixed language spoken in greater Pretoria, South Africa. *Sociolinguistic Studies* 12 (3–4). 439–459.

Aycard, Pierre. 2014. *The use of Iscamtho by children in White City-Jabavu, Soweto: Slang and language contact in an African urban context*. Cape Town: University of Cape Town dissertation.

Bembe, Magdeline P. and Anne-Marie Beukes. 2007. The use of slang by black youth in Gauteng. *Southern African Linguistics and Applied Language Studies* 25 (4). 463–472.

Brookes, Heather. 2004. A repertoire of South African quotable gestures. *Journal of Linguistic Anthropology* 14 (2). 186–224.

Brookes, Heather. 2014. Urban youth languages in South Africa: A case study of tsotsitaal in a South African township. *Anthropological Linguistics* 56 (3–4). 356–388.

Brookes, Heather and Tshepiso Lekgoro. 2014. A social history of urban male youth varieties in Stirtonville and Vosloorus, South Africa. *Southern African Linguistics and Applied Language Studies* 32 (2). 149–159.

Bornman, Elirea, Pedro Álvarez-Mosquera and Vuyo Seti. 2018. Language, urbanisation and identity: Young Black residents from Pretoria in South Africa. *Language Matters: Studies in the Languages of Africa* 49 (1). 25–44.
Calteaux, Karen V. 1994. *A sociolinguistic analysis of a multilingual community*. Johannesburg: Rand Afrikaans University dissertation.
Calteaux, Karen. 1996. *Standard and non-standard African language varieties in the urban areas of South Africa: Main report for the STANON research programme*. Pretoria: Human Sciences Research Council.
Cook, Susan E. 2009. Street Setswana vs. school Setswana: Language policies and the forging of identities in South African classrooms. In Jo A. Kleifgen and George C. Bond (eds.), *The languages of Africa and the Diaspora: Educating for language awareness*, 96–116. Bristol: Multilingual Matters.
Cronjé, A.P.J. 1955. *Die Sotho-tale in die Bantule-lokasie van Pretoria*. Pretoria: University of Pretoria MA thesis.
Deumert, Ana. 2018. Tsotsitaal online: The creativity of tradition. In Cecelia Cutler and Unn Røyneland (eds.), *Multilingual youth practices in computer mediated communication*, 109–126. New York: Cambridge University Press.
Ditsele, Thabo. 2012. Language contact in urban settings in Africa: The case of Sepitori in Tshwane. Paper presented at the 2012 Colloquium on African Languages and Linguistics (CALL 2012), Leiden University, the Netherlands, 27–29 August.
Ditsele, Thabo. 2013a. Sepitori: A Pretoria mixed language that could help revive interest in two Bantu languages in South Africa. Poster presented at the 5th International Conference on Bantu Languages, INALCO, France, 12–15 June.
Ditsele, Thabo. 2013b. Sepitori: A Pretoria non-standard variety that could do more than enrich vocabularies of Setswana and Sepedi. Paper presented at the 1st African Urban and Youth Languages Conference, University of Cape Town, South Africa, 5–6 July.
Ditsele, Thabo. 2014. Why not use Sepitori to enrich the vocabularies of Setswana and Sepedi? *Southern African Linguistics and Applied Language Studies* 32 (2). 215–228.
Ditsele, Thabo. 2018. Social media assessments of Sepitori: Some preliminary data from #LearnPitori. Paper presented at the 49th Annual Conference on African Linguistics (ACAL 49), Michigan State University, USA, 22–25 July.
Ditsele, Thabo. 2019. Assessing social media submissions presented as Sepitori on #LearnPitori. *Arusha Working Papers in African Linguistics* 2. 1–21.
Ditsele, Thabo and Charles C. Mann. 2014. Language contact in urban settings: The case of Sepitori in Tshwane. *South African Journal of African Languages* 34 (2). 159–165.
Ditsele, Thabo and Ellen Hurst. 2016. Travelling terms and local innovations: The tsotsitaal of the North West province, South Africa. *Literator* 37 (2). 1–8.
Githinji, Peter. 2006. Bazes and their shibboleths: lexical variation and Sheng speakers' identity in Nairobi. *Nordic Journal of African Studies* 15 (4). 443–472.
Gunnink, Hilde. 2012. *A linguistic analysis of Sowetan Zulu and Sowetan Tsotsi*. Leiden: University of Leiden MA thesis.
Hurst, Ellen. 2008. *Style, structure and function in Cape Town Tsotsitaal*. Cape Town: University of Cape Town dissertation.
Hurst, Ellen. 2015. Overview of the tsotsitaals of South Africa; their different base languages and common core lexical items. In Nico Nassenstein and Andrea Hollington (eds.), *Youth language practices in Africa and beyond*, 169–184. Berlin: De Gruyter Mouton.

Hurst, Ellen. 2019. South African urban youth language research: The state of the nation. In Gratien Gualbert Atindogbé and Augustin Emmanuel Ebongue (eds.), *Linguistic and sociolinguistic perspectives of youth langauge practices in Africa: Codes and identity writings*, 3–20. Cameroon: Langaa RPCIG.

Hurst, Ellen and Mthuli Buthelezi. 2014. A visual and linguistic comparison of features of Durban and Cape Town tsotsitaal. *Southern African Linguistics and Applied Language Studies* 32 (2). 185–197.

Hurst, Ellen and Rajend Mesthrie. 2013. 'When you hang out with the guys they keep you in style': The case for considering style in descriptions of South African tsotsitaals. *Language Matters: Studies in the Languages of Africa* 44 (1). 3–20.

Hurst-Harosh, Ellen. Forthcoming. South Africa: Tsotsitaal and urban vernacular forms of South African languages. In Paul Kerswill and Heike Weise (eds.), *Urban contact dialects and language change: Insights from the Global North and South*. London: Routledge.

Kamanga, Chimwemwe M.M. 2015. *A descriptive analysis of Chibrazi, the urban contact vernacular language of Malawi: A focus on the lexicon and semantic manipulation*. Pretoria: University of Pretoria dissertation.

Kießling, Roland and Maarten Mous. 2004. Urban youth languages in Africa. *Anthropological Linguistics* 46 (3). 303–341.

Kioko, Eric M. 2015. Regional varieties and 'ethnic' registers of Sheng. In Nico Nassenstein and Andrea Hollington (eds.), *Youth language practices in Africa and beyond*, 119–148. Berlin: De Gruyter Mouton.

Kone, A'ame. 2010. Politics of language: The struggle for power in schools in Mali and Burkina Faso. *International Education* 39 (2). 6–20.

Kouega, Jean-Paul. 2003. Word formative processes in Camfranglais. *World Englishes* 22 (4). 511–538.

Madingwaneng, Lebogang M. 2019. *Linguistic contributions of Northern Sotho to Sepitori: Perspectives of Northern Sotho home language speakers brought up in Tshwane*. Pretoria: Tshwane University of Technology MA thesis.

Makalela, Leketi. 2013. Translanguaging in kasi-taal: Rethinking old language boundaries for new language planning. *Stellenbosch Papers in Linguistics Plus* 42. 111–125.

Malimabe, Refilwe M. 1990. *The influence of non-standard varieties on the standard Setswana of high school pupils*. Johannesburg: Rand Afrikaans University MA thesis.

McLaughlin, Fiona. 2001. Dakar Wolof and the configuration of an urban identity. *Journal of African Cultural Studies* 14 (2). 153–172.

Mesthrie, Rajend. 2008. "I've been speaking Tsotsitaal all my life without knowing it": Towards a unified account of tsotsitaals in South Africa. In Miriam Meyerhoff and Naomi Nagy (eds.), *Social lives in language*, 95–110. Amsterdam: John Benjamins.

Mesthrie, Rajend. 2014. English tsotsitaals? – An analysis of two written texts in Surfspeak and South African Indian English slang. *Southern African Linguistics and Applied Language Studies* 32 (2). 173–183.

Mesthrie, Rajend and Ellen Hurst. 2013. Slang, code-switching and restructured urban varieties in South Africa: An analytic overview of tsotsitaals with special reference to the Cape Town variety. *Journal of Pidgin and Creole Languages* 28 (1). 103–130.

Mesthrie, Rajend, Ellen Hurst-Harosh and Heather Brookes (eds). forthcoming. *Youth language practices and urban language contact in Africa*. Cambridge: Cambridge University Press.

Mfusi, M. J. H. 1990. *Soweto Zulu slang: A sociolinguistic study of an urban vernacular in Soweto*. Pretoria: University of South Africa Honours dissertation.

Molamu, Louis. 2003. *Tsotsitaal: A dictionary of the language of Sophiatown*. Pretoria: University of South Africa.

Mous, Maarten. 2009. The development of urban youth languages in Africa. In Carme Junyent (ed.), *Transferences: The expression of extra-linguistic processes in the world's languages*, 215–232. Barcelona: University of Vic.

Msimang, Christian Themba. 1987. Impact of tsotsitaal. *South African Journal of African Languages* 7 (3). 82–86.

Mulaudzi, Phalandwa A. and George Poulos. 2001. The 'Tsotsi' language variety of Venda. *South African Journal of African Languages* 21 (1). 1–8.

Namyalo, Saudah. 2017. The sociolinguistic profile and functions of Luyaaye within its community of practice. In Augustin Emmanuel Ebongue and Ellen Hurst (eds.), *Sociolinguistics in African contexts: Perspectives and challenges*, 225–245. Cham: Springer.

Nassenstein, Nico. 2015. The emergence of Langila in Kinshasa (DR Congo). In Nico Nassenstein and Andrea Hollington (eds.), *Youth language practices in Africa and beyond*, 81–98. Berlin: De Gruyter Mouton.

Ndlovu, Sambulo. 2018. *A comparative analysis of metaphorical expressions used by rural and urban Ndebele speakers: The contribution of S'ncamtho*. Cape Town: University of Cape Town dissertation.

Nkosi, Dolphina M. 2008. *Language variation and change in a Soshanguve high school*. Pretoria: University of South Africa MA thesis.

Ntshangase, Dumisane K. 1993. *The social history of Iscamtho*. Johannesburg: University of the Witwatersrand MA thesis.

Ntuli, Nonhlanhla. 2016. *Gesture and speech in the oral narratives of Sesotho and Mamelodi lingo speakers*. Johannesburg: University of the Witwatersrand MA thesis.

Rudwick, Stephanie. 2005. Township language dynamics: isiZulu and isiTsotsi in Umlazi. *Southern African Linguistics and Applied Language Studies* 23 (3). 305–317.

Schröder, Anne. 2007. Camfranglais – a language with several (sur)faces and important sociolinguistic functions. In Anke Bartels and Dirk Wiemann (eds.), *Global fragments: (Dis)orientation in the new world order*, 281–298. Amsterdam: Rodopi.

Schuring, Gerard K. 1981. Die basilek van flaaitaal. *Tydskrif vir Geesteswetenskappe* 21 (2). 122–130.

Schuring, Gerard K. 1985. *Die omgangs-Sotho van die swart woongebiede van Pretoria*. Johannesburg: Rand Afrikaans University dissertation.

Spitulnik, Debra. 1998. The language of the city: Town Bemba as urban hybridity. *Journal of Linguistic Anthropology* 8 (1). 30–59.

Wagner, Valencia K. 2018. *Transfer effects of Sepitori on the language performance of Setswana Home Language high school learners in Tshwane: Some case studies*. Pretoria: Tshwane University of Technology MA thesis.

Webb, Vic. 2010. The politics of standardising Bantu languages in South Africa. *Language Matters: Studies in the Languages of Africa* 41 (2). 157–174.

Ziervogel, Dirk. 1969. Die taal van Atteridgeville. In R. D. Coertze (ed.), *Atteridgeville: 'n stedelike Bantoewoonbuurt*, 429–454. Pretoria: University of Pretoria.

Alexandra Y. Aikhenvald
7 Innovation and change in a multilingual context: The Innovative Tariana language in northwest Amazonia

The world over, younger generations speak differently from older people and show deviations from the established norm. In many communities, younger peoples' ways of speaking appear to bear an indelible impact from national languages and linguas francas. Patterns of change in Innovative varieties of traditional languages spoken by people at least a generation younger than the bearers of the norm can be internally motivated. Or their origins can be traced to the increased impact of contact with linguas francas or national languages, regularizing paradigms and creating new forms and expressions. The Innovative Tariana spoken by younger generations is a case in point. Tariana is the only Arawak language spoken in the Brazilian part of the multilingual linguistic area of the Vaupés River Basin (which spans Brazil and Colombia). The language is spoken by about 100 people. The region is known for its obligatory multilingualism based on linguistic exogamy: you have to marry someone whose father speaks a different language than your father (and thus belongs to a different language group). Languages within the multilingual marriage network are Tariana (Arawak) and a number of East Tucanoan languages, including Tucano, Wanano, Piratapuya, etc. The Tariana used to be fluent in several East Tucanoan languages. Now, Tucano is gaining ground as the main language of the region (mostly thanks to the Catholic education policies); and many younger people use it on a day-to-day basis. There is a marked difference between the "Traditional Tariana" (now almost gone; documented by the author in the 1990s-early 2000s) and the "Innovative Tariana", currently spoken, which bears an increasing impact of Tucano, especially as concerns syntax and discourse patterns and also morphology. I provide a systematic investigation of the Innovative Tariana, focusing on internally motivated changes (including 'anticipatory changes') and changes due to the impact of Tucano and Portuguese, the national language. Traditional Tariana used to be a predomi-

---

Acknowledgments: I am grateful to the Brito, Muniz and Lopes families for teaching me their Tariana language. Special thanks go to Pier Marco Bertinetto, Luca Ciucci, R. M. W. Dixon, Chris Holz, Yann LeMoullec, and Nico Nassenstein for comments on this paper, and to Brigitta Flick for proofreading it.

Alexandra Y. Aikhenvald, Central Queensland University, e-mail: a.aikhenvald@cqu.edu.au

nantly oral language, with literacy developed in the early 1990s. All speakers of the Innovative Tariana are literate in the language. I also focus on newly emergent genres – including written stories, personal letters, and communication by e-mail, messenger, Facebook, and WhatsApp – and concomitant language change.

1 The Tariana language in its present setting

Worldwide, younger generations speak differently from older people and show deviations from traditions and norms. In many communities, younger people's ways of speaking appear to bear an indelible impact from majority languages. Alternatively, patterns of change in innovative varieties of traditional languages can be internally motivated. A variety spoken by younger people may display language changes which have already taken place in a more innovative related language, or languages, without the influence of language contact (see Aikhenvald 2019). The situation can be further complicated by the impact of language obsolescence. An innovative variety may become a badge of linguistic identity for the speakers, setting them apart from an older generation. In addition, innovative patterns may spread across all generations of speakers within a community, obliterating the differences between traditional and innovative varieties. Cross-linguistic studies of spontaneously emerging younger speaker varieties, and the motivations for individual changes in them, hold the clue to the ways in which languages may evolve under different circumstances, and the direction younger people's varieties may take. As modern means of communication – including internet and social media – become available to younger generations of speakers, we see the rise of new genres and new ways of saying things as part and parcel of younger speakers' speech practices (in agreement with the tendencies outlined in Yannuar et al., this volume).

Most – if not all – of these factors are at play in the development and usage of Innovative Tariana, spoken in the Vaupés area in northwest Amazonia (Brazil). In view of the scarcity of studies on the language of young people and of generational differences in Amazonia (one of the hot-spots of linguistic diversity worldwide), the special features of Innovative Tariana, their emergence, motivation and spread open an additional avenue for offering a global view and a global perspective on youth languages in their many guises. We start with a brief snapshot of the language and its speakers.

Tariana is an endangered North Arawak language spoken by about 70 people in two villages (Santa Rosa and Periquitos) in the Vaupés River basin in northwest Amazonia. The dialectal differences between the two villages are minor (comparable to those between British and American English). Tariana is a member of the linguistic area of the Vaupés River Basin. The area is known for its institutionalized multilingualism based on the principle of linguistic exogamy between speakers of Tariana (the only Arawak language) and its East Tucanoan neighbours (including Tucano (or Ye'pâ Masa), Piratapuya (or Waikhana), Wanano (or Kotiria), Desano, and Tuyuca). In agreement with the principles of the traditional language-based exogamy, one is always supposed to marry someone who belongs to a different language group and thus has a 'right' to identify with the language. Language identity and ownership are inherited from one's father. There is a traditional inhibition against mixing languages, viewed in terms of using recognizable loan forms, especially from Tucano or any other East Tucanoan language (more on this is in Aikhenvald 2010).

Intensive language contact between Tariana and East Tucanoan languages has resulted in the diffusion of numerous structural patterns. Comparison between Tariana and closely related Arawak languages of the Uapuí subgroup (especially Baniwa of Içana-Kurripako dialect continuum, Piapoco, Yucuna, and Guarequena) helps distinguish features diffused into Tariana from Tucanoan languages and those inherited from the proto-language. This paper, just like all my work on Tariana, is based on extensive fieldwork with numerous speakers (from 1991 onwards). The total corpus consists of 40 transcribed hours of audiorecordings, in addition to fieldnotes collected during participant observation. This is constantly being augmented via communication with the remaining speakers. Tariana examples are given in the practical orthography adopted in the Tariana school in the mission centre of Iauaretê, Amazonas, Brazil.

The Tariana used to be fluent in several East Tucanoan languages. Throughout the history of the Vaupés linguistic area in Brazil in the 20th century, Tucano – the majority East Tucanoan language – has spread at the cost of other indigenous languages (including Tariana). The main reason for this was the Catholic education policies in the area (for further discussion, see Aikhenvald 2010, 2015). Currently, Tucano is effectively the main indigenous language of the region, and all the extant Tariana use it on a day-to-day basis. In the 1990s and early 2000s, older and traditionally-oriented Tariana spoke Tariana with their children. Now that most elders are gone, the majority of ethnic Tariana speak Tucano at home most of the time; those who have moved to São Gabriel da Cachoeira – the capital of the Federal Territory of the Upper Rio Negro, which encompasses the Vaupés Basin – also speak regional Portuguese. The language is emblematic for people's identity – this is an important reason for its maintenance among speakers of different generations (see also Aikhenvald 2010, forthcoming).

There are notable differences between "Traditional Tariana" (now almost gone; documented by the author in the 1990s-early 2000s) and "Innovative Tariana", currently spoken by those born from 1950 onwards.[1] A comparison between Innovative and Traditional Tariana demonstrates the tendencies typical of generational differences in language evolution. Innovative Tariana bears an increasing impact of Tucano in the structure of words, clauses, and sentences, in addition to discourse devices (see Aikhenvald 2010; the analysis of a recent impact of language contact on the verb structure can be found in Aikhenvald 2016). Also, in many ways, Innovative Tariana sounds differently from the traditional language – this is our main focus here. Some of the phonetic and phonological differences can be considered internally motivated, while others can be traced to the impact of Tucano. The attitudes of the speakers towards these two types of change differ sharply. We turn to these issues in Section 2. Some innovative speakers – aware of the generational differences – make an effort to use more traditional forms, and even apply processes of hypercorrection, in an attempt to follow the ways the elders used to speak.

At present, the Tariana language is endangered. Very few children are learning the language in the domestic setting. Speakers of Innovative Tariana display many tell-tale signs of language attrition (following the trends outlined by Campbell and Muntzel 1989; see also Aikhenvald 2010: 249–259). As the number of traditional speakers goes, some features of the innovative language spread to the remaining elders: the innovative language is what they hear around them, and this affects their language habits. This phenomenon of levelling age or generation differences has been documented in other parts of the world: For instance, Dixon (2015: 327) notes the use of forms typical for innovative speakers of Dyirbal, an Australian language, by a few remaining elders.

Following Tsitsipis' (1998: 34) classification of linguistic changes, phonological changes in Innovative Tariana are on-going, or continuous. They are subject to inter-speaker variation and can be considered unstable. In contrast, completed changes do not allow any synchronic variation. A further type of change, labelled "discontinuous changes", are one-off deviations characteristic of individual speakers, and are a typical feature of obsolescent languages. A number of individual changes in Innovative Tariana can be considered discontinuous. These are the topic of Section 3.

---

[1] Tariana is currently being learnt by a limited number of children who are exposed to the innovative variety and speak it fluently.

2 Phonological features of Innovative Tariana

Phonological changes in Innovative Tariana come about as a result of language-internal processes or as a result of external influence – the impact of contact with Tucano as a major language of the area (see Gerritsen and Stein 1992). A clear case of internally motivated phonological change in Tariana involves 'anticipatory change' which 'anticipates' the changes which had already occurred in other, more innovative, languages of the family with which the innovative variety is not in contact (see other examples in Aikhenvald 2019[2]). This is the topic of Section 2.1. In 2.2, we turn to a number of phonological features of Innovative Tariana which can be accounted for by an increasing impact of Tucano. Speakers' attitudes and reactions to the two kinds of changes are contrasted in 2.3.

2.1 Internally motivated phonological changes in Innovative Tariana

A marked feature of Innovative Tariana is monophtongization of a falling diphthong *ai* > *e* and *ãi* > *ẽ* within roots – a cross-linguistically common phenomenon. Examples are in (1). If monophtongization occurs at the end of a word, the resulting vowel is lengthened to /e:/, as shown in the last two examples.

(1) | Traditional Tariana | Innovative Tariana | Translation |
|---|---|---|
| *haiku* | *heku* | 'tree, wood' |
| *maipuku* | *mepuku* | 'fish trap' |
| *kaiwači* | *kewači, kewasi* | 'sorubim catfish' |
| *mhãida* | *mhẽda* | 'prohibitive marker' |
| *mhãisiki* | *mhẽsiki* | 'hunger' |
| *hunay* | *hune* | 'manioc Solanum tuberosum Doré' |
| *hipay* | *hipe* | 'land' |

The process of monophtongization within roots in Innovative Tariana does not take place if the word contains /i/ in the syllable following the erstwhile diphthong, e.g. Traditional and Innovative Tariana *paiči* 'frog', *mhaičida* 'a ceramic stand for a cooking pot', *aini* 'mosquito'. A frequently used word *daikina* 'after-

---

[2] A further example of anticipatory change comes from Young People's Dyirbal. The masculine interrogative noun marker in absolutive form was *wuñjiñ* in all dialects of Dyirbal, but it was then reduced in northern dialects to *wuñji*. In recent times, younger speakers of the southern dialects have shortened *wuñjiñ* to *wuñji*, mirroring the change in northern dialects (Dixon 2015: 243, 328).

noon' is an exception to this: Innovative speakers variably pronounce it as [deikina], [de:kina], or [dekina]. This is an instance of a further application of the monophtongization rule.

The Traditional Tariana forms are shared with the archaic members of the Uapuí subgroup of Arawak (to which Tariana belongs), namely, the Baniwa-Kurripako dialect continuum *haiku* and Piapoco *aiku* 'tree' (Ramirez 2001, Klumpp 1995). The Innovative Tariana form is shared with Guarequena, another language from the same subgroup of Arawak, which has *héku* 'tree'. There is no evidence of any contact between Tariana and Guarequena (González-Ñánez 2005). Monophtongization of a diphthong in Innovative Tariana is 'anticipating' the change which has already occurred in its innovative relative Guarequena.

The process of monophtongization of the falling diphthong within roots in Innovative Tariana is an extension of the same process regularly applied in other contexts. Change *a-i* to *e* across affixal boundaries can be considered an instance of completed change. For instance, the Tariana underlying form *dipitana-ita* (his.name-CAUS) is always realised as *dipitaneta*, and the underlying *na-ima* (3pl-stand) is realised as *nema* 'they stand' (further examples are in Aikhenvald 2003: 48–9). Monophtongization has also taken place, as an instance of completed change, within the plural suffix of nouns: compare Tariana *-ne* with Baniwa-Kurripako *-nai* and Piapoko *-nái* (González-Ñáñez 1997: 67; Aikhenvald 1999: 84). The process of monophtongization across affixal boundaries in Tariana appears to be relatively recent. Evidence for this comes from a Tariana shamanic chant recorded in the 1950s, in which the form *wa-pa-ita* (1pl-rot/die-CAUS) 'we make rot' has an alternative form *wapeta*. Language-conscious purists — all of them innovative speakers themselves — diphtongize the vowel *e* to *ai* in root internal position as a matter of hypercorrection, in their attempt to sound like their elders (see §3).

Simplification of the rising diphthong *wa > a* in an unstressed position is another feature of Innovative Tariana. Some examples are in (2).

(2) | Traditional Tariana | Innovative Tariana | Translation |
|---|---|---|
| -keñwa | -keña | 'begin' |
| yakolekwa | yakoleka | 'door (entrance)' |

This process did not take place in more archaic languages, e.g. Baniwa-Kurripako *-kéñoa* (Ramirez 2001: 172) and Karo variety of Kurripako *-keñua-* (Bezerra 2012) 'begin'. It has occurred in the more innovative Yucuna *keño-* 'begin' (Schauer et al. 2005: 87). This allows us to interpret the process in Innovative Tariana as an instance of anticipatory change.

The process of word-final vowel assimilation (or vowel harmony) within enclitics is a further characteristic of Innovative Tariana. Speakers assimilate the penultimate vowel within enclitics – which are stressed on the last syllable – to the one in the stressed syllable. Then, the Traditional Tariana =*nakú* 'topical non-subject' is pronounced as =*nukú*, and =*nuká* 'present visual evidential' as =*naká*.

The late Ismael and a few other innovative speakers extend the vowel assimilation to the negative suffix, both word-finally and before a clitic. The forms from a story by Ismael – with innovative forms – are shown in (3a) and (4a). In a comment on the story, his father, the late Cândido, a speaker of Traditional Tariana, repeated the form cited in (3a) as its more archaic version, (3b). The archaic form in (4b) was produced by Cândido on a different occasion (as a reply to a question).

(3a) ne=nuku   nhesiri-kede   *Innovative Tariana*

(3b) ne=naku   nhesiri-kade   *Traditional Tariana*
      then=TOP.NONSUBJ like-NEG
      'Then (he) didnt't like (it)'

(4a) ma-ni-kede=naka   *Innovative Tariana*

(4b) ma-ni-kade=nuka   *Traditional Tariana*
      NEG-do-NEG=PRES.VIS
      '(I) don't do (anything)'

The case form =*naku* in Traditional Tariana is cognate to Baniwa of Içana -*naku* 'locative (on the surface)' (see further discussion in Aikhenvald 2010: 308). The present visual form goes back to the grammaticalized verbal form *nu-ka* (1sg-see) 'I see'. Vowel assimilation within enclitics has no parallels in related languages. This process in Innovative Tariana can be considered an independent innovation.

2.2 Contact-induced phonological changes in Innovative Tariana

Phonological changes in Innovative Tariana under the influence of Tucano are either on-going (if used by several people), or discontinuous (if specific to individual speakers). A recurrent type of on-going change involves gradual neutralization and loss of phonological distinctions absent from Tucano (see also Aikhenvald 2010: 39–51).

Similar to other related Arawak languages, Traditional Tariana has two sibilants: an alveo-palatal voiceless fricative /s/ and a lamino-palatal voiceless affricate /tʃ/ (č in the practical orthography). Tucano has just one alveolar fricative s. All innovative speakers of Tariana display a strong tendency to neutralize the distinction between the two sibilants s and č, especially in front of a high vowel, and for them the two sibilants appear to be allophones in free variation. This variation appears in the form *kewasi, kewači* 'sorubim catfish' in (1).

Traditional Tariana (just like the closely related Baniwa of Içana-Kurripako) has a set of aspirated stops, nasals, and the bilabial glide [wʰ]. These are absent from Tucano. As a consequence, speakers of Innovative Tariana display free variation between aspirated and non-aspirated consonants. For instance, *di-nu-mha* (3sg-come-PRES.NONVIS) 'he comes (unseen)' is often pronounced as [di-nu-ma], and *Kumatharo* 'personal name' as [Kumataro]. The loss of aspiration among innovative speakers results in the creation of homonyms: the phonetic form [-ma] now covers the marker of excessive action *-ma* and the erstwhile *-mha* 'present nonvisual'. Alternatively, a new pattern of polysemy can arise. The phonetic form [-ne] covers the instrumental case marker *-ne* and the erstwhile *-nhe* 'focussed subject'. The form *ãdaru-ne* (parrot-INST/FOC.SUBJ), in Innovative Tariana, can mean either 'with the parrot' (Traditional Tariana *ãdaru-ne*) or 'the parrot (not anyone else) (did something)' (Traditional Tariana *ãdaru-nhe*). The two meanings are easily distinguishable by context. At least for some speakers, the merger of the two nasals results in a new pattern of polysemy.

On one occasion, Jovino, an innovative speaker, told a story about a parrot, using the Innovative form for the focused subject, *ãdaru-ne*, in (5).

(5) ãdaru-ne   di-a=pidana   *Innovative Tariana*
    parrot-FOC.SUBJ 3sgnf-say=REM.P.REP
    'The parrot (not anyone else) spoke'

He then translated the sentence into Portuguese as *ele falou, com papagaio*', literally, 'he spoke, with parrot'. The translation reflects the fact that, for Jovino, the form *-ne* could refer to the instrumental case as well as the focused subject (a cross-linguistically common polysemy). A traditional speaker used *ãdaru-nhe* in a story similar to that in (5).

Speakers of Innovative Tariana vary as to the degree of their loss of aspirated nasals. The late Ismael (1950–2008) carefully maintained aspirated nasals – as seen in (3a) – in contrast to his younger brother, Jovino (born 1963).

Speakers of Innovative Tariana display Tucano-like patterns of allophonic variation. The alternation between the voiceless apico-dental stop [d] and the flap [ɾ] in intervocalic position is a case in point. In Tucano, an intervocalic *d* regularly surfaces as a rhotic flap after a front vowel (Ramirez 1997: 31). A similar phenomenon occurs in Innovative Tariana, especially in rapid speech; for instance, the negation *-kaɖe, -ɖe* is pronounced as *-kaɾe*, or *-ɾe, kiɖa* 'ready, finished' as *kiɾa*, and *-piɖana* 'remote past reported evidential' as *-piɾana*. Some innovative speakers occasionally pronounce *ɾ* as *ɖ* between two high front vowels in Portuguese personal names, e.g. the Portuguese name *Emílio* is pronounced as [Emiɾio] or as [Emiɖio]. The process appears to be expanding. In the 1990s-early 2000, Emílio pronounced his own name as [Emiɖio] only occasionally. Ten years on, this became his main pronunciation, illustrating the spread of the Tucano-induced allophonic process.

Palatalization of the glide *y* in word-initial and root-initial position is another case in point. In Tucano, ^{d}*y* is a regular variant of *y* word-initially, before high and central vowels (West and Welch 1967: 15–16). Speakers of Innovative Tariana tend to pronounce [y] as [^{d}y] or [ʤ] in the same position, e.g., Traditional Tariana *yeka*, Innovative Tariana ^{d}*yeka, ʤeka* 'sap', Traditional Tariana *di-yena*, Innovative Tariana *di-^{d}yena, di-ʤena* 'he exceeds'.

2.3 Phonological awareness and attitudes to changes

Similar to many peoples the world over, the Tariana – and other members of the Vaupés River Basin linguistic area – are aware of the ways their language is spoken, often judging other's speech as "good" or "bad", or "correct" or "incorrect" (see the discussion and references in Aikhenvald 2010: 214–221). The ways in which the Tariana formulate and rationalize their intuitions concerning 'correct' language relate to language structure, language attitudes, and relationships of authority (along the lines of Silverstein 1981). Language awareness among the Tariana speakers relates to most parts of the language. Most speakers display a high degree of lexical awareness – following the cultural inhibition against recognizable loan forms, especially those from Tucano (cf. Aikhenvald 2015: 82–83). Those who are seen as 'mixing languages' are referred to, behind their backs, as *mẽdite* 'useless'.

A further mechanism through which Tariana speakers identify potential tokens of language mixing and evaluate the language is phonological awareness (as defined in Aikhenvald 2010: 215). A form which sounds Tucano-like tends to be branded as 'foreign'. The principle of phonological awareness underlies the differences in attitudes to those features of Innovative Tariana which are due to language-internal changes and those which can be traced to the recent impact of Tucano. Contact-induced phonological changes are recognised as tokens of 'incorrect' language by the extant speakers of Traditional Tariana and by the younger purists. This is what sets them apart from internally motivated changes.

Innovative forms discussed in Section 2.1 are accepted as "correct" variants (Tariana *páwali*) by speakers of all generations. Both appear in the pedagogical materials and in the dictionary thoroughly checked by speakers of Traditional and of Innovative Tariana.

The attitude towards innovative forms which bear phonetic and phonological impact from Tucano (see Section 2.2) is different. Those who display an alternation between *s* and *č* are corrected (that is, a traditional speaker would repeat back the form they consider correct). The loss of aspiration in nasals and the bilabial glide is openly criticized as 'mixing with Tucano' (*na-ñamura na-sape-nipe* 3pl-mix 3pl-speak-NOM), and so are the alternation between the stop *d* and the flap *ɾ* and palatalization of the glide *y*.

We can recall from (3a) and (4a) that some innovative speakers apply vowel assimilation to the negative suffix -*kade,* pronouncing it as -*kede*. This was not considered incorrect by traditional speakers. However, an innovative speaker who started pronouncing [kede] as [kere] (applying a Tucano-sounding phonological process) was pointed out to me as someone who 'mixes his language up with Tucano'.

Contact-induced phonological phenomena in Innovative Tariana – perceived as tokens of foreign influence – can be considered "anti-emblematic". This attitude does not apply to the completed contact-induced phonological changes in Tariana, which are now part of the repertoire of all generations of speakers (such as the central vowel *o*, as shown in Aikhenvald 2010: 42–43).

3 Hypercorrection, individual variation, and the spread of Innovative Tariana

A further facet of language attitudes among the Tariana is special respect for "the ways our grandfathers, or ancestors, spoke": the forms attributed to the older generation are considered well and truly "good language". This was described as "generational awareness" in Aikhenvald (2010: 217–220). Puristically inclined speakers of Innovative Tariana make an effort to use Traditional Tariana forms – including those listed in (1) and (2) – especially so in carefully prepared narratives rather than in casual conversations.

An attempt to sound "traditional" results in the emergence of hypercorrect forms containing spurious diphtongization of *e* into *ai*. The late Graciliano and Ismael pronounced the word *pe(:)the* 'manioc bread' as [paithe] (some younger speakers continue to do so). The latter form was never used by traditional speakers. Cognates in related languages and in other dialects of Tariana show that the original form was *pe:rithe with a variant *pe:the rather than *paithe: compare Baniwa of Içana and Kurripako péethe, Karutana and Katapolitani Baniwa pērite (Koch-Grünberg 1911: 206), and Kumandene Tariana perithe.

A further process at work is the spread of Innovative Tariana forms to the elderly and erstwhile traditional speakers – a "linguistic contagion" of sorts. In the late 1990s-early 2000s, such contagion was characteristic of those elders, for whom Tucano was the main language of communication within their families. The late Américo Brito (ca. 1915–2004), then the oldest and the most knowledgeable speaker of Tariana, used to display Tucano-induced phonetic features, such as variation between [d] and [ɾ] between two high vowels and occasional palatalization of the initial glide. He also used to occasionally code-switch with Tucano (provoking negative reactions behind his back; see Aikhenvald 2010: 47; 193–195). Now that only three speakers of the traditional language are still alive, Traditional and Innovative varieties are in the process of being merged. The remaining elders – exposed to Tucano in their homes – have only innovative speakers with whom they can speak Tariana. In casual and unplanned discourse, they employ Innovative speech forms (cited in ex. (1), (2), and (3)). The Traditional forms tend to be maintained in narratives and discussions dealing with traditional practices. For instance, in his narratives dealing with the origins of Tariana and with traditional practices, Leo, a knowledgeable elder, consistently used the Traditional topical non-subject marker =naku (164 occurrences in ca. 4000 words). In a casual tale about Fish-people and a man rejected by women – a recurrent story told by the Tariana of all ages – the number of occurrences of =naku and its innovative variant =nuku were roughly equal (51 of =naku and 49 of =nuku in a 3000 word-long story).

Innovative Tariana speakers, most of whom use mostly Tucano in their day-to-day life, display numerous individual innovations – similar to what Tsitsipis (1998) described as one-off discontinuous changes, typical of obsolescent languages falling into disuse. The process of changing -wa to -a (illustrated in (2)) does not usually apply to the vowel sequence u-a; so, the inherently negative verb kurípua 'there is absolutely nothing' is never pronounced as *kurípa. In the 1990s-early 2000s, one innovative speaker, Jovino, pronounced this word as [kurúpua], over-applying the process of vowel assimilation (illustrated in (3)). Ten years on, he started pronouncing the same word as [kurupá], with simplification of the vowel sequence, in addition to stress shift.

Individual one-off changes go beyond phonological changes. An illustrative example comes from Jovino's reanalysis of the postposition dalipa 'at, near to'. In Traditional Tariana, the personal prefix on a postposition is replaced by the placeholder indefinite i- when the postposition is used with a noun. The Traditional pattern is shown in (6a–6b).

(6a) di-dalipa   *Traditional and Innovative Tariana*
      3sgnf-near
      'near him'

(6b) e:ni   i-dalipa   *Traditional Tariana*
      chief INDEF-near
      'near the chief'

Innovative speakers no longer use the indefinite prefix *i-* (as this feature is absent from Tucano). Instead, they employ the personal prefix on the postposition, as shown in (6c), or omit the prefix altogether, as in (6d).

(6c) e:ni   di-dalipa   *Innovative Tariana*
      chief 3sgnf-near
      'near the chief'

(6d) e:ni   dalipa   *Innovative Tariana*
      chief near
      'near the chief'

Jovino goes a different way: the form *dalipa* is reanalyzed as *d-alipa* (3sgnf-near), and a new nonce form *alipa* is created, as in (6e).

(6e) e:ni   alipa   *JvB's Innovative Tariana*
      chief near
      'near the chief'

This personal innovation is not considered wrong by other speakers, as it is not an instance of "mixing" with Tucano. (Further individual phenomena in morphology, syntax, and also discourse of Innovative Tariana speakers were addressed in Aikhenvald 2010).

A high degree of personally-patterned variation among the Tariana is one of the consequences of language obsolescence. Similarly to the situation among the last speakers of Gaelic (Dorian 2010: 298), variability among the Tariana does not mark group membership, nor does it have a social boundary-marking function. The high degree of individual variation among the Innovative Tariana offers a challenge to a radical position whereby individual grammatical and phonological patterns are excluded from consideration in linguistic analysis. In Johnstone's (2000: 411) words, synchronically, speakers "have different grammars". We now turn to the creativity of innovative speakers in the ways the language is applied to the new contexts.

4 New phenomena in new contexts

The world over, younger generations have access to technological advances – internet, social media, radio, television, and mobile phones. Innovative speakers of Tariana exposed to the new means adapt their language use to the new information sources. Evidentials reflect how one knows things. Their use correlates with different kinds of access to information. In the early 1990s, a phone was a rarity. Since information acquired via a phone conversation was heard, speakers used to relate it using the nonvisual evidential. Currently, those who do not have continuous access to a mobile phone still use the nonvisual evidential. Those who use a mobile phone on a day-to-day basis treat phone interactions on par with face-to-face chats and use the visual form.

Short-wave radio has been the main means of communication with remote villages (including some of the Tariana villages), and partly remains so. Information obtained via the radio is treated as "nonvisual". Innovative Tariana speakers who live in the mission centre Iauaretê and in the regional centre – the town of São Gabriel da Cachoeira – have access to Brazilian TV and watch it a lot. The information received is recounted as "seen", with the visual evidential. More and more Tariana – especially those who live in the mission and the regional centre – have Internet and use Facebook messenger, "chat" and WhatsApp. The visual evidential is the normal choice.

Traditional Tariana used to employ chains of clauses, reflecting sequences of subevents in all genres. A new speech style appears to be developing for communication via messenger, social media and WhatsApp. Sentences are short and consist of sequences of individual declarative sentences interspersed with commands. An example of a recent post by Rafael illustrates this. (The post has been recast in practical orthography).

(7) Mača=naka   Sacha   nu-pheru-pasi   *Innovative Tariana on*
    good=PRES.VIS Sasha   1sg-older.sister-AUG *messenger*
    numa   iñe   iha   pi-panoa   ma:či
    1sg+wish,look.for devil   faeces   2sg-send   bad
    nu-rena=ka=mha
    1sg-feel=DECL=PRES.NONVIS
    'It is good, Sasha my big older sister, I want money (lit. devil's faeces), send, I am in a bad way.'

The author uses the innovative form of the present visual evidential =*naka* (see Section 2.1 and (4a)). He also uses the new formation *iñe iha* (devil excrement) 'money' recently devised by innovative speakers (Rafael being one of the authors). Rafael explained to me that this was based on Tucano, wãtĩ ɨ 'tá (evil spirit excrement). The message consists of three simple clauses, with no clause chaining markers. In the 1990s, similar requests either spoken or sent in letters by traditional speakers contained at least one dependent clause, as shown in (8).

(8) mači nu-rena-whyume   *Traditional Tariana*
  bad 1sg-feel-DEP
  yarumakasi-tupe nu-na pi-panoa
  clothing-DIM   1sg-OBJ 2sg-send
  'As I am in a bad way, send me a few clothes.'

Employing short independent sentences in lieu of clause chaining is a feature of written stories in Innovative Tariana (collected over the years during pedagogical workshops). The ways in which newly emergent genres are going to further develop – and how viable they will be – are difficult to predict, in view of the impending language obsolescence.

5 Innovation and change in Innovative Tariana: What can we conclude?

Innovative Tariana – spoken by younger generations – differs from the Traditional language in numerous ways, including its phonology – the focus of this contribution. The Innovative language displays several internally-motivated changes. Some of these can be considered 'anticipatory', as they replicate those changes that have already occurred in related languages. Contact-induced changes in Innovative Tariana are due to the increasing influence of Tucano, nowadays the major language of the area. Traditional Tariana bears the impact of numerous East-Tucanoan languages (as shown in Aikhenvald 2010, 2015, and references there). In contrast, contact-induced changes in the Innovative language are limited to those from Tucano.

  Patterns of linguistic awareness of the speakers distinguish two types of change. Contact-induced developments are condemned as token of language-mixing with Tucano. Internally-motivated changes are treated as accepted ways of speaking. They are the ones that play a role in the processes of hypercorrection applied by some Innovative purists. The processes of linguistic contagion within the community result in a rapid spread of Innovative Tariana at the expense of the Traditional language. A further feature of the current state of the art is a high degree of individual variation between speakers, exacerbated by the limited use of the language and the impending language obsolescence of Tariana.

The advent of modernity brings in new genres and new ways of saying things. As a consequence, markers of information source are applied to e-mail, internet, social media and WhatsApp. All of these are treated as face-to-face communication, resulting in the expansion of the visual evidential. The language used in social media involves short sentences rather than clause chains – creating a new genre, different from oral narratives and conversations. We hypothesize that these new ways of speaking carry the seeds of language change – the direction the language is likely to take.

List of abbreviations

1	first person
2	second person
3	third person
AUG	augmentative
CAUS	causative
DECL	declarative
DEP	dependent clause marker
DIM	diminutive
FOC.SUBJ	focused subject
INDEF	indefinite person prefix
INST	instrument
NEG	negation
NOM	nominalization
OBJ	object marker
PL	plural
PRES.NONVIS	present nonvisual
PRES.VIS	present visual
REM.P.REP	remote past reported
sg	singular
sgnf	singular nonfeminine
TOP.NONSUBJ	topical nonsubject

References

Aikhenvald, Alexandra Y. 1999. The Arawak language family. In R. M. W. Dixon and Alexandra Y. Aikhenvald (eds.), *The Amazonian languages*, 65–105. Cambridge: Cambridge University Press.

Aikhenvald, Alexandra Y. 2003. *A grammar of Tariana, from northwest Amazonia*. Cambridge: Cambridge University Press.

Aikhenvald, Alexandra Y. 2010. *Language contact in Amazonia*. Oxford: Oxford University Press.

Aikhenvald, Alexandra Y. 2014. Language contact, and language blend: Kumandene Tariana of northwest Amazonia. *International Journal of American Linguistics* 80. 323–370.
Aikhenvald, Alexandra Y. 2015. *The languages of the Amazon*. Oxford: Oxford University Press.
Aikhenvald, Alexandra Y. 2016. Language contact and word structure: A case study from northwest Amazonia. In Berez-Kroeker, Andrea L., Diane M. Hintz and Carmen Jany (eds.), *Language contact and change in the Americas. Studies in honor of Marianne Mithun*, 297–313. Amsterdam: John Benjamins.
Aikhenvald, Alexandra Y. 2019. The legacy of youth: the seeds of change and the diversity of voices in Papua New Guinea. A plenary address. *Proceedings of LSPNG Conference (Language and Linguistics in Melanesia)*, Port Moresby, September 2019.
Aikhenvald, Alexandra Y. forthcoming. The Amazon basin: Linguistic areas and language contact. In Salikoko S. Mufwene and Anna María Escobar (eds.), *The Cambridge handbook of language contact*. Cambridge: Cambridge University Press.
Bezerra, Zenilson A. 2012. *Dicionário Kuripako/Português*. Mimeographed. Missão Novas Tribos do Brasil.
Campbell, Lyle and Martha C. Muntzel. 1989. The structural consequences of language death. In Nancy Dorian (ed.), *Investigating obsolescence. Studies in language contraction and death*, 181–196. Cambridge: Cambridge University Press.
Dixon, R. M. W. 2015. *Edible gender, mother-in-law style, & other grammatical wonders. Studies in Dyirbal, Yidiñ, & Warrgamay*. Oxford: Oxford University Press.
Dorian, Nancy C. 2010. *Investigating variation. The effects of social organization and social setting*. New York: Oxford University Press.
Gerritsen, Marinel and Dieter Stein. 1992. Introduction: On "internal" and "external" in syntactic change. In Marinel Gerritsen and Dieter Stein (ed.), *Internal and external factors in syntactic change*, 11–15. Berlin: De Gruyter Mouton.
González-Ñánez, Omar. 1997. *Gramática de la lengua Warekena*. Caracas: Universidad Central de Venezuela dissertation.
González-Ñánez, Omar. 2005. *Los Warekena, indígenas Arawakos del Guainía-Río Negro: mitología y vida cotidiana*. Centro de Investigaciones Etnológicas, Universidad de los Andes.
Johnstone, Barbara. 2000. The individual voice in language. *Annual Review of Anthropology* 29. 405–424.
Klumpp, Deloris. 1995. *Vocabulario Piapoco-Español*. Santafé de Bogotá: Asociación Instituto Lingüístico de Verano.
Koch-Grünberg, Theodor. 1911. Aruak-Sprachen Nordwestbrasiliens und der angrenzenden Gebiete. *Mitteilungen der Anthropologischen Gesellschaft* 41. 203–282.
Ramirez, Henri. 1997. *A fala Tukano dos Yepâ-masa. Tomo I. Gramática*. Manaus: Inspetoria Salesiana Missionária da Amazônia CEDEM.
Ramirez, Henri. 2001. *Dicionário Baniwa-Português*. Manaus: Universidade do Amazonas.
Schauer, Stanley, Junia Schauer, Eladio Yucuna and Walter Yucuna. 2005. *Meke kemakánaka puráka'aloji. Wapura'akó chu, eyá karíwana chú. Diccionario bilingüe Yukuna-Español, Español-Yukuna*. Bogotá: Editorial Fundación para el Desarrollo de los Pueblos Marginados.
Silverstein, Michael. 1981. *The limits of awareness*. Working Papers in Sociolinguistics 84. Austin: Southwest Educational Development Laboratory.
Tsitsipis, Lukas D. 1998. *A linguistic anthropology of praxis and language shift. Arvanítika (Albanian) and Greek in Contact*. Oxford: Clarendon Press.
West, Birdie and Betty Welch. 1967. Phonemic system of Tucano. *Phonemic Systems of Colombian Languages*, 11–24. Oklahoma: SIL, University of Oklahoma.

Part II: **Specific purposes**

Young speakers creatively "do things with words" (Austin 1962) and employ youth language in very specific settings that are commonplaces of group activities, communities of practice and identity formation. Youth around the globe play with language in ways that often display emergent resistance identities (in Castells' sense), enhance the development of subcultures with their own signs and styles, and may eventually lead to the creation of antilanguages (in Halliday's sense). While these are commonly known and cited contexts of emergence of young people's language practices, the purposes for which they are used are more diverse and prone to global influences and local (re)definitions of youth culture and language. In a recent book chapter, Mitchell and Neba (2019) label the ways of speaking associated with specific groups and motivated by ideologies of differentiation and identity-formation as "special-purpose registers", which may include avoidance languages, linguistic *rites de passage*, jargons of specific professional groups – and also youth languages. In a similar turn, Hurst-Harosh (forthcoming 2022) categorizes youth's ways of speaking as "registers" which are "restricted to particular domains, contexts and speakers" and she refers to Jaworski and Coupland (2009) who relate the term to the communicative purpose that the linguistic practice serves. When the public image and social types associated with specific registers become more prominent and, as a process of higher-order indexicality (in Silverstein's sense), attract other youth to emulate their peers, "enregisterment" occurs. The purposes of youth adopting enregistered styles are often based on associations of linguistic fashion and novelty, triggered by a fashionable reputation as well as by charismatic leaders of these groups.

Young speakers, as illustrated in the various chapters in this section, display diverse motivations, and their language practices may simultaneously serve divergent purposes related to their identities. Some purposes are more playful and include joking, mockery and crossing, while others are more serious and may include exclusionary styles, ostracisms and mimicry. Most are group-oriented, but some intend to promote individual actors within a group and invert hierarchies and regulations of social structure. All these purposes that trigger young speakers' linguistic creativity, their play with forms, sounds and structures (see the preceding section), have in common that they include processes of creative semiosis, involving (re)defined signs and meaning making processes that contribute to the emergence of new 'styles'.

Young Congolese and South African speakers employ different patterns of conversational joking in order to change the pragmatic context of their interaction and reminisce, strengthen their interpersonal bonds and enhance group identity (Hurst-Harosh and Nassenstein). Ugandan youth use linguistic manipulations as decolonial critique; their special purpose is the usage of deviant lexemes and the modification of songs and prayers (in sports groups) to initiate decolonial thinking (Hollington and Akena). Young Nigerian speakers have creatively coined new expressions within the lexical field of tobacco consumption, transforming a liminal and often stigmatized practice verbally into trendy practice (Mensah). Youth in New Ireland, Papua New Guinea, employ ludlings and complex syllable play in order to achieve concealment – and to have fun (Holz). Similarly, Spanish-speaking youth from Spain, Argentina and Chile employ rude vocatives as transgressive in-group practice, strengthening in-group solidarity and community cohesion by transgressing verbal norms, thus excluding the "societal excluders" who favor more conventional speech styles (Stenström).

References

Austin, John L. 1962. *How to do things with words*. Cambridge, MA: Harvard University Press.
Castells, Manuel. 1997. *The information age. Economy, society and culture. Vol. 2: The power of identity*. Oxford: Blackwell.
Halliday, Michael. 1976. Anti-languages. *American Anthropologist* 78 (3). 570–584.
Hurst-Harosh, Ellen. forthcoming 2022. Youth language and registers. In Lutz Marten, Nancy C. Kula, Jochen Zeller and Ellen Hurst-Harosh (eds.), *The Oxford guide to the Bantu languages*. Oxford: Oxford University Press.
Jaworski, Adam and Nicholas Coupland. 2009. *The new sociolinguistics reader, 2nd edition*. London: Red Globe Press.
Mitchell, Alice and Ayu'nwi Neba. 2019. Special-purpose registers of language in Africa. In H. Ekkehard Wolff (ed.), *The Cambridge handbook of African linguistics*, 513–534. Cambridge: Cambridge University Press.
Silverstein, Michael. 2003. Indexical order and the dialectics of sociolinguistic life. *Language & Communication* 23. 193–229.

Ellen Hurst-Harosh and Nico Nassenstein

8 On conversational humour in South African and Congolese youth's interactions: A pragmatic approach to youth language

Youth languages have been treated as a mostly sociolinguistic phenomenon, while the present chapter turns the focus to pragmatic approaches. The pragmatics of humour often circle around the three theoretical concepts "incongruity", "superiority" (grounded in sociological theory), and "relief" (according to psychoanalytical theory) (Dynel 2013b: vii) with an emphasis on the incongruity approach. Besides the study of jokes, humour has increasingly been investigated in its manifold conversational contexts, or as part of language in interaction across different discourse domains – however, mostly without taking young speakers' language practices into account. This chapter analyses humour in interaction in African youth languages by specifically looking at conversational storytelling in South Africa (focusing on Tsotsitaal/isiTsotsi speakers), and by looking at humorous anecdotes as practice of joint reminiscing in DR Congo (by speakers of Lingala ya Bayankee/ Yanké). The suggested "pragmatic turn" in the study of African youth languages is based on the analysis of structural aspects of conversational humour, its stylisation and transgressive function. The chapter offers an outlook onto the study of humour as a new and relevant field of study not only for African youth's performances and interactions but also as a promising component in more global approaches.

1 Introduction to (youth) language and humour

Research on humour in language[1] has yielded a vast number of relevant publications over the past two decades, with different foci and manifold theoretical research questions. However, the attempt to define the actual nature of humour

---

[1] We are considerably grateful to all research assistants and interlocutors who assisted during fieldwork in DR Congo and South Africa. The anonymous reviewers are warmly thanked for their ideas and support.

Ellen Hurst-Harosh, University of Cape Town, e-mail: ellen.hurst@uct.ac.za
Nico Nassenstein, Johannes Gutenberg-Universität Mainz, e-mail: nassenstein@uni-mainz.de

often fails: In an early framework, Attardo (1994: 4) summarises humour as a phenomenon "to be an all-encompassing category, covering any event or object that elicits laughter, amuses, or is felt to be funny". This summary provides no suggestion of logical subdivisions but encompasses humour variously as a literary phenomenon (including parody, irony, satire, farce – or appearing as a "genre" of joke, humorous anecdote, tale etc.), as psychological phenomenon (differentiated as being either scatological, aggressive, sexual etc.), or as serving either incongruity or incongruity plus resolution. At times, the field of humour is pictured as an open "semantic field" encompassing the four directions "wit", "humour", "fun" and "ridicule" (see ibid.: 4–7). This already shows the inherent complexity of this hard-to-define concept and field of study due to the fact that every community defines what they perceive as funny, hilarious or comic. The difficulty of competing disciplines contributing to the study of humour, such as philosophy, literature, sociology, psychology and linguistics, make the object of study even fuzzier.[2]

More recent studies have continued these early efforts to elaborate on the theoretical foundations of humour (Dynel 2013a), or have focused on the pragmatics of humour across different discourse domains (Dynel 2011), on the psychology of humour (Martin 2007), or mediatised humour (Chovanec and Ermida 2012) and humour in narratives (Ermida 2008), among numerous other directions. Other approaches include the analysis of humour in conversations, a direction recurrent in studies that focus on humour in everyday narratives such as Norrick (2003, 2009), Dynel (2009) and Norrick and Chiaro (2009). The humorous exchanges that are subject to our analysis follow the same incentive, because "an interactional theory of humor must go beyond a purely pragmatic description of jokes and joking" and "any complete theory of humor must include its exploitation in and effects on interaction" (Norrick 2009: 261). Norrick analyses humour against a background of everyday language use, and understands especially conversational joking as a bonding strategy, which with some adaptations is also postulated by Boxer and Cortés-Conde (1997) with focus on in-group teasing. Bonding as intended output of conversational humour is also part of the analyses in Section 3 below.[3] Rather than humour employed in stand-up comedy programmes and

---

[2] In another early study, Attardo and Raskin (1991) work out a general theory of humour that is perceived as essentialist, as "identification of those features that make a situation, a text, or an object funny" (Attardo 1994: 9–10), and ground their analysis on six knowledge resources. This essentialisation of humour is not further discussed in this concise, analysis-based and mostly ethnography-oriented chapter.

[3] There are also studies on language and humour with a very different focus, and specifically dealing with various forms of 'laughter': "improper laughter" as found in Goldstein (2013),

theatre (staged, directed), films and cartoons (starred, rehearsed) or as in public jokes (working toward a punchline, with clear speaker-hearer roles), humour in youth's interaction deals with "incongruity" in (mostly) spontaneous storytelling and anecdotes. Incongruity is based on "a mismatch/contrast between two meanings" from a linguistic perspective or as "deviation from a cognitive model of reference" from a more psychology-oriented view (Dynel 2013b: vii) and will be further applied to contexts in which verbal humour[4] is used by African youth.

2 Pragmatics and youth language as a methodological turn

While African youth language practices have been approached from various angles and research perspectives, focusing on either language variation, manipulative speech and linguistic change, identity constructions and communities of practice, mediatisation and semiotics, pragmatic perspectives have often been left out, and questions about "language in use" mostly been left unanswered. This does not come as a surprise as a few major topics have been very prominent in youth language research, yet they have only been investigated in their social/sociological dimension: "Identity" has often been over-emphasised and under-theorised in African youth language research, with language use often attributed broadly to "identity performance" or to essentialised social categories at the cost of systematic analyses of actual conversational and interactional behaviours. Indexicality, metaphor analysis and style have been usefully applied in some recent research on African youth practices (Nassenstein and Hollington

---

Norrick and Chiaro (2009), Billig (2005), Rowe (1995), "ludicrous laughter" as dealt with by Barasch (1985), or "bitter laughter", as studied by Storch and Nassenstein (2020: 16). These will not be included in the present overview of bonding strategies through conversational humour by African youths. Also, a much more general distinction has to be made which clarifies the scope of the present chapter: while youth language practices (or what non-speakers categorize as youth language) are often dealt with in metahumorous formats, i.e. comedy and sitcoms, performed jokes and parodies, these are in most cases not authentically represented by communities of practice that *use* youth language but by those who perform and consume youth language, often individuals who are otherwise part of the mainstream society (i.e. professional comedians, musicians, actors etc.).

4 While verbal humour and non-verbal humour are oftentimes treated as different phenomena (Dynel 2013b), the analysis of the two African case studies mostly centres around verbal humour, while acknowledging that style and multimodal language use of youths also includes non-verbal and non-linguistic features.

2016, Hurst-Harosh 2020, Mesthrie, Hurst-Harosh and Brookes forthcoming), but this work has, in some ways, fallen short of detailed interactional stylistics such as studies undertaken elsewhere by *inter alia* Eckert (1989, 2000), Bucholtz (2011) and Rampton (1995, 2006). These interactional perspectives (as shown by Eckert and others), alongside conversation analytical approaches, could yield new and important insights into African youth language practices.

Apart from conversation, interaction and indexicality, more pragmatically-oriented studies necessarily will equally have to look at ambiguity (Hurst-Harosh 2020), more profoundly into humour, (im)politeness and taboo speech, irony and sarcasm, swearing and cursing (see among others Stenström 2020), speech act theory, and the pragmatics of digital communication.

Why turn to pragmatic perspectives now (an endeavour already rudimentarily suggested by Hollington and Nassenstein 2015: 348–349)? We believe this kind of work will add to a growing body of literature looking at youth and their role in patterns of speech action, bringing along studies focusing on "implied and inferred meanings, and communicative principles that connect meanings with actual contexts" (Bublitz and Hübler 2007: 5–6). It will enable deeper understanding of the actual *context* of language practices of youth taking place in African languages. Conversely, it will also add depth to pragmatics approaches themselves, to weigh their usefulness and theoretical framing in the often richly multilingual contexts of Africa. Can the pragmatics approaches used elsewhere such as in the USA, benefit from refinement and/or expansion when considering different contexts, languages and interactional dynamics?

Methodologically speaking, a 'pragmatic turn' also means turning away from angles that approach youth language as deviant speech, and view it rather as young people's everyday practice in its conversational context: especially critical youth language studies (Hollington, Nassenstein and Storch 2018) have argued that youth language is often exoticised, commodified, selectively stimulated and reappropriated. A focus on "everyday language" recorded by speakers themselves, is preferred over staged recordings – also as a turn toward a conceptualisation of youth language as a "decolonial option" (Hurst-Harosh 2019). The analysis of everyday language and common contexts of interactions, as done in conversation analysis or interactional sociolinguistics, requires a shift of paradigm, and a methodological focus on the context of speech (acts). Naturalistic and authentic[5] data such as those being dealt with in Hurst-Harosh and Mensah (forthcoming) is critical to this project, and is reflected in the data in Section 3 below.

---

5 Both natural/istic and authentic are complex and contestable terms, and are discussed in full in Hurst-Harosh and Mensah (forthcoming).

The two discussed case studies in this chapter intend to show how incongruity is treated and processed by young African speakers, a concept not new to humour studies and already used by Plato and Aristotle (Attardo 1994). Incongruity is often defined as either divergence from expectations, breaking the perception of a (harmonic) whole, as consequence of a visual stimulus based on specific laws of visual arrangement, as play with (visual) ambiguities, or as discrepancy between speaker's and addressee's cognitive expectations – just to partially break down a few definitions recurrent in the literature (for a more fine-grained analysis see Canestrari and Bianchi 2013: 4–6). The latter also differentiate between "global contrariety", "additive contrariety" and "intermediate contrariety" in the field of incongruity (ibid.: 7–8). In addition, the two case studies assess the relationship of humorous speech and social cohesion and community-building (3.1; including "basic" conversation analysis), showing how performed humour in interaction is a bonding strategy in a community of practice in South Africa. Moreover, the second case study asks for the role of shared anecdotes, the structure of anecdotes and their linking, and also for the role of taboo topics in processes of social bonding (3.2), based on interactions among two Congolese youth.

3 Concise case studies from Africa

In the following subsections, two case studies from South Africa and the DR Congo are discussed to offer insights into humour and conversational storytelling (3.1) and street youth's humorous anecdotes as a strategy of indulging in reminiscences (3.2), both highlighting strategies of social bonding and enhanced sociability. In the following section, they are then applied to the concept of incongruity and to taboo speech in interaction. Besides the "canned joke", conversational humour occurs frequently but is less prominently studied – and can be understood as

> an umbrella term for various verbal chunks created spontaneously or repeated verbatim for the sake of amusing the recipient, either directly contributing to the semantic content of the ongoing conversation or diverting its flow into a humorous mode/frame/key, in which speakers need not genuinely mean what their humorous verbalisations convey
> (Dynel 2009: 1286).

In conversational humour, different strategies are pursued by speakers in order to increase the humorous potential of an interaction, amongst them: register clashes (Dynel 2009: 1291), banter (Norrick 1993: 29), forms of teasing directed at a participant in the conversation (Boxer and Cortés-Conde 1997), and many more. In the presented case studies, the focus lies on storytelling (Norrick 2007), its narrative structure and anecdotes (Dynel 2009: 1295) intended to strengthen the social bond between hearer and listener.

3.1 Humorous conversational storytelling in isiTsotsi

The example in this section comes from a 2012 video recording of a peer group of young men (approximately 18–20 years old) in a township called KwaMashu just outside the city of Durban in Kwa-Zulu Natal. The young men are friends who gather in the evenings at a local soccer field to smoke (cigarettes and marijuana) and drink, and to chat and listen to music (mostly local and international house music). They draw on resources from the local Tsotsitaal stylect[6] "isiTsotsi" in interactions during their gatherings. isiTsotsi in and around Durban relies on isiZulu for its base language or morphosyntactic frame (Rudwick 2005), and involves many relexicalisations, including borrowings, metaphors, neologisms, archaisms etc., in keeping with youth language practices elsewhere. The stylect is used by young men and women to index a streetwise identity, as well as for fun and humour within peer groups (Hurst and Buthelezi 2014, Hurst 2016, Hurst-Harosh 2020).

The excerpt focused on here involved one of the peer group members undertaking conversational storytelling (Norrick 2007) to tell his friends about an incident that had taken place a few days previously. To summarise the narrative, the young man had been drinking with a friend, and then was supposed to go and meet with his girlfriend. He is very drunk, and goes in the wrong direction, and then accidentally gets into a communal taxi, which is also going the wrong way. While in the taxi he realises he does not have the money to pay. When he finally does meet up with his girlfriend, for some inexplicable reason he has two bags of spinach, despite having no money in the taxi. Then when he and his girlfriend get back home, he accidentally calls her by his ex-girlfriend's name.

3.1.1 Narrative structure and humour

The storytelling follows a typical narrative structure (Norrick 2007). The storyteller initially provides an abstract, or orientation signalling what the story is about – how drunk he was on Saturday.

---

[6] "Stylect" is a term developed in Hurst (2008) and Hurst-Harosh (2020) to refer to youth language practices which involve the styling of resources (including extra- and paralinguistic) to achieve (indexical) social meaning.

Abstract/orientation:
P2: *Uyabona lendlela beng'phuze ngayo ngoMqibelo zange ng'bon' ukuthi ng'dale kanjani. Ngahlala noSipho mfethu nalomjita uSfiso mfethu uyamfojela?*

'You see how drunk I was on Saturday, I didn't even see what I did. I sat with Sipho[7] bro and that guy, Sfiso. You know him?'

Next, the storyteller reiterates that he has a story he wants to tell because his friends are not paying attention properly.

Opening:
P2: *Lalela, lalela, ngina ngendaba mfethu, listen dog.*

'Listen, listen. I have – I have a story, listen dog.'

Now he has their silence and attention, he provides orientation to the story, describing how he was supposed to meet his girlfriend, who he calls Cherry, at West Street, but he is already late.

Orientation
P2: *Uyagcwala! Eh wena mfethu uCherry unglinde ngase Edgars ngivele sengilate wena mfethu. Uphume ngo 2, yabo. Lapho u past 2. Ngehle mfethu kuQuantam bes'marsha ngayo wena mfethu, ngithi sho kubo kubo lova, heh ngiyamarsha. Ngidakwe ngi-fucked ang'boni. Ngiyamarsha mfethu, kumele mina mfethu ngiye kuWest Street ngiyoland' uCherry, yabo.*

'You check! So bro Cherry is waiting for me by Edgars and I'm already late bro. She left at 2. At that time it's past 2. I get out of the Quantam we were in and say bye to the gents and I go. I am drunk, I am fucked up I can't see. ((background snigger)) I'm walking man, I had to, I had to go to West Street to go get Cherry you see.'

Next in the narrative, he provides a complicating action, which involves him getting into a taxi instead of going to West Street.

---

[7] Names in both case studies have either been changed, shortened or omitted to guarantee our research assistants' anonymity.

Complicating action #1:

P2: *Ngiyamarsha ngiyaw'dlul'uWest Street. Ngimarshelaphi? Ngimarshela kuSmith Street. Yabo labo s'caba lab' bakbiza ngish'ungafuni mfethu? Bang'donsa mfethu eh ngamarsha ngadwadl' eteksini. Ngaph'ang'na nyuku mfethu. Ngidakwe lapho mfethu, ang'bon' emehlweni ngendlele ngiduzuke ngayo mfethu. I-flop isuka lapho ke wezwa.*

'I go and pass West Street. Where am I going? I'm going to Smith Street. ((short background laugh)) You see the door guys that call you even if you don't want to? They pull me in and I leave and get into the taxi. ((everyone laughs loudly)) At that time, I don't have money bro. I am drunk, ((laughter ongoing)) I can't see the way I was so finished. The problem starts there you hear. ((laughter ongoing))'

His foolhardiness by getting in the taxi due to being drunk, puts him in danger, as he does not have the money to pay, and the taxi operators become threatening. In South Africa, communal taxis are often operated by dangerous 'gangs' who have been known to engage in violence. After a long description of the trouble he gets himself in, he provides a resolution of the first complicating action in the form of humour.

Resolution #1:

P2: *Ngikhumbulukuthi ngehl'eteksini, iyona yodwa into engiy'khumbulayo mfethu. Mengizwa mfethu uCherry wang'dlula ngeteksi ngisemakethi ngihamba nge-ynyawo mfethu. Ngipheth'oplastic abawu two bes'spinashi kanjani. Amakhulu mfethu. Way'mis'iteksi wayemarsha ngayo mfethu, wang'getha. Wathi "manje baby z'thini." Ngiphethe wena mfethu amaplastic awutwo wespinashi. Waqhuma kanjalo.*

'I just remember getting out of the taxi, that's all I remember bro. When I hear Cherry says she passed me as she was in a taxi, I was walking by foot bro. I was holding two plastics with spinach. ((speaker laughs)) Huge ones. ((speaker laughing)) She stopped the taxi she was in and gets to me and she's like "and now baby what's up?" ((speaker laughs, others join in)) I have two bags of spinach bro. So, she bursts out laughing. ((speaker laughing while talking, background laughter))'

This initial resolution of the narrative is then followed by a second complicating action, when the storyteller calls his girlfriend by his ex-girlfriend's name:

Complicating action #2:
P2: *Ha bafethu ngaflopa, uthi ngavela ngaflopa.*

'Then I made a mistake. I made a mistake'

P4: *Ha udala otherwise heh!*

'((laughs)) You're doing things differently hey!'

P2: *Uthi ngavele ngam'biza ngoBontle mfethu. Kabili, ngiqhuma kanjalo.*

'She says I called her Bontle bro. ((someone gives a long whistle)) Twice as I got up.'

The resolution of the second complicating action comes in the form of an evaluation of himself, by both himself and his friends, who consider that perhaps he still likes his ex-girlfriend, but it only emerges when he is very drunk.

Resolution #2/coda/closing:
P4: *Ha usay'shaya ngoBontle imember, isagcwele.*

'This member still likes Bontle.'

P2: *Cabanga mfethu subconsciously dog, ak'yona into enzeka. Yabo manje phambi kwami intwengiy'cabangayo yabo mangiy'fojela, hai lutho mfethu. Ngisuka ngingekho engqondweni. Kuvele kwenzeke nje bang'tshel'ukuthi kade usuthi, wathi, uyabona. Manje mina ang'shayisani. Ngiyay'phika mina ngithi ayikho lento. Kodwa hai ingathi kuyibona mfethu.*

'Think about it, subconsciously dog it's not what should happen. You see in front of me what I see when I look at her – nothing. But when I'm out of it, it just happens. Then someone tells me what I was saying and I said this, you see. But no, I don't understand. ((speaker laughs)) I deny this, I say it's not there. But it seems it's there, bro.'

Broadly, the narrative serves to build on common experiences of drunkenness and draws on discourses around getting into trouble with girlfriends (men as hapless, subject to desire, women as jealous), as well as discourses relating to violence in South Africa.

The moments for humour or comedy in this narrative are multiple, and involve incongruity – for example, the narrator being lost and drunk; forgetting to meet his girlfriend; going the wrong way; being *blasé* in the face of dangerous taxi gangs; the presence of two inexplicable bags of spinach (discrepancy between hearer's/speaker's cognitive expectations); and saying the ex-girlfriend's name to his current girlfriend, which on its introduction as a second complicating action, breaks the perception of a (harmonic) whole.

Throughout the narrative, his friends offer supporting interjections and agreement regarding the various scenarios he finds himself in. The humorous moments are presented as experiences that his peers will have in common, having also been drunk and in trouble with their girlfriends. These comedic common experiences appear to develop social cohesion and community-building amongst the peer group, and his friends often interject agreement into the narrative. The narrative is also accompanied by laughter from both the speaker and his friends, sometimes raucous. The gestures of the speaker are muted, but he sometimes covers his face with his hands and shakes his head disbelievingly, while narrating the trouble he gets into. The video could benefit from an analysis mapping these interactional features including gestures and the function of laughter in the narrative, using a software such as ELAN which enables annotation of para- and extralinguistic features including pitch of voice, gestures, body posture and so on alongside the audio transcription.

3.1.2 Linguistic styling

Despite the prominent role and status of English in Kwa-Zulu Natal, there are only a few isolated borrowings from English (*listen, fucked, subconsciously, member, all along, beyond repair, story, sober*), with the majority of the narrative taking place in isiZulu and no sentential code-switching. Meanwhile, the language throughout is peppered with stylectal words and phrases (see Table 8.1). For example, in the excerpts above we see the following lexical items which are associated with the isiTsotsi stylect in KwaMashu, and some with Tsotsitaal more broadly (Hurst and Buthelezi 2014):

Table 8.1: isiTsotsi lexical items in KwaMashu narrative.

isiTsotsi lexical item	Translation	Etymology
-*fojela*	'to see/ know'	unknown
-*marsha*	'to walk'	Eng. *march*
lova	'guys/ gents'	poss. Eng. *loafer*
nyuku	'money'	poss. Xitsonga 'sweat'
iflop	'a problem'	Eng. *flop*
-*qhuma*	'to laugh'	Zulu 'explode'
-*hlaba*	'to have sex'	Zulu 'stab'

In reported speech (imitated speech) during the narrative, the main speaker (P2) represents different people using different styles of talking, particularly in reference to the use of isiTsotsi markers. The taxi operator on the one hand is represented by 'deeper' isiTsotsi, while P2 represents his girlfriend's speech using relatively few stylectal markers.

In the following excerpt, the taxi operator's reported speech begins with *eh mfethu ek se* 'hey, bro, I say', which is a stylistic rendition of densely packed discourse markers typical of deeper forms of isiTsotsi. *Ek se* is from Afrikaans and more commonly encountered in Cape Town Tsotsitaal than in Durban Tsotsitaal in the collected data, so it may be indexical of the taxi operator's speech here.

Taxi operator:
P2: Eh us'gcaba mfethu ethi "eh mfethu ek se, kad' ihamba iteksi ngicela lo four randi" Eh ngiphenduke ngimbuke, udriver ang'buke ahleke eh mang'fojel'usgcaba. Mfethu ngimbheka mfethu kuvela amasekeni. Ngithi "eh mfethu ang'naw' ufour randi" Ethi "heh wena mfethu usanocka? Ngendlela wena uhleli mahala eteksini".

'Then the door guy bro says "Hey bro, the taxi's been going please bring the four rand". ((short background laugh)) Then I turn around and look at him, the driver looks at me and laughs. When I look at the door guy bro I get scared. ((ongoing sniggers in background)) I say "my man I don't have four rand" ((background laugh)) Then he says "hey are you that drunk? You're just sitting here thinking the taxi moves for free."'

On the other hand, his girlfriend's speech is interlaced with endearments such as *baby*, and rather than using isiTsotsi lexical items, her speech is represented as closer to urban isiZulu. For example, 'did you walk' is reported as *uhambe ngenyawo*, whereas during the narrative, the speaker generally uses the term *-marsha*, the isiTsotsi for 'to walk'. Thus the female speech is represented as more conventional isiZulu, although she is at one point reported to use *shap* (from English *sharp*) which is a now-common urban form for *okay*, although originating in Tsotsitaal.

Girlfriend's reported speech:
P2: Way'mis'iteksi wayemarsha ngayo mfethu, wang'getha. Wathi "manje baby z'thini?" Ngiphethe wena mfethu amaplastic awutwo wespinashi. Waqhuma kanjalo.

'She stopped the taxi she was in and gets to me and she's like "and now baby what's up?" ((speaker laughs, others join in)) I have two bags of spinach bro. So she bursts out laughing. ((speaker laughing while talking, background laughter))'

P2: *Wathi, wathi "manje zthini?!" (...) Ngiyamarsha, uCherry uyang'qhuma uthi "udakwe kanje". Ngithi "hai baby kade ngphuza", uthi "hai ke shap". Wath' "uhambe ngenyawo?"*

'She said, she said "and now?". (...) So I go. Cherry is laughing at me saying "you're so drunk". ((ongoing background laughter)) I'm like "No babe I had been drinking", she's like "okay, fine." And she says "Did you walk".'

The narrative style also draws heavily on discourse markers, which are often used to direct hearer attention and to keep listeners engaged (Fraser 1999). For example throughout the narrative, *mfethu* is used, a shortened form of *umfowethu*, 'my brother' in isiZulu, translated here as 'bro'. In the excerpt below, the speaker also uses *ke wezwa* 'you hear', *uyabona* 'you know', and *yabo* 'you see'.

P2: *Bang'donsa **mfethu** eh ngamarsha ngadwadl' eteksini. Ngaph'ang'na nyuku **mfethu**. Ngidakwe lapho **mfethu**, ang'bon' emehlweni ngendlele ngiduzuke ngayo **mfethu**. I-flop isuka lapho **ke wezwa**. Ngimarshe ngeteksi wena **mfethu**, futhi ngihleli ngaphambili kwi Quantam angith' **uyabona** – kube u-driver besekube nale seat ngala? Ziwutwo ngaphambili. Ngihleli la. Eh us'gcaba **mfethu** ulokhethi "Ek se wena mfethu shayisis imala phela wean **mfethu**" yabo "uwena wedwa ongakhokhile". Ngithi "hai sure mfethu" yabo.*

'They pull me in and I leave and get into the taxi. ((everyone laughs loudly)) At that time I don't have money bro. I am drunk bro, ((laughter ongoing)) I can't see the way I was so finished bro. The problem starts there you hear. ((laughter ongoing)) I get into the taxi, bro, I'm sitting in the front, you know in a Quantam there's the driver then there's the seat? ((one participant still laughing)) There's two in the front. I'm sitting there. So the door guy keeps saying "Hey bro bring the money guy" you see, "you must pay for it yourself". And I say "okay bro" you see.'

The analysis above goes some way towards describing youth language practice and styling within a peer group, including the use of stylect resources, as well as the use of a typical narrative structure for humorous storytelling. Further analysis of such rich naturalistic data however could furnish us with even greater detail on interactional and conversational behaviours including the use of extra- and paralinguistic features in the achievement of humour.

3.2 Memories and transgressive topics: Humour in Lingala ya Bayankee/Yanké

The second excerpt is a taken from a longer audio recording of a conversation[8] of two 15–16-year old friends in Kinshasa (DR Congo), who were both former street children (so-called *bashegé, baphaseur* or *bayankée*) and were by then sharing a small flat. After having lived in the streets of Kinshasa for a number of years, they were now trying to get back to school and organise their lives (with financial support by international friends). After having bought a small TV, they would sit together in the evenings and drink beer, smoke cigarettes and either speak about the day at school or about their memories a few years back in Kinshasa's streets. In their daily conversations, they would often use Lingala ya Bayankee (also called Yanké, hereafter thus shortened to LyB/Y; see also Kunzmann, this volume), a Lingala-based[9] stylect widespread among young people with modest backgrounds in the crowded neighborhoods of the Congolese capital (van Pelt 2000, Nassenstein 2014). LyB/Y speakers make use of specific phonological, morphological and especially semantic manipulations, and language users' multilingual repertoires including lexemes from Congo Swahili, Cilubà, Kikongo-Kituba, French and increasingly English. Despite deliberate manipulations, LyB also reveals changes in its noun and verb morphology (Nassenstein forthcoming), specifically in the noun class system (e.g. in the use of morphological diminutives) and in its tense-aspect system (e.g. in employing grammaticalised forms).

Dynel (2009: 1296) defines humorous anecdotes as follows, also referring to Norrick's (1993, etc.) groundbreaking work:

> This is a humorous narrative by means of which the speaker regales the hearer with a story deriving from his/her personal experience or other people's lives [. . .]. Anecdotes are delivered in a colourful style abounding in witty lexemes and phrasemes, coupled with rich non-verbal expression (the tone of voice, facial expression and gestures), which contribute

---

[8] The recording stems from longitudinal fieldwork carried out in Kinshasa, DR Congo, in 2009–2010, and refers back to events that mainly occurred in 2004 and 2005.
[9] Lingala is a Bantu language (of Bantu group C) spoken in parts of the DR Congo, the Republic of Congo and to some extent in northern Angola. It serves as most widely known national language in DR Congo and it is said to have as many as 20 million native speakers and another 20–25 million non-native speakers (Meeuwis 2020: 15).

to the humorous effect. It is not uncommon for such stories to refer to events which were hardly humorous and even dramatic, but are, however, recounted jovially to elicit a humorous response in the addressee.

The presented anecdotes coincide with Dynel's typology as far as the colourful style, accompanying gestures and the recurrent phrasemes that are frequently used by Congolese (street) youth are concerned. Witty lexemes in Dynel's sense are realized in the recorded anecdotes as creative manifestations of youth language, i.e. stylized and manipulated lexemes originating from many different languages and "flavouring" the speech. What Dynel describes as "dramatic" and only "hardly humorous" (ibid.) topics, occur in Lyb/Y anecdotes as explicitly or implicitly addressed taboo topics.[10]

Breaching of verbal taboos is typical of youth language, and transgressive genres of communication (mobbing, sexting, swearing and cursing, shouting etc.) are frequently employed by youths for different reasons (see also Stenström, this volume). The recorded anecdotes address (1) body hygiene and bodily effluvia, (2) food and gluttony, (3) women and sex, (4) vanity and bragging, and (5) racism and exclusion. In their influential study, Allan and Burridge (2006) list all but the fourth theme as cross-linguistically recurrent semantic fields in taboo speech. In humorous anecdotes, the reference to taboo topics and incidents that show transgressive communicative behaviour intend to strengthen the relationship and social bond among speakers. The indexical value of tabooed speech can be understood as creating a liminal bond and reviving a cheeky kind of reminiscence among male youth.

3.2.1 Sequence and structure of humorous anecdotes in interaction

The first speaker introduces the first anecdote in French, which refers to a moment in time six years earlier, with an initial phatic statement 'do you remember/you remember . . .', while opening a beer bottle and taking a seat on the couch in the small apartment.

---

10 As suggested by one reviewer, it should be added here that humour is always culture-specific. What appears as "dramatic" or "hardly humorous" in one context, may not necessarily be perceived as such in another cultural setting.

P1: *Tu te rappelles, à Niangara . . . on faisait beaucoup de blagues sur la propreté, sur manger . . .*

'You remember, while at Niangara [name of an orphanage in Kinshasa], we joked a lot about cleanliness, about eating . . .'

P2: *Ouais.*

'Yeah.'

The initial stock phrase serves as introduction of a narrative from the past (in analogy with the formula *once upon a time* in English stories), and is held in French in most anecdotes that were recorded in this conversation. The second speaker accepts the orientation/invitation (with a short marker of confirmation *ouais*). The first humorous anecdote about one of their former peer's body hygiene is then narrated in Lingala:

P1: *Nga na Ogune, tozaláki na Paul, on disait: Baó ba'á[11] batshara-venda, tshara-venda fort! Paul ó alinga'a kovela té. Ya sóló, alinga'a kovela té. Nga pé, jour wâná nayókákí a'ólumba fort.* ((shaking his head)) *Paul?! A'á tshara-venda, vraiment.* ((laughing))

'Ogune and I, we were with Paul, we said: These ones are dirty, very dirty! This guy Paul does not want to shower. Really, he does not like showering. I also noticed that day how he was smelling ((shaking his head)) Paul?! He was [is] really dirty. ((laughing))

P2: *Ouais, ouais* ((laughing)) *Na Trickpa pé! Azá venda fort! Omóna ká'a, a'otíka basolo nzóto na banini na badraps. Sókí ayé boyé, afazé, donc, omóna basolo. Yé, alingí kovela té! Sikóyo to'osála ndé níni?*

'Yeah, yeah ((laughing)) And Patrick, too! He was [is] so dirty! You see just he will leave body smells on anything and on bedsheets. If he came like this and slept, then, you would notice the smells. He does not want to shower! So, what are we gonna deal with it?'

---

11 Apostrophes mark shortened syllables or morphemes, for instance due to haplology in the interlocutors' speech. Square brackets either represent literal translations or indicate the omission of parts of the citation. Round brackets contain logical additions and non-literal expressions. Double round brackets either denote laughter, gestures or the manner in which an utterance is expressed.

P1: *Ah, sókí omóní bôngó ... il fallait tolobéláki yé káka que non, il fallait aveláki. Il fallait tolobéláki yé, sókí té, ah ...*

'If you see it this way ... it would have been necessary to tell him, no, that he would have to shower. One would have needed to tell him, otherwise, ah ...'

P2: *Ah nga, kútu yaya ó nga esí nabayé yé. Niveau moto alingí avela té, nzóto nayé ageré yangó ndé níni? Alingákí limba té. Et ... quand les gens étaient en train de manger ...*

'As far as I am concerned, this buddy, I am already tired of him. The extent to which he does not shower, how did he manage his body? He did not like water. And ... whenever guys were eating ...'

The second theme, dealing with food, is introduced by another French intervention by Speaker 2 toward the end of the anecdote on body hygiene (*en train de manger ...*), signalling to Speaker 1 that another humorous topic is brought up in the conversation. He triggers the first speaker to renarrate more memories from a few years earlier. He also begins in French, and then switches to Lingala right after the initial statement and connecting passage is uttered.

P1: *Et puis, mosúsu, d'autre ... Kabamba, tá'á adamjam! Tá'á ndéngé a'ódamjam! Adamjam monéné bakolánda yó, ba-grand-mobokilo! Kútu jour wâná, niveau yé abandákí kodamé tsenge, nalobákí bakolánda yé to níni ...*

'And then, another [one], apart ... Kabamba, look how ate [eats]! Look how he was [is] eating! He ate [eats] to an extent as if they followed [will follow] him or what, gluttons! Moreover, that day, the way/extent to which he began to eat rice, I said (as if) they were to follow him or what ...'

P2: *Ah, yaya wâná aleláki kodamé fort, aleláki damaz fort, aleláki kodamé fort! Oui, yaya aleláki mbengele fort. Donc, azaláki grand mobokilo. Eh, ndéngé adundákí!*

'That guy loved eating, he loved food, he loved eating so much! Yes, the guy loved foodstuff a lot. So, he was a big glutton. Man, the way he stuffed himself!'

P1: ((laughing)) *Bon, ezaláki makambo nayé-eeh!*

((laughing)) 'Well, those were his [lengthened/emphatic] problems!'

P2:   *Ahh.* ((laughing))

   'Ah/Well.' ((laughing))

A third theme is sex and often misogynist talk about women.[12] In front of the apartment in the crowded neighborhood Matongé there was a busy main street, where both young men would often watch their friends pass by with new girlfriends, or, occasionally at night, female sex workers. They would then comment upon their changing relationships and affairs, and sometimes also address aspects of beauty or body shape of the respective young women. In the course of the conversation, they remember their former friends who would often be engaged in new relationships. The new topic starts with an exclamation that directs the focus right onto the main protagonist of the anecdote:

P1:   *Pedro na banzele! Depuis Niangara, alingaka kochangé banzele fort. Leló namóní yé na momí móko boyé.*

   'Pedro and girls! Since (the orphanage) Niangara he likes changing girls. Today I saw him with a girl.'

P2:   *Ah, nabulékí néti y'omónaka yé té. Ah, nga pé, nabandá komóna yé fort. Kútu leló alékí na bor mókó boyé, bor'angó, tálá sima gayard!*

   'Ah I thought you had not seen him. I, too, saw him a lot (like this). Besides, today he passed with a girl [thing], this very girl, imagine [look at] her bum!'

P1:   *Nókó wâná alela bamomí fort. Leló butú mobimba akobámba na kobámba. Eh, nókó, père ó, eh eh eh. Yaya ó a mystique. Leló omóní yé na momí óyo, lóbí namóní yé na tipete wâná.*

   'That buddy [uncle] loves girls. Today all night long he will be banging. Ah, uncle, that guy [father], [interjection of astonishment]. That guy is unbelievable. Today you see him with this girl, tomorrow you see him with that girl.'

---

12 This third topic is not starting with a French phrase. While there is a general tendency to use French when initiating a new theme, this pattern is prone to exceptions and does not reflect the only possible narrative structure. We are grateful to one reviewer for comments on this.

P2: *Ahh, Pedro. Heure [ɛR] nyónso ká'a na badamuna na badamuna. Alela bor fort. Alinga'a ká'a koremorqué na remorqué.*

'Oh boy, Pedro. All the time only with girls and girls. He likes the thing (meaning here: 'sex') a lot. He only likes fucking.'
((both laughing))

A fourth theme identified in conversations among the two young men is vanity and pride. They remember a young guy, a former friend and his style, and begin the new anecdote again in French, then switch to Lingala after setting the scene.

P2: *Ah, tu rigoles. Des gens qui aiment se faire voir . . . rappelle-toi de Zuma. Yaya ó alingí komimóna fort, azómóna néti yé a'á danzé.*

'You are making fun. People who like to be seen . . . remember Zuma. This guy liked [likes] to show himself a lot, he considered [considers] it as if he was hot/special.'

P1: *Ah, yé abúlaka néti alela minéne fort, néti a'óléka, néti a'óbudé bato nyónso.*

'Ah, he thinks as if he was proudly showing himself, as if when he was [is] passing, he was [is] arrogantly ignoring everyone.'

P2: *Ah alela ba-fier epolá! Sókí kútu amóní bato ba'ótámbola néti a'óbudé bato tout.*

'He has a wrong sense of vanity/pride! If moreover he sees people walking it is as if he was arrogantly ignoring all people.'

P1: *Ah, a'á nayé pé na rien! Sókí otálí yé, kútu a'á na position [pojisjɔ̃] té.* ((laughing))

'Ah, what concerns him, he has actually nothing on him! If you look at him, he has no reputation/prestige. ((laughing))'

P2: ((laughing)) *Tálá kútu bambati alátí! Yé kútu moto mókó boyé mais sókí alekí boyé káka minéne na minéne.*

'Look moreover at the pants he wears! He appears as somebody but when he passes like this, only false pride/pomposity.'

Eventually, a fifth recurrent theme is xenophobic mockery of foreign-looking (especially Asian) passersby, a common raciolinguistic phenomenon in Kinshasa

(Nassenstein 2020). A few hours later, in their conversation, the two youth recall a situation where they saw an Asian couple walking past them at the market Gambela, while they were staring at the woman's behind.

P2: *Oyébí lisúsu . . . un jour on était en train de marcher près de . . . près de Marché Gambela. On a vu des chinois . . .*

'You still know . . . once we were walking near Gambela market. We saw some Chinese . . .'

P1: *Nalobákí óh yangó ba-shisho ó ba'á penzá na mabáya na sima.*

'I said: Therefore (it is that) these Chinese really have flat buttocks.'

P2: *Ah grave! Ba'á penzá mabáya.* ((laughing))

'Massive! They are indeed flat-behinds.'

The humorous anecdotes show a specific structure (that can be analysed in more detail in future studies) and initiatives or key phrases to move from one anecdote to the next one, mostly held in French, as pointed out above (in analogy with Norrick's concept of "story-rounds"). This code-switching strategy has the sense of signaling to the addressee the moment to move forward. It also identifies one "lead narrator" for each anecdote and the one who, as *"le deuxième ou troisième ajoute juste les commentaires"* [the second or third one adds only comments],[13] as expressed by one of the two speakers. Moreover, the anecdotes put more emphasis on their incongruent parts and the humorous or often transgressive content through repetitions of almost exactly the same wording (see, for instance, the anecdote on food and gluttony). Interjections such as *ah* or *eh* signal turn-taking and often mark the second speaker's turn, and signal mostly affiliative stance. Overlaps and interruptions are less common in the recorded conversations than in other interactions, and less instances of repair. In the anecdotes, the speaker-hearer roles are expressed through terms of endearment, which usually derive from Lingala and French kinship terms such as *nóko* 'maternal uncle' (who has a specific symbolic function) and *père* 'father' (see also similar strategies in the isiTsotsi excerpt in 3.1). These can also be inverted and be applied to the protagonists of the humorous anecdotes when this appears suitable.

---

[13] In Rühlemann's (2013) sense, this third person could be classified as "responsive recipient". We are grateful to one reviewer for this comment.

3.2.2 Linguistic styling

Apart from a specific structure of the interactions, also linguistic styling in LyB/Y contributes largely to the humorous effect of shared anecdotes. Table 8.2 contains some of the stylectal lexical items that show the manipulative strategies, borrowing and coinage that occur in African youth language practices and has been subject to numerous studies (see, for instance, Kießling and Mous 2004). While this paper focuses on pragmatic matters, also stylisation plays a role in interactions due to the addressee's implicit assumptions (or, presupposition) about the narrated incident in question and a speaker's stance when making use of e.g. euphemistic and dysphemistic semantic strategies. While presuppositions are generally known and shared among speaker and addressee, the choice of wording or a specific linguistic construction can trigger different presuppositions.

The recorded conversation mostly uses present tense (expressed with the suffix -í) or, more often, present progressive aspect (expressed with the shortened prefix 'ó- from Kinshasa Lingala zó-), despite the point of reference lies in the past. This can be considered a narrative strategy when remembering and retelling vivid memories.

Moreover, the following stylectal lexical terms are used to flavour the anecdotes and increase their humorous potential, especially due to relexicalisation.

Table 8.2: Lingala ya Bayankee/Yanké lexical items in the humorous anecdotes (selection).

Lyb/Y lexical item	Translation	Etymology
tshara-venda	'very dirty person, dirty'	Portuguese *cara* 'face', *venda* 'dirty' (brought with migrants from Angola)
-vela	'to shower, to bathe'	Fr. *laver* 'wash'
-fazé	'sleep'	possibly Fr. *phase* 'phase (of sleep)'
limba	'water; fuel; sperm'	unclear
-damjam	'to eat'	Fr. *Jeu de Dames* 'checkers' (eating adversaries' game pieces)
tsenge	'rice'	coinage?
nzele	'girl'	Fr. *mademoiselle*
momí	'girl(friend)'	Engl. *Mom* or Engl. *mummy*
bor	'thing; girl; sex'	possibly Fr. *bord* 'edge'
tipete	'girl(friend)'	Fr. *petite* 'little one, girl'
damuna	'girl'	Fr. *dame* 'lady'
-boulé	'to think; to work'	Fr. *boule* 'head' (colloq.)
ba-fier epólá	'wrong sense of vanity'	Fr. *fier* 'proud' and Ling. *-póla* 'to rot'
position [pojisjɔ̃]	'prestige, reputation'	Fr. *position*

Table 8.2 (continued)

Lyb/Y lexical item	Translation	Etymology
mbati	'pants'	coinage?
shisho	'Chinese person'	onomatopoiea
mabáya	'flat behind'	Swahili adj. *-baya* 'bad'

4 Conclusions

In his article on the theoretical foundations of humour in interaction, Norrick (2009: 274) comes to the conclusion that "jokes are not the only funny narratives in conversation" and that by "exchanging anecdotes about our personal lives, we present personal identities for ratification by the other participants in the conversation [. . .,] to the extent that we accept the identities presented in the personal narratives we tell each other, we create solidarity and rapport." Apart from solidarity and group identity, Norrick (ibid.) also stresses the fact that storytelling and the narration of specific anecdotes disrupt the flow of conversation to a lesser extent than for instance jokes with a punchline; moreover, the endeavour can be collaborative and gives room for (funny) evaluative comments, sarcasm and much more.

Humour in African youth languages is not only expressed through genre, following specific conversational structures that correspond with conversational patterns in other languages (cf. Norrick and Chiaro 2009) but also stylistically by inserting specific manipulated or stylectal lexemes. Both the manipulation and stylisation of lexical items (assembling different words for drunkenness, food, body parts, sex etc.), due to their creative synonymy, innovative character and the ritualised turn-taking and conversational structure of humorous narratives, lead to incongruity. What is presented as story with a dramatic (cf. Dynel 2009) or serious content, turns into a semi-serious, ironic or hilarious tale or anecdote, with incongruent patterns (e.g. urban nighthawks lost in the city, drunkards with spinach in their hands, self-confident street boys with smelly bodies, styled up Chinese passersby with "flat behinds", etc.). Incongruity is here triggered by implicature in the retelling of stories, implicating that something may not be adequate, fitting or "right" in the anecdotes. The social function of indulging in reminiscences among users of African youth language practices targets the strengthening of social cohesion, enhancing ritual sociability, and reliving witty and jocular moments in contexts of experienced marginality and liminality in the streets (i.e. in the margins of society, conversing about indecent topics, narrating actions with transgressive behaviour).

The analysis of the conversational storytelling narratives highlights the numerous ways in which pragmatic approaches can contribute to an understanding of youth language practices, such as through interactional stylistics, conversation analysis, and approaches which consider indexicality. Such analyses could be further extended through approaches which incorporate paralinguistic and extralinguistic features, made possible by the use of naturalistic video recorded data. The above analyses also take us a step further towards our aim of understanding "everyday language use" amongst youth. Our emphasis here has been on humour yet indicates a rich field of study for researchers applying the full range of pragmatics approaches to youth language data.

References

Attardo, Salvatore. 1994. *Linguistic theories of humour*. Berlin: De Gruyter Mouton.
Attardo, Salvatore and Victor Raskin. 1991. Script-theory revis(it)ed: Joke similarity and joke representation model. *Humor. International Journal of Humor Research* 4 (3–4). 293–347.
Barasch, Frances K. 1985. The grotesque as a comic genre. *Modern Language Studies* 15 (1). 3–11.
Billig, Michael. 2005. *Laughter and ridicule*. London: Sage.
Boxer, Diana and Florencia Cortés-Conde. 1997. From bonding to biting: Conversational joking and identity display. *Journal of Pragmatics* 27. 275–294.
Bublitz, Wolfram and Axel Hübler (eds.). 2007. *Metapragmatics in use*. Amsterdam and Philadelphia: John Benjamins.
Bucholtz, Mary. 2011. *White kids: Language, race, and styles of youth identity*. Cambridge: Cambridge University Press.
Canestrari, Carla and Ivana Bianchi. 2013. From perception of contraries to humorous incongruities. In Marta Dynel (ed.), *Developments in linguistic humour theory*, 3–24. Amsterdam and Philadelphia: John Benjamins.
Chovanec, Jan and Isabel Ermida (eds.). 2012. *Language and humour in the media*. Newcastle: Cambridge Scholars.
Dynel, Marta. 2009. Beyond a joke: Types of conversational humour. *Language and Linguistics Compass* 3 (5). 1248–1299.
Dynel, Marta (ed.) 2011. *The pragmatics of humor across discourse domains*. Amsterdam and Philadelphia: John Benjamins.
Dynel, Marta (ed.). 2013a. *Developments in linguistic humour theory*. Amsterdam and Philadelphia: John Benjamins.
Dynel, Marta. 2013b. A view on humour theory. In Marta Dynel (ed.), *Developments in linguistic humour theory*, vii–xiv. Amsterdam and Philadelphia: John Benjamins.
Eckert, Penelope. 1989. *Jocks and burnouts: Social categories and identity in the high school*. New York: Teachers College Press.
Eckert, Penelope. 2000. *Linguistic variation as social practice*. Oxford: Blackwell.
Ermida, Isabel. 2008. *The language of comic narratives: Humor construction in short stories*. Berlin: De Gruyter Mouton.
Fraser, Bruce. 1999. What are discourse markers?, *Journal of Pragmatics* 31 (7). 931–952.

Goldstein, Donna. 2013. *Laughter out of place*. Berkeley: University of California Press.
Hollington, Andrea and Nico Nassenstein. 2015. Conclusion and outlook: Taking new directions in the study of youth language practices. In Nico Nassenstein and Andrea Hollington (eds.), *Youth language practices in Africa and beyond*, 345–356. Berlin: De Gruyter Mouton.
Hollington, Andrea, Nico Nassenstein and Anne Storch (eds.) 2018. Critical youth language studies – rethinking concepts. *The Mouth* 3.
Hurst, Ellen. 2008. Style, structure and function in Cape Town Tsotsitaal. Cape Town: University of Cape Town dissertation.
Hurst, Ellen. 2016. Metaphor in South African tsotsitaal. *Sociolinguistic Studies* (Special Issue: The Dynamics of Youth Language in Africa) 10 (1–2). 153–176.
Hurst-Harosh, Ellen. 2019. Tsotsitaal and decoloniality. *African Studies* 78 (1). 112–125.
Hurst-Harosh, Ellen. 2020. *Tsotsitaal in South Africa: Style and metaphor in youth language practices*. Cologne: Rüdiger Köppe.
Hurst, Ellen and Mthuli Buthelezi. 2014. A visual and linguistic comparison of features of Durban and Cape Town tsotsitaal. *Southern African Linguistics and Applied Language Studies* 32 (2). 185–197.
Hurst-Harosh, Ellen and Eyo Mensah. 2021. Authenticity and the object of analysis: Methods of youth language data collection. In Rajend Mesthrie, Ellen Hurst-Harosh and Heather Brookes (eds.), *Youth language practices and urban language contact in Africa*, 182–200. Cambridge: Cambridge University Press.
Jay, Timothy. 2000. *Why do we curse? A neuro-psycho-social theory of speech*. Amsterdam and Philadelphia: John Benjamins.
Kießling, Roland and Maarten Mous. 2004. Urban youth languages in Africa. *Anthropological Linguistics* 46 (3). 303–341.
Martin, Rod A. 2007. *The psychology of humor. An integrative approach*. Burlington: Elsevier.
Meeuwis, Michael. 2020. *A grammatical overview of Lingála*. Revised and extended edition. Munich: LINCOM.
Mesthrie, Rajend, Ellen Hurst-Harosh and Heather Brookes (eds.). 2021. *Youth language practices and urban language contact in Africa*. Cambridge: Cambridge University Press.
Nassenstein, Nico. 2014. *A grammatical study of the youth language Yanké*. Munich: LINCOM.
Nassenstein, Nico. 2020. Mock Chinese in Kinshasa: On Lingala speakers' offensive language use and verbal hostility. In Nico Nassenstein and Anne Storch (eds.), *Swearing and cursing: Contexts and practices in a critical linguistic perspective*, 185–208. Berlin: De Gruyter Mouton.
Nassenstein, Nico. forthcoming. Lingala ya Bayankee/Yanké. In Paul Kerswill and Heike Wiese (eds.), *Urban contact dialects and language change: Insights from the Global North and South*. London: Routledge.
Nassenstein, Nico and Andrea Hollington. 2016. Global repertoires and urban fluidity: Youth languages in Africa. *International Journal of the Sociology of Language* 242. 171–193.
Norrick, Neal 1993. *Conversational joking: Humor in everyday talk*. Bloomington: Indiana University Press.
Norrick, Neal. 2003. Issues in conversational joking. *Journal of Pragmatics* 35. 1333–1359.
Norrick, Neal. 2007. Conversational storytelling. In David Herman (ed.), *The Cambridge companion to narrative*, 127–141. Cambridge: Cambridge University Press.
Norrick, Neal. 2009. A theory of humor in interaction. *JLT* 3 (2). 261–284.
Norrick, Neal and Delia Chiaro (eds.). 2009. *Humor in interaction*. Amsterdam and Philadelphia: John Benjamins.

Rampton, Ben. 1995. *Crossing: Language and ethnicity among adolescents*. London: Longman.
Rampton, Ben. 2006. *Language in late modernity: Interaction in an urban school*. Cambridge: Cambridge University Press.
Rowe, Kathleen. 1995. *The unruly woman*. Austin: University of Texas Press.
Rudwick, Stephanie. 2005. Township language dynamics: IsiZulu and IsiTsotsi in Umlazi. *Southern African Linguistics and Applied Language Studies* 23 (3). 305–317.
Rühlemann, Christoph. 2013. *Narrative in English conversation. A corpus analysis of storytelling*. Cambridge: Cambridge University Press.
Stenström, Anna-Brita. 2020. English- and Spanish-speaking teenagers' use of rude vocatives. In Nico Nassenstein and Anne Storch (eds.), *Swearing and cursing: Contexts and practices in a critical linguistic perspective*, 281–301. Berlin: De Gruyter Mouton.
Storch, Anne and Nico Nassenstein. 2020. "I will kill you today": Reading swearing and bad language through Otherness, mimesis, abjection and camp. In Nico Nassenstein and Anne Storch (eds.), *Swearing and cursing: Contexts and practices in a critical linguistic perspective*, 3–35. Berlin: De Gruyter Mouton.
van Pelt, Frank. 2000. *Lingala ya Bayankee: een beschrijving van het Lingala Argot*. Leiden: Leiden University MA thesis.

Andrea Hollington and Dennis Gengomoi Akena
9 Youth language manipulation as decolonial practice in Uganda

Ever since the 15th century, when the various societies of present-day Uganda were established, sports education, which also included music, dance and drama (MDD), has been an integral part of the education system for the training of young people, with language always being an important means of instruction. The combination played a fundamental role in the processes of nation building and state formation. With the introduction of "modern" schooling and education by the Christian missionaries in the 1890s, and the enactment of the first official education policy of the British Colonial Government in 1925, the combination of sports education with MDD has developed into one of the most important aspects of schooling, used to educate, indoctrinate and produce citizens of the colonial and the national system. For example, the recent introduction of traditional sports including wrestling commonly known as *Ekigwo*, shows how sports education has been used to educate the young generation that traditional sport is equally important. Meanwhile the use of music in military education commonly refered to as *Mchakamchaka* demonstrates how sports education has been used for political indoctrination by the current ruling government of the National Resistance Movement. In this chapter, we will illustrate how youth language and language manipulation in the context of sports education has formed part of the institutional and historical processes that have constituted the current education system, as well as forming part of everyday practices and rituals in school assemblies, classes, sports and school ceremonies. We will discuss how the youth use the linguistic manipulation of colonial, national and school rituals as a tool of resistance and as a decolonial practice. In particular, we will look at the linguistic strategies, and show the ways in which youth language practices and music have been playing and continue to play a significant role in the context of education and politics in Uganda.

Andrea Hollington, University of Cologne, e-mail: andrea.hollington@yahoo.de
Dennis Gengomoi Akena, University of Cologne, e-mail: akenaug@yahoo.com

1 Introduction – another aspect of African youth language practices

This contribution constitutes a collaborative work that brings together our research on *"Sports education practices in Uganda: Ideologies, interests and strategies of key actors"* (Akena forthcoming) and on African youth language practices and sociolinguistics. By combining our perspectives, we aim to present a fresh look at African youth language practices through a focus on the ways in which young Ugandans deal with the country's colonial linguistic heritage, as well as the colonial and neo-colonial education system. The study of African youth languages (AYL) has enjoyed increasing popularity over the last couple of years. A major focus has been on the description of African youth language varieties (such as Sheng, Camfranglais, Yarada K'wank'wa, Nouchi, Yanké, Luyaaye, and so on) and the ways through which they deviate from other "standardized" or "traditional" languages. Studies of AYL have often focused on strategies of language manipulation, on linguistic creativity, on identity, ideology and language attitudes, etc., usually by focusing on African linguistic repertoires. However, the colonial legacies have left many African societies with colonial languages as official languages and these (European) languages continue to dominate in society and education. While the colonial languages also impact the linguistic varieties of youth, there are other ways in which young people use and play with normative colonial education and language practices. In Uganda, English has been the main medium of education and teaching in the school system since British colonialism. Moreover, the education system and language use therein have been heavily influenced by missionary activities in the country, which preceded official colonialism (see Nankindu 2014). Standards and practices in today's education system still reflect the European missionary and colonial discourses that shaped the development of Uganda's school system.

Against this background, young students in Uganda manipulate and use language to react to the established (linguistic) norms and to negotiate political attitudes and reactions. In this regard, youth language practices can be seen as an agentive way of dealing with the colonial legacy in language and education policies, which can be regarded as a decolonial practice, as we will argue in the following.

The next section will present a short overview of the history of sports education and the current background to the language practices observed. Data for this contribution was collected through ethnographic field work in Uganda in 2014 and involved research at the following schools: 1) Makerere College School, a mixed boys' and girls' day school, founded in 1945 by the British Protectorate government, and currently owned by the Protestant Church of Uganda; and 2)

Namilyango College School, an all-boys' Catholic school founded in 1901 by the Mill Hill Fathers Missionaries, currently owned by the Roman Catholic Church.

It needs to be stated that the short historical summary presented in the following is by no means complete, but rather highlights certain events relating to the interplay of sports education, missionary activities and colonial politics.

After that we will look at manipulated songs that students sing, particularly during sports events, and see how these practices express resistance to the established religious and political norms, whose foundations lie in imperialism and colonialism. As this constitutes a first preliminary study, we will only introduce two examples and discuss how this can be seen as a decolonial practice.

2 Background to sports education in Uganda 1500–2018

This section summarizes sports education perspectives and practices of the following four political eras: pre-colonial Buganda, the missionary era, British colonialism, and independence. This section outlines the key political events, including policy changes, regime changes and conflicts that have affected or influenced institutional changes in sports education practices. It's important to note that in discussing sports under the different governmental regimes, we focus on sports education (physical education syllabus) and key sports events/disciplines in which youth and manipulation were expressed and became evident. We therefore observe that the sports education practices during the different governmental regimes were determined by the sports education syllabus and were not homogenous across the various schools and regions. This ranges from pre-colonial sports such as wrestling, boat competitions and hunting to modern sports including football, athletics, netball, cricket, volleyball, basketball, and boxing among others.

2.1 Pre-colonial era: Wrestling in the Buganda Kingdom

Prior to European colonialism, there were various historical kingdoms in what is now known as Uganda, in particular Bunyoro-Kitara, Buganda, Ankole, Tooro and Busoga. These societies participated in leisure and sports activities mainly as part of cultural practices. Traditional sports were closely related to socio-economic and livelihood activities but did not require specific or formally defined and constructed sports facilities. They were, rather, adapted to the natural environment of the respective communities (Ministry of Education and Sports 2009), were inclusive in nature and allowed the participation of different members of society.[1] Some of the pre-colonial sports included wrestling, jumping, throwing, shooting, dodge ball, hunting, *Omweso* board games, boat competitions among many other forms. In the Buganda Kingdom, which we look at as an example here,[2] wrestling was considered the main sport: it was part of everyday life, with all men, young and old, including the king himself, having a keen interest in it. (However, it was unacceptable to defeat the king in a wrestling match; doing so would result in immediate execution.) Young men used wrestling to negotiate their status both within their peer groups and in society. Women participated in wrestling as spectators. The participation of women as spectators generated fun and amusement. Songs of victory as well as songs expressing sexuality were sung during wrestling festivals to either inspire or provoke participants. It is through such contexts that songs, youth language and manipulation took form to express interest, positions but also resistance. Importantly, language manipulation was used during this epoch as a means of resistance. In Buganda, songs and poems performed at sports festivals were one of the few means for people, especially adolescents, to express their dissatisfaction with the Kabaka.[3]

Exceptional wrestling skills earned a man an opportunity to ascend the societal hierarchies, including recruitment by the leadership school at the king's court, qualification to join the standing army, the *batongole,* and deployment as a chief or administrator. There were regular clan wrestling competitions attended by the king and his chiefs. By the 1500s, wrestling had played an important role in establishing socio-political order by creating harmony, unity and peace among the various clans in the kingdom (Roscoe 1914).

2.2 The missionary era

When the missionaries first arrived in Buganda towards the end of the 19th century, the practices of traditional sports such as wrestling and others were criticized and the sport was regarded as ruthless and barbaric (see Alegi 2010).

It was against this background that the missionaries sought to introduce modern sports as a form of "civilization", thus shaping the missionary political intention through intervention in sports education (similar developments in colo-

---

[1] While many of the known pre-colonial sport activities included only boys, some games for girls also existed. The active participation of girls was restricted especially with regard to their age and ended when they reached womanhood. A more nuanced picture of gender issues with regard to pre-colonial sports education will require more research.
[2] There are five historic and contemporary kingdoms in the territory of Uganda.
[3] We would like to thank the anonymous reviewer for highlighting this point.

nial sports education can be observed in other African countries, such as Nigeria and South Africa; see Akena forthcoming). Sports played an important role in enhancing gender identities and status in many pre-colonial African societies. With the introduction of modern sports (including football, netball, athletics, gymnastics among other modern sports), such practices were transformed by the various respective governmental regimes.

The end of the 19th century, with internal conflicts and wars, as well as the growing influence of missionaries and British colonial ambitions, constituted quite an unstable era. A religious civil war broke out in Buganda, based on a conflict between the Protestant and Roman Catholic missionaries. This also led to rivalries between the various Christian-run schools, which were played out in sports competitions. The rivalries and sports competitions between Catholic and Protestant missionaries are deeply rooted in Uganda and can be traced back to the times of Kabaka Muteesa, who invited European teachers to Buganda (1875).

During this time, sports competitions between the various religious groups became battle grounds where the "proxy wars" between the various political factions were fought out. As the dominating religious schools (Catholic and Protestants) sought to extend their dominance, the rival schools (marginalized schools) sought to resist their subordinate positions through sports by adopting various strategies which up to the present day have been dismissed as sports hooliganism. These dynamics can be traced back to 1875, when Kabaka Muteesa invited European teachers to come to Uganda to teach new knowledge and new skills that would help his kingdom cope with the local situation and also to connect with European governments. So that he could defend Buganda more effectively against external invasion. His invitation attracted both Catholic and Protestant Christian missionaries. Although the teaching of the Protestants was in some ways similar to that of the Catholics, there was antagonism and conflict between them, to the extent that each missionary group established its own programs and school within the King's Courts. Each group sought to win the king's favor and extend its influence in the Buganda Kingdom through education and schooling.

2.3 The British colonial government and the King's College Budo riots

During colonial times, the mandate of the education system of the British Empire, to educate, construct and produce citizens, was placed in the hands of the various Christian missionary organizations who owned the schools. The British colonial government maintained direct control and supervision of the schools, but the actual implementation was done by the missionaries and it was them who adapted sports ideologies to the British colonial government's educational policy. It's worth noting that as sports education and its policy was used to indoctrinate and educate youth, sport events, and football in particular, at Kings College Budo, were used by students as platforms of expression and site under which resistance, linguistic manipulation and mobilization took place. For example Kabaka Muteesa II, the king of Buganda was a footballer and used football to mobilize his supporters.

During colonial times, there is also a record of resistance by students and staff of the King's College Budo (a school for educating the sons of chiefs and kings to become regional leaders under the British colonial government), who, in 1942, broke into unexpected school strikes and riots that brought the whole of Buganda Kingdom to a standstill, leading to the immediate closure of the school. The strike was a battle between the Buganda Kingdom and its allies (various students across the various ethnic groups) under the leadership of Kabaka Muteesa II on the one hand, and the British colonial government and the Protestant church under the leadership of Dennis Herbert, who was the headmaster of Budo at the time, on the other (see Summers 2006 for more details).

In 1942, the prefects, who had been influenced by the Christian morals and values of honesty, obedience and discipline, the basis on which they had attained their leadership positions, rebelled against the school administration. They sided with the Kabaka, who had questioned the authority of the colonial government and the school administration over the leadership roles and positions within the school context. The school system favored meritocracy and personal achievements in games and sports as the basis for rewarding students with leadership positions in school, as compared with the notion of inherited leadership in Buganda.

2.4 Independence era and the language education policy

Uganda became independent in 1962. Since then the language policy has continued to focus on a monolingual education policy, prioritizing English over African languag (Nankindu, Kirunda and Ogavu 2015). While local African languages are used as a medium of instruction in primary schools, especially in the rural areas, secondary education relies on the use of the colonial language, English, which continues to constitute a variety with high prestige and is a necessary asset in career opportunities (see ibid.). The authors state: "[. . .] the hegemony of English comes out very strongly from the Government White Paper on education [1992] as shown above. The seed of this ideology was planted in the colonial period" (ibid.: 191).

Moreover, it is worth noting that with the introduction of the 1963 Education Act, the state took away the ownership and the responsibility of managing and governing schools from the religious and cultural institutions who had founded and owned them. Moreover, during the early independence era, the conflicts between the Buganda kingdom and the central government were also partly played out in school sports competitions, particularly in the Buganda Cup of 1964, which resulted in the so-called Buganda Cup tragedy in which twelve students of St. Mary's College Kisubi lost their lives on their way back home after winning the cup.[4] Table 9.1 summarizes the history of sports education in Uganda in the context of the country's history.

Table 9.1: Sports education in Uganda (Akena forthcoming).

Year	Sports and Education Landmarks	Political Change Landmarks	Governmental Era
2030			
2020			
2010	Compulsory Physical Education		Current Government
2000	Universal Secondary Education	2005 Election	
1990	Enactment of Physical education Policy	2000 Election 1995 Uganda Constitution 1986 Coup d'Etat	
1980	Government White paper		
1970	Political Education	1971 Coup d'Etat	
1960	Enactment of 1964 Education Act	1966 Buganda Crisis	Independent Uganda
1950	Kings College Budo Riots	1963 Referendum	
1940	Introduction of Gils Education		
1930	British Education Policy		British Government
1920			
1910			
1900		1900 Buganda Agreement	

---

4 A truck which was transporting the students back to St. Mary's College Kisubi after the Cup was hit by a military truck. The truck overturned and 12 students lost their lives in this tragic accident. As the incident occured in a heated political climate between the central government and the Buganda Kingdom, some accounts say that the jubilant students had been mistaken for pro-Buganda agitators and therefore met by the military on purpose; see [https://observer.ug/features-sp-2084439083/57-feature/34942-50-years-later-kisubi-remembers-tragic-12] (accessed 20 June 2020).

Table 9.1 (continued)

Year	Sports and Education Landmarks	Political Change Landmarks	Governmental Era
1890	Introduction of Missionary Education	1890 Uganda British Protectorate	British Protectorate
1880		1886 Uganda Martyrs	
1870		1884 Religious war	Missionary Agencies
1860			
1850			
1840			
1830			
1820			
1810	Buganda Leadership School		Pre-Colonial
1800			Buganda Kingdom
1790	Life Skills Education linked to		
1780	sports and natural environment		
1770			

3 Resistance through youth language use in contemporary Uganda: Decolonial practices and epistemic disobedience

Songs, chants and anthems have always been an integral part of sports education in Uganda. Students have often made use of songs to express criticism and challenge the status quo through language manipulation and choice of songs. Songs in these contexts can be a way of expressing things that could not otherwise be said or communicated easily. For instance, in the 1990s, it was common for students of Makerere College to sing the Buganda anthem during sports competitions, although the kingdom had not yet been reinstated (this happened at a time when it was still illegal to sing the anthem). The students usually sang the first stanza and reworded it accordingly (see below). While the students celebrated their own school's houses[5] rather than the kings and chiefs of Buganda, the use of the anthem itself constitutes an act of resistance to the government, which had

---

5 The "schools" comprise "houses of residence" as part of their organizational structure, to which the students belong.

abolished the kingdoms in 1967 and reinstated them in 1993 (except for Ankole, but now including Rwenzururu).

Buganda Anthem (with author's rough translation)

Original version	**Students' version**
Twessimye nnyo x 2	*Twessimye nnyo* x 2
('We are blessed')	
Olwa Buganda yaffe	*Olwa Muteesa [Lumumba, Kabalega] waffe*
('For our kingdom Buganda')	
Ekitiibwa kya Buganda kyava dda	*Ekitiibwa kya Mutesa [Lumumba, Kabalega] kyava dda*
('The pride of Buganda dates back in time')	
Naffe tukikuumenga	*Naffe tukikuumenga*
('Let us preserve it')	

It is vital to note that youth language manipulation took many forms depending on the context, school location, and language. For example, at Makerere University the Buganda anthem was manipulated according to the university environment. One example is the famous *Gongom* anthem sung by Lumumba Hall residents. Here, language is manipulated to praise the *Gongom* statute which is Lumumba Hall's symbol and represents the hall "Lumumba" itself. This shows that the practice of manipulating songs and anthems in the context of sports education in schools is very common and versatile as it reveals different local contextualizations in various parts of the country.

The space for the resistance practices is in fact provided within the official regulations of sports education, though the students use it in subversive ways. The Ministry of Education and Sports directive, as well as the rules regarding the organisation of sports events, indicate that songs and music are part of sports education. However, during sports events, schools and sports education administrators are cautioned to play the "right" music and songs. Yet within the same events, students have gone on to create their own music and songs, which express their interests but also contest the rules of school and state. Here, music constitutes a space for creativity and subversion. Johnston's (2005) study on mobilization, resistance and repression is relevant in understanding the political articulation of sports. Johnston suggests that soccer matches, in which uncommonly intense crowd enthusiasm, chants and songs (including prohibited ones) occur, impart a clear message to the authorities that something beyond fans supporting their teams is going on. Students and activists may use symbolic songs and anthems in articulating their (political) statements, attitudes and positions through sports (Johnston 2005: 127–128). The political grievances between the state and cultural institution (the kingdom) were often negotiated through sports and in school. Students from the various cultural institutions held their campaigns in schools, and used sports events, songs and anthems to assert their positions and reclaim their cultural identity.

Following the Buganda Cup crisis of 1964, schools and students adopted the use of sports houses as spaces in which to preserve their cultural identity but also to protest against the state. Schools across the various regions of Uganda, which were opposed to the state, adopted the names of the traditional and religious leaders (who had been abolished) as a means of protest and resistance, and used the house structure of the schools as a means of preserving cultural values and memories. Johnston (2005) provides insights into understanding how opposition groups accomplished their political interests in repressive regimes. He suggests that under repressive regimes, an opposition accomplishes important cultural work in free spaces, reframing what is possible, defining collective identities, articulating grievances, preserving oppositional norms and values, but also reshaping mobilization structures through network bridging and network extension. The names of the houses appeared as a free space for the opposition to use to preserve its values. Mr. Mugisha, the former sports teacher of Makerere College, said in an interview that the names of houses were not only symbolic but that they played a key role in preserving the cultural identity of school and students during that period, especially after the kingdoms were abolished in 1967. The case of students of Makerere College School in the 1990s demonstrates how the students and the school used sports events to protest and campaign for the restoration of cultural institutions (the kingdoms).

Another example of a subversive practice is the manipulation of the Lord's Prayer, which is known as the "Ngonian Rugby Prayer", recorded in 2014 at a Rugby competition between two rival schools, Namilyago College and St. Mary College Kisubi. Their positions go back to the colonial era when schools were divided along lines of religion (Tyler 1989). Despite the fact that both schools were Catholic, they belonged to two different Roman Catholic factions. Namilyago College was founded by the Mill Hill Fathers and St. Mary College Kisubi was founded by the Italian missionaries (White Fathers). Since the schools are deeply rooted in missionary activities and ritual practices, based on Christian norms and values that have developed during the missionary and colonial eras in Uganda, a manipulation of this well-known and highly emblematic Christian prayer can be regarded a violation of the established norm. Communal prayer and the use of the Lord's Prayer was a ritual practice established during colonialism at Namilyago College and at many other Christian schools in Uganda. A manipulation of this Christian-colonial ritual would be expected to be strongly reprimanded. However, school sports seem to constitute a special space in which the expression of thoughts and manipulation of norms is acceptable. Listening to the way the language and message of the prayer was manipulated by the students, there is a strong link to control, power relations, domination and resistance that cut across different levels, for example between the schools involved, between the students and the school administration and between students of both schools:

Ngonian Rugby Prayer
"Our players, who art on pitch,
Allowed be your strength,
Thy victory come.
May your anger be displayed onto your opponents,
As it is shown on the weevils!
Give us a broken jaw,
Forgive them not for their would be side steps,
But plant them to the glory of thy merciless cries of the true Ngonian.
For thy broken jaws, experienced and injured souls
Forever and ever
Remain victims of thy power of the mighty Ngonian."

The Ngonian Rugby Prayer follows the structure of The Lord's Prayer and often uses the same verbs or verbal semantics. It replaces metaphors and requests for forgiveness, kindness and provision, with anger, mercilessness and brutality. The prayer not only reflects a linguistic violation of one of the classical holy texts, but also a manipulation that breaks with Christian values and promotes rivalry. It also plays with (the continuations of) linguistic colonialism. It's worth mentioning that the manipulation of the Lord's Prayer exists in many forms and in different schools as well as in the various languages including Luganda, Lusoga, Runyankore, among others. Besides the Lord's Prayer, school songs, school anthems have been manipulated and songs of victory, war songs but also songs of amusement have been adapted, and new ones were composed by students to express their position and interests in different school contexts. Although we discuss only two examples here, the existence of many other forms of linguistic manipulative practices in these contexts encourages more research in this field.

As outlined in this chapter, the norms of sports education and the school system have been produced by the joint missionary-colonial project and their "mission" to create a modern education system based on Eurocentric paradigms. In fact, missionary schools and the colonial government and politics transformed the Ugandan education system and set linguistic norms that still impact education in the country to the present day. They also created tension between different schools, groups and regions of the country. One context in which that became manifest is rivalry in school sports. Given the missionary-colonial basis of the educational ideologies and practices in the schools, the youth's appropriation and manipulation of expressive forms can be regarded as a form of *epistemic disobedience* in this regard (Mignolo 2011: 45). Based on the writings of Quijano, *epistemic disobedience* is a necessary step of extrication from coloniality and modernism and its system of power. Mignolo writes:

> Epistemic disobedience leads us to decolonial options as a set of projects that have in common the effects *experienced* by all the inhabitants of the globe that were at the receiving end of global designs to colonize the economy (appropriation of land and natural resources), authority (management by the Monarch, the State, or the Church), and police and military enforcement (coloniality of power), to colonize knowledges (languages, categories of thoughts, belief systems, etc.) and beings (subjectivity). (Mignolo 2011: 45)

This perspective seems suitable on two levels: the youth challenge the established educational norm that represents the missionary-colonial project in Uganda by using an illegal anthem that invokes a pre-colonial political system[6] that symbolizes cultural identity. This counter-discourse and conscious identity construction can be regarded as a decolonial option in the sense of Mignolo. Following the ideas of post-colonial thinkers, the subversive practices of Ugandan youth, their ways with dealing with English and their colonial linguistic heritage, can be regarded as a way of "speaking back" (in analogy to "writing back") which is regarded as "an effective means of escaping from the binary polarities implicit in manichean constructions of colonization and its practices" (Ashcroft, Griffith and Tiffin 1995: 10). Here, young people seize the options not to follow the colonial linguistic norms and to break the chain of linguistic obedience.

In this regard, by manipulating linguistic norms, even in a Christian prayer, the youth engage in an act of emancipation and voice their own interests. This can also be regarded as a way of dealing with their colonial linguistic heritage. Sugirtharajah (2012), who investigates post-colonial Biblical Studies and sheds light on resistance and speaking back practices in the contexts of imperial Christianity and Bible translations, makes a similar observation, by showing how various colonized people resisted imperializing Christianity by creating their own adaptations and translations of the Bible (Sugirtharajah 2012: 71).

---

6 Which was, though upheld, used by the colonial government to impose its own colonial politics through the Ugandan kingdoms.

4 Conclusion and outlook

Sports events and sports education seem to open up a third space for the students in which they can negotiate power relations, political interests and identity. The relationship between youth language practices and colonial linguistic legacies, the subversive and creative ways in which adolescents deal with colonial languages and play with the attitudes and ideologies attached to them, constitutes a large field, with many more aspects to research in the future. This contribution is a first attempt to see the language use and manipulation of Ugandan students as a form of decolonial intervention, and to present a fresh perspective on Ugandan youth language practices and the sports education system in the historical context. Moreover, it also shifts the focus in research on African youth language practices to the ways in which youth deal with their European colonial linguistic heritage. Investigating what happens with colonial languages like English, French, Spanish, Portuguese and others has mainly been studied through post-colonial linguistic approaches or in the field of Creole studies, often with a focus on agency and language contact (see for instance Faraclas 2012, Hollington 2015, Anchimbe & Mforteh 2011, Schneider 2007). On the other hand, studies on youth language practices in Africa have often focused on "indigenous" African languages rather than on colonial European languages. This contribution may therefore pave the way for a decolonial youth language perspective that looks at (linguistic) subversion and agency with regard to young people's ways of dealing with colonial language. More studies in these contexts could reveal how (young) people use conscious language practices as a means of empowerment. As hinted at, in Uganda alone there are many other related practices of subversion and resistance to be found in the linguistic manipulation of students who express their discomfort with the (aftermath of) the missionary-colonial education system. While the context of sport education is a very fruitful one where many other insights could be gained (e.g. in different sports, and beyond schools in other sport contexts), there are also many other domains and contexts in which the intersection between youth language practices and colonial and decolonial language can yield new and challenging results, for instance in music, activism (such as Black Lives Matter), formal education (e.g. colonial curricula) and many other areas.

References

Akena, Dennis. forthcoming. *Sports education politics and practices in Uganda 1500–2020. Ideologies, interests and strategies of Key Actors.* Cologne: University of Cologne dissertation.

Alegi, Peter. 2010. *African soccerscapes. How a continent changed the world's game.* Ohio: Ohio University Press.

Anchimbe, Eric A. and Stephen A. Mforteh (eds.). 2011. *Postcolonial linguistic voices. Identity choices and representations.* Berlin: De Gruyter Mouton.

Ashcroft, Bill, Gareth Griffith and Helen Tiffin. 1995. Introduction to part one. In Bill Ashcroft, Gareth Griffith and Helen Tiffin (eds.), *The post-colonial studies reader,* 9–13. London and New York: Routledge.

Johnston, Hank 2005. Talking the walk: Speech acts and resistance in authoritarian regimes. In Christian Davenport, Hank Johnston and Carol Mueller (eds.). *Repression and mobilization,* 108–137. Minneapolis: University of Minnesota Press.

Mignolo, Walter D. 2011. Epistemic disobedience and the decolonial option: A manifesto. *Transmodernity* 1 (2). 44–66.

Ministry of Education and Sports. 2009. *Proposal for sports for development.* Government of Uganda.

Nankindu, Prosperous. 2014. *Language in education policy and literacy acquisition in multilingual Uganda: A case study of the urban district of Kampala.* Cape Town: University of the Western Cape dissertation.

Nankindu, Prosperous, Rebecca F. Kirunda and Tutus Ogavu. 2015. Language in education in Uganda: The policy, the actors and the practices. A case of the urban district of Kampala. *Paripex – Indian Journal of Research* 4 (5). 190–193.

Roscoe, John. 1911. *The Buganda. An account of their native costums and beliefs.* London: MacMillan & Co.

Schneider, Edgar W. 2007. *Postcolonial English. Varieties around the world.* Cambridge: Cambridge University Press.

Sugirtharajah, Rasiah S. 2012. *Exploring postcolonial biblical criticism. History, method, practice.* Malden and Oxford: Wiley-Blackwell.

Summers, Carol. 2006. 'Subterranean evil' and 'Tumultuous riot' in Buganda: Authority and alienation at King's College, Budo, 1942. *Journal of African History* 47 (1). 93–113.

Eyo O. Mensah

10 "Whenever I smoke, I see myself in Paradise": The discourse of tobacco consumption among rural youth in Nigeria

Among rural male youth in Southern Cross River State, South-eastern Nigeria, smoking behaviour is an essential everyday cultural practice and part of a way of life. Smoking is an important form of sociability that signals "self-liberation" and proper manhood in their social universe. They use this practice to construct and command new social sites for creative agency and positioning. This article examines the social and cultural aspects of smoking ritual among these youth by analysing subjective narratives and locally constitutive ideologies enacted in their discourse of smoking such as articulating various dimensions of masculinity, using acts of smoking to enact different identities, and relating smoking prevalence to the experience of duress and lifestyle factors. The study is rooted in the community of practice framework, a sociolinguistic tool that is concerned with a group of people who come together around mutual engagement, shared passion and jointly negotiated enterprise. The study adopts an ethnographic linguistic approach, focusing on participant observation, focus group, semi-structured interviews and metalinguistic conversations. The results show that young men utilise smoking culture and its accompanying linguistic codes as forms of style that enable them to articulate other male-centred subcultural capital in their rural space and to connect with urban identity and modernity. I consider the implications of the study for global perspectives on youth language and tobacco control, especially the demarketing of tobacco products in Nigeria.

Acknowledgements: I wish to thank two anonymous reviewers for contributing ideas and perspectives that really strengthened the argument of this paper. I thank all the participants in this study, especially Effiom Bassey and Offiong Edem for acting as liaisons between the researcher and the participants in the study areas. I am equally grateful to Idorenyin Attah for interviewing and recording assistance and Crystal Mensah for referencing assistance. The remaining errors are mine.

Eyo O. Mensah, University of Calabar, e-mail: eyomensah2004@yahoo.com

1 Introduction

In 2018, the Federal Government of Nigeria announced a new tax regime for tobacco products in order to check their abuse, prevent their smuggling into the country, seek innovative ways of mobilising revenues, and promote the campaign against tobacco by implementing the World Health Organization's (WHO) Framework Convention for Tobacco Control. One of the consequences of the new tax policy was the increase in a unit cost of a packet of cigarette from N60 (16¢) to about N250 (65¢), which is believed to have had a marginal positive impact on public health and a larger impact on government revenue (Akanonu et al. 2018). Evidently, the new tax regime for tobacco products was primarily intended to boost government revenue. It corroborates the claim by Nichter and Cartwright (1991) that tobacco is an appealing cash crop and an immediate source of tax revenue and profit to First and Third World governments, who surreptitiously support the tobacco industry even while speaking publicly in favour of antismoking initiatives. In spite of this new law and several warnings on packets of cigarette such as "smokers are liable to die young", "smoking is dangerous to your health", and "smoking causes lung cancer, heart disease, emphysema and may complicate pregnancy", not much has changed in terms of tobacco consumption or the demarketing of its products in the community of practice in which this study is situated.

In some rural contexts in Nigeria, tobacco is an essential commodity, and its consumption has varying cultural meanings and involves a set of learned, patterned social behaviour (Marshall 2008). Smoking, as part of a social lifestyle, is embedded in the socio-cultural fabric of everyday life. It is a form of pleasure, leisure and relaxation that conveys different connotations for different people. Smoking is a social behaviour and a source of leisure that is associated with relational and symbolic benefits (Pourtau et al. 2019), and smoking behaviour is used to negotiate identity, foster group integration and enhance solidarity within the community of smokers. It can also be adopted as a resistance identity to reinforce anti-establishment behaviour (Mensah 2012, 2016). Haines et al. (2009) describe smoking as a collective social practice given that it offers smokers the benefits of belonging to a micro- or isolated group within a larger network of people (non-smokers) where a specific type of sociability can be fostered. Most contemporary research on smoking and tobacco consumption in Nigeria has been concerned with socio-cultural influences and medical risks (Egbe et al. 2014), and others are concerned with use, prevalence and perception (Oyewole et al. 2018, Gana et al. 2018). For some researchers, antismoking campaigns and interventions are their primary focus (Egbe et al. 2016) and the impact of gender is the target of other works (Egbe et al. 2017). Little is known about the socio-cultural influences of tobacco on young people's lives, especially in the rural setting where smokers deploy language to reinscribe situated agency and identity. The present study aims to fill this gap.

In this study, I examine the phenomenon of youth smoking and/or tobacco consumption from more nuanced social and cultural perspectives, taking into account the social functions of smoking, the motivations, and the subjective discourses associated with this practice. I also investigate the locally-framed ideologies and specialised slanguage and metaphor that are linked with established smoking traditions. The study aims to highlight the importance of smoking behaviour as a less studied youth subculture, particularly in the rural sociolinguistic domain, where the act of smoking can manipulate social relations among smokers and fellow smokers on the one hand, and with the non-smoking others on the other hand. The study is based conceptually on the community of practice theory "which has proved to be a robust framework for the investigation of language in use" (King 2014: 62). The theory is concerned with the discursive practice of a group of people who have come together to share common interests and goals (Lave and Wenger 1991). Such a community shares a common passion, experience and concerns around which participation is organised and meaning negotiated. In the context of the present study, rural youth who share common traits such as gender, sexual identity, and marginalised social status participate in smoking as a social activity that adds "value" to their social life in terms of knowledge sharing and mutual interests. This smoking experience also contributes to defining their enterprise and social identity. It is, however, imperative to note that smoking is not the only social activity that indexes group belonging among participants in this study. Drinking culture, music/dance, dress codes and local sports, especially wrestling and football, are other markers of social identity. Among girls and young women, membership in friendship groups and engagement in church activities are important sources of socialisation and belonging. I aim to increase our understanding of complex socio-cultural practices that merge with youth agency, social exclusion and inequality in situated rural spaces, and explore the symbolically constructed meanings within these interactions that are attributed to the smoking ritual. Smoking behaviour is embedded in a broader context in this community of practice. It is a highly central practice in expressing and strengthening the sense of togetherness, belonging, pride, and masculinity.

2 The socio-cultural context of smoking among Nigerian youth

Smoking is an essential socialising tool for young people in Africa and beyond, especially in the rural context where tobacco consumption is weaved into the cultural fabric of society. A part of this acceptance or normalisation of smoking is its reconstruction as a healthy activity. Egbe et al. (2017) report that tobacco products are essential requirements in some traditional ceremonies (marriage, rite of passage, purchase of land or other property) in Nigeria, in order to strengthen the identity (of men) that is associated with smoking. Some rural farmers and traders depend on tobacco for survival, and for maintaining their local economy. They cultivate tobacco, process its leaves into snuff and cigars, distribute and market these products to eke out a living. The prevalence of smoking has also been reported among young people in and out of schools, with significantly low risk perception of its inherent danger to smokers' health and well-being. According to Oyeniran et al. (2019), smoking is a disturbing health-threatening behaviour among students in tertiary institutions of learning in Nigeria, and there is an urgent need to establish intervention and health awareness campaigns. Gana et al. (2018) maintain that cigarette smoking is on the increase among out of school adolescents in Nigeria and that the trend needs to be swiftly arrested. Many studies (Oyewole et al. 2018, Egbe et al. 2017) have reported that smoking prevalence was higher among males than females in southern Nigeria. This claim resonates with an essential observation in this study, which clearly views engagement with smoking as a male domain contrary to the scenario in developed countries with decreasing smoking rates among men and increasing rates among women (Flandorfer et al. 2010).

In certain gatherings, like evening parties and other activities, smoking is a common social ritual among young people. They use such events to delineate their social space, bond and reaffirm friendship. Partying may also be used to depict the notion of "enjoyment" or the "good life", which involves celebrating with cigarettes, alcohol and women. Demant and Ostergaard (2007) argue that the social logic of a party is to consume alcohol (and cigarettes) collectively as it symbolises commitment to both the party and to a specific group of friends. Such outings provide outlets to connect, communicate and socialise, and offer strong reasons for smoking. During important celebrations like Christmas, New Year, and other festival periods, young people naturally have reasons to smoke. These events are usually heralded by activities such as dancing, music, masquerading, and feasting (food, alcohol and tobacco), and provide platforms for "maximised social, political and religious interactions for cultural and philosophical manifestations" (Nzewi 1979: 168). It is during such occasions that the people's culture is recreated, and communal solidarity regenerated. Based on these accounts, smoking, in the rural context in focus, is a way of life and plays a central role in everyday cultural practices of young men irrespective of their social disadvantage and poor economic status. By the very act of smoking, identity is discursively constructed and different modes of belonging negotiated. Meaning is framed in relation to the experience of smoking, which ultimately has become a symbolic resource for the cultural reproduction of otherness. Consequently, microinteractional discourses involving smoking can lead to a better understanding of the construction and maintenance of solidarity, friendship and social bonding. Slang, metaphors and sociolect are used stylistically to index group ideology and give meaning to young people's social experiences.

3 Methods, setting, data and participants

This study is based on six months of qualitative ethnographic fieldwork in two districts of the Southern Cross River State of southeastern Nigeria, namely Ikot Ekriba (Akpabuyo) and Esighi (Bakassi). I collected data ethnographically, using focus groups, participant observation and personal interviews. Fifteen young men within the age range of 20–32 were purposively selected for the study in each of the areas. A total of 30 male youth were consulted for the research because, in this community of practice, smoking lies predominantly in the social domain of male youth. Two field assistants, who also acted as the liaison between the researcher and the participants, selected the participants in their respective areas. The primary criteria for selection were first and foremost the participants' willingness to participate in the study, their involvement as smokers, and their familiarity with the social utility and discourses of smoking. Participants were classified into heavy smokers and light smokers, and members of the two categories were familiar with slanguage associated with smoking. I recorded the metadata and socio-biographical profiles of each participant such as name (pseudonym as used in the text), gender, age, job status, income, religion, educational status and marital status. Three participants lived in the rural area but worked in the city. The dominant language spoken in the study area is Efik, but participants' linguistic repertoires also include Nigerian Pidgin and another specially invented language (a mixture of slang, metaphors and sociolect) that is used to foster group membership, negotiate boundaries and enforce social inclusion and exclusion. Some of the demographic characteristics of participants were useful in defining agency in tobacco consumption and in influencing consumption rate. The study was approved by the ethics committee of the University of Calabar, and participants gave informed consent for all interviews and recordings. Two focus group panels were also conducted, involving a group of ten participants in each of the areas. The interviews and discussions were guided and controlled by the researcher based on open-ended questions. This approach enabled the researcher to elicit detailed information on the participants' subjective narratives on smoking experience. It also provided participants the platform to offer insights on the slang and metaphors they used in describing smoking-related experiences. They shared their opinions, ideas and perspectives on some of their motivations for smoking. This collaboration also allowed participants to share their experiences, reactions and perceptions freely about the kinds of situations they faced that prompted consumption of tobacco. I also sought to know how smoking culture is used to create social space, construct identities and engage different modes of belonging.

Participant observation enabled the researcher to gain insights into the participants' community of practice first by establishing the relevant rapport and close bond and being integrated as a group member. From this vantage position, the researcher gained detailed knowledge of their local situations and practices that were related to smoking, and observed how they interrelate socially and conceptualise values, meanings, and viewpoints about cigarettes, *kanja* and marijuana. The researcher joined the participants in many social gatherings where cigarettes were smoked, and probed further. He sought to understand the beliefs and ideologies in relation to smoking through local history and culture in addition to these field observations. Generally, the researcher got used to their way of life with smoking, while also engaging participants in personal semi-structured interviews and metalinguistic conversations. These approaches afforded him the opportunity to interact with the participants in order to dig deeper into their personal experiences with smoking and related norms, and to gain other contextual information that could not be brought to light through the other modes of enquiry. The researcher asked questions about participants' individual history of smoking, the frequency of smoking, the influence of smoking habits on their lifestyle, and their attitude towards smoking. The researcher also probed into what they smoked (cigars, cigarettes, marijuana or locally prepared grass called *kanja*) and the types or brands of cigarette that were their favourite. I asked questions about the nature of their characteristic smoking behaviour. This approach also helped me to capture non-verbal cues, emotions and gestures, which featured prominently in the course of the interaction with participants. I also engaged participants to understand their perceptions and attitudes towards smoking, and how the act of smoking challenges or conforms to their stereotyped norms and social conventions.

Data were coded into relevant categorial frames and themed. Interviews, focus group discussions and field notes were transcribed verbatim and subsequently checked for accuracy. The coding and categorisation processes involved an identification of the different tropes that emerged from the data and the relationship between them. Labels and numbers were assigned to recurring themes for easy organisation. The scope of the relevant data was limited to smoking-related discourses involving slang, metaphors and sociolect. The descriptive approach has been adopted in data analysis, interpretation and discussion. It is aimed to interpret the main features of the data and to offer in-depth explanations based on insights into participants' views, actions and perceptions of the phenomenon of tobacco consumption.

4 Results

In the analysis and discussion that follow, I categorise the discourse of smoking among rural youth into five interrelated themes. These include social motivations for smoking, smoking as a resource of masculinity, as a source of modernity, as a form of emotional relief, and the specialised slanguage of smoking. I analyse each of these sub-themes in greater detail.

4.1 Social motivations for smoking

Smoking initiation is a mark of independence that enables young people to take the position of leadership or responsibility that is required of a man. In the community of practice where this study is situated, smoking is regarded by young people as a rite of passage, which marks the transition from adolescence to manhood. When a young man begins smoking, it is a mark of self-liberation from parental influence and control. Attaining the status of a "real man" entails not just freedom from parental control; it is the ability to grow into a person one feels authentically fits his social path. This ability also entails being economically empowered to assume responsibilities such as fending for oneself and supporting one's family. A participant emphasised the point further during the interview session as follows:

> When a *guy* [young man] starts smoking in this village, it shows that he's no longer feeding from his parents' pots, indicating that he has come of age and can take care of himself as a man. You see, smoking initiation comes with a sense of responsibility [laughing].
>
> (Effiom, 25)

This evidence details the fact that smoking confers autonomy and a transition to "real manhood", which comes with some degree of responsibility and which young men genuinely struggle to define and honestly claim (Pickhardt 1993). It makes one become his own governing authority and entails the freedom to interpret one's own actions and experiences. This liberty is essential for social progress and promotes a sense of individuality, which is essential for the cultivation of the self. This expression of autonomy and enforcement of individuality are not matters of parental approval. The concept of "real manhood", which can also be marked by one's initiation into cigarette smoking, therefore, is all about owning oneself and being able to live as a responsible member of the society. Another participant (Effiong, 32) remarked that smoking initiation also signals one's desire to be in the driver's seat in one's life, that is, to reposition one's self to shoulder responsibilities towards oneself, one's family and community members. A primary component of this transition to manhood includes one's ability to acquire farmland, a fishing net, a boat or a gun to show one's level of preparedness to begin an occupation in farming, fishing or hunting. Ultimately, it also entails one's intention to marry as soon as possible in order to begin one's own family as a mark of accomplishment and a passage into a new phase of life. Participants' comments reveal that young people want to feel special and different through the use of cigarettes in order to categorize themselves as increasingly independent in their social world.

Based on the focus group interactions, the study also found that smoking is mainly used to reinforce identity and to enact belonging. In this way, it is an important form of bonding among rural youth. It promotes friendship and creates a network of smokers who are united by a common positive sense of belonging (Pourtau et al. 2019). Non-smokers are usually labelled and stigmatised in certain social circles. Participants generally believe that young people who do not smoke are children, women or left-handed. This stereotyped perception tends to be responsible for their social exclusion of non-smokers in certain gatherings within their local community. When a participant was asked to expatiate on this point in the focus discussion, he stated as follows:

> *Chairman* [Researcher], *it makes sense to bass* [it is good to smoke cigarette] for brotherhood and community development. If you *no bass* [don't smoke] in this community, it means you never grow *na* [as you ought to know]. That is why we collect packets of *cigar* [cigarette] and football for the youth in any traditional event in this community from marriage, chieftaincy, burial and other shows. (Okon, 22)

This claim points to the fact that smoking enhances solidarity and fosters group solidarity, which participants described as "brotherhood". It unites them more firmly in executing community development initiatives for their people, and to establish the importance of smoking among the youthful population; they collect packets of cigarettes, ounces of tobacco and footballs from families that celebrate important events in their community. In this community of practice, it is the norm for any family which is celebrating an important event like a traditional marriage to set aside tobacco products, liquor, cash and other items for young men in the community. The belief is that they are crucial stakeholders in the socio-political affairs of the community and deserve a recognition. This practice is one of the ways in which tobacco and alcohol consumption are socially and culturally endorsed. The construction of identity with smoking has a penetrating pattern of sociability in a variety of ways: It helps smokers to gain social space and share male-centred subjectivities. Smoking is an important aspect of young people's transformational pathways and is used for cementing inter and intra-group bonds of conviviality (Black 1984, Russell 2019). This conviviality is clearly demonstrated with the concept of *show love* in which a group member who is broke can be sustained with sticks/packets of cigarettes by other group members until he is able to recover financially and may also extend the goodwill to others. A participant (Eteyen, 28) said that *show love* could also entail lighting a cigarette and sharing with one or more group members within a particular social circle. This account further reveals that tobacco plays an important role in development and maintenance of social relationships and cooperation (Roulette et al. 2016). Smoking behaviour in this community of practice is not categorised as a form of deviance or a source of "slow death" in spite of its attendant high health risk; it is widely accepted as a normative behaviour among young people.

4.2 Smoking as a resource for the performance of masculinity

Young men's smoking behaviour is correlated with their performance of stereotyped gender roles and the negotiation of gendered and other intersecting identities. In fact, smoking has become a masculinised activity. Women in this community of practice do not smoke, although they have other means of consuming tobacco, especially through snuffing. Masculinity describes the way men behave in order to assert or define their manliness. Among the participants, there is a pre-conceived notion that links smoking behaviour to the performance of masculinity, which is connected to the image of toughness, competitiveness and dominance (Mensah 2017, 2020, 2021). Since smoking is the "stuff of men", it has become a source of gendered social identity that confers genuine masculine personalities on smokers. Non-smokers are regarded by smokers as children or women, which carries a connotation of powerlessness or weakness, and a position of subordination and submissiveness based on the prevailing gender stereotype. Participants enact masculinity in the discourse of smoking in many ways. Smoking is believed to be a source of physical strength. Some participants averred that smoking has been an energy booster to them during farm work, from clearing farmland to cultivation and harvesting. A participant corroborated the views of others during the focus group interaction as follows:

> Whenever I need to work on my farm, I smoke about six sticks of *cigar* [cigarette] and a rap of *Igbo* [marijuana]. I'll start with the *Igbo* [marijuana] and three sticks, intermittently, then, I'll take the other sticks. *Bros* [Brother], I'll work like a jackass. I can do the work of four men in a day.
> (Eteka, 27)

Another participant (Abasi Udo, 25) further admitted that he gained a lot of stamina from smoking whenever he had physically demanding manual labour to do. The demonstration of physical strength is a stereotyped gender identity that is associated with men, given their daily engagements with activities that are sources of their economic empowerment such as fishing, hunting, blacksmithing and farming, and given their roles as breadwinners in their various families. In this context, masculinity is defined and shaped by smoking practices.

Another way in which many participants assert masculinity through smoking rituals was the rejection of association with feminine attributes. Smoking is a key presence in social gatherings and interactions involving group members. Masculinity is the unspoken requirement in such social circles. Certain brands of cigarettes are labelled "womanish" or "feminine" because they are believed to have lighter taste, and young men are "naturally" not expected to identify with such brands in order to save face in the midst of the social others (Zhoa and Davey 2015). Participants argued that "real men" affiliate with fine filter and strong taste, which makes a whole lot of difference. There is a pattern of holding the cigarette (with the thumb and index finger) that can be described as feminine or crude. Participants argued that real smokers hold the cigarette in-between the index finger and the middle finger. This pattern, according to them, exudes masculine confidence and projects the smoker as an authoritative paternal figure. A participant explained the concept more clearly in the course of informal conversation as follows:

> It is women in Nollywood [Nigeria's home movie industry] who hide cigarettes from their husbands that hold it like this [with thumb and index finger]. The real *mafias* [smokers] put it here [in-between index finger and middle finger] to show you the stuff they are made of.
> (Ekpatuka, 30)

Further evidence of performance of masculinity is one's ability to inhale the fume deeply and exhale it through the nose with a sustained release of the smoke. Such a style is believed to consolidate smokers' experience as old smokers. Participants also argue that real men smoke up to half a packet of cigarettes a day. This reveals that masculinity could be enacted through various styles, patterns and degrees of smoking. Every participant tends to be aligned with manly character in smoking because it is believed to be a symbol of status and identity. In this way, different styles of smoking are gendered. This shows that, through smoking, one can be doing or undoing gender (Triandafilidis et al. 2017).

A regional group of participants also portrayed smoking rituals as a positive masculine trait with particular reference to their vigilante group, which is comprised of thirty-five youth who are all smokers. The vigilante groups guard and secure the villages at night against robbery, burglary and kidnapping activities. Participants maintained that smoking and vigilante work are manly activities and part of their gender role identity. When asked why all the vigilante members were smokers, the head of the group responded as follows:

> We didn't select ourselves. Each compound [household] contributed a member and it turned out that all strong men in this village are the smokers. We already know ourselves and with our identity as *bass men* [smokers], our tasks have been very easy. (Eyo Edem, 32)

This participant shows how the practice of smoking is used to reaffirm masculinity and generally maintain protective identity. Smoking is highly significant to participants in their everyday cultural activities, and there is a strong cultural norm that favours and promotes smoking. Therefore, smoking has become a source of cultural identity to rural youth. As a result of a strong acceptance and tolerance of smoking as a normalised part of culture in this community of practice, smoking is also a form of sexual attraction especially in projecting the image of idealised masculinity. As a result of smokers' propensity for hard work, they believed that they are more attractive, stronger and more desirable to young women than non-smokers. A participant justified this claim during an informal chat as follows:

> Every young woman needs a strong guy as a husband or *bobo* [boyfriend]. In this village, strong guys are those that *bass* [smoke], and we have enough *supplement* [strength]. It is people like us that can take them into extra time and make them to ask for more.
> (Iniko, 23, single)

Tinkler (2001: 120) describes this kind of attraction as "heterosexualisation of smoking" which is shaped by ideals of masculinity. Participants talked about the potency of tobacco as male sexual stimulant, which they called *supplement* and which sustains their erection for a longer time during sexual intercourse. This shows that they also associate tobacco with improved sexual health of smokers.

4.3 Smoking as a source of leisure and alignment with modernity

Many participants perceived their smoking behaviour as a source of leisure, pleasure and fun. Smoking is a way of articulating situated agency and sustaining a leisured lifestyle in their community of practice. Smoking is generally a social practice among the participants and is useful in social bonding and every other form of social engagement. Participants believed that smoking is cool and gives a pleasant and comforting feelings. On why he is projecting the image of a leisured smoker, a participant argued as follows:

> Smoking is not food to me as some of these old-fashioned guys are doing. It is merely a relaxed leisure experience to feel cool and encounter some happy moments. It is calming and takes you to this happy place where everything is okay. (Ita Udo, 28)

This participant acknowledged himself as a stylish smoker in opposition to "old-fashioned" smokers who find pleasure in consuming tobacco as an alternative to food without an awareness of its harmful health implications. This account further reveals that some participants engage in smoking as a pastime to create a bit of happiness for themselves irrespective of what is smoked. On why they feel that smoking was pleasurable, participants generally attributed the good feeling when smoking to the taste, smell, or sensation of smoking and the physical effect or neurochemistry of smoking. They contended that a combination of these factors creates a buzz of pleasure and energy. Participants also identified the periods of smoking when it is most pleasurable. Some said this is when smoking is combined with alcohol, others said it is when they smoke as a first thing in the morning, and to others, it is after every meal.

One set of participants utilised smoking as a symbol of modernity and a way of responding to social change. These are those with paid work as teachers in government-owned schools, clerks in health clinics, transporters, agricultural extension officers and local government workers. Other participants have affiliations with the city and showed interest in some urban youth subcultures associated with wearing sagged jeans and with stylish haircuts. This category of participants has exposure to urban life, although their educational level is low. They also have access to both social and conventional media through their mobile phones and other electronic devices. To this group of participants, smoking is a reflection of the reality of modern life, and as a result of their advantaged socio-economic status, they perceive smoking as a symbol of affluence and glamour. Based on their accounts, it is evident this category of smokers tends to be aware of the harmful effects of tobacco to health in spite of its normative acceptance in their community of practice, given the benefits of education and exposure to the media, especially smoking adverts and cessation campaigns.

4.4 Smoking as a form of emotional relief

A significant psychological factor in the smoking experience of the sampled population of rural youth was the use of smoking to either enhance good mood or relieve tension, stress and depression. Participants reported that they became conditioned to smoking when they were happy, excited or satisfied. To these young men, smoking enhances positive mood and pleasure. In this rural context, young men usually celebrate each other's achievements, like the acquisition of new property such as farmland, a bicycle, or a motorcycle, or even marrying a wife or having children. This act is commonly referred to as *washing*, which is a formal occasion to celebrate one's achievement. Alcoholic beverages and tobacco are freely consumed on such occasions. Participants believed that a combination of these stimulants reinforces their joy and excitement. When asked why he smoked so heavily during the *washing* of his motorcycle, a participant recounted as follows:

> *Oga* [Master], it has not been easy. I started this *journey* [saving for this project] many years ago. Today, I am very happy to have accomplished that dream. I am expressing my joy with the cigarettes. They're for cool relaxation and make my head to be calmer. (Nnasia, 26)

This account emphasises the fact that smoking is used to lift mood and express light-headedness that comes with a sense of achievement. In this way, smoking helps to modulate positive affect. Other participants reported a different kind of mood-relation with respect to their smoking experience. To these participants, smoking is used to escape stressful events and situations. It is a powerful tool that enables them in coping with physical pressure or emotional upset and in managing the rigours of daily life. Participants talked about smoking in this context as a source of relief from stress and tensions, and an escape from situations that produce trauma-related symptoms. A participant resorted to chain-smoking when he realised that his fishing nets were stolen at the sea bay. He explained his attitude and smoking behaviour during an interview session as follows:

> Whenever I smoke, I see myself in Paradise. Smoking is good for the body and the soul. It elevates my status and sends criminals after me. They are liars because nobody can stop *reggae* [my fishing business] and bring me to my knees. (Akanowo, 26)

Based on this account, the participant indulged in heavy smoking to push away distressing memories after a traumatic experience of losing his fishing nets. Smoking is therefore used to suppress difficult emotions like anger and frustration. It creates a feeling of temporary withdrawal and calmness in the wake of a depression. Another participant (Bassey Etim, 22) remarked that it is only the cigarette that can provide such emotional succour and relief to his friend at a difficult point in time. It was apparent that no consolation from anyone could fill the emotional gap or vacuum the participant (Akanowo) was experiencing at the moment.

4.5 The specialised language of smoking

Smoking is a unique social practice by participants who have evolved special vocabulary comprising sociolectal slang, and metaphors to capture their experience of tobacco and marijuana consumption. The linguistic resources are drawn from Nigerian Pidgin, English, Efik (language of the immediate environment), Igbo and other Nigerian languages. Nigerian Pidgin is the most efficient means of interethnic communication in Nigeria. The three major languages Hausa, Igbo and Yoruba serve as the regional lingua francae for the northern, eastern and western regions respectively. English is the official language in Nigeria, particularly with government circles, education and the media industries. A plethora of small languages spread across the length and breadth of the country serve domestic and localised functions in the areas where they are mainly spoken. Some of the smoking vocabulary include conventionalised terms or expressions, while other terms have been invented by the group and are peculiar to their community of practice. To smoke is to *bass* or to *meditate*. This reflects the belief by participants that smoking offers an opportunity to relax and think clearly. Marijuana is popularly called *wewe* (coined from *weed*), *grass* or *ikọñ ekpo* 'ghost's leave' and a combination of marijuana and a local gin (*ufọfọp*) is commonly called *combine*. Participants also have special names for the different brands of cigarettes they smoke, for example, St. Moritz (*Momo*), Benson and Hedges (*Benz*), Rothmans (*Blue label*), Chesterfield (*Big chest*) and Oris (*Pinky*), and brands that contain menthol are generally regarded as *ladies' cigarettes*.

One who smokes and gradually sustains the release of the fume through his nose is called *John Wayne*, after the famous Hollywood actor of the 1980s. This terminology reveals the influence of the movies on addictive smoking behaviour among young people. One that smokes and coughs consistently is called *inwañ* 'novice' (lit. 'farm'). The lexeme *nico* is a clipped form of *nicotine*. It has been contextualised by a participant (Okokon, 30) in the example below:

(1) *Nico   no   jell   for   this   bass.*   Nigerian Pidgin
    nicotine NEG   jell   PREP   DET   cigarette
    'Nicotine is not sufficient in this cigarette.'

A participant (Ekpri, 26) explained that insufficient nicotine is usually found in the brand of cigarette they call *ladies' brand*. He further maintained that *nico* is the thing that keeps them afloat and sustains their interest in smoking. According to him, "[i]t creates the sensation that takes one to the mountain top and back". This claim details the calming effect of nicotine as a sedative or stimulant. Participants also have a special register for law enforcement agents, especially the police who often comb their community of practice for drug offenders. The police are called *ukara* 'government' because, according to a participant (Togo, 32), "they represent the government which has declared marijuana cultivation, sale, distribution and consumption as illegal and a criminal offence". The police cell where offenders are usually kept after arrest is called *twang*, which is an onomatopoeic creation after the sounds of the iron bar door of the cell. A participant (Etete, 25) further contextualised some of these terms this way:

(2) *E-si-de-dibe   e-bass   ikon ekpo,   mmidihe*   Efik
    3PL-ASP-REDUP-hide   3PL-smoke   marijuana   CONJ
    ukara   e-mum   fi,   o-duk   twang.
    police   3PL-arrest PRO   3SG-enter cell
    'We usually hide to smoke marijuana, else if police arrest you, you'll find yourself in a cell.

A person who is suspected to be an informant to the police is called *alaba* 'one without a job'. Participants argued that it is only idle people that monitor who smokes or does not smoke (marijuana) to report to the police. Such people are not just labelled, they are often threatened. A policeman who is willing to *play ball* 'accept a bribe' and set his suspect(s) free is called a *guy man* but one that is uncompromising is labelled *aruba* or *eyen eku* 'son of a rat'. Young men who are non-smokers are stereotyped as women or children or *ufien* 'left-handed', which depict their oppositional stance to smoking. This stigmatisation is based on the perception of women as "weaker vessels", children as immature, and the cultural conceptualisation of left-handedness as signifying fruitlessness, unproductivity, lack of progress, darkness, and evil generally (Mensah et al. 2020).

Group members' specialised smoking vocabulary also involves the use of slang, which is a part of their inherent capacity for creativity to enliven their language and sustain their identity as smokers. Slang is sourced from cultural items and their engagement with other youth's subcultural capital, for example, interests in football, mobile telephone technology, dance and music. Cigar is *ike* 'power' and cigarette is *ikañ* 'fire'. These words are rooted in Igbo and Efik languages respectively. There are unique slang terms to define the multiple smoking identities of group members in this community of practice: A light or new smoker is called *ekpep* 'a learner', an old smoker is *okpo eset* 'old masquerade' and an ex-smoker is a *retired general*. Local grass that is rolled in paper and smoked is *kanja*, and when it is combined with marijuana, it is called *kanja-hemp*. This mixture is usually recommended for people with a "light brain" who cannot cope with the effect of marijuana while the plain *kanja* is usually meant for beginning smokers. I observed the following dialogue between two group members, which involved contextual slang as part of the smoking lexicon:

(3) Speaker A: *Chairman, abeg you fit lay me small pass?*
'Boss, can you pass me your cigarette?'
Speaker B: [smoking cigarette] *No be free kick be dis, Bros.*
'It is not a free cigarette, pal.'

The practice of passing one's lighted cigarette to another is reconceptualised as the *laying of a pass*, and such a gesture is often regarded as a "free kick" because the beneficiary does not need to part with any money. Based on interview responses, a *pass* could be either small or complete. A *small pass* requires the beneficiary to borrow, smoke a little and return the cigarette to its owner. A *complete pass*, on the other hand, does not get back to the donor. This is football register, which is popularised by participants' interest in football, especially the English Premier League (EPL), which is a strong source of socialisation for group members. This dialogue also shows that the concept of *show love* is relative and may not apply in all situations. A cursory examination of the structure of the dialogue also reveals power dynamics between the group members given the use of non-reciprocal address terms. *Chairman* ('boss') has a higher social scale as the man with power and influence than *Bros* ('pal'), the man who is limited economically. Further probing however attributes the low economic status of Speaker A to be responsible for the exaltation of Speaker B. Group members' use of contextual slang offers another way to understand their subjectivities about smoking and prevent non-smokers from understanding their linguistic repertoire.

Widely connected to the use of slang is the choice of metaphors in the smokers' vocabulary. Metaphors project operational knowledge about concrete phenomena and experiences onto a wide range of more abstract ones (Steen 2011). Metaphorical creativity allows group members access to coherent organisation of experience from a source domain to a target domain through a mapping process.

Participants draw metaphorical expressions from their cultural vocabulary from which they are adapted and integrated to their own specialised meaning. The prevalence of metaphors is illustrated in the following Nigerian Pidgin data recorded during an observation:

(4) Speaker A: *Bros, you carry stick der?*
'Pal, do you have any (stick of) cigarette with you there?'
Speaker B: *Bros, stick don finish, na ghost remain.*
'Pal, cigarettes have finished but I still have marijuana."
Speaker A: *Oluwa! I no get miss call.*
'Thank God! I have not been disappointed.'

In this dialogue, there is explicit comparison between *stick* and *ghost* with 'cigarette' and 'marijuana' respectively, where two conceptual domains have been linked. *Stick* and *cigarette* may share a similar lexical field in terms of shape, size and length, and are connected semantically to the mind. In the Efik language, where the metaphor for marijuana originates, it is called *ikon ekpo* 'ghost leaves' (see ex. (2)) and group members simply call it 'ghost.' It is believed that certain attributes of a ghost, like being scary and evil, are also conceptually represented in marijuana. The use of the form *Oluwa* ('God' in Yoruba) is an exclamation for 'Thank God!'. The expression *I no get miss call* originates from mobile phone technology, which many participants can access. The semantic import is that one who gets a missed call is often disappointed, and if one doesn't have a missed call, he has not been disappointed. The implication of this expression is that Speaker will be glad to have marijuana since the cigarette he asked for was not available.

From these accounts, it is evident that smoking is a social action that is profoundly entrenched in participants' everyday reality and language use; hence, they have (re)created meaning as part of their social construction of their smoking ritual. The inscription of meaning is a fundamental principle that defines their social world. In this context, cigarettes and other abused substances are symbols with subjectively defined meanings based on the perception of the smokers. Other social actors like the law enforcement agents, informants and non-smokers are classified and given internal referentiality and attributions which may not be conventional in the target metaphoric or slangy domain. These terms and expressions are deeply rooted in the cultural experience of smokers. There are coded smoking lexemes which are a part of participants' street drug expressions which "gives access into their dark and secretive world of drugs" (Ghounane 2020: 419). This position shows that language plays a central role in young people's social development and the enactment of subcultural capital.

5 Global perspectives on youth language: Insights from smoking practices

A few scholarly works on the relationship between language and smoking practices by young people have interrogated language as a predictor of smoking prevalence (Chen 1999, Dusenbury et al. 1992, Dusenbury et al. 1994, Epstein et al. 1998), mainly from the perspective of linguistic acculturation. Most results have shown that highly linguistically acculturated individuals smoke more often than less acculturated individuals (Epstein et al. 1998). Research has also shown that language use among peers during the acculturation process increased the risk of smoking by young people more than language use with parents (Unger et al. 2000). In this regard, language is an aspect of smoking-based socialisation. Young people exert their agency through language use in order to define their social circumstances. In the context of smoking (and other substance abuse), this agency is primarily manifested in the creation of slang and metaphors, which are "tools for exclusion and to disrupt ideological and mainstream linguistic order" (Mensah 2016: 2). Gyuro (2016) has investigated how slang words associated with substance abuse (in the *Drug Slang Dictionary*) are conceptualised through metaphors. In her classification, marijuana is categorised under the metaphor of happiness and is widely referred to as *joy smoke*. It is further classified under subthemes of colour (as *red cross*, *bud*, or *yellow submarine*) and love (as *baby* or *love leaf*), and to smoke marijuana is to *fly Mexican airline*. This categorisation is based on linguistic evidence that the ordinary conceptual system is metaphorical in nature (Lakoff and Johnson 1980). This is usually achieved through a mapping process from the source domain (where the metaphorical expression is drawn) to the target domain (what we try to understand). Gyuro (2016) argues that this class of metaphors is connected to the expression of novelty, as emerging forms and phrases can express contents that open new dimensions in meaning.

In South Africa, Hurst (2016) reports that the metaphor *smoko* in Tsotsitaal is derived from English *smoke* but means 'trouble' or 'problem', which is entirely different from the English referent. Gibbs and Nagaoka (1985) also provide an account in American slang in which the expression *he's on a trip* means 'he is using drugs'. *Sniping* is an American slang term for scavenging cigarette butts and filters in public ashtrays or on the street and then smoking the castoffs or using the contents to make a "new" cigarette (Tucker and Shadel 2015). This high-risk practice is prevalent among homeless youth and is occasioned by harsh living conditions. In the German slang dictionary *kiffen* is 'to smoke marijuana', and marijuana itself is *weed*. Marijuana leaves rolled into a cigarette for smoking are called *spliff*. In Britain, the slang for cigarette is *fag*, *ciggy* or *butt*. Marijuana is *skunk*, *peng* or *zoot*. In Israel, the slang form for marijuana is *hash* or *marihuana*. In Switzerland, it is *hasch*, *ganja* or *pétard*. In Brazil, the slang for marijuana is *maconha*. It is called *Gras* in Germany and *dagga* in South Africa (Chopra 2009, Sawler et al. 2015). Through the use of these terms, smokers find social meanings and narratives behind their social actions and experiences. The use of smoking-related slang, therefore, is a symbolic action which has been ascribed some social meaning and an organising principle that is acquired in the course of a situated social experience (Bourdieu 1984, 2000).

For the participants in this study, the creative use of language in relation to tobacco consumption is, therefore, a platform for initiating social and symbolic actions and a strategy for distinction. Slang and sociolect creation is inspired by the need to be different, and indexes varying modes of belonging among group members while excluding others. Global patterns of consumption such as through the Internet, mobile phones, (hip hop and popular) music, and social media in addition to local and trans-local social experiences have provided the resources for creating some of these modes of expression. Lukose (2005) contends that youth consumption practices have become an index of the presence and reach of globalisation. Young men explore these new forms as cultural forces to define their modernity, identity and social spaces. This is what Bucholtz (2004: 130) describes as "distinctiveness-centred model of language", in which verbal style is used in the creation and maintenance of distinctiveness. In this way, their distinctive use of sociolect, slang, and metaphors is based on their linguistic ideology which is closely tied to gender ideology and identity.

6 Conclusion

In this chapter, I have demonstrated how rural youth in southeastern Nigeria navigate their experience of smoking in the construction of identity and hegemonic masculinity. I identified five thematic tropes – social motivations for smoking, smoking as a resource for the performance of hegemonic masculinity, smoking as a source of leisure and modernity, smoking as a form of emotional relief and the specialised smoking-related slanguage. The study shows that young people's smoking behaviour is deeply steeped in the cultural sensitivity of their rural context. With reference to our conceptual framework, community of practice, smoking is an activity in which young people participate on a regular basis and share a social identity (Eckert and McConnell-Ginet 2007), and their engagement with smoking is a social practice with a shared meaning. Every participant understands the values, norms and principles of his community of practice, which are mediated by three core elements of engagements: joint enterprise, mutual engagement and shared repertoire (Lave and Wenger 1991, Wenger 1998, King 2014). Joint enterprise ensures that participants work towards a common goal, in this case the pursuit of smoking as a social behaviour/practice. Mutual engagement involves coming together as a social unit and developing shared norms and tasks over a period of time, for example, participants' involvement in vigilante services, sporting activities and festivals. A shared repertoire is concerned with the creation of shared meaning and referents, which promotes shared tacit knowledge. This includes the creation of smoking-related slang and metaphors like the concept of *show love*, which are symbolic resources used to transport semiotic nuances. The consumption of tobacco holds different appeal to young rural men in Nigeria, especially in achieving their perceived ideals of hegemonic masculinity, mood altering, relief from tension, and leisure. Smoking has thus become an essential aspect of their everyday life that is endorsed by their culture. It has also become a collective social practice and an expression of "habitus" (a set of bodily dispositions acquired over time in their everyday activities that dispose them to act in certain ways) (Bourdieu 1984, 2000). Young people use smoking to open up space and time, and to reconfigure social relations. To these young people, smoking is a form of situated agency that sustains their shared interests and locally originating ideologies about smoking. No tier of the Nigerian government – federal, state or local – seems to note or respond to the dangerous effect of tobacco addiction on the health of these vulnerable youth. It is important to articulate smoking cessation campaigns that will shift focus to both individual behaviour and community behavioural change, driven by an understanding of the social history of the practice as a normative cultural practice. Smokers' lifestyle model has to change positively in response to public health challenges posed by tobacco consumption in order to transform young people's lives.

List of abbreviations

3	third person
ASP	aspect
CONJ	conjunction
DET	determiner
NEG	negation
PREP	preposition
PRO	pronoun
PL	plural
REDUP	reduplication
SG	singular

References

Akanonu, Precious, Joseph Isiaku and Chukwuka Onyekwena. 2018. The implications of recent changes to Nigeria's tobacco policy. [https://www.africaportal.org/features/implications-recent-changes-nigerias-tobacco-tax-policy/] (accessed 12 January 2020).

Black, Peter. 1984. The anthropology of tobacco use: Tobian data and theoretical issues. *Journal of Anthropological Research* 40 (4). 475–503.

Bourdieu, Pierre. 1984. *Distinction: A social critique of the judgment of taste*. Cambridge: Harvard University Press.

Bourdieu, Pierre. 2000. Making the economic habitus: Algerian workers revisited. *Ethnography* 1 (1). 17–41.

Bucholtz, Mary. 2004. Styles and stereotypes: The linguistic negotiation of identity among Laotian American youth. *Pragmatics* 14 (2–3). 127–147.

Chen, Xinguang, Jennifer Unger, Tess Cruz and C. Anderson Johnson. 1999. Smoking patterns of Asian-American youth in California and their relationship with acculturation. *Journal of Adolescent Health* 24 (5). 321–328.

Chopra, Gurbakhsh. 2009. Man and marijuana. *International Journal of Addictions* 4 (2). 215–247.

Demant, Jakob and Jeanette Ostergaard. 2007. Partying as everyday life: Investigations of teenagers' leisure life. *Journal of Youth Studies* 10 (5). 517–537.

Dusenbury, Linda, Jennifer Epstein, Gilbert Botvin and Tracy Diaz. 1994. The relationship between language spoken and smoking among Hispanic-Latino youth in New York City. *Public Health Report* 109 (3). 421–427.

Dusenbury, Linda, Jon Kerner, Eli Baker, Gilbert Botvin, Susan James-Ortiz and Ann Zauber. 1992. Predictors of smoking prevalence among New York Latino Youth. *American Journal of Public Health* 82 (1). 55–58.

Eckert, Penelope and Sally McConnell-Ginet. 2007. Putting community of practice in their place. *Gender and Language* 1 (1): 27–38.

Egbe, Catherine, Anna Meyer-Weitz, Kwaku Asante and Inge Petersen. 2017. A woman is not supposed to smoke: Exploring gender stereotypes in smoking patterns in a Nigerian Setting. *Journal of Psychology*. 5 (1). 1–7.

Egbe, Catherine, Elizabeth Egbochukwu, Inge Petersen and Anna Meyer-Weitz 2016. Cigarette smoking among Southern Nigerian youth and what geographical zones got to do with it. *Vulnerable Children and Youth Studies* 11 (3). 251–262.

Egbe, Catherine, Inge Petersen, Anna Meyer-Weitz and Kwaku Asante. 2014. An exploratory study of the sociocultural risk influences for cigarette smoking among Southern Nigerian youth. *BMC Public Health* 14 (1204). DOI: [https://doi.org/10.1186/1471-2458-14-1204].

Epstein, Jennifer, Gilbert Botvin and Tracy Diaz. 1998. Linguistic acculturation and gender effects on smoking among Hispanic youth. *Preventive Medicine* 27. 583–589.

Flandorfer, Priska, Christian Wegner and Isabella Buber. 2010. Gender roles and smoking behaviour. *Vienna Institute of Demography Working Paper* 7: 1–23.

Gana, Godwin, Suleiman Idris, Kabiru Sabitu, Mansure Oche, Aisha Abubakar and Patrick Njuku. 2018. Prevalence and perception of cigarette smoking among out of school adolescents in Birnin Kebbi, North Western Nigeria. *Pan Africa Medical Journal*. 30. 1–12.

Ghounane, Nadia. 2020. A thorough examination of teens drug slang in Algeria. *Arab World English Journal* 11 (1). 419–431.

Gibbs, Raymond W. and Annette Nagaoka. 1985. Getting the hang of American slang: Studies on understanding and remembering slang metaphors. *Language and Speech* 28 (2). 177–194.

Gyuro, Monika. 2016. Conceptualising the metaphors of drug abusers. *Topics in Linguistics* 17 (1). 81–91.

Hurst, Ellen. 2016. Metaphor in South African Tsotsitaal. *Sociolinguistic Studies* 10 (1–2). 153–175.

King, Brian. 2014. Tracing the emergence of a community of practice: Beyond presupposition in sociolinguistic research. *Language in Society* 43 (1). 61–81.

Lakoff, George and Mark Johnson. 1980. Conceptual metaphor in everyday language. *The Journal of Philosophy* 77 (8). 453–486.

Lave, Jean and Etienne Wenger. 1991. *Situated learning: Legitimate peripheral participation*. Cambridge: Cambridge University Press.

Lukose, Ritty. 2005. Consuming globalization: Youth and gender in Kerala, India. *Journal of Social History* 38 (4). 915–935.

Marshall, Mac. 2008. Carolina in the Caroline: A survey of pattern and meanings of smoking in a Micronesian Island. *Medical Anthropology Quarterly* 19 (4). 365–382.

Mensah, Eyo. 2012. Youth language in Nigeria: A case study of the Agaba Boys. *Sociolinguistic Studies* 6 (3). 367–419.

Mensah, Eyo. 2016. The dynamics of youth language in Africa: An introduction. *Sociolinguistic Studies* 10(1–2). 1–14.

Mensah, Eyo. 2017. Proverbial nicknames among rural youth in Nigeria. *Anthropological Linguistics* 59 (4). 414–439.

Mensah, Eyo. 2020. He has committed a drinkable offence: The discourse of alcohol consumption among rural youth in Nigeria. *Linguistics Vanguard* 6 (s4). 20190036.

Mensah, Eyo. 2021. To be a man is not a day's job: The discursive construction of hegemonic masculinity by rural youth in Nigeria. *Gender Issues* 38 (1). 1–23.

Mensah, Eyo, Ekawan Silva and Idom Inyabri 2020. An ethnopragmatic study of libation rituals among the Kiong-speaking Okoyong people in South-eastern Nigeria. *Journal of Anthropological Research* 76 (3). 347–366.

Nichter, Mark and Elizabeth Cartwright. 1991. Saving the children from the tobacco industry. *Medical Anthropology Quarterly* 5 (3). 236–256.

Nzewi, Meki. 1979. Some structural features of the Igbo festival. *The Black Perspective in Music* 7 (2). 168–181.

Oyeniran, Oluwatosin, Terkuma Chia and Abayomi Ajagbe. 2019. Prevalence of drug and alcohol use among undergraduate medical students in a Nigerian private university. *Asian Journal of Medicine and Health* 16 (1). 1–6.

Oyewole, Bankole, Victor Animasahun and Helena Chapman. 2018. Tobacco use in Nigeria. A systematic review. *Plos One*. [https://journals.plos.org/plosone/article?id=10.1371/journal.pone.0196362] (accessed 20 April 2020).

Pickhardt, Carl. 2013. *Surviving your child's adolescent*. New York: Wiley.

Pourtau, Lionel, Elise Martins, Gwenn Menvielle, Fabienne El Khoury-Lesueur, and Maria Melchior. 2019. To smoke or not to smoke? A qualitative study among young adults. *Preventive Medicine Report* 15. 1–5.

Roulette, Cassey, Edward Hagen and Barry Hewlett. 2016. A biocultural investigation of gender differences in tobacco use in an egalitarian hunter-gathering population. *Human Nature* 27 (2). 105–129.

Russell, Andrew. 2019. *Anthropology of tobacco: Ethnographic adventures in non-human worlds*. London and New York: Routledge.
Sawler Jason, Jake Stout, Kyle Gardner, Darryl Hudson, John Vidmar, Laura Butler et al. 2015. The genetic structure of marijuana and hemp. *PLoS ONE* 10(8): e0133292. DOI: 10.1371/journal.pone.0133292 (accessed 20 April 2020).
Steen, Gerard. 2011. The contemporary theory of metaphors – now, new and improved! *Review of Cognitive Linguistics* 9 (1). 26–64.
Tinkler, Penny. 2001. Rebellion, modernity and romance: Smoking as a gendered practice in popular young women magazine, British 1918–1939. *Women's Studies International Forum* 24 (1). 111–122.
Triandafilidis, Zoi, Jane Ussher, Janette Perz and Kate Huppatz. 2015. Doing and undoing femininities: An intersectional analysis of young women's smoking. *Feminism and Psychology* 27 (4). 465–488.
Tucker, Joan and William Shadel. 2015. Sniping: Homeless youths' high-risk smoking practice. [https://www.rand.org/blog/2015/10/sniping-homeless-youths-high-risk-smoking-practice.html] (accessed 20 January 2020).
Unger, Jennifer, Tess Cruz, Kurt Ribisi, Lourdes Baezconde-Garbanati, Xinguang Chen, Dennis Trinidad and C. Anderson Johnson. 2000. English language use as a risk factor for smoking initiation among Hispanic and Asian American adolescents: Evidence for mediation by tobacco-related benefits and social norms. *Health Psychology* 19 (5). 403–410.
Wenger, Etienne. 1998. *Community of practice: Learning, meaning and identity*. Cambridge: Cambridge University Press.
Zhao, Xiang and Gareth Davey. 2015. Contesting modernity: Tobacco use and romanticism among older Dai farmers in Xishuangbanna, China. *Sociology of Health and Illness* 37 (8). 1173–1190.

Christoph Holz
11 Notes on children's secret language games in New Ireland, Papua New Guinea

Secret languages play an important role in Melanesian communities. Traditionally, they are more commonly found among men who want to keep their secrets from uninitiated social groups. This chapter, in contrast, presents secret language codes primarily used by school girls in New Ireland – three language games that can be played in many local languages, in Tok Pisin and in English. Schools, often accommodating children from various linguistic backgrounds, harbour a creative environment for the development of language games and their spread within the province, and apparently also further into the country. This chapter will also focus on how young speakers deal with applying a fixed set of game rules to a variety of phonotactically unlike languages.

1 Origin of secret languages

Aufinger (1942: 630) distinguishes two types of language in Melanesia: "straight language" (*gerade Sprache*) and "secret language". Whereas straight language is the normal language used in daily life and is understood by everyone in the speech community, secret language is a register only known to initiated people, unintelligible to others. Secret languages fall into two further categories: a "figurative secret language" (*Bilder-Geheimsprache*) uses the same words as the straight language but adds a new secondary meaning to them; and a "secret language proper" replaces parts of the vocabulary with items from foreign languages or newly constructed words (Aufinger 1942: 630–632).

Secret languages are a common phenomenon world-wide, found under a variety of names, including "language game", "play language", "argot", "code

---

Acknowledgements: I am grateful to Geraldine Batsinuk, Joseph Kombeng, Kendle Susuvin and the grade 9 and 11 students from Madina High School for teaching me these three language games, and to Craig Alan Volker for helping me organising the interviews at Madina High School.

Christoph Holz, Central Queensland University, e-mail: christoph.holz@cqumail.com

language", "speech disguise", "word game", "ritual language", "speech play", "disguised speech", "linguistic game" and "ludling" (e.g., Bagemihl 1995: 698, Sherzer 1967: 20). Secret languages may use grammatical operations to conceal speech and derive new words. These operations seem unlike ordinary language operations superficially, but in fact they differ quantitatively rather than qualitatively, in the extent of their application (Bagemihl 1995: 697), as they may be applied multiple times within a word. Storch (2017: 292–299) describes six strategies for manipulating words in secret languages:

1) Inserting strategy: New segments are affixed or inserted into a word.
2) Templatic strategy: Original segments are rearranged according to a fixed templatic pattern.
3) Replacement strategy: Original segments are replaced by another segment.
4) Speaking backwards: Original segments or syllables are partially or totally reversed.
5) Truncation: Words are shortened by deleting segments.
6) Repetition: Words become longer by reduplication.

Regarding the inserting strategy, Botne and Davis (2000: 320) further distinguish between an insertion-type and imposition-type strategy: Insertion-type games insert a fixed set of segments, such as a CV template, at a certain position within a syllable; imposition-type games impose a consonant on the prosodic peak of a syllable, which splits the syllable into two demisyllables, with the peak vowel being part of both demisyllables (see Section 3).

More than one strategy may be employed in a secret language: the historic *Nyōbō Kotoba* register of Japanese adds the polite prefix *o-* and occasionally the suffix *-moji* (inserting strategy) to words and removes the final syllable (truncation) (Blake 2010: 232). The *Louchébem* register of French replaces the onset of a word with /l/ (replacement strategy), moves the original onset to the end of the word (speaking backwards) and adds a suffix (inserting strategy) (Blake 2010: 237). Although many secret languages are based on a single strategy in a straightforward manner, others exhibit more fluid language practices through which the same word may generate a variety of possible outputs, as in *Chibende* from Zimbabwe (Hollington 2019: 36–37).

One important motivation for speaking a secret language is to exclude outsiders from understanding private group-internal speech. In Melanesia, the excluded groups may be other clans (Laycock 1977: 136), foreigners, and a certain gender or age group (Aufinger 1942: 630). Camron Pidgin English in Milne Bay, for instance, was created by school boys to prevent being overheard by their female schoolmates, who they thought to be involved in witchcraft (Volker 1989: 22). Secret languages may also serve to hide one's intention from animals while hunting, from plants during harvest (Laycock 1977: 137), or to avoid the attention of ghosts (Aufinger 1942: 630). They can be linked to a certain geographical area or activity as special languages related to taboo, as for instance the use of the pandanus languages in the New Guinea Highlands when harvesting pandanus nuts (Franklin and Stefaniw 1992: 1). They can be strategies for avoiding names of certain relatives (Foley 1986: 42) or for replacement of lexical items in songs (Foley 1986: 45), or they can originate from the principle of parallelism as the "other side" song register in Manambu (Aikhenvald 2014: 90).

In more recent times, schools have become a fertile ground for the creation and spread of secret languages among children and teenagers, with functions that are somewhat different from traditional or ritualised secret languages such as pandanus languages. While retaining its function of expressing an in-group identity among peers and excluding outsiders, "[t]he young people's code-speak is a very different type of concealed speech; probably faddish rather than traditional, and with the aims of circulating gossip and snide remarks rather than protecting against spirits" (Sarvasy 2019: 21). Additionally, it helps "to practise language in a skilful way in order to deepen one's linguistic knowledge" (Storch 2017: 292).

Language games are not a new phenomenon in Papua New Guinea. Playful renderings of language have been described in older literature, in which workers and school boys were reported to reverse words from Tok Pisin and local languages for their own entertainment rather than secrecy (Aufinger 1942: 632). Substitution of phonemes has been found in Kuma and Chimbu (Laycock 1977: 134). Two language games have been described for Buin, one featuring metathesis of single phonemes or whole syllables, and one based on phoneme deletion and affixation (Laycock 1977: 134–135).

This chapter presents data on similar recent language games in Papua New Guinea, based on my fieldwork in New Ireland between February and October 2019, with a focus on Tiang, an Oceanic language spoken on Djaul Island (see Section 3). Additional data has been gathered from interviews at Madina High School in the Nalik area on 18 October 2019 with grade 9 and 11 students from eleven other language groups, allowing for an overview of language game uses in other New Ireland languages (Section 4), Tok Pisin (Section 5), and English (Section 6). Each language group interviewed at Madina High School consisted of three to six students, who were asked about their use of the games. They were then encouraged to produce sentences in the languages of their choice; each group provided up to nine sentences.

2 Current linguistic situation in New Ireland

New Ireland has a patchwork of more than twenty languages. With the exception of Kuot, the only non-Austronesian language of New Ireland in the centre of the province, all New Ireland languages belong to the Oceanic language family. The present chapter is based on interviews with students from twelve language groups: Tungag (Lavongai), Tigak, Tiang, Kara and Nalik of the Tungag-Nalik family in northern New Ireland; Mandara (Tabar), Lihir and Notsi of the Tabar linkage on the east coast and the islands northeast of the province; non-Austronesian Kuot; Madak and Barok of the Madak linkage in central New Ireland; and Patpatar of the St George linkage in the south (Figure 11.1).

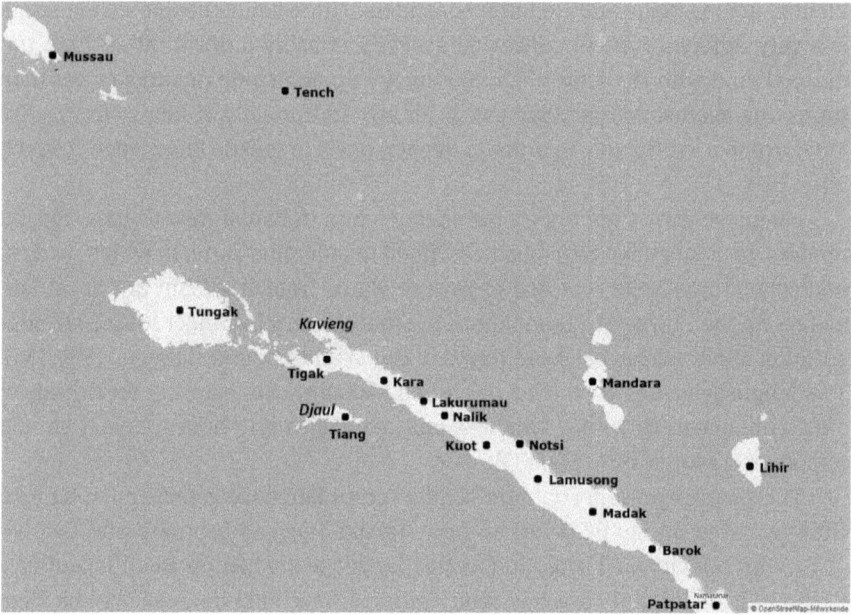

Figure 11.1: Languages in the area of investigation (adapted from openstreetmap).

People from New Ireland are generally multilingual. They grow up with a local language and may acquire knowledge of neighbouring languages through traveling or family relations. In addition, almost everyone has learned Tok Pisin as a second mother tongue, and those who attended school are familiar with English. However, knowledge of the local languages is in decline, particularly on the more developed east coast. The highway along the east coast offers easy access to the capital city Kavieng, so that east coast people deal more often with outsiders than do members of less accessible communities on the west coast.

Language games are very common in New Ireland. Among the students interviewed on Djaul Island and at Madina High School, everyone was familiar with at least one game that they would usually play in Tok Pisin, and, depending on the language group, also in their local language and English. Students who reported the use of a language game in their local language, Tok Pisin and English were speakers of Tungag, Tigak, Tiang, Kara, Notsi and Patpatar. Children from the Lihir and Madak area reported playing language games only in their local language and Tok Pisin, but not in English. While Nalik and Mandara students would not play any games in their local language, they reported, however, doing so in Tok Pisin and English. Kuot and Barok children knew games only for Tok Pisin. Additionally, Kendle Susuvin, a consultant from Mussau in the very north of New Ireland, reported that children played such games in Tok Pisin on his home island too.

Three language games have been identified, each consisting of breaking up all syllables of a word by inserting a labial obstruent, two velar consonants, or the sequence of a lateral and velar stop, following Storch's (2017) inserting strategy, or, more precisely, Botne and Davis' (2000) imposition-type strategy. Generally familiar with all three games, each language group has one favoured version. By far the most common one is imposition of [p]. The only language group in which all three games are played is Tiang (see Section 3), but even Tiang speakers prefer imposition of a labial or velar consonant over using the more complex pattern of a lateral–velar stop sequence. The preference for labial consonants in language games is a common phenomenon cross-linguistically; according to Botne and Davis (2000: 328), a labial consonant "permits the tongue position for the vowel to remain nearly constant throughout the vowel gesture. In other words, a labial gesture does not interrupt the vowel articulation and can be viewed as an imposition upon the vowel articulation."

When asked for their motivation for using these games, the students unanimously answered: to tell secrets among friends that not everyone should hear. Additionally, "[t]he code-speak could be interpreted as thus subverting the usual hierarchical social structure in which people aged in their late twenties and older held most power and commanded most respect" (Sarvasy 2019: 26). Some older people have indeed remarked to be not fond of children using code speak and stated that in past situations they have scolded them for not speaking intelligibly and using so many unnecessarily long words.

The language games are learned from friends and family members roughly of the same age. Although most young people are familiar with these games, girls most frequently play them; boys more commonly have a passive knowledge only. Some middle-aged women from the Tiang, Kara and Mussau areas were said to have been playing these games also, when they were children, probably as first-generation users. Further evidence that the language games might have originated in the northern half of New Ireland comes from the Nalik area: Joseph Kombeng from Djaul first heard girls talking that way in 2000 when he was a student at Mongop High School in the Nalik area. The earliest report dates back to the early nineties, when school girls were first heard using such games for Tok Pisin in the Nalik village Madina. Taking into account that certain persons of the older generation are able to understand the secret language codes of the younger generation, one wonders to what degree they still fulfil the purpose of keeping secrets today. Perhaps their primary function nowadays is rather as an identity marker for young females.

The role of school girls in authoring such speech modifications is interesting, as gender-based secret languages in Papua New Guinea have more commonly been described for men, e.g., among the Tolai in New Britain (Volker 1989: 20) and language groups near Madang (Aufinger 1942: 633). In other cases, they are used by the whole community regardless of sex, as in the pandanus languages in the Highlands (Franklin and Stefaniw 1992: 1), or are reserved for a certain clan (Laycock 1977: 136). Senft (1996: 232) argues that female adolescents show a much more playful and unconventional use of classifiers in Kilivila than do male adolescents. Boys have to obey social and linguistic constraints at a younger age than girls to gain social status, whereas girls only become fully integrated members of the society after marriage. The female prominence in language games in New Ireland might thus correlate with a higher linguistic creativity resulting from a looser social integration.

Outside New Ireland, an almost identical game has been found in Morobe Province for Tok Pisin and Nungon (Finisterre-Huon, non-Austronesian), which uses insertion of [b] into each syllable of a word. The game is known as *Long Pidgin* and *Girls' and boys' language* and is used by speakers under the age of thirty throughout the Highlands and Huon region (Sarvasy 2014: 58). Nowadays, Long Pidgin has fallen out of use in the Highlands and has been replaced with a new game in Tok Pisin, which involves altering vowels (Sarvasy 2019: 26). As a school girl, a teacher at Madina High School said she had also heard such games in the Kuanua area of East New Britain, although she had never actively used them herself. In the Austronesian world outside Melanesia, similar secret languages are found, with somewhat different rules, for instance, in Tagalog (Blust 2013: 143), Malay, Indonesian (Blust 2013: 145) and Javanese (Sherzer 1967: 27–30).

Not only are children's secret languages thus omnipresent in New Ireland, they seem rather like a country-wide phenomenon. As the game rules are almost identical, one may assume a mutual influence of various speech communities via Tok Pisin, for which schools seem to play an important role. The schools as a place of language innovation is not a new phenomenon. Apart from the aforementioned Camron Pidgin English, another boarding school language, the German-based *Unserdeutsch* from East New Britain, was created by students who wanted to distinguish themselves from other groups at school in the first half of the twentieth century (Volker 1989: 19–20). As the language games presented here are used in many parts of the country, it is hard to establish where they originated. High schools in Papua New Guinea are often boarding schools, attracting children of different linguistic backgrounds from many different parts of the province, with Tok Pisin as their only common language. Once an innovation such as a language game is created for Tok Pisin in one school and becomes in vogue among its students, the children will naturally use it with friends from their language community when visiting their home village. The innovation will thus spread easily across the province and apparently even beyond.

The following sections illustrate the application of the language games in a variety of phonotactically diverse languages, starting with Tiang in Section 3. Games in other local languages from New Ireland are described in Section 4. Section 5 provides data on games in Tok Pisin, and Section 6 on games in English as performed by young speakers in New Ireland.

3 Tiang

3.1 Regular syllables

All three aforementioned language games are used by Tiang-speaking children. (1a) shows the frequently asked question "Where are you going?" in its normal shape, as it would be uttered by every member of the Tiang community. *No=k* is the fused form of *no* '2SG' and *ik* 'IPFV'. (1b–d) show the same sentence after applying the game rules. In (1b), [p] is inserted; in (1c) it is the cluster [ŋk]; and in (1d) the sequence of [l] and [g]. Insertion takes place for every syllable in the sentence and causes repetition of one vowel per syllable. Tiang examples are giving in IPA.

(1) a. no=k pən əma? (no=k < no ik)
 2SG=IPFV go where
 'Where are you going?'
 b. no\<p\>o i\<p\>ik pə\<p\>ən ə\<p\>ə.ma\<p\>a?
 c. no\<ŋk\>o i\<ŋk\>ik pə\<ŋk\>ən ə\<ŋk\>ə.ma\<ŋk\>a?
 d. no\<l\>o\<g\>o i\<l\>i\<g\>ik pə\<l\>ə\<g\>ən ə\<l\>ə\<g\>ə.ma\<l\>a\<g\>a?

In all cases, it is not the fused form *no=k* that is preferred, but the underlying forms *no* '2SG' and *ik* 'IPFV'. Although (1b–d) are all in use, my consultants strongly favoured the simpler versions (1b) and (1c) over the more complex game in (1d), as the latter was harder to produce and understand.

The regular syllable structure in Tiang is (C)V(C), where C represents a consonant, and V a single vowel, a diphthong or triphthong. Diphthongs and triphthongs must begin or end in the high vowels /i/ or /u/, which serve phonetically as on- and off-glides around the syllable peak vowel. All other vowel sequences belong to separate syllables (Holz forthcoming). A syllable must consist at least of a vowel, optionally followed by a coda consonant, preceded by an onset consonant, or both. Table 11.1 illustrates the application of the three games on the four types of regular Tiang syllables; the original unmanipulated word of the ordinary speech is found in the "normal" row.

Table 11.1: Regular Tiang syllables.

	V	VC	CV	CVC
normal	*ə* 'ART'	*ik* 'IPFV'	*no* '2SG'	*pən* 'to go'
\<p\>	ə\<p\>ə	i\<p\>ik	no\<p\>o	pə\<p\>ən
\<ŋk\>	ə\<ŋk\>ə	i\<ŋk\>ik	no\<ŋk\>o	pə\<ŋk\>ən
\<l-g\>	ə\<l\>ə\<g\>ə	i\<l\>i\<g\>ik	no\<l\>o\<g\>o	pə\<l\>ə\<g\>ən

As the games are played, one of the three infixes \<p\>, \<ŋk\> and \<l-g\> is imposed on the syllable peak vowel, with the effect of splitting the original syllable into subparts, which Botne and Davis (2000: 327) call "demisyllables". In the case on *\<p\>* (2a) and *\<ŋk\>* (2b), the original syllable splits into two demisyllables: The first one consists of all the segments before the peak vowel, and the second of everything after the peak vowel. The peak vowel itself acts as the breaking point and is hence part of both demisyllables. In the case of \<l-g\> (2c), two distinct impositions take place: After the imposition of \<l\> on the syllable peak, \<g\> is imposed in a second round on the peak vowel, creating a third demisyllable (cf. Botne and Davis 2000: 333–334). This behaviour is remarkable, as Tiang otherwise does not feature infixation. However, "[p]lay languages based on the insertion of an element into the base word are a world-wide common type" (Storch 2017: 292). Imposition is always performed on the vowel in the syllable peak, but never on the on- and off-glides of diphthongs and triphthongs (2).

(2)

		Demi-σ₁	Infix₁	Demi-σ₂	Infix₂	Demi-σ₃
a.	tuïi 'snake'	tuï	<p>	ïi		
b.	tuïi 'snake'	tuï	<ŋk>	ïi		
c.	tuïi 'snake'	tuï	<l>	ï	<g>	ïi

Tuïi 'snake' in (2) has the triphthong /uïi/ phonemically. Although all parts of the triphthong belong to the nucleus, only the syllable peak /ï/ is part of all demisyllables. Phonetically, pre-syllable peak /u/ and post-syllable peak /i/ are realised as approximants, which occur outside the syllable peak just like onset and coda consonants (3).

(3)

		Demi-σ₁	Infix₁	Demi-σ₂	Infix₂	Demi-σ₃
a.	pən 'to go'	pə	<p>	ən		
b.	pən 'to go'	pə	<ŋk>	ən		
c.	pən 'to go'	pə	<l>	ə	<g>	ən

In multisyllable words, the rules must be applied to each syllable (4). As a result, every modified syllable of the original word is perceived as a separate phonological word, sometimes pronounced with a pause to buy time for applying the rules to the next syllable.

(4)

		Syllable₁			Syllable₂		
		Demi-σ₁	Infix	Demi-σ₂	Demi-σ₁	Infix	Demi-σ₂
a.	mə.lai 'village'	mə	<p>	ə	lə	<p>	əi
b.	tə.i 'conch shell'	tə	<p>	ə	i	<p>	i
c.	ai.us 'to relax'	a	<p>	ai	u	<p>	us

Secret languages have a long history as tools for investigating the psychological reality of phonological units (Bagemihl 1995: 705). To mention one prominent example, with the help of the language game "Rabbit Talk", Breen and Pensalfini (1999) delivered evidence for the underlying syllable structure of VC(C) in Arrernte, a Pama-Nyungan language from Australia. Also in Tiang, language games are a helpful tool for establishing what a syllable is. As shown in (4b) and (4c), not every vowel combination necessarily forms a diphthong or triphthong. In most words, the combination /ə/ and /i/ makes up the diphthong [əi] as in (4a). In (4b), /ə/ and /i/ do not go into one syllable but form two separate syllables, giving [tə.i] with a hiatus instead of *[təi] for 'conch shell'. In (4c), the hiatus appears between /ai/ and /us/, resulting in the form [ai.us] instead of *[a.ius] for 'to relax'. The occurrence of a hiatus is in many cases unpredictable but may follow phonotactic criteria as illustrated below.

3.2 Unstable syllables

Apart from regular syllables, there are unstable syllables, which occur in fast speech, especially in the phonologically more innovative western dialect of Tiang. Unstable syllables are superheavy syllables that consist of an off-glide diphthong or triphthong followed by a coda consonant (Table 11.2). In careful speech, particularly in the more conservative eastern dialect of Tiang, superheavy syllables are eschewed and usually realised as two syllables; i.e., the post-syllable peak vowel is parsed as the nucleus of a separate syllable.

Table 11.2: Unstable Tiang syllables.

normal	bɔ.rɔ(.)*is* 'to steal'	kə.ka(.)*is* 'fresh water spring'	niɨu=k '1SG=IPFV' (< niɨu ik)
<p>	bɔ<p>ɔ.rɔ<p>ɔis	kə<p>ə.**ka<p>ə.i<p>is**	niɨ<p>ɨu i<p>ik
<ŋk>	bɔ<ŋk>ɔ.rɔ<ŋk>ɔis	kə<ŋk>ə.**ka<ŋk>ə.i<ŋk>is**	niɨ<ŋk>ɨuk
<l-g>	bɔ<l>ɔ<g>ɔ.rɔ<l>ɔ<g>ɔis	kə<l>ə<g>ə.**ka<l>ə<g>ə.i<l>i<g>is**	niɨ<l>i<g>ɨu i<l>i<g>ik

The instability of superheavy syllables in the everyday register is reflected in the variable ways they are treated in the language games. Of the tested words with unstable syllables, only the unstable syllable /rɔ(.)is/ in *bɔrɔis* 'to steal' was given with a preference for a superheavy [rɔis]. Unstable syllables in other words were usually split up into two syllables, as is the syllable /kə(.)is/ in *kəkais* 'fresh water spring'. In the case of *niɨu=k* '1SG=IPFV', a superheavy syllable was sometimes accepted, as in *niɨ<ŋk>ɨuk*, and sometimes split up, as in *niɨ<p>ɨu i<p>ik*. *Niɨu=k* is special in that it is the contraction of *niɨu* '1SG' and *ik* 'IPFV', hence its rendering as *niɨ<p>ɨu i<p>ik* based on the underlying form, instead of **niɨ<p>ɨ.u<p>uk*.

A second type of unstable syllables occurs in words in which two high front or back vowels occur in front of another vowel. In *iuai* 'two' (5), either of the two initial high vowels can become a glide, resulting in two acceptable versions, [i.uai] and [iu.ai], with the first one being more commonly heard. Maybe due to its frequency, [i.uai] serves in (5) as the base to which the language game rules are applied; thus we get *i<p>i.ua<p>ai* from [i.uai] rather than ?*iu<p>u.a<p>ai* from the otherwise acceptable [iu.ai].

(5)

	Syllable₁			Syllable₂		
	Demi-σ₁	Infix	Demi-σ₂	Demi-σ₁	Infix	Demi-σ₂
i.uai ~ iu.ai 'two'	i	<p>	i	ua	<p>	ai

In (6), two identical high vowels are adjacent to one another. Often, such homophonic sequences are simplified by deleting one of the high vowels, while the retained high vowel changes into a glide. *Kuuɨl* 'together' in (6a) has two realisations, the full form [ku.uɨl] and the shortened form [kuɨl]. Both forms are acceptable, although the first would be preferred by more conservative speakers and the latter by younger speakers. As the presented games are played by younger speakers, it does not come as a surprise that the shorter form [kuɨl] serves as the base, explaining the form *kuɨ<p>ɨl* from [kuɨl] instead of ?*ku<p>u.uɨ<p>ɨl* from [ku.uɨl]. In (6b), in turn, shortening is not an option because this would affect the meaning. Bisyllablic *tiɨ* with double /iɨ/ means 'to dance', while monosyllablic *tɨ* with single /ɨ/ is a kind of fish; the distinction must be kept.

(6)

		Syllable₁			Syllable₂		
		Demi-σ₁	Infix	Demi-σ₂	Demi-σ₁	Infix	Demi-σ₂
a.	*ku.uɨl ~ kuɨl* 'together'	kuɨ	<p>	ɨl			
b.	*ti.ɨ ~ *tɨ* 'to dance'	ti	<p>	i	ɨ	<p>	ɨ

The phonological boundaries do not always correspond to the grammatical boundaries. *Bɔi-ən* 'food' (7) is composed of the verb *bɔi* 'to eat' and the nominaliser *-ən*. Phonetically, however, its boundaries are [bɔ.iən], with the final /i/ of the lexeme *bɔi* becoming the on-glide of the next syllable. If the language games were played based on the word-internal grammatical structure, one would expect forms such as **bɔ<p>ɔi-ə<p>ən* from /bɔi-ən/. Instead, my consultants produced *bɔ<p>ɔ.iə<p>ən* based on [bɔ.iən]. In other words, it is not the word-internal underlying form but its phonetic realisation that matters here.

(7)

	Syllable₁			Syllable₂		
	Demi-σ₁	Infix	Demi-σ₂	Demi-σ₁	Infix	Demi-σ₂
bɔ.iən 'food' (< *bɔi-ən*)	bɔ	<p>	ɔ	iə	<p>	ən

Example (8) shows two distinct cases in which two grammatical words are fused into one phonological word. *Liuɨn* 'beach' (8a) is the fusion of *lə* 'in' and *uɨn* 'sand'. During fusion, vowel harmony takes place with the raising of /lə/ 'in' to [lɨ]; the bisyllablic syllable structure is retained. Again, the phonetic realisation is the base for the language games, as we get *lɨ<p>i.uɨ<p>in* from a vowel-harmonised [lɨ.uɨn] instead of **lə<p>ə.uɨ<p>in* from the underlying /lə uɨn/. *No=k* '2SG=IPFV' behaves differently (8b). It is the fusion of *no* '2SG' and *ik* 'IPFV', but when fusing, the syllable structure is changed into one monosyllabic word [nok] through the deletion of /i/ from *ik*. This time it is interestingly not the phonetic realisation that is favoured as the base but the underlying form with two separate words, *no* and *ik*. Thus, we get *no<p>o i<p>ik* from /no ik/ rather than ?*no<p>ok* from its phonetic realisation [nok].

(8)

		Syllable₁			Syllable₂		
		Demi-σ₁	Infix	Demi-σ₂	Demi-σ₁	Infix	Demi-σ₂
a.	lɨ.uin 'beach' (< lə uin)	lɨ	<p>	ɨ	uɨ	<p>	in
b.	no=k '2SG=IPFV' (< no ik)	no	<p>	o	i	<p>	ik

To conclude, normally the phonetic realisation serves as the base for applying the language game rules. Morpheme boundaries of affixes within one grammatical word do not have an influence on the game (7). Word boundaries of two grammatical words, in turn, do have an effect in that fused syllables will preferably be restored into their original bisyllabic shape (8b), although changes of their vowel quality are retained (8a). Even though restoration of the original bisyllablic shape is preferred, it seems to be optional as my consultants produced both nɨɨ<ŋk>ɨuk from fused nɨɨu=k '1SG=IPFV' and nɨɨ<p>iu i<p>ik from an unfused /nɨɨu ik/ (Table 11.2).

4 Other New Ireland languages

Apart from Tiang, I was able to collect data for more New Ireland languages through interviews with grade 9 and 11 students of Madina High School. Most of the students were familiar with all three language games. The students who reported using them in their local mother tongue were asked to provide sample sentences of their choice, all of which were formed using the labial strategy. The majority of the sentences follow the rules described for Tiang in Section 3, i.e., a <p> infix is imposed on every syllable peak vowel of a word, with diphthongs and triphthongs being treated as glides outside the syllable peak. This is the case for Tigak (9), Kara (10), Madak (11) and Patpatar (12).

(9) **Tigak** (glossed after Beaumont 1979)
    a. kara   inang lo kono
       1PL.INC go   in sand
       'Let's go to the beach.'
    b. ka<p>a.ra<p>a i<p>i.na<p>ang lo<p>o ko<p>o.no<p>o

(10) **Kara** (glossed after Dryer 2013; digraph *aa* represents /a/)
    a. laak   maan
       enter come
       'Come inside.'

  b. *laa\<p\>aak maa\<p\>aan*

(11) **Madak** (glossed after Lee 2005)
  a. *l-asen taram nege?*
    NM-name POSS.2SG who
    'What is your name?'
  b. *la\<p\>a.se\<p\>en ta\<p\>a.ra\<p\>am ne\<p\>e.ge\<p\>e?*

(12) **Patpatar** (glossed after Condra 1989)
  a. *iau wara sisiu*
    1SG PUR bathe
    'I want to wash.'
  b. *ia\<p\>au wa\<p\>a.ra\<p\>a si\<p\>i.si\<p\>iu*

The games in three other languages were slightly different from the Tiang rules. Tungag students were inserting [p] only sporadically; more often, they produced a bilabial fricative [ɸ] (13), which is in free variation to [p] (Fast 2015: 15).

(13) **Tungag** (glossed after Fast 2015)
  a. *tara pasal ane nei akalit*
    1PL.INC go toward in school
    'Let's go to school.'
  b. *ta\<ɸ\>a.ra\<p\>a pa\<ɸ\>a.sa\<ɸ\>al a\<ɸ\>a.ne\<ɸ\>e ne\<ɸ\>ei a\<ɸ\>a. ka\<ɸ\>a.li\<ɸ\>it*

In Lihir, \<p\> seems to be only inserted into the last syllable of a word. In (14b), the students rendered *o=le* '2SG=want' thus as *o.le\<p\>e* instead of the expected *?o\<p\>o.le\<p\>e*. When playing the game in Tok Pisin (Section 5), however, they were following the general rule of inserting infixes into every syllable. This leads to the assumption that Lihir children might have different rules for the games in Lihir. However, as (14) is the only example in my corpus with disyllablic words in Lihir, more research is needed to prove this assumption.

(14) **Lihir** (glossed after Neuhaus 2015)
  a. *o=le wa ka tu e?*
    2SG=want 2SG go toward where
    'Where do you want to go?'
  b. *o.le\<p\>e wa\<p\>a ka\<p\>a tu\<p\>u e\<p\>e?*

Example (15) from Notsi is interesting, not only because the diphthong [ai] in *la=ita* 'go=where' is made up across morpheme boundaries, but also because both vowel segments apparently occur inside the syllable peak. When imposing <p> on the syllable peak, the complete diphthong is repeated, and we get *lai<p>ai.ta<p>a* instead of the expected ?*la<p>ai.ta<p>a*. This is in clear contrast to all other languages in this chapter, which means that Notsi speakers might have a different phonological representation of dipthongs than speakers of other New Ireland languages. As this is the only Notsi example with diphthongs that I was able to collect (the examples of Tok Pisin and English from Notsi children did not contain diphthongs either), more research is necessary.

(15) **Notsi** (glossed after McCarthy 2000)
    a.   u   la=ita?
          2SG go=where
          'Where are you going?'
    b.   *u<p>u lai<p>ai.ta<p>a?*

5 Tok Pisin

The three language games are also known for Tok Pisin, as demonstrated in (16), which is based on the sentence *yumi (i) go nau* 'let's go now' as produced by a Tiang speaker. The predicate marker *i* as well as its derivations *i<p>i*, *i<ŋk>i* and *i<l>i<g>i* are optional.

(16) a.   *yumi*   *(i)*   *go*   *nau*
          1PL.INC PM   go   now
          'Let's go now.'
     b.   *yu<p>u.mi<p>i (i<p>i) go<p>o na<p>au*
     c.   *yu<ŋk>u.mi<ŋk>i (i<ŋk>i) go<ŋk>o na<ŋk>au*
     d.   *yu<l>u<g>u.mi<l>i<g>i (i<l>i<g>i) go<l>o<g>o na<l>a<g>au*

Tok Pisin features a more elaborate syllable structure than New Ireland languages in allowing for initial consonant clusters. Information from Verhaar (1995: 6–8) and Mosel (1980: 18) reveal a syllable structure of (S)(C)(L)V(C), where S stands for the sibilant /s/, L for the liquids /l, r, j, w/, and V for a vowel or diphthong. All elements, save the vowel, are optional to create well-formed syllables. Table 11.3 lists a selection of available syllables in Tok Pisin in which the three language games are performed by young Tiang speakers. Examples are written in the common Tok Pisin orthography. The rules are the same as for other New Ireland languages: One of the game infixes is imposed on the syllable peak, thus creating new demisyllables.

Table 11.3: Some Tok Pisin syllables.

	V	CVC	CLVC	SCV
normal	i 'PM'	taun 'town'	blong 'of'	sto 'shop'
<p>	i<p>i	ta<p>aun	blo<p>ong	sto<p>o
<ŋk>	i<ŋk>i	ta<ŋk>aun	blo<ŋk>ong	sto<ŋk>o
<l-g>	i<l>i<g>i	ta<l>a<g>aun	blo<l>o<g>ong	sto<l>o<g>o

As no fully accepted standard form of Tok Pisin exists, there is a high degree of speaker variation (Verhaar 1995: 3). The syllable structure (S)(C)(L)V(C) is an idealised construct, which is, in fact, not available to many speakers. Initial consonant clusters of lexical items are frequently broken up through insertion of an epenthetic vowel; *brus* 'tobacco' and *sto* 'shop' are thus commonly heard as [bu.rus] and [si.tɔ], respectively. Grammatical items, in turn, show the opposite variation in promoting the creation of syllable-initial clusters by eliding unstressed vowels, as in *bilong* 'of' becoming [blɔŋ], or *dispela* 'this' becoming [dis.pla]. Note that although syllables in Tok Pisin may start with /spl/, *disp(e)la* is syllabified as [dis.pla], not *[di.spla], likely due to its internal structure as *dis* 'this' and the noun modifier marker *-pela* (Verhaar 1995: 13), or because initial fricative–stop combinations are marked structures that violate syllable sonority principles (cf. Treiman et al. 1992 for similar findings on /s/-initial syllables in English). This fluctuation is evident when playing the language games (Table 11.4).

Table 11.4: Unstable Tok Pisin syllables.

normal	b(u.)rus 'tobacco'	s(i.)to 'shop'	b(i.)long 'of'	dis.p(e.)la 'this'
<p>	bu<p>u.ru<p>us	sto<p>o	blo<p>ong	di<p>is.pla<p>a
<ŋk>	bu<ŋk>u.ru<ŋk>us	sto<ŋk>o	blo<ŋk>ong	di<ŋk>is.pla<ŋk>a
<l-g>	bu<l>u<g>u.ru<l>u<g>us	sto<l>o<g>o	blo<l>o<g>ong	di<l>i<g>is.pe<l>e<g>e.la<l>a<g>a

Which syllables can be produced in Tok Pisin generally depends on the phonotactics of the speaker's mother tongue. It is hence not surprising that a Tiang-speaking child favours forms such as *bu<p>u.ru<p>us* from [bu.rus] 'tobacco', with an epenthetic vowel, over ?*bru<p>us* from the short form [brus], as Tiang does not allow for syllable-initial consonant clusters. However, the short [stɔ] 'shop' and [blɔŋ] 'of' were used to form *sto<p>o* and *blo<p>ong*. Madak children, in turn, produced *bi<p>i.lo<p>ong* from the longer [bi.lɔŋ] 'of'. Table 11.4 also shows speaker-internal variation within one item: *di<l>i<g>is.pe<l>e<g>e.la<l>a<g>a* derives from the full form [dis.pɛ.la] 'this', whereas *di<p>is.pla<p>a* and *di<ŋk>is.pla<ŋk>a* come from the shortened [dis.pla]. Such variety of possible outputs promotes the idea that individual speakers of the games have different underlying phonological representations of the same word, cf. the different treatment of off-glides in superheavy syllables in Tiang (Table 11.2). Sherzer (1967: 33) came to the same conclusion for language games in Kuna, a Chibchan language spoken in Panama.

Depending on which language the games are played in, the same speaker will treat the same segment string differently. Superheavy syllables are stable in Tok Pisin, even if spoken by a multilingual Tiang child (17a), whereas superheavy syllables are unstable in Tiang and are often broken up into two syllables (17b).

(17) a. *taun* 'town'　　　　　　　　*ta<p>aun*　　　　　(Tok Pisin)
　　　b. *kə.kə(.)is* 'fresh water spring'　*kə<p>ə.kə<p>ə.i<p>is* (Tiang)

What has been said about the language game use in Tok Pisin by Tiang speakers was generally reproduced as such by children from other language groups of New Ireland. The most commonly used game involves imposition of *<p>*, which is the case for the Tok Pisin variety used by Tigak, Kara, Nalik, Notsi, Kuot, Mandara, Lihir and Madak speakers. Tungag children also insert a labial consonant, but they use [ɸ] instead of [p] (18b), which is most likely influenced by their mother tongue in which [ɸ] and [p] are allophones (Fast 2015: 15). Mussau-speaking (Kendle Susuvin, p.c.) and Barok-speaking children claimed to prefer *<l-g>*.

(18) a. *yumi　　go　long　skul*
　　　　　1PL.INC　go　in　school
　　　　　'Let's go to school.'
　　　b. *yu<ɸ>u.mi<ɸ>i go<ɸ>o lo<ɸ>ong sku<ɸ>ul*

6 English

When playing language games in English, children most commonly used, again, the *<p>* infix. The rules are almost identical to what we have seen in the previous sections, but the complexity of English phonology and its realisation in a New Ireland accent require a few adaptations. These are illustrated in Table 11.5 using

IPA. While English phonotactics are similar to Tok Pisin, they differ in allowing for more complex consonant clusters in coda position, e.g., [ts] in *let's*. Syllabic sonorants as in *bottle* [bɒ.tl̩] are not available in New Ireland English and are treated as CVC syllables with an epenthetic vowel.

Table 11.5: Some New Ireland English syllables.

	CV	CVC	CVCC	CLV
normal	*də* 'the'	*bɔ.tɔl ~ bɔ.təl* 'bottle'	*lɛts* 'let's'	*krai* 'to cry'
<p>	*də<p>ə*	*bɔ<p>ɔ.tɔ<p>ɔl*	*lɛ<p>ɛts*	*kra<p>ai*
<ŋk>	*də<ŋk>ə*	*bɔ<ŋk>ɔ.tə<ŋk>əl*	*lɛ<ŋk>ɛts*	*kra<ŋk>ai*
<l-g>	*də<l>ə<g>ə*	*bɔ<l>ɔ<g>ɔ.tə<l>ə<g>əl*	*lɛ<l>ɛ<g>ɛts*	*kra<l>a<g>ai*

Initial consonant clusters are much more stable than in Tok Pisin. In fact, the same multilingual speaker who would insert an epenthetic vowel for initial clusters in Tok Pisin, would easily produce English clusters. Example (19) shows how the same lexical item 'to cry' is rendered differently depending on which language the games are played in. In (19a), English *cry* is treated as one syllable with a complex onset, resulting in the form *kra<p>ai*. Bisyllablic *ka<p>a.ra<p>ai*, in turn, is the preferred outcome of *k(a)rai* in Tok Pisin, with an epenthetic vowel between the initial consonants (19b).

(19)   a.   *cry*   *kra<p>ai*   (English)
       b.   *k(a.)rai* 'to cry' *ka<p>a.ra<p>ai*   (Tok Pisin)

One minor divergence was found in use by Tungag students. As shown in (13) for Tungag and (18) for Tok Pisin, Tungag children consistently produced [ɸ] and [p] in free variation, also for games played in English (20).

(20)   *let's go to school   lɛ<p>ɛts gɔ<ɸ>ɔu tu<p>u sku<ɸ>ul*

7 Conclusion

This chapter has presented three secret language games from New Ireland that are played among younger speakers for several different languages, including local languages from New Ireland, Tok Pisin and English. These games are special in that they are mainly played by girls with their friends, as opposed to other gender-based secret languages in Papua New Guinea, which have been more commonly described for adult men. Schools, accommodating many children from various parts of the province, harbour a creative environment for linguistic innovation and its spread across the whole province and even beyond.

The games feature segmental manipulation of words by imposing the consonantal infixes <p>, <ŋk> and <l-g> on a vowel. Storch (2017: 299) writes that "play languages help us to analyse phonological and morphological rules of individual base languages, which are often paradigmatically manipulated in language games and thereby made more transparent in their regularity". They provide evidence for the syllable structure and boundaries, for instance, in determining whether vowel sequences are real diphthongs and triphthongs, or whether they form separate syllable nuclei divided by a hiatus, and also evidence for how speakers have represented these structures mentally. Grammatical structures play only a minor role in the New Ireland games; thus, it is the phonetic realisation on which the game rules are based, usually ignoring morpheme boundaries. The exception is the fusion of two grammatical words, in which case the games are most frequently performed on the underlying unfused structure.

"Another achievement of the descriptive and typological research on play languages lies in the contribution to insights into language acquisition and multilingual practices" (Storch 2017: 300). With multilingualism being the norm in New Ireland, children are able to perform games in various languages with unlike phonotactics. Depending on which language a multilingual child is playing the games in, the child may treat the same string of segments differently. Tiang speakers have different stabilities of certain syllable structures in Tiang, Tok Pisin and English; syllables that are stable in one language can be unstable in another. On the other hand, multilingualism can spread allophonic variation from one language to another, as seen with Tungag children, who apply lenition of /p/ also to games in other languages.

Furthermore, having a language game in one's local language is an indicator that a language is still vital. If no one could speak or understand even the everyday register, there would be no need for creating a secret version of it. Indeed, languages are less likely to be used for language games when the youth have stopped acquiring their local language, as is the case in the Nalik (Volker 1994: 31) and Kuot areas (Lindström 2002: 81), where children reportedly play language games only in Tok Pisin or English.

Several questions remain. Why do children from the Lihir (14) and Notsi (15) areas have games that are inconsistent with the other language communities? Is it because of language-specific game rules, do they have a different mental representation of the segments, or have they not yet fully acquired the game rules and made mistakes in applying them?

What is the motivation behind secret language games in New Ireland? The simple answer would be that it is a means of private in-group communication among young females, for sharing secret information and gossip that are to remain unknown to outsiders. However, the game rules are also known by some boys and adults, which contradicts the idea of a secret language code. The use of language games seems more likely to be a mark of identity for initiated speakers. Bagemihl (1995: 700) offers an interesting view on this aspect of language games with the observation that although language games often add new morphology to a word, the added segments do not carry any meaning; rather, they are markers of a special register that classifies the speech act participants as belonging to a certain social group.

After all, language games also serve as entertainment for the speaker and the audience, and as a form of verbal art to practice one's language skills and manipulate language in a creative way – as Blake (2010: 227) puts it, "as much for fun as for real secrecy".

List of abbreviations

1	first person
2	second person
ART	article
INC	inclusive
IPFV	imperfective
NM	noun marker
PL	plural
PM	predicate marker
POSS	possessive
PUR	purpose marker
SG	singular
σ	syllable
?	uncertain form

References

Aikhenvald, Alexandra Y. 2014. 'Double talk': Parallel structures in Manambu songs, and their origin. *Language and Linguistics in Melanesia* 32 (2). 86–109.

Aufinger, Albert. 1942. Die Geheimsprachen auf den kleinen Inseln bei Madang in Neuguinea, *Anthropos* 37/40. 629–646.

Bagemihl, Bruce. 1995. Language games and related areas. In John A. Goldsmith (ed.). *The handbook of phonological theory*, 697–712. Oxford: Blackwell.

Beaumont, Clive H. 1979. *The Tigak language of New Ireland*. Canberra: Pacific Linguistics.
Blake, Barry J. 2010. *Secret language: Codes, tricks, spies, thieves, and symbols*. Oxford: Oxford University Press.
Blust, Robert A. 2013. *The Austronesian languages*. Canberra: Asia-Pacific Linguistics.
Botne, Robert and Stuart Davis. 2000. Language games, segment imposition, and the syllable. *Studies in Language* 24 (2). 319–344.
Breen, Gavan, and Rob Pensalfini. 1999. Arrernte: A language with no syllable onsets. *Linguistic Inquiry* 30(1), 1–25.
Condra, C. Edwin. 1989. *Patpatar grammar essentials*. Unpublished manuscript.
Dryer, Matthew S. 2013. *A grammatical description of Kara-Lemakot*. Canberra: Asia-Pacific Linguistics.
Fast, Karin E. 2015. *Spatial language in Tungag*. Canberra: Asia-Pacific Linguistics.
Foley, William A. 1986. *The Papuan languages of New Guinea*. Cambridge: Cambridge University Press.
Franklin, Karl J. and Roman Stefaniw. 1992. The 'pandanus languages' of the Southern Highlands Province, Papua New Guinea: A further report. In Tom Dutton (ed.), *Culture change, language change: Case studies from Melanesia*, 1–6. Canberra: Pacific Linguistics.
Hollington, Andrea. 2019. Chibende: Linguistic creativity and play in Zimbabwe. *International Journal of Language and Culture* 6 (1). 29–44.
Holz, Christoph. Forthcoming. *A comprehensive grammar of Tiang*. Cairns: Central Queensland University dissertation.
Laycock, Donald C. 1977. Special languages in parts of the New Guinea area. In Stephen A. Wurm (ed.), *New Guinea languages and language study* 3, 133–149. Canberra: Pacific Linguistics.
Lee, Robert. 2005. *Sentences in Madak*. Unpublished manuscript.
Lindström, Eva. 2002. *Topics in the grammar of Kuot: A non-Austronesian language of New Ireland, Papua New Guinea*. Stockholm: Stockholm University dissertation.
McCarthy, Joe. 2000. *Notsi interlinear grammar texts*. Unpublished manuscript.
Mosel, Ulrike. 1980. *Tolai and Tok Pisin: The influence of the substratum on the development of New Guinea Pidgin*. Canberra: Pacific Linguistics.
Neuhaus, Karl. 2015. *Grammar of the Lihir language of New Ireland, Papua New Guinea*. Translated and edited by Simon Ziegler. Port Moresby: Institute of Papua New Guinea Studies.
Sarvasy, Hannah S. 2014. *A grammar of Nungon: A Papuan language of the Morobe Province, Papua New Guinea*. Cairns: James Cook University dissertation.
Sarvasy, Hannah S. 2019. Taboo and secrecy in Nungon speech. *The Mouth* 4. 20–30.
Sherzer, Joel. 1976. Play languages: Implications for (socio)linguistics. In Barbara Kirshenblatt-Gimblett (ed.), *Speech play: Research and resources for the study of linguistic creativity*, 19–36. Philadelphia: University of Pennsylvania Press.
Senft, Gunter. 1996. *Classificatory particles in Kilivila*. New York and Oxford: Oxford University Press.
Storch, Anne. 2017. Typology of secret languages and linguistic taboos. In Alexandra Y. Aikhenvald and R. M. W. Dixon (eds.), *The Cambridge handbook of linguistic typology*, 287–321. Cambridge: Cambridge University Press.
Treiman, Rebecca, Jennifer Gross and Annemarie Cwikiel-Glavin. 1992. The syllabification of /s/ clusters in English. *Journal of Phonetics* 20. 383–402.

Verhaar, John W. M. 1995. *Toward a reference grammar of Tok Pisin: An experiment in corpus linguistics*. Honolulu: University of Hawai'i Press.

Volker, Craig A. 1989. The relationship between traditional secret languages and two school-based pidgin languages in Papua New Guinea. *Horizons: Journal of Asia-Pacific issues* 3. 19–24.

Volker, Craig A. 1994. *Nalik grammar (New Ireland, Papua New Guinea)*. Honolulu: University of Hawai'i dissertation.

Anna-Brita Stenström
12 Three "bad" favourites in Spanish-speaking teenagers' conversation

This chapter discusses how three recurrent "bad" words with a comparable origin, *huevón/a, boludo/a* and *gilipollas*, are used in spontaneous conversation by teenage students in Santiago de Chile, Buenos Aires and Madrid, respectively. Special emphasis is put on how the youth use these words when addressing each other and when talking about each other. The Latin-American words *huevon/a* and *boludo/a* turn out to be far more frequent than the peninsular word *gilipollas*, which, on the other hand, has a wider range of uses. The repeated use of these words has the effect that their "badness" is disappearing in people's minds. Chilean *huevón* constitutes a special case due to its recurring position at critical points in the ongoing conversation, which is turning it into a discourse marker.

1 Introduction

The three "bad" words to be discussed in this paper, Chilean *huevón/a*, Argentinian *boludo/a* and peninsular *gilipollas,* are very common, but what makes them even more interesting is that they have a comparable origin. This chapter illustrates how they are used by today's teenage students in Latin-American Santiago de Chile and Buenos Aires and peninsular Madrid, as reflected in COLA (*Corpus Oral de Lenguaje Adolescente*).

Incidentally, a preliminary survey of the conversations in the corpus revealed that both *huevón/a* and *boludo/a* turn up in the following conversation in which five Madrid boys are chatting about the use of Spanish bad words (abbreviated). This excerpt is preceded by a long passage in which the boys are trying to beat each other by uttering the most exaggerated taboo expressions.

(1) G07   *hola hola chicos palabrotas en español hijo de puta hijo de puuuta*
          'hello hello pals swearwords in Spanish son of a bitch son of a bitch'
    G03   [*je je*]
          'he he'

Anna-Brita Stenström, University of Bergen, e-mail: stenstrom.ab@gmail.com

https://doi.org/10.1515/9781501514685-014

G07 [*caabrón*]
'baastard'
G05 *me cago en tu puuta puuta maaadre*
'to hell with your bloody mother'
G05 *ahora palabrotas en colombiano hijo puta mama**huevo** cornudo*
'now taboo words in Columbian son of a bitch egg sucking cuckold'
G02 [*tu madre*][1]
'your mother'
G01 [***boludo***]
'arsehole'
G05 [***boludo** pelotudo*]
'stupid arsehole'
G01 *argentino*
'Argentinian' (MALCE2[2])

These Madrid boys are probably fully aware that *huevón/a* and *boludo/a* are the most popular bad words in Chile and Argentina, but there is no evidence in the COLA corpus that the Latin-American teenagers are familiar with the peninsular word *gilipollas* (see the epigraph below). For "bad" words, see Andersson and Trudgill (1990), Ramírez Gelbes and Estrada (2003), Stenström (2014).

J01 *sabes grabar*
'can you record'
G02 *no. soy gilipollas*
'no, I'm an idiot'
J01 *vale*
'okay' (MABPE2)

Corpus Oral de Lenguaje Adolescente (COLA) consists of three subcorpora, all collected at the beginning of the 21st century in Madrid (COLAm), Buenos Aires (COLAba) and Santiago de Chile (COLAs). Each subcorpus consists of spontaneous, unsupervised everyday conversations or chats, recorded by students who were willing to record their encounters with classmates and friends for a few days in various informal situations, for instance, when they met in the school yard, in the street, in a park, at a cafe, or at home.

---

[1] For swearing by mother, see Danbolt Drange, Hasund and Stenström (2014: 29–59).
[2] Refers to the text the dialogue is taken from.

The students who took part in the conversations were 13 to 19-year-old boys and girls with varying socio-economic backgrounds and living in the same area. They were all aware of being recorded, which seems to have had an effect on their sometimes rather offensive choice of vocabulary.

2 Origin and development

Huevón/a, *boludo/a* and *gilipollas* have a partly comparable origin and similar functions.

2.1 Huevón/a

Voy muy huevón para la casa de la huevona
'I often go 0[3] to the girl's house' (SCEAB8)

The origin of *huevón/a* is the singular form *hueva* ('testicle') and the masculine suffix *on*. Originally, it referred to a 'courageous man', but as time went by the meaning of 'courageous' changed to 'stupid' and 'coward' (cf. Ramírez Gelbes and Estrada 2003: 337, Rojas 2012: 143–154, Stenström 2020). Today, *huevón* can refer to a person who is not only lazy, stupid and slow but also a coward (*Collins Spanish English Dictionary*), to a person who is so lazy that his testicles drag on the ground (*Urban Dictionary*). According to *Wiktionary*, the size "of a man's balls" is indirectly proportional to his intelligence in many Latin countries.

Huevón/a is used in nearly any situation and context as an insult and/or as a greeting. What it signifies, depends entirely on who is spoken to, when, where and in what contextual situation. If it is said in a derogatory way, it means 'asshole', 'dickhead', 'dumb', and 'slow'. Used in a friendly way it means 'friend', 'mate', 'bro(ther)' and 'guy'.[4] Whether *huevón/a* is intended to be friendly or unfriendly can only be interpreted in actual use (Mateo and Yus 2000). It is not perceived to be as rude today as it used to be, though it is still regarded as a "bad" word by some adults.

Huevón/a has given rise to the derivatives *huevada* ('stupidity', 'nonsense'); *huevear* ('bother', 'have fun', 'joke'), *ahuevonado* ('fool', 'dumbass'), as in *saca esa* **huevada ahuevonado** ('stop this nonsense dumbass') and *deja de* **huevear**

---

[3] '0' indicates that the Spanish word would probably not correspond to an English word.
[4] See [http://www.spanish.cl/chilean/huevon-weon-gueon.htm].

huevones ('stop joking idiots'), which all occur in COLAs. Whether the Chilean students use the short forms *weón/a, weon* and *wn* cannot be attested, since they do not appear in the transcripts.

2.2 Boludo/a

J01   *Yo cada dos minutos digo* **boludo** *hablo mucho*
'every second minute I say boludo I talk a lot'
pero la mitad son malas palabras
'but half of it is bad words' (BABSU2)

Like *huevón/a*, *boludo/a* is extremely common and "so important that it nearly defines the sociolinguistic identity of the pueblo argentino, or the Argentine people".[5] Similarly to *huevón/a*, the origin of *boludo/a* is a word for 'testicles', the plural form *bolas* to which is added the suffix *-udo*. It comes from the Argentine dialect Lunfardo and has developed from a noun used to indicate somebody with disproportionally big testicles to a noun representing somebody who is really stupid, and later into a word that can be used even in a friendly way (Ramírez Gelbes and Estrada 2003: 337). Like *huevón/a*, *boludo/a* is not always negative; depending on the speaking situation, it may be a strong insult or a term of great affection.

As a friendly term it corresponds to 'mate', 'girl, or 'dude' and as an insult to 'arsehole' or 'dumbass'. The word is generally used among friends of the same age as the speaker, among girls in particular. Since it can be quite an insult, it should be used with caution but like *huevón/a*, it is losing its status as a "bad" word (Ramírez Gelbes and Estrada 2003: 337).

Boludo/a has given rise to *bolu*, which is short for *boludo/a*, as in *te haces la bolu u uda ja ja ja* ('they call you bolu u uda ha ha ha'), and *boludez* ('stupidity', 'something trivial', 'unimportant'), as in *yo no quiero que nos peleamos por una boludez* ('I don't want us to fight for a trifle'), expressions that occur in COLAba.

2.3 Gilipollas

According to *Diccionario de la Real Academia Española*, *gilipollas* is an adjective meaning 'silly' and 'stupid'. *Urban Dictionary* states that it is a compound of the vulgar adjective *gili* ('innocent', 'stupid') and the vulgar noun *polla* ('penis'),

---

5 See [https://www.fluentu.com/log/spanish/boludo-argentina/].

originally with reference to a person who "thinks with his penis and not with his head", and "somebody who is less of a man, who does not act like a man". The closest English equivalents to *gilipollas* would be *dickhead* or *arsehole*. In the middle ages, *gili* ('stupid') and *polla* ('penis') referred to men who only managed to generate girls, signalling that the man's penis was so stupid that it did not know how to produce boys.[6]

A witty description in folk etymology of the origin of *gilipollas* goes back to the end of the 16th century and a certain don Baltasar Gil Imón de la Motga, who occupied a high position in the Spanish Finance Department. When appearing at important festivities organized for the Madrid society, he used to be accompanied by his daughters, hoping to attract the attention of some suitable cavaliers. People attending the festivities used to comment on the appearance of father and daughters by saying *ahí va don Gil con sus pollas* ('here comes don Gil with his maidens'). At the time, the word *polla* was used for 'maiden', 'girl'. The suggestion is that this gave rise to the word *gilipollas*.[7] The following dialogue seems to reflect J01's awareness of the origin of *gilipollas* suggested in this paragraph:

(2) J02 [*mira quién hay <nombre> ju ju ju*][8]
 'look who it is <name> hi hi hi'
 J04 [*quién hay/ no le había visto*]
 'who is it/ I didn't see him'
 J01 *tía pues ese es un **gilipollas gil i pollas** palabra compuesta*
 'O cos he is a blockhead gil i pollas a compound' (MALCE2)

Only one derivative occurs in the COLAm conversations: *gilipollez*. No derivative verb such as **gilipollear* occurs, for instance. With regards to the meaning of *gilipollas*, on the other hand, a great number of alternatives have been generated. *The Multilingual Dictionary Term Bank* lists as many as 176 meanings, divided into 'general' (*dumb, jerk*), 'idioms' (*nerd, twat*), 'colloquial' (*arsehole, prick*) and 'slang' (*wanker, dickhead*), including the sub-section 'British slang' (*dickfuck, cunt*).

An additional section lists a number of 'idioms': *quedar como un gilipollas* ('make an arse of oneself'), 'colloquial': *hacerse el gilipollas* ('bum/idle about') and 'slang': *hacer el gilipollas* ('screw off', 'dick around'). The most common phrases are considered to be *eres gilipollas* ('you're an arsehole') and *gilipollas de mierda* ('fucking arsehole').[9]

---

[6] See [http://etimologias.dechile.net/?gillipollas].
[7] See [http://www.secretosdemadrid.es/].
[8] Indicates simultaneous speech.
[9] See [http://www.spanishdict.com/translate/gilipollas].

3 Frequencies

The three subcorpora differ considerably in size, with COLAm consisting of 456.340 words and COLAs and COLAba of no more than 70.534 and 68.579 words, respectively. In other words, the difference in size between the two Latin American corpora on the one hand and the peninsular corpus on the other hand is striking. COLAm is more than six times as large as both COLAs and COLAba. Consequently, a different distribution than the one presented in Table 12.1 might have been expected:

Table 12.1: Frequency of *huevón/a* and *boludo/a* and *gilipollas* in relation to corpus size.

Corpora	COLAs	COLAba	COLAm
Corpus size	70.534	68.579	456.340
Bad words	huevón/a	boludo/a	gilipollas
Total occurrences	384/29	81/186	204
Per cent of corpus size	0.59 %	0.39 %	0.04%

However, despite the comparatively large size of COLAm compared to the far smaller size of COLAs and COLAba, the Madrid teenagers' most common bad word *gilipollas* turned out to be much less common than both Chilean *huevón/a* and Argentinian *bulodo/a*. A factor that contributes to the difference between COLAm and the smaller corpora is undoubtedly the Madrid teenagers' preference for a neutral word, most often *tío/a* or *tronco/a* ('boy/girl'), instead of a potentially bad word when addressing or talking about somebody (Rodríguez González and Stenström 2011: 245).[10] Table 12.2 sums up the students' use of *huevón/a*, *boludo/a* and *gilipollas*:

Table 12.2: Frequency of *huevón/a*, *boludo/a* and *gilipollas* in the three corpora.

	Boys	Girls
gilipollas	79	125
huevón	345	39
huevona	13	16
boludo	70	11
boluda	7	176
Total	514	367

---

10 Participants in COLA are roughly 53.6 percent girls and 46.4 percent boys.

As Table 12.2 shows, the overall distribution of Chilean *huevón/a* is strikingly different from that of Argentinian *boludo/a*. In COLAs, the male form *huevón* dominates, and in COLAba, the female form *boluda*. Moreover, *huevón* is more than thirteen times as frequent as the female form *huevona*, while *boluda* is slightly more than twice as common as the male form *boludo*. This points to a specific role in the discourse for *huevón* (cf. Section 5), while *boluda* is characterised as a term of endearment that is frequent in girls' conversations (cf. Section 2.2).

The fact that the female forms *huevona* and *boluda* are most often uttered by girls and the male forms *huevón* and *boludo* by boys seems to point to a majority of girls only and boys only conversations. The form *gilipollas*, which does not reveal the sex of the addressee, turns out to be a girls' word, more often uttered by girls than by boys. A survey of the female-male distribution showed that it is more often used in girls only than in boys only conversations, but also that it occurs most often in mixed-sex conversations (cf. Stenström 2017: 161). Unlike *huevón/a* and *boludo/a*, *gilipollas* often has a 'neutral' meaning, neither addressing nor talking about somebody, as in *nos divertimos un rato haciendo el gilipollas* ('let's enjoy ourselves a little while dicking around').

4 Two levels

The use of *huevón/a*, *boludo/a* and *gilipollas* can be seen in a syntactic perspective: how they are arranged to form phrases and sentences – and in a pragmatic perspective: how they are related to meaning in use.

4.1 The syntactic level

Huevón/a, *boludo/a* and *gilipollas* can all serve as adjectives, although there are extremely few instances of *huevon/a* and *boludo/a* in this function:

está boluda esta niña	('she is stupid this girl')
serías muy huevón	('you would be very stupid')
son muy gilipollas	('they are very stupid')

All three terms also appear as nouns, serving as subject, subject complement and direct object:

Subject:
la huevona empezó a llorar ('the stupid girl started to cry')
la boluda vino ('the girl came')
lo dice el gilipollas ('that's what the dickhead says')

Subject complement:
es un huevón impotente ('he is a weakling')
como si fuese una boluda ('as if it was a girl')
porque es un puto gilipollas de mierda ('because he is a bloody bastard').[11]

Direct object:
me presentó un huevón ('he introduced a guy to me')
...para dejar otro boludo ('to leave another idiot')
...para decirle gilipollas tronca ('to tell him nonsense dumbass')

4.2 The pragmatic level

On the pragmatic level, *huevón/a, boludo/a* and *gilipollas* are used as vocatives, addressing somebody directly (Jørgensen and Martínez 2010, Stenström 2020), or talking about somebody who is not present or not within hearing.

4.2.1 Addressing somebody

For the use of the three terms in direct address, consider examples (3) to (5):

(3) *Cállate gilipollas!* 'Shut up dickhead'

(4) *Me voy a quedar en mi casa huevona* 'I'm going to stay at home 0'

---

[11] Notice that there are two versions of BE in Spanish: SER and ESTAR. ESTAR is used to indicate position: estamos en Madrid ('we are in Madrid'). Otherwise the choice of SER or ESTAR depends on whether the subject complement is seen as a characteristic feature: **son** muy gilipollas estos tíos ('they are very stupid these guys') or a situation-bound feature: hay veces que cuando **está** gilipollas... ('there are times when he is stupid'). Sometimes the boundary line between characteristic and situation-bound is vague and seems to go against the rule: estoy pensando que **he sido** gilipollas ('I'm thinking that I've been an idiot'), in which the speaker probably thinks that she has been stupid for quite some time and not at a particular moment.

(5) *Qué quieres que haga boludo?*   'What do you want me to do man/silly ass'

The imperative in (3) invites a rude interpretation, the simple statement about the speaker staying at home as in (4) does not, while the question in (5) opens for either a neutral or a negative interpretation depending on the circumstances. As demonstrated in (4), the Spanish vocative, here *huevona*, will not always be translated into English. In Madrid Spanish, it generally corresponds to a neutral word such as *tía* ('girl'), as demonstrated by Stenström and Jørgensen (2011: 265) and Rodríguez González and Stenström (2011: 245). The extent to which *huevón/a*, *boludo/a* and *gilipollas* are used as vocatives differs a great deal between the corpora, as Table 12.3 shows:

Table 12.3: Percentage vocatives in COLAs, COLAba and COLAm.

Word	Percentage
huevón	73.9
huevona	41.4
boludo	74.1
boluda	83.3
gilipollas	33.8

The forms *huevón*, *boludo* and *boluda* predominate as vocatives. A closer observation shows that *huevona* generally refers to a girl who is being talked 'about' (*la huevona, esa huevona*, etc.). Whether a boy or a girl is being addressed by the 'gender neutral' *gilipollas* does not show for obvious reasons. Moreover, it tends to be used not only as a noun (*el gilipollas*) but also as an adjective (*es muy gilipollas*).

The comparatively low figures for the Chilean female form *huevona* may seem surprising compared to the much higher figures for Argentinian *boluda*. This raises the question whether there are more male than female speakers in COLAs and more female than male speakers in COLAba, which turns out not to be the case. The gender distribution is roughly the same in the two corpora, with slightly more girls than boys, and has nothing to␣ with the number of boys and girls in the respective corpus. The answer seems simply to be that *boluda* is a more frequent way of addressing a girl in Buenos Aires than *boludo* is to address a boy, while the frequency of *huevón* is due to its special function in the conversation (cf. Section 5).

In their role as a vocative, *huevón/a, boludo/a* and *gilipollas* may be intended as insults: *Tonto huevón, huevón maricón* ('stupid bastard'), *huevón de mierda* ('bloody idiot'); *sos*[12] *un pene boludo* ('you are a bastard'), *tu eres feo gilipollas* ('you are ugly dumbass'). But a scrutiny of the three corpora, judging by the effect in the actual context, shows that the insulting effect is extremely rare, which indicates that their rudeness is weakening, that they express company and camaraderie rather than offense. This is emphasised by Vigara Tauste (2002: 230), who regards the bad vocatives as "apelativos cariñosos" ('friendly address terms') in line with Zimmermann (2002: 15). All three terms can occur in expressions of appreciation or displeasure and as interjections. For the use of vocatives in youth language in Madrid, Buenos Aires and Santiago de Chile, see Jørgensen (2011).

Concerning their position: As vocatives, *huevón/a, boludo/a* and *gilipollas* are found in initial, medial or final position in an utterance/turn, or as a turn of their own in the exchange, with a different function depending on where they occur. This is demonstrated in examples (6) to (9) (cf. Stenström 1984, 1994, Leech 1999, Stenström 2008, 2014). In *initial* position, the vocative links up with the previous speaker's utterance or initiates new information:

(6) G02   *no no es así*
          'no it's not like that'
    G01   **huevón** *cállate*
          'shut up man'
    G02   *no me acuerdo*
          'I don´t remember' (scawm4)

In *medial* position the vocative establishes or maintains contact between speaker and interlocutor:

(7) J04   *nadie nadie nadie entiende que es ese aparato* **boluda** *pasan y miran*
          'nobody nobody nobody understands that it is this equipment they pass and watch' (BABAS4)

Here *boluda* acts as a "marcador de control de contacto" [contact check] (Briz 2000: 34) and as a conversational "filler", helping to keep the conversation going, closely in line with Chilean *huevón*, Madrid Spanish *tío/a* and BrE *you know*. In *final* position the vocative invites a reaction, as indicated in (8).

---

[12] The form *sos* corresponds to peninsular Spanish *are*.

(8) G04 *casi me rompes las gafas **gilipollas***
         'you almost ruined my spectacles bastard'
    G03 *es lo que intento*
         'that's what I intend to' (MALCC2)

When *standing alone*, the vocative reacts, agrees, and confirms:

(9) G15 *es un pájaro negro así*
         'it's a blackbird'
    G01 **huevón**
         'thickhead'
    G15 *dice tui tui tui tui tui tui*
         'it says tui tui tui tui tui tui' (scawm4)

4.2.2 Talking about others

In addition to serving as vocatives, *huevón/a, boludo/a* and *gilipollas* are used for talking about others, for instance, persons who are not present in the speaking situation or not within hearing:

tan delicada la huevona	'she is so sensitive the girl'
es una boluda	'she is a fool'
y se lo dice el gilipollas	'that's what the jerk says'

An interesting question from a gender perspective is to what extent the girls talk about boys and the boys talk about girls, as reflected in the corpora. A scrutiny of COLAs and COLAba showed that *huevón* was mentioned ten times by the girls and *huevona* twelve times by the boys in COLAs, while *boludo* occurred only once and *boluda* not at all in reference to the opposite gender in COLAba. Whether that indicates that the Argentinian teenagers are less interested in the other sex than the Chilean teenagers is of course an open question. Obviously, *gilipollas* does not permit any speculations of this kind.

5 From vocative to discourse marker

As was demonstrated in Table 12.3, the frequency of the male form *huevón* in the Santiago conversations far exceeds that of the female form *huevona*. This reflects the gradual development of *huevón* into a discourse marker, the aim of which is to maintain the contact between speaker and addressee and facilitate the continuation of the current speaker's speaking turn. Romero Trillo (2002: 774) characterises discourse markers as "elements that have undergone a process of discourse grammaticalization and have included in their semantic/grammatical meaning a pragmatic dimension that serves for interactive purposes". This development, grammaticalisation, which is "a process of language change by which words representing objects and actions (i.e. nouns and verbs) become grammatical markers" (Wikipedia) involves semantic, syntactic and phonetic change and is described in detail for *huevón* by Rojas (2012: 156–162). No less than eighteen percent of the *huevón* instances in COLAs appear to be undergoing this change. They are generally preceded by (*po/pues*) or simply *pues* (cf. Section 4.2) and occur in the following positions:

- At the beginning of an utterance, helping the speaker to get started: *ah sí **(po/pues) huevón** (tenís / tienes) suerte huevón* ('oh yes cos man you're lucky man')
- In the middle of an utterance signalling hesitation: *tienes posibilidades **pues huevón** o sea no no no porque . . .* ('you have possibilities cos man or no no no because')
- As a filler, giving the speaker more time: *no las cargo **(po/pues) huevón** sencillamente hablo con ellas* ('I don't accuse them cos man seriously I'll talk to them')
- At the end of an utterance, indicating that the speaker has no more to say: *sí pues arriesgas tu vida **pues huevón*** ('yes cos you risk your life man')

Judging by occurrences in the COLAba conversations, the grammaticalisation process is also affecting *boluda*, which occurs as a conversational filler, helping the speaker keep the conversation going without interruptions:

(10) J01 *míralo boluda que están todas son todas se ponen en pedo boluda van vestidas tipo putas*
'look 0 all are they are all getting drunk 0 they are dressed like prostitutes' (BABSU2)

Gilipollas, by contrast, shows no signs of being affected by this process. As pointed out in connection with example (4), the "filler" function in the Madrid youngsters' language is generally realised by a "neutral" word, in particular *tía* (girl) or *tío* (man/boy), as in (11) and (12).

(11) A   *por qué estás todo el rato con Manuel*
         'why are you all the time with Manuel'
     B   *porque **tía** porque le quiero mucho*
         'because 0 I like him very much' (MALCE2)

(12) A   *sí te lo juro*
         'yes I swear'
     B   *pero **porque tío** que le conozco joder es mi vecino*
         'but cos 0 I know him for fuck's sake he's my neighbour' (MAMTE2)

The closest corresponding expression in English would be *you know*, a typical discourse marker.

6 Conclusions

Both *huevón/a* and *boludo/a* are typical language exponents of their respective countries. Visitors to Santiago or Buenos Aires can hear these words frequently, which indicates that they are not only used by the young. *Gilipollas*, by contrast, will probably go largely unnoticed by the Madrid visitor. Yet, there are strong reasons for treating the three together: their comparable origin, their further development, and their largely parallel everyday use as a means for speakers to address and talk about each other.

A noticeable difference is that *huevón/a* and *boludo/a* are far more common as address terms than *gilipollas*, which tends to be substituted by a neutral term in that function, in particular by *tío/a*. Yet another difference is that *gilipollas* is both personal, as in *los gilipollas que somos* ('the fools that we are') and impersonal, as in *tus cagadas gilipollas* ('your bloody stupidities'). Moreover, only *gilipollas* is used as an interjection: *Ah por gilipollas!* ('Oh for god's sake'). In other words, *gilipollas* is more versatile than both *huevón/a* and *boludo/a*.

Finally, the way *huevón/a*, *boludo/a* and *gilipollas* are used in COLA, mainly as a friendly address term and a phatic device, helping to keep the conversation going, makes the epithet "bad" largely outdated.

References

Andersson, Lars and Peter Trudgill. 1990. *Bad language*. Oxford: Blackwell.
Briz Gómez, Antonio. 1998. *El español coloquial en la conversación*. Madrid: Ariel Lingüística.
Drange, Eli-Marie Danbolt, Ingrid Kristine Hasund and Anna-Brita Stenström. 2014. "*Your mum!*" Teenagers' swearing by mother in English, Spanish and Norwegian. *International Journal of Corpus Linguistics* 19 (1). 29–59.
Jørgensen, Annette Myre. 2011. Formas de tratamiento: los vocativos en el lenguaje juvenil de Madrid, Buenos Aires y Santiago de Chile. In Leticia Rebollo Couto and Célia Santos Lopez (eds.), *As formas de tratamento em português e em espanhol: variação, mudança e funções conversacionais*, 127–150. Rio de Janeiro: UFF.
Jørgensen, Annette Myre and Juan Martínez. 2010. *Vocatives and phatic communion in Spanish teenage talk*. Cambridge: Cambridge Scholars Publishing.
Leech, Geoffrey. 1999. The distribution and functions of vocatives. In Hilde Hasselgård and Signe Oksefjell (eds.), *Out of corpora*, 107–120. Amsterdam and Atlanta: Brill and Rodopi.
Matéo, José and Francisco Yus. 2000. Insults: A relevance-theoretic taxonomical approach to their translation. *International Journal of Translation* 12 (1). 97–130.
Ramírez Gelbes, Silvia and Andrea Estrada. 2003. *Annuario de Estudios Filológicos* 26. 335–353.
Rodríguez González, Félix and Anna-Brita Stenström. 2011. Expressive devices in the language of English- and Spanish speaking youth. *Alicante Journal of English Studies* 24. 235–256.
Rojas, Darío. 2012. *Huevón* como marcador de discurso en el español de Chile. Huellas de un proceso de gramaticalización. *Revista de Humanidades* 25. 145–164.
Romero Trillo, Jesús. 2002. The pragmatic fossilization of discourse markers in non-native speakers of English. *Journal of Pragmatics* 34. 769–784.
Stenström, Anna-Brita. [1984] 1994. *An introduction to spoken interaction*. London: Longman.
Stenström, Anna-Brita. 2008. Algunos rasgos característicos del habla de contacto en el lenguaje de adolescentes en Madrid. *Oralia* 11. 207–226.
Stenström, Anna-Brita. 2014. *Teenage talk. From general characteristics to the use of pragmatic markers in a contrastive perspective*. Basingstoke: Palgrave Macmillan.
Stenström, Anna-Brita. 2017. Swearing in English and Spanish. *Advances in Swearing Research*, 157–162. Amsterdam: John Benjamins:
Stenström, Anna-Brita. 2020. Los Vocativos. In M. E. Placencia and Y.X. Padilla (eds.), *Guía práctica de pragmática del español*, 70–80. London and New York: Routledge.
Stenström, Anna-Brita. 2020. English and Spanish teenagers' use of rude vocatives. In Nico Nassenstein and Anne Storch (eds.), *Swearing and cursing: Contexts and practices in a critical linguistic perspective*, 281–302. Berlin: De Gruyter Mouton.
Stenström, Anna-Brita and Annette Myre Jørgensen. 2011. La pragmática contrastiva basada en el análisis de corpus: Perspectivas desde el lenguaje juvenil. In Lars Fant and Ana María Harvey (eds.), *El diálogo oral en el mundo hispanohablante*, 251–276. Frankfurt am Main: Vervuert.

Vigara Tauste, Ana Maria. 2002. Cultura y estilo de los niños bien: radiografía del lenguaje pijo. In Félix Rodríguez Gonzáles (ed.), *El lenguaje de los jóvenes*, 195–242. Barcelona: Ariel.
Zimmermann, Klaus. 2002. La variedad juvenil y la interacción verbal entre jóvenes. In Félix Rodríguez González (ed.), *El lenguaje de los jóvenes*, 137–163. Barcelona: Ariel.

Electronic references

Collins Spanish-English Dictionary online: [https://www.collinsdictionary.com/dictionary/spanish-english] (accessed 1 June 2020).
Diccionario de la Academia Española: [https://dle.rae.es/] (accessed 6 June 2020).
Fluentu: [http://www.fluentu.com/log/spanish/boludo-argentina] (accessed 1 June 2020).
Secretos de Madrid: [http://www.secretosdemadrid.es] (accessed 1 June 2020).
Spanish.cl: [http://www.spanish.cl/chilean/huevon-weon-gueon.htm] (accessed 1 June 2020).
Spanish.dict: [http://www.spanishdict.com/translate/gilipollas] (accessed 1 June 2020).
The Multilingual Dictionary Term Bank: [https://termbank.com/en/spanish-english/gilipollas] (accessed 9 June 2020).
Urban Dictionary: [http://www.urbandictionary.com] (accessed 06 June 2020).

Part III: **Ideologies and belonging**

While all of the studies in this volume have something to do with linguistic forms and social purposes as emphasized in the previous sections, the following chapters have a particular focus on the belief systems and sense of group belonging that underlie youth language practices. Youth languages reflect young people's ideologies and their in-group and out-group behavior. Nowadays the new media are an omnipresent feature of youths' way of life, being important carriers of synchronous communication in spoken mode, as well as of asynchronous communication, the more formal written mode (Busch and Sindoni). Many forms of socialization depend now on the use of digital media (Sindoni et al. 2019), which helps youth to adapt to and integrate into the different national and international communicative communities, without disintegrating themselves from their local urban communities but continuing to use local ways of speaking (Tropea, Vaughan and Carter). Feelings of belonging to the local community makes youths' ways of speaking attractive for use in advertisements (Kariuki et al. 2015, Nassenstein 2020) and movies (Febrianti and Yannuar). Youth may even transfer their languages abroad, using them in the diaspora and keeping contact with the community at home, as can be observed in Italy with Camfranglais (Machetti and Siebetcheu 2013). These language varieties have become valuable not only as identity markers but also as socially acceptable and valuable media of communication. New ways of communication expand the functions of youth languages and have an impact on their status, forcing modification of our definitions of youth language. The question of what is to be considered a youth language (its typical or diagnostic characteristics and its boundaries) arises also when seeing that speakers of a given "low-status" youth language like Sango Godobé (CAR) do not define their way of speaking as such, but consider it a hardly deviant variety of the common language (Nassenstein and Pasch). Youth make choices about being segregated or integrated into various "imagined communities" (Anderson 2006). Oftentimes, musicians adopt and engage in the creation of youth language in their presentations trying to raise its prestige and that of the respective youth. In Rufumbira (Uganda) the hip hop style Amahoro Fleva, characterized by many innovations, is quite generally associated with positive prestige and it has become an inverted emblem of local culture and pride (Nassenstein and Pasch). The question of defining youth language also arises with regard to the authorship of specific features of "high-status" youth languages that were not created by youth themselves but retained from school books which had the purpose of spreading these features as part of a language planning program as is the case with Ruyaye (Nassenstein and Pasch) or from languages of culture and higher education like Latin or French as in *Burschensprache* used by German students in the 18th and 19th centuries, and promoted for the purpose of building their character and conforming their political values and attitudes to ruling ideology (Storch).

There is need to extend the boundaries of the thematic area "youth language" to situations in the past and into new domains. Linguists also have to make clear why given ways of speaking are called youth languages and by whom, and whether the speakers should have a say in that. Further contesting and expanding the boundaries of existing scholarship on youth languages, the chapters by Nassenstein and Pasch and by Storch conclude this volume, offering a gateway for discussion into the future of research on youth languages.

References

Anderson, Benedict. 2006. *Imagined communities: Reflections on the origin and spread of nationalism*. London/New York: Verso.

Kariuki, Annah, Fridah Erastus Kanana and Hilda Kebeya. 2015. The growth and use of Sheng in advertisements in selected businesses in Kenya. *Journal of African Cultural Studies* 27 (2). 229–246.

Machetti, Sabrina and Raymond Siebetcheu 2013. The use of Camfranglais in the Italian migration context. *Tilburg Papers in Culture Studies* 55. [https://pure.uvt.nl/ws/portalfiles/portal/30358652/TPCS_55_Machetti_Siebetcheu.pdf] (accessed 03 July 2021).

Sindoni, Maria Grazia, Elisabetta Adami, Styliani Karatza, Ivana Marenzi, Ilaria Moschini, Sandra Petroni and Marc Rocca. 2019. *Common framework for intercultural digital literacies*, 1–255. [https://www.eumade4ll.eu/wpcontent/uploads/2019/09/cfridil-framework-MG3_IM_4-compresso.pdf] (accessed 03 July 2021).

Nassenstein, Nico. 2020. Tokooos! as a linguistic fashion: The recontextualization and appropriation of Lingala youth language. *Linguistics Vanguard* 6,s4: 20190035.

Florian Busch and Maria Grazia Sindoni
13 Metapragmatics of mode-switching: Young people's awareness of multimodal meaning making in digital interaction

Young people's social relationships are increasingly established and maintained through digital media. Today's communicative engagements parallel the continuous challenge to deploy a range of semiotic resources that can be arranged in various media platforms for different communicative events. The use of popular applications, such as WhatsApp and Skype, is characterized by varying combinations of speech and/or writing as well as the orchestration of other semiotic resources. The chapter aims to expand the original notion of *mode-switching* (Sindoni 2013) to empirically focus on these patterns of resources in a data set of Skype video calls between international University students, on the one hand, and a data set of WhatsApp threads between German secondary school students, on the other. Drawing on the concept of *media ideology* (Gershon 2010a), the study examines the metapragmatic awareness on which these multimodal practices are based as shown in the data. The chapter thus develops an understanding of mode-switching as a communicative practice that is functionally shaped by participants and discusses similarities and differences of such practices between video calls and text messaging data.

1 Introduction: Digital practices in the social life of young people

Digital practices are currently so pervasive in the lives of teenagers[1] that most forms of socialization are established, built, and maintained by and with digital media, texts, and practices (Sindoni et al. 2019) – boosted by the growing use of smartphones (Lenhart et al. 2015), which allow increasingly open and free access to networked and rapidly evolving web scenarios (boyd 2014). In the European context

---
[1] In this paper, we will follow the UN definition that includes in the category of young people those between 15 and 24.

Florian Busch, Martin Luther University of Halle-Wittenberg,
e-mail: florian.busch@germanistik.uni-halle.de
Maria Grazia Sindoni, University of Messina, e-mail: mariagrazia.sindoni@unime.it

https://doi.org/10.1515/9781501514685-016

in 2016, 91% of young people engaged with digital-based activities (in comparison to 71% of the overall European population), while 83% used mobile phones to access the internet away from home, work, and school (Eurostat 2017). The most current and frequent digitally interconnected services, in which young people are most likely involved, can be grouped around three loose and overlapping categories, distinguished by the European Commission (2018), namely: (1) email and communication; (2) chat and messaging media; and (3) social networking websites and social media platforms. By using these various online services, children and young people today are the most connected generation ever – provided with virtually endless kinds of digital entertainment, for example as they stream videos, listen to music, and use game-related materials (Childwise 2019). However, a significant portion of young people's online activities still involves talking with others through emails, instant messaging, or other chat systems (Frydenberg 2018, Nadkarni and Hofmann 2012). Chat is a general term used to describe interactive communication that takes place on a dedicated discussion channel that includes two or more people, typically in informal contexts, by means of different digital tools with a range of media affordances (including typing, video and audio streaming, and instantaneous message exchange). WhatsApp, Kik, Snapchat, Viber, Telegram, or iMessage are currently the most popular messaging apps, whereas software programs, such as Skype, MSN, and Facetime, are some of the most used for live conversations. Real-time infrastructures, such as the services mentioned, imply very low latency at a global level and provide experiences that are perceived as happening *now*. These may include any kind of live data, or a live interaction like chat or customer support which can be regarded as an "open, bi-directional, synchronous, channel of communication" (Friedlein 2016).

In this paper, we will consider two forms of real-time interactions: (1) live conversations via software programs, such as Skype, that are synchronous by default and (2) text-based interactions through messenger apps, such as WhatsApp, that may not involve live interaction but that nonetheless give real-time feedback on what other participants are doing – thus putting social pressure to respond immediately as the unmarked choice. In the following, we examine how participants in these two media environments use semiotic resources differently to sustain collaborative interactions by taking on a two-fold perspective: (1) we explore communicative patterns by unpacking the use of different semiotic resources, such as speech, writing, visuals (e.g., emojis, gifs, pictures),[2] and media affordances (Skype vs.

---

[2] Following van Leeuwen (2005: 285), *semiotic resources* are understood as "the actions, materials and artefacts we use for communicative purposes [. . .] together with the ways in which these resources can be organized. Semiotic resources have a meaning potential, based on their

WhatsApp platforms) and (2) we investigate young people's media ideologies and their metapragmatic awareness within these digital communicative scenarios.

To this end, we will first introduce the concept of mode-switching (Section 2) as well as that of media ideologies (Section 3) to develop a view on the metapragmatics of multimodal practices in digital interactions (Section 4). Drawing from this, we give examples from qualitative observations of digital interaction between young people from two different data samples: The first sample consists of twenty-one mostly informal video calls (via Skype and Facetime), involving students using English as the language of communication in international contexts (Section 5). The sample contains multimodal transcriptions of the video calls, which were developed by the students themselves and thus provide access to their metacommunicative awareness. The second sample includes 47 informal WhatsApp threads involving German adolescents between the age of 13 and 18 (Section 6). In addition, interviews were conducted with 16 of the participants, who reflected on their habits and perceptions of digital communication. Both samples allow us to conduct sequential analyses that trace how young people use different semiotic resources in digital interactions and metapragmatically motivate these choices. Through exemplary case studies on these data, we will discuss similarities and differences between video calls and text messaging data, as well as similarities and differences between different communities of practice, defined as groups of people who share a common interest and engage in regular activities by following patterned social rules (Wenger-Treyner and Wenger-Treyner 2015). In our data sets, these communities are made up of young people who regularly interact employing digital platforms/apps for social purposes, such as peer-to-peer conversations. Based on our exploration of these communities' interactions, we discuss the metapragmatics of mode-switching (Section 7).

2 Mode-switching

In spontaneous, live and real-time digital interactions, several resources can be creatively combined by participants in communication. The notion of *mode-switching* originally paraphrased code-switching, but drawing on systemic-functional grammar, in particular on one of the three components of register, defined by Halliday (1978) as "mode". He derived this notion from Pearce's "mode" as "the channel of communication adopted: not only the choice between spoken and written medium

---

past uses, and a set of affordances based on their possible uses, and these will be actualized in concrete social contexts".

but much more detailed choices" (Doughty, Pearce and Thornton 1972), further explained by Halliday as the role played by language in the situation, whereas the medium is a "functional variable" (Halliday 1978: 110). Hence mode-switching was devised in the first place to describe patterns of alternation between spoken and written modes in digital live chats in one-to-one or one-to-many platforms (Sindoni 2012). The label "switching" tries to capture dynamics that imply mode change, that is, a specific moment in time in which one or more participants decide to switch from the spoken to the written mode, or vice versa. Even though in interactions the impression of simultaneity may be strong, time-sensitive transcriptions (i.e., sensitive to seconds or inferior time measures) prove that there is always a time-lag, albeit minimal. In the case of video-mediated and live-streamed interactions, such as Skype or Facetime conversations, research has shown the overall prevalence of the spoken mode, with occasional use of the written mode interspersed in the main spoken thread of conversation for specific communicative purposes, such as to repair trouble in conversation or to manage technical issues, as is the case of audio or video stream issues that halt smooth conversation (Sindoni 2013, 2019).

We wish to extend our analysis to a wider sample of environments with different media, including Skype and WhatsApp, and to discuss the whole repertoire of semiotic resources used by participants by extending the original label of mode-switching to other patterns of alternation, combination, and conflation. Guided by recent studies on digital communication, this might include, *inter alia*, how writing is enriched by pictorial signs such as emoji, stickers, and gifs (Herring and Dainas 2017), how voice messages are sequentially integrated into chat threads (König and Hector 2019) and how spoken video interactions are accompanied by text messages and images (Sindoni 2019). Given this semiotic complexity, we argue for heuristics that are not limited to language-derived phenomena and agenda in their phenomenology.

3 Media ideology

Explaining choices of resources solely by technical restrictions or technology-inherent resource preferences would be a highly limited perspective. Resource choice is always a selection from a variational range and thus always entails the potential to be interpreted communicatively and socially. Starting from this theoretical premise, participants' metapragmatic beliefs and attitudes towards semiotic resources (and thus also towards mode-switching in ongoing interactions) become crucial. To understand these ascriptions of meaning, it is worthwhile to examine the concept of *media ideology* (Gershon 2010a, 2010b).

Media ideologies – derived from the concept of language ideologies (Silverstein 1979, Woolard 1998, Irvine and Gal 2000) – constitute the ideas and attitudes with which participants and observers socially interpret selective processes of mediation, i.e., the selection of "all semiotic means by which people relate to each other within frameworks of communicative activity" (Androutsopoulos 2014: 11). The concept focuses on "how people understand both the communicative possibilities and the material limitations of a specific channel, and how they conceive of channels in general" (Gershon 2010a: 283). As with linguistic practices, participants' metapragmatic conceptualization of media practices defines the appropriateness and contextualizing effects of semiotic resources in interaction. Mediational means can be perceived as rather formal or rather informal by the participants and are associated with certain distinct linguistic, but also multimodal, styles (cf. ibid.: 290, Busch 2018, 2021). In this sense, media ideologies are always inherently comparative, implicitly raising the question: What would have been if not this but that medium and/or resource had been used for a communicative event? (cf. Gershon 2010a: 287). For example, the extent to which a voice message is considered more appropriate than a text message for a particular communicative activity (or vice versa) is gradually enregistered by the metasemiotic activities of a social population – for example, commenting metapragmatically on a resource choice as 'inappropriate' or demanding the choice of a specific resource in a particular situation (cf. Agha 2007).

Following on from this, we draw on the concept of media ideologies by adopting three interrelated assumptions in our research on mode-switching in digital interactions: First, we assume that semiotic resources afforded by any digital medium can be deployed for meaning making (Kress and van Leeuwen 1996). Second, and consistent with our first assumption, we point out that media choice is grounded in media ideologies, i.e., the shared attitudes and beliefs about mediational means within a community of practice. And third, we therefore locate these media ideologies in the communication processes themselves, in which implicit and explicit reflexivity towards the social value of semiotic resources can be observed (cf. Agha 2007).

4 Metapragmatics of mode-switching: Theoretical framework

By bringing together both strands of our previous discussion, we gain theoretical access to the metapragmatics of mode-switching. Digital media of interpersonal communication offer possibilities to combine different semiotic resources in ongoing interactions. We assume that all digital interactions are shaped by the orchestration of different semiotic resources and that switching from one resource to another is a communicative default. Therefore, an analysis of digital interactions limited to linguistic resources seems reductionist and will be supplemented in the following by a closer look at the selective processes of mode choice and mode-switching. In order to understand contextualization through semiotic resources, it is essential to trace metapragmatics in interaction, i.e., to reconstruct the displayed media ideologies of the participants. Focusing on both (I) the sequential and simultaneous embedding of mode-switching and (II) the metapragmatic ideology regarding these selective processes, our analysis is modeled on a two-fold theoretical framework:

I. Drawing on the concept of *mode-switching*, we investigate how mode (i.e., only verbal) and resource (i.e., other than verbal) choices are embedded in digital interactions, including how and if verbal language modes are integrated or substituted by non-verbal resources, such as visuals and other forms of embodied practices. The analysis adopts a perspective on multimodal interactions guided by the basic principles of Conversation Analysis (CA), used for the transcription of spoken turns, even though the granularity of the analysis is low, in consideration of the fact that the students themselves were not trained in CA. In our first data set, students transcribed conversations following only some basic CA conventions (Sindoni 2013). More specifically, we adopted the principles of "mutual elaboration" (Goodwin 1981) from CA that posits that any resource other than language, such as gestures or kinesics, does not make meaning in itself, but needs to be understood in combination with other resources. For example, gestures cannot be analyzed in isolation, but need to be viewed in their mutual elaboration with other resources that in our multimodal approach are not limited to language, but embrace others, such as emojis, gestures, and gaze. This method resonates with the notion of affordance (Gibson 1979), which recognizes that each resource, such as those listed above, has a different potential to make meaning.

II. Based on the interactional reconstruction, we trace the *metapragmatics of observed mode-switching*. Therefore, we analyze mode-switching with consideration of the sequentially preceding and following communicative actions, as well as the parallel semiotic displays. Only in the collaborative interweaving of these actions does mode-switching unfold its contextualizing indexicality, i.e., serving to signal contextual qualities of the on-going interaction and thus enabling mutual understanding of situated utterances, as Gumperz (1982) has described with the notion of *contextualization cues*. Our approach seeks to locate mode-switching in the temporal course of interaction and interpret it in relation to its surrounding semiotic context. While contextualization cues in the sense theorized by Gumperz (1982) are traditionally assumed to be unconscious or subconscious, we are particularly interested in choices and switches for which metapragmatic awareness is explicitly articulated by participants. In particular, we focus on moments of explicit metacommunicative thematization (e.g., when self-initiated or other-initiated mode-switching is explicitly referenced by at least one interlocutor) that provide information about the interactional functions of mode-switching, here interpreted as a meaning-making change of mode.

In the following sections, we discuss examples from our two data sets. In Section 5, we present two examples from two video interactions between participants using English as the main language of communication, but with occasional use of Italian. In Section 6, we present an example from a WhatsApp thread between two German speakers. We aim to select instances of mode-switching and problematize students' mode and resource choices with a view to unearthing media ideologies that go beyond technical and semiotic media affordances.

5 Metapragmatics of mode-switching in the Skype data

The first data set includes twenty-one video calls in a multilingual[3] context, involving students who use English as the language of international communication. The clips and related study materials were produced within a European-funded research project, "EU-MADE4LL: European Multimodal and Digital Education for Language Learning".[4] The students' final assignments included: 1) a recording of a video conversation of any length[5], with tools such as Skype or Facetime, between the student and another external participant[6], 2) a multimodal transcription of a short chunk of their video interactions (max. 3 minutes) using a pre-compiled grid with columns, where the student was asked to tran-

---

[3] Most participants had Italian, Danish or English as their first language, but other first languages are also present in the data set, such as German and Brazilian Portuguese.
[4] Project ref.: 2016-1-IT02-KA203-024087; website: [http://www.eumade4ll.eu].
[5] Submissions included clips from a minimum of 0:48 seconds to a maximum of 25:48 minutes. However, all students had to produce a multimodal transcription using a common grid and selecting a much shorter chunk (minimum 30 seconds – maximum 180 seconds) of the recorded clip.
[6] All participants had been previously informed about the project's research aims and all signed an informed consent form that complied with GDPR.

scribe spoken and written turns, occurrences of mode-switching, proxemics and kinesics patterns, gaze, etc., and 3) a written paper that commented on their conversations and related transcriptions.

The EU-MADE4LL data set is approximately 5 hours long and includes 14 informal video calls and 7 job interviews, involving 44 participants, who were all informed about the main research purposes of the project. However, only the students were fully aware of the interactional patterns under scrutiny in contrast to their recruited friends or relatives, who were external to the project. The students had been previously taught about the semiotic resources they needed to focus on and, subsequently, transcribe. Considering that this data set includes a detailed report of how all primary participants set up the conversation, which tools they used, and who they involved in the conversation and that, additionally, they had to motivate all their semiotic choices, we also have access to students' metareflections and media ideologies. Even though primary participants (i.e., those involved in the project and thus aware of the communicative practices they would be asked to reflect on in their assignments) cannot be considered completely spontaneous in their interactions, our main concern in this paper is about the media ideologies they manifest in their conscious choices and motivations, as explicitly addressed and discussed in their written assignments. For example, in their assignment, they all had to justify which segment of the conversation they had decided to transcribe from their raw full-length clip, how they made specific choices in their transcription task and how they solved technical or conversational issues. The two main and often co-occurring reasons for the segment's selection were: 1) both participants seemed to show looser self-monitoring, in terms of increase of self-correction, pauses, hesitations, fillers, vague words, and 2) mode-switching occurred at least once. These two arguments provided by the students reveal that they clearly understood the importance of focusing on more spontaneous excerpts and the significance of mode-switching to understand the affordances of video interactions. Additionally, not only do written assignments grant access to students' priorities, ideologies and learning strategies activated to make sense of a random conversation, but transcriptions as well provide insights into how they critically reflected on their own interactions. Since students were not fully trained multimodal or conversation analysts, they were provided, as part of their course content, with some basic tools for carrying out multimodal transcription and annotation, as well as some guidelines with reference to basic CA transcription conventions. The transcription grids are simple tables organized in pre-given vertical columns that give indications for turn, time, participant's name, speech, writing, examples of mode-switching (indicated with a +, if present), proxemics patterns, kinesics action, gaze, setting and visual units (i.e., a screenshot). All horizontal rows had to be filled in by students using verbal descriptions, except for the last column, where students had to insert a screenshot that best represented the moment captured in the row. We will provide some examples of these interactions, with a focus on mode-switching, and how these were critically explained by students.

In an example selected for analysis, one occurrence of mode-switching, from speech to writing, between Tilly, the student analyst (Leeds, UK) and Sara, another student participating in the project (Rome, Italy) is shown in Figure 13.1 in turn 8, 6th column, with the conventional symbol +. This is a case of *self-initiated mode-switching*, that is, when the transition from speech to writing is initiated by one participant on her own initiative, without being directly prompted to do so (see Sindoni 2013). In previous research (Sindoni 2013, 2019), the distinction between *self-initiated* and *other-initiated mode-switching* has been shown to be fairly loose and only useful for heuristic purposes, but this case can be easily classified as self-initiated because Sara anticipates her mode-switching by saying "[Okay] I am writing to you" in turn 6. In this case, Sara claims in advance that she will change mode to facilitate Tilly's understanding. However, typical features of conversation, such as overlapping in this case, may cause trouble in turn-taking, hence mode-switching is used as a facilitator to compensate for trouble in communication. Tilly recognizes overlapping in Sara's turn, somehow prioritizing her stance as transcriber. In other words, this transcription seems to implicitly create a hierarchy between the two participants in interaction, with the transcriber placed in "superordinate" position and the interlocutor as the participant who "does" the overlapping, or, we may venture to say, the interruption. This is visible because, in her transcription, Tilly attributes overlapping only to Sara (turn 6), and signals this is the case by applying square brackets only in Sara's turn. Overlapping is thus understood as the contemporary utterance of some word or phrase on the part of the *other* participant, and, more specifically in this case, as one interruption of the participant Sara. Overlapping could have been signaled by square brackets in both participants' turns if Tilly had recognized that overlapping is reciprocal and not "attributable" to one participant only.

A creative resource that Tilly uses to visually show the affordances is shown in Figure 13.1, turn 8, last column "Visual units": the screenshot does not merely include the video screen, but, significantly, the text chat box in left position. Tilly understands that the visual unit is another resource that can be operationalized to show the example of mode-switching in its full repertoire. Additionally, the crying smiley <😢> can be identified, even though it was sent before the moment captured in turn 8, and its context of use is lost.

All the examples of mode-switching in the overall data set can be ascribed to the attempt to facilitate conversation in a context in which one participant is an English native speaker, while the other is using English as a foreign language,

	Time	Participant	Speech	Writing	Mode-switching	Proxemics patterns	Kinesic action	Gaze	Setting	Visual units (screenshots)
6	11:02,04	Sara	[Okay] I am writing it to you		-	Left side of face and left shoulder visible.	Moves towards camera and begins typing.	Gaze directed at keyboard.	Bedroom.	
7	11:04	Tilly	Okay		-	Head and shoulders visible.	Looks down.	Looks towards the instant messaging tab.	Bedroom.	
8	11:05	Sara	Okay	Gelato	+	Head and shoulders visible.	Smiles and moves away from camera. Presses send on message.	Looks towards instant messaging tab.	Bedroom.	

Figure 13.1: Tilly's transcription (unedited).

thus spending considerably more effort in trying (sometimes unsuccessfully) to communicate. Unlike previous research (Sindoni 2013), mode-switching seems here exclusively used for intercultural facilitation. This is perfectly realized and recognized by Tilly, who, in her assignment, writes:

> T used the most accommodation features such as asking more questions and repeating the answers of S to accommodate for the language barrier, as S was not a native speaker of the conversational language (5, 11, 16, 21, 26, 32, 35, 41, 44 and 48). S tended to use more mode-switching to facilitate intercultural communication when the words she needed to communicate were in Italian.

Mode-switching is here recognized by the student as a meaning-making resource in itself, as changing mode from spoken to written language is interpreted as a useful strategy to illustrate foreign language words, in this case Italian. In the basic exchange of easy words from one language to another one, both students perceive writing as a way to pin down language, make it easier, storable, and thus retrievable for future use. The underlying ideology at work here seems to indicate the primacy of writing in contexts of foreign language use and intercultural communication, as perceived by students. In this example, Tilly appears to believe that using the mode of writing is more effective to communicate a foreign word and Sara follows suit.

In another example, the student Mariangela (Messina, Italy) argues that code-switching was a frequent occurrence in the video interaction with Tonino, a Canadian friend with Italian parents. Code-switching was mostly associated with *self-initiated* mode-switching, as shown in Figure 13.2. Tonino mode- and code-switches at the same time when he says and writes "al volo" (i.e. *hurriedly, on the spot*) in turn 27 (termed "row" by Mariangela). Even though Mariangela fails to transcribe change of language and of mode at the same time, she understands in her assignment that this is a strategy used to "express exactly what he [Tonino] feels, using the Italian language and using writing to be clearer." Mariangela creatively exploits the affordances of the transcription table itself by adding the column "code-switching" alongside the column "mode-switching", even though she forgets twice to add +, one in the column "code-switching" and the other in the column "mode-switching". In turn 29, Tonino ironically says "thank you" as if responding to some past criticism received at a job interview in real-time. On that occasion, he had been asked to react "al volo", that is, *impromptu*, Italian-style. With this humorous innuendo, Tonino indirectly rejects the implication that Italians can improvise under any circumstances. By ironically and *a posteriori* thanking the interviewer in front of the audience/Mariangela, Tonino is dramaturgically re-impersonating himself, while mentally thanking the interviewer for demanding an excessively prompt reaction. Hence he is somehow placing himself aside, as if re-impersonating himself (Goffman 1959). Mariangela, at least at some level, recognizes the irony of Tonino who *a posteriori* thanks the interviewer, to the point that she transcribes his self-quotation by exploiting the affordances of both spoken conventions // (used for beginning and ending of a spoken turn) and written conventions ". . ." (used for (self)reported speech).

Row	Time	Participant	Speech	Writing	Mode-switching	Code-switching	Proxemics patterns	Kinesic action	Gaze	Setting (built environment)	Visual units (screenshots)
27.	01:43	Tonino	//Everything Italian is / everything is al volo and I'm [like]/	-	-	+		Keeps smiling while moving his hands	Looks at the screen		
28.	01:45	Mariangela	//[Yeah!]//	-	-	-		Smiles and nods while shrugging	Looks at the screen		
29.	01:46	Tonino	//"Thank you"//	-	-	-		Smiles jokingly	Looks at the screen		
30.	01:48	Mariangela	//That's true//	-	-	-	Turns on her seat before going back to the previous position	Laughs	Looks at the screen then bottom right then back at the screen		

Figure 13.2: Mariangela's transcription (unedited).

In the example of the video interaction between Tilly and Sara, communication between two people speaking different languages is facilitated by means of writing as a disambiguating strategy. In the second example, the co-occurrence of mode-switching and code-switching points to the extra communicative power that changes, in mode or resource, can add to the interaction. A similarity in the two examples can be illustrated by referring to media ideologies. All participants in the project seem to implicitly confirm primacy to writing as the channel that can confer stability, clarity and expressive power to communication. As exemplified in our qualitatively selected examples, the data set shows the preference for writing to disambiguate and/or clarify chunks of conversation. Participants resort to writing in all the analyzed data as a conversational facilitator of some kind or at some level, for example to explain, make more explicit or, more generally, to solve trouble in conversation. In the next section, we will discuss whether the same applies to a different data set and whether the ideology of writing as a stabilizer in communication works along the same lines.

6 Metapragmatics of mode-switching in the WhatsApp data

The second data set we examine was collected in the course of a doctoral research project on adolescents' registers of digital writing (Busch 2021). Twenty-three German high school students between the ages of 13 and 18 were recruited, each providing at least two WhatsApp threads (mostly one-to-one chats with friends from school). The data includes 47 chatlogs with 39,176 messages and a total of 301,987 word tokens. While the vast majority of messages are actually text messages, the sample contains 1,454 voice messages (which make up about 3.7% of the sample). Even though the contents of the voice messages are not available for our investigation, the voice messages can be localized in their sequential position in the flow of interaction by means of placeholders. In addition to this primary data, seven semi-structured group interviews were conducted with 16 of our participants to discuss their metapragmatic awareness of semiotic variation in WhatsApp communication and to gain an ethnographic understanding of their language and media ideologies in relation to daily literacy practices.

Both the interview data and the chatlogs reveal a remarkable awareness regarding practices of media choice and mode-switching. The participants repeatedly associate prototypical addressees (for instance friends, parents, and teachers) with specific media choices. While WhatsApp is considered a medium of social closeness, appropriate for friends and family, for example, the interviewees reported that WhatsApp interactions with a schoolteacher must be considered inappropriate (cf. Busch 2018). These conceptualizations of media choices are not only deterministically oriented towards social roles but are themselves resources for defining social relationships. For example, 14-year-old students Anne and Lea reflect on their use of voice messaging in WhatsApp, noting that the use of this affordance is characteristic of communicating with "very best friends". Here it is not only the presumed social closeness that makes voice messages appear appropriate, but the frequent realization of voice messages indicates a socially highly relevant relationship in the community of practice observed.

The guiding principle of such underlying media-ideological rationalization is the degree of mediation that the participants enregister to media practice. For example, the fact that a voice message entails a particularly "familiar" relationship is explained by the participants regarding its quality of embodiment. Due to its bodily trace, a voice message appears to be less mediated than a text message – a media ideology that we have traditionally known regarding handwriting (cf. Gredig 2019). Just as the significance of handwriting is dependent on the contrast to typewriting, the media-ideological "directness" of a voice message unfolds its indexical effectiveness only in direct contrast to the text messages that accompany it.

These media-ideological interpretations compete with the negotiation of the extent to which different semiotic resources are suitable for the accomplishment of various communicative tasks. For example, voice messages require less input effort on the technical device than a typed message: more words are transmitted in less time. For this reason, there seems to be a tendency for voice messages among adolescents, especially for more complicated or longer contributions. In communicative practice, however, a conflict arises in the metapragmatics of voice messages – on the one hand, voice messages indicate a close social relationship, on the other hand, they are perceived as effective when it comes to dealing with complex problems, which are more often dealt with in the context of professional tasks or social tensions.

In the following excerpt, this can be exemplified in a WhatsApp interaction between the classmates Lea and Konrad (reproduced slightly shortened, all original typos are retained). The sequence is typical for the communicative everyday life of our young participants in that the interaction involves helping each other with homework for school. Both interlocutors have a math worksheet in front of them, with which Lea asks for help in message 01.

01	19:01:	Lea:	Hey Konni kannst du mir die Aufgaben noch mal erklären?
			Hey Konni can you explain the homework again?
02	19:02:	Konrad:	Ähh 😅
			Uhh 😅
[...]			
09	19:05:	Konrad:	Hmm moment ich überlege kurz wie ich das erklären soll 😅
			Hmm just one second I'll figure out how to explain it 😅

10	19:05:	Lea:	Mach Sprachnachicht geht schneller
			Send a voice message it's faster
11	19:05:	Konrad:	Ja ich weiß nicht wie ich das erklären soll 😅
			Well I do not know how to explain this 😅
12	19:06:	Konrad:	Ich weiß nur das es 20l ist 😋
			I just know it's 20l 😋
13	19:06:	Lea:	Ok das ist egal und beim 2. bild?
			Okay, that's not important, and the second picture?
14	19:06:	Konrad:	Also
			So
15	19:07:	Konrad:	Teil 60 durch 10 dann haste 10 prozent? 😂
			Divide 60 by 10 then you get 10 percent? 😂
16	19:08:	Konrad:	Das sind 6–10 prozent
			That's 6–10 percent
17	19:08:	Konrad:	Haltbieren wir das sind es 3 mg und ähh 5prozent xD
			If we cut that in half it's 3 mg and uhh 5 percent xD
18	19:09:	Lea:	Hä ich verstehe gerade nichts bei welcher Aufgabe wir sind 🥺
			Huh I just don't understand what task we are at 🥺
19	19:09:	Konrad:	Bei 2
			At 2
20	19:09:	Konrad:	Beim O-Saft
			At the orange juice
21	19:09:	Konrad:	😅 😅
22	19:10:	Lea:	Ok kannst du vllt Sprachnachicht machen weil ich kapiere das sonst echt nicht 🙏😅
			Ok can you maybe send a voice message because otherwise I really don't get it 🙏😅
23	19:10:	Konrad:	Naja wenn du wüstest wie meine stimme sich anhört per sprachnachricht 😅😋
			Well if you knew what my voice sounds like on voice message 😅😋
24	19:11:	Konrad:	Gannz anders 🥴😶😅
			Completely different 🥴😶😅
25	19:11:	Lea:	Egal ist bei mir auch so 😅
			No worries it's the same with me 😅
26	19:11:	Konrad:	dann mach ich galileo aus 😈
			then I'm turning off galileo [a TV show] 😈

27	19:12:	Lea:	Das wäre voll nett 😂
			That would be very nice 😂
28	19:12:	Konrad:	Ok ih hoffe ich spreche deutlich genug 😂
			Okay I hope I'm speaking clearly enough 😂
29	19:13:	Lea:	Schaffst du schon 😂
			You can do that 😂
30	19:13:	Konrad:	[Sprachnachricht]
			[voice message]
31	19:14:	Konrad:	Beste!!
			Best!!
32	19:14:	Konrad:	Ganz deutlich!!!
			Very clearly!!!
33	19:15:	Konrad:	Und ganz erwachsen 😄
			And very grown up 😄
34	19:15:	Konrad:	Irgentwie verständlich? 😂
			Somehow understandable? 😂
35	19:16:	Lea:	[Sprachnachricht]
			[voice message]

We can observe how Konrad struggles to realize the most effective explanation or instruction for the relatively complex math problems in the written mode. He refers to this cognitive planning process metacommunicatively through interjections (messages 02 and 09) and indicates that it is somehow difficult. Lea takes up this difficulty by trying to explicitly initiate a mode-switch (message 10). In a voice message, the explanation would be "faster". Konrad ignores this explicit reference to another mode and explicates his formulation problems instead (message 11). This is followed by a very fragmented sequence in which mathematical operations and results are communicated by Konrad through written messages. Lea in turn asks back for further information and expresses that she fails to understand (for example in message 18). She evaluates the written explanatory sequence as failed and tries to initiate a mode switch again (message 22). Konrad can no longer ignore this initiation and explains why he has not sent a voice message so far: He is uncomfortable with his recorded voice (messages 23–24). What follows are some affirmations by Lea that Konrad has nothing to worry about, so that he finally sends a voice message, in which he most likely explains the task again (message 30). Directly following, Konrad evaluates his own voice message with written contributions wittily as "Best!!", "Very clearly!!!" and "very grown up" (messages 31, 32, 33). By doing so, Konrad implicitly refers to his concern about appearing vulnerable through the voice message. The bodily trace of his voice opens up interpretative frames, which he obviously does not like to have in his conversation with Lea (as for example sounding like a "child"). Only after this contextualization work, Konrad checks whether Lea has finally understood the math task (message 34). The superficial communicative task of explaining thus recedes temporarily behind the social contextualization of the spoken mode. The sequence thus clearly shows that mode and resource choices are never neutral but are negotiated by the participants. Different media-ideological attitudes collide, which can make the collaborative metapragmatics of mode-switching necessary.

7 Discussion and conclusion

The examples from the two data sets allow to gain insights about media ideologies of youth in peer-to-peer educational contexts. Young people have been captured in the act of co-constructing meanings in contexts where effective communication was somehow hindered or had come to a halt. The Skype data set includes multilingual environments where English was used as the language of communication but asymmetrically indexed: one participant was a native English speaker, whereas the other spoke English as a foreign language, thus creating an imbalance that participants tried to manage in order to facilitate conversation. Additionally, the Skype data set incorporates another form of power asymmetry, as one participant was a student involved in the project, thus being fully aware of the patterns under investigation, such as mode-switching, and hence active in prompting and eager to transcribe, describe, and eventually interpret expected or unexpected relevant interactional patterns. Conversely, in the WhatsApp data set, participants spoke German as their native language, thus being neither in communicative trouble nor in positions of language power asymmetry. WhatsApp spontaneous conversations add to interactional symmetry, with no pressure or prior knowledge of an overt or covert research agenda, as was the case in the Skype data set. These differences, rather than constituting a limit in our research, have allowed us to uncover participants' use of semiotic resources in mediated interactions, as well as their media ideologies, both explicitly and implicitly – irrespective of their native language and relative a/symmetrical power position.

If Skype conversations have the spoken mode as the preferred choice determined by media affordances, WhatsApp exchanges mostly used the written mode.[7]

---

[7] This is the case at least for the sample under investigation. The fact that WhatsApp threads in some other communities are primarily made up of voice messages will not be denied here (cf. König and Hector 2019).

Changes from the preferred, "in-built" mode are *marked choices*, that is, deviation from what is pre-afforded by the medium and consequently perceived and reproduced by users as standard. In other words, there is no conversational or interactional reason why speech is more used than writing in Skype video calls and why it is the opposite with WhatsApp text chats. The establishment of a "standard mode" is, on the one hand, facilitated by medium affordances that may, on the other hand, nonetheless be creatively changed, or even overturned, by users. The choice of mode and resources in digital interactions is thus always in a tense relationship of pre-configured affordances of the medium and their metapragmatically calibrated appropriation by the interlocutors. It is this tension that is the source of meaning making.

In the Skype data set, we have shown self-initiated examples of mode-switching. Contrary to previous research, self-initiation is not ambiguous, as is explicitly anticipated: "I am writing to you". These conversation facilitators are employed in contexts where clarity and lack of ambiguity were acknowledged as essential by participants. In another example, mode-switching and code-switching co-occurred, once more showing that deviation from what is in-built in the medium is a marked choice, and, as such, meaningful: Mariangela recognizes that combining code-switching from English to Italian and mode-switching adds clarity and expressive power. For different but consistent reasons, writing seems to grant stability, clarity, and permanence. Writing is ideologically given prominence both implicitly (in conversational patterns) and explicitly (in the transcription tasks and written assignments about both conversations and transcriptions).

Conversely, in the WhatsApp data set, the conversational patterns seem to run counter what was observed in the Skype data set. The use of voice is perceived as a signal of familiarity and closeness; as the informants Lea and Anne contend, it is a resource available for "very best friends". Even though media affordances of WhatsApp text chats seem to make full use of speech resources by means of voice messages, at closer inspection, these do not simulate face-to-face spoken interactions as video instant message systems, such as Skype and WhatsApp video calls, do. In other words, an only-voice message thread would lose most speech-like qualities (e.g., real-time, other-paced, overlapping, etc.). Recordings follow the syntagmatic organization of discourse, akin to written discourse. Consistent with this view, informants implicitly notice this difference and in fact refer to "voice" and not to "speech" – of course also following the app developer's labeling as "voice message". This choice nonetheless implicitly highlights the vocal components that the informants understand and perceive as meaningful in themselves, thus further encouraging our reflections on how resources, media and affordances are interwoven in the fabric of interaction. In the WhatsApp data set, recorded voice can be considered a resource on its own, with its distinct properties and grammar, and implicitly recognized as such by participants. Its bodily quality, with all its attached connotations, such as tone, rhythm, timbre, volume, etc., makes it less mediated and more personal and thus considered a resource mostly apt to family and close friends. Its use can be activated only under specific circumstances and participants seem to implicitly identify them, as these represent a deviation from the unmarked, "regular" use.

Even though writing embodies the standard and unmarked mode choice in the WhatsApp environment, it is perceived, at least by Lea, as a less effective resource to achieve the communicative goal, that is, explaining the mathematical operational task, and she is quick in prompting Konrad to mode-switch. However, Konrad is reluctant to change mode, and the reasons why he does so are explained in terms of voice: "Well if you knew what my *voice* sounds like on voice message 😅😬" (message 23, our italics). Konrad attempts to smooth down Lea's social imposition by procrastinating and finally sending the voice message, but it takes him seven turns to meet Lea's explicit request. The visual resources of emojis are consistently used as hedging devices. He justifies his delay in meeting his interlocutor's expectations with a few arguments, such as pointing out that the recorded voice is completely different from the "real" one. The two emojis reinstate the concept that he does not like and/or is embarrassed by his recorded voice (message 24). In message 26 and 28, Konrad again takes time and anticipates possible troubles in understanding, respectively. Recorded voice, however, appears to point to stability along with those affect components explicitly mentioned by participants. The math explanation most likely requires resources that are ingrained in speech as elaboration – whereas text messages are less apt to in-depth analysis, probably when longer explanations/elaborations of any kind are needed.

This exchange is indicative of the different nature of resources, as implicitly and explicitly perceived by participants in comparable situations, that is when informal learning is involved. Instead of positing a preferential mode for communication in peer contexts between young people, we argue that in digitally mediated communication, resources do not have a standard value and meaning in themselves. We contend that resources are components of meaning making in the interlaced dynamics of media affordances (e.g., Skype vs. WhatsApp), thus producing media ideologies, which are constructed and co-negotiated in different communities of practice. Seen from this angle, spoken, written and visual resources play roles that may seem contradictory but should be analyzed and interpreted against the backdrop of media affordances (i.e., what tools are meant to do and how by those who designed them in the first place) and media ideologies (i.e., what individual participants think they can do and which practices are developed within and across different communities of practice). We believe that it is at this intersection that research should find new lines of investigation.

References

Agha, Asif. 2007. *Language and social relations*. Cambridge: Cambridge University.
Androutsopoulos, Jannis. 2014. Mediatization and sociolinguistic change. Key concepts, research traditions, open issues. In Jannis Androutsopoulos (ed.), *Mediatization and sociolinguistic change*, 3–48. Berlin: De Gruyter Mouton.
boyd, danah. 2014. *It's complicated: The social lives of networked teens*. New Haven and London: Yale University Press.
Busch, Florian. 2018. Digital writing practices and media ideologies of German adolescents. *The Mouth* 3. 85–103.
Busch, Florian. 2021. *Digitale Schreibregister. Kontexte, Formen und metapragmatische Reflexionen*. Berlin: De Gruyter.
Childwise. 2019. Childhood 2019 press release. [http://www.childwise.co.uk/uploads/3/1/6/5/31656353/childwise_press_release_-_monitor_2019.pdf] (accessed 2 November 2021).
Council of Europe. 2017. *Internet literacy handbook*. Strasbourg: Council of Europe.
Doughty, Peter, John Pearce and Geoffrey Thornton. 1972. *Exploring language*. Schools Council. Programme in Linguistics and English Teaching. London: Edward Arnold.
European Commission, Directorate General for Education, Youth, Sport and Culture. 2018. *Developing digital youth work. Policy recommendations and training needs for youth workers and decision-makers: Expert group set up under the European Union Work Plan for Youth for 2016–2018*. [https://op.europa.eu/en/publication-detail/-/publication/fbc18822-07cb-11e8-b8f5-01aa75ed71a1] (accessed 2 November 2021).
Eurostat. 2017. Being young in Europe today – digital world. Last update December 2017.. [https://ec.europa.eu/eurostat/statistics-explained/index.php/Being_young_in_Europe_today_-_digital_world] (accessed 2 November 2021).
Friedlein, Ashley. 2016. What does realtime web, or realtime data, actually mean? In *Medium*, May 19, 2016. [https://medium.com/ably-realtime/i-what-does-realtime-web-or-realtime-data-actually-mean-cd6603562876?#.77qu69l3h] (accessed 2 November 2021).
Frydenberg, Erica. 2018. *Adolescent coping*. 3rd edn. London and New York: Routledge.
Gershon, Ilana. 2010a. Media Ideologies. An introduction. *Journal of Linguistic Anthropology* 20 (2). 283–293.
Gershon, Ilana. 2010b. Breaking up is hard to do. Media switching and media ideologies. *Journal of Linguistic Anthropology* 20 (2). 389–405.
Gibson, J. J. 1979. *The ecological approach to visual perception*. Boston: Houghton Mifflin.
Goffman, Erving. 1959. *The presentation of self in everyday life*. New York: Doubleday.
Goodwin, Charles. 1981. *Conversational organization: Interaction between speakers and hearers*. New York: Academic Press.
Gredig, Andi 2019. Die Spur der Gefühle. Kulturanalytische Überlegungen zum emotionalen Wert der Handschrift. In Stefan Hauser, Martin Luginbühl and Susanne Tienken (eds.), *Mediale Emotionskulturen*, 39–56. Bern: Lang.
Gumperz, John J. 1982. *Discourse strategies*. Cambridge: Cambridge University.
Halliday, Michael A. K. 1978. *Language as social semiotic. The social interpretation of language and meaning*. London: Arnold.
Herring, Susan C. and Ashley Dainas 2017. 'Nice picture comment!' Graphicons in Facebook comment threads. In *Proceedings of the Fiftieth Hawai'i International Conference on System Sciences* (HICSS-50), 2185–2194. Los Alamitos: IEEE.

Irvine, Judith T. and Susan Gal. 2000. Language ideology and linguistic differentiation. In Paul V. Kroskrity (ed.), *Regimes of language. Ideologies, polities, and identities*, 35–84. Santa Fe: School of American Research.

König, Katharina and Tim Moritz Hector. 2019. Neue Medien – neue Mündlichkeit? Zur Dialogizität von WhatsApp-Sprachnachrichten. In Konstanze Marx and Axel Schmidt (eds.), *Interaktion und Medien*, 59–84. Heidelberg: Winter.

Kress, Gunther and Theo van Leeuwen. 1996. *Reading images. The grammar of visual design*. 2nd edn. London: Routledge.

Lenhart, Amanda, Maeve Duggan, Andrew Perrin, Renee Stepler, Lee Rainie and Kim Parker. 2015. *Teens, social media & technology overview 2015: Smartphones facilitate shifts in communication landscape for teens*. [http://www.pewinternet.org/files/2015/04/PI_TeensandTech_Update2015_0409151.pdf] (accessed 2 November 2021).

Nadkarni, Ashwini and Stefan G. Hofmann. 2012. Why do people use Facebook? *Personality and Individual Differences* 52 (3). 243–249.

Silverstein, Michael. 1979. Language structure and linguistic ideologies. In Paul R. Clyne, William F. Hanks and Carol L. Hofbauer (eds.), *The elements. A parasession on linguistic units and levels*, 213–226. Chicago: Chicago Linguistic Society.

Sindoni, Maria Grazia. 2012. Mode-switching: How oral and written modes alternate in video chats. In Mariavita Cambria, Cristina Arizzi and Francesca Coccetta (eds.), *Web genres and web tools: With contributions from the Living Knowledge Project*, 141–153. Como and Pavia: Ibis.

Sindoni, Maria Grazia. 2013. *Spoken and written discourse in online interactions. A multimodal approach*. London and New York: Routledge.

Sindoni Maria Grazia. 2019. Mode-switching in video-mediated interaction: Integrating linguistic phenomena into multimodal transcription tasks. *Linguistics and Education*. [DOI: 10.1016/j.linged.2019.05.004] (accessed 2 November 2021).

Sindoni, Maria Grazia, Elisabetta Adami, Styliani Karatza, Ivana Marenzi, Ilaria Moschini, Sandra Petroni and Marc Rocca. 2019. *Common framework for intercultural digital literacies*, 1–255. [DOI: 10.13140/RG.2.2.20064.43520] [https://www.eumade4ll.eu/wp-content/uploads/2020/02/cfridil-framework-linked-fin1.pdf] (accessed 2 November 2021).

van Leeuwen, Theo. 2005. *Introducing social semiotics*. London and New York: Routledge.

Wenger-Trayner, Etienne and Beverly Wenger-Trayner. 2015. Introduction to communities of practice – A brief overview of the concept and its uses. [https://wenger-trayner.com/wp-content/uploads/2015/04/07-Brief-introduction-to-communities-of-practice.pdf] (accessed 2 November 2021).

Woolard, Kathryn A. 1998. Language ideology as a field of inquiry. In Bambi B. Schieffelin, Kathryn A. Woolard and Paul V. Kroskrity (eds.), *Language ideologies. Practice and theory*, 3–47. Oxford: Oxford University Press.

Nico Nassenstein and Helma Pasch

14 Whose way of speaking? Youth's self-reflexive voices and language ideologies in Uganda and Central African Republic

While the study of African youth language practices has yielded exciting results over the past two decades, speakers who do not use specifically labeled youth registers have seldom been in the center of scholarly attention. The present chapter focuses on self-reflections of Ugandan and Central African youth with regard to their language practices and looks at language ideologies of young people who do not consider themselves as using "deviant" or "non-conformist" speech. By approaching the question of speakerness and non-speakerness we focus on language ideologies, i.e. "conceptualizations about languages, speakers, and discursive practices" (Irvine 2011/2012). We investigate, based on field research carried out in the three communities among youth in Bangui (Central African Republic), Mbarara and Kisoro (both Uganda), how metalinguistic "talk about talk" and the metapragmatics of stylized youth language reveal imaginations about and desire for specific languages, conceptualizations of rap as stylized practice and how the blurry boundary between speakers and non-speakers and between youth language and common speech is addressed in self-reflexive statements. In future research on language ideologies, we suggest enhancing the scholarly focus on voices from the Global South and their emic judgments and evaluations.

Acknowledgments: We are considerably thankful to our interview partners Nick Lee, Capher Nsabiyumva and numerous others during our research, to our colleague Germain Landi for his assistance, as well as to musicians from Kisoro, Uganda. We are indebted to Paulin Baraka Bose's help during the research trip to Mbarara, western Uganda. Cynthia Groff is warmly thanked for giving us helpful suggestions on improving our English. We are indebted to reviewers of this chapter for their valuable comments and ideas. All remaining shortcomings are our own.

Nico Nassenstein, Johannes Gutenberg-Universität Mainz, e-mail: nassenstein@uni-mainz.de
Helma Pasch, Universität zu Köln, e-mail: ama14@uni-koeln.de

https://doi.org/10.1515/9781501514685-017

1 On everyday speech and youth's ideologies: An introduction

Young people's registers or ways of speaking[1] in different African contexts (often labeled 'youth languages' by linguists) often underly complex self-reflexive explanations. It appears that some of them cannot be categorized as separate languages or registers in the narrow sense of the word by their speakers, to whom their language appears less deviant from other practices than described in the respective literature. In this chapter, we investigate the blurry boundary between categorizations of youth language vs. other ways of speaking and the contrast between youth's fluid everyday speech and its underlying language ideologies vs. the often static concept of "youth languages" as distinct entities or fixed varieties (for numerous criticisms of this static approach see Brookes and Kouassi 2018, Nassenstein and Hollington 2016, Hurst-Harosh 2020, etc.). We are specifically interested in the ways youth's language practices are conceptualized by speakers as non-deviant and as conforming to everyday routines. Studying youths' self-reflexive utterances about their language based on metalinguistic and metapragmatic comments, narratives and explanations means redirecting the angle, focusing on the same questions that Gal and Irvine (2019: *book cover excerpt*) pursue in a recent influential contribution on ideology and semiotic processes:

> How are people's ideas about languages, ways of speaking, and expressive styles shaped by their social positions and values? How is difference, in language and in social life, made – and unmade? How and why are some differences persuasive as the basis for action, while other differences are ignored or erased?

For a long time, language ideologies constituted an understudied phenomenon in youth language research (see Section 2 for a brief literature review), a situation which has only recently begun to change. Hollington (2016: 136), in her study on ideologies of young speakers from Ethiopia, observes that "the relationship

---

[1] The concept of "ways of speaking" is attributed to Dell Hymes (1964) and his "ethnography of speaking", later relabeled to "ethnography of communication". In his framework, language is understood as a system of cultural practices and behaviors (with a focus on speakers' communicative competence) and different ways of speaking (Hymes 1989) are shared by a speech community. Also, the study of language ideologies derives from Hymes' initial framework in the 1960s, as explained by Irvine (2011/2012), and was strengthened in the 1980s when the relation of language to power and political economy was addressed; then, later it became more prominent also due to Silverstein's (1979) work. Judith T. Irvine herself has, as much as Paul V. Kroskrity (2004, 2016, and many more), greatly contributed to advances of this field of study within linguistic anthropology.

between linguistic practices and language ideologies is very complex and sometimes ambivalent; they can reflect and influence each other, but can also contradict or undermine each other, as fluid practices and discourses evolve in unlimited ways." An analysis of speakers' ideologies therefore reflects "the complexity, fluidity and elaborateness of speakers' ideas about, and ways with, language" (ibid.).

In the present contribution, in order to yield more adequate scholarly results, we suggest the inclusion of individual local speakers' voices in the study of language ideologies of African youth, their beliefs and judgments. While youth language research has often been an endeavor inspired and pursued by linguists, many of whom are based in the Global North, we aim to highlight voices and epistemologies from the Global South. This "decolonial option" (Mignolo 2012, for its application to youth language see Hurst-Harosh 2019) can be part of an incentive to de-essentialize ideas around youth language and to treat practices as social and cultural processes and as the outcome of speakers' choices and ideologies (Lüpke and Storch 2013) rather than as fixed codes or sociolects. Based on fieldwork in Uganda (2012–2016), Central African Republic (CAR) (1990–1991) and with speakers from CAR in the diaspora (2016–2019), we focus on self-reflexive language, metapragmatic awareness (cf. Verschueren 2000), and alternative ways of researching youth's beliefs and ideas about their language use as part of a critical analysis of youth language ideologies.

We have investigated three communities of African youth in western and southwestern Uganda, and in the Central African Republic, whose contexts of language usage may be considered different from what is commonly described in the literature on the topic. We base our arguments on expressions of speakers' agency, their views and judgments about "youth speech", and their folklinguistic attitudes toward standardized language and other kinds of more formal speech.[2]

---

2 As a clarification, the present chapter focuses mainly on language ideologies, a field of study in linguistic anthropology, and less on language attitudes, a prominent field of research in sociolinguistics and social psychology. While both have a specific overlap in their objectives and the phenomena they investigate, they stem from different traditions and are based on different methods. In contrast with language ideologies, language attitudes often contain judgments about good and correct language use from an in-group vs. an out-group's perspective (Garrett, Coupland and Williams 2003), and they are understood to constitute "an evaluative orientation to a social object of some sort" (Garrett 2010: 20). They reflect "[. . .] people's reactions to language varieties [and] reveal much of their perception of the speakers of these varieties" (Edwards 1982: 20). In the present chapter, we are less concerned with attitudes toward specific (other) varieties or languages but more interested in speakers' feelings and ideas about their own ways of speaking, i.e., their language ideologies, researched on the basis of ethnographic fieldwork, not relying on questionnaires, perceptual dialectology, stereotyping or categorizations based on linguistic cues such as accents. The prime aim of this chapter is to show whether and in what

The first community are Banyankore youth from Mbarara in western Uganda who *declare* Ruyaye to be a supraregional youth language, although Ruyaye – as our investigations have revealed – does not really exist as a homogenous practice.[3] The second community are youth in southwest Uganda who claim not to speak or know of a distinctive youth register and even contest that Rufumbira, as used by young people, could be seen as "youth language." Rather, they express sociospatial belonging to youth culture through their local hip hop style, Amahoro Fleva. The third group are street children in Bangui, CAR, who play with fuzzy and blurry boundaries between in-group and out-group. They are stigmatized as criminal youth and their language is regarded by society as "gangster slang", but they themselves do not make a clear distinction between everyday language and their own way of speaking.

The paper is organized as follows: Section 2 introduces the reader to general matters of youth language and language ideologies, while Section 3 presents three case studies from southwestern Uganda (on Rufumbira, a Bantu language close to Kinyarwanda), from western Uganda (Runyankore, a Bantu language), and from the Central African Republic (Sango, a Ubangian language). In Section 4, African youth's speech styles are presented from a decolonial perspective, highlighting "local" ideologies from the Global South. Section 5 evaluates semiotic processes and Section 6 provides a summary and eventually concludes the chapter with an outlook onto further studies.

2 Studying youth's language ideologies

"Who talks to whom, in what place and what situation, in what way, in order to achieve which goal?" are the fundamental questions of sociolinguistics (Fishman 1965) and of the ethnography of speaking or communication (Hymes 1964). The investigation of language ideologies, which may be shared or resisted by some or all members of given speech communities (Morgan 2004: 7), tries to explain why people talk to certain other people at specific moments and why they do this in specific ways. Language attitudes, in contrast, may often be determined by the prevailing ideologies.

---

way speakers count themselves to be the "makers and breakers" (Honwana and de Boeck 2005) in processes of linguistic innovation – or not.

3 It must, however, be taken into consideration that this language practice is understudied; for Ugandan youth language practices, see Namyalo (2015), Rüsch and Nassenstein (2016), Nassenstein, Hollington and Storch (2018) and Hollington and Akena (this volume).

The "how" and "why" of linguistic deviation has for long been addressed with diverse research approaches. The study of language ideologies in urban Africa has until today been dominated mostly by ideological research foci originating in the Global North and oriented towards youth's linguistic practices in the Global North, which are based on manipulated varieties of the local standard languages. The study of language ideologies among young people from Africa, however, requires a different approach, based on perspectives from the south, including a postcolonial take on language. Generally, language ideologies can be defined as "the ways in which speakers perceive and shape their language behavior and as the entirety of their underlying motivations to use a specific kind of language as a tool for either social cohesion or social distance" (Rüsch and Nassenstein 2016: 185) or as "sets of belief about language articulated by users as a rationalization or justification of perceived language structure and use" (Silverstein 1979: 193).

Oral communication is normally understood as an exchange of utterances which intends to convey – besides emotions, expectations and attitudes – specific content, which a third person may overhear or understand. There are, however, always situations in which a speaker wants to share a given content only with his/her interlocutor(s) but not with an outsider. Manipulating language is an efficient way of concealing meaning and making an utterance unintelligible. This is particularly important for speakers who operate most of the time in public space, as is the case with street children. While the function of manipulated forms and structures is to guarantee some secrecy towards outsiders, within a community of practice, they indicate insiderness, and they are proof of playful creativity. The ongoing manipulation of forms and constructions and the creation of novel expressions, which exceed given needs of secrecy, develop features of a specific fashion. Fashion is based on the imitation of models, which are, however, emulated in a way that shows one's own originality, so that Otherness, including imperfection, becomes obvious (Esposito 2001: 56). With regard to the alleged secret character of youth languages, this means that manipulations are not sufficiently cryptic to guarantee absolute incomprehensibility because they are based on the grammatical structures of the base language (e.g., as is the case for Sheng drawing from Swahili, Nouchi drawing from French, Lingala ya Bayankee/Yanké drawing from Lingala; see also Kunzmann, this volume). Youth communities in African urban settings do not live in isolation from the rest of the population but in close contact to other communities, hence manipulated forms are rapidly diffused and used outside their speech community.

Linguistic manipulations in youth languages often make use of given grammatical forms, constructions and rules. While normally new forms and constructions obey these rules so that new forms are transparent, the rules are transgressed in the context of secret manipulations to the effect that forms are not transparent but must be learned or acquired through initiation. In the long run, they may lexicalize and replace the original forms and become instances of language change (Storch 2011: 9). Numerous studies on youths' linguistic practices have so far left out a detailed analysis of language ideologies. Among the few exceptions in the field are Ag and Jørgensen (2012), who focus on language ideology in their study of youths' polylanguaging processes in multiethnolectal[4] European cities. Lytra (2015) provides a detailed insight into Turkish-speaking adolescents' ideological choices in the British and Greek diasporas, and Bucholtz (2009) takes a closer look at stance and style in Mexican immigrant youth slang in the United States. Style – a salient feature of fashion – in general plays a central role when assessing youth's language ideologies, and so does stylization of performances (Eckert 2012, Hurst-Harosh 2020, among others). Most of these studies lack, however, the postcolonial or – in Mignolo's (2012) terms – decolonial approach to linguistic differentiation that we suggest.

Scholarly work on African youth language practices hangs onto the notion of resistance identities and associates young people's speech styles with motivations of non-conformity correlating with creativity, which then produces so-called anti-languages, a concept introduced by Halliday (1976). Resistance is to some extent part of adolescents' ideological fundament– yet, it is by far not all youth's key motivation. Hollington (2016) analyzes the language practices of young Ethiopians in different neighborhoods of Addis Ababa with reference to Irvine and Gal's (2000) concept of "fractal recursivity" as semiotic process of differentiation, while Rüsch and Nassenstein (2016) look at a northern Ugandan scenario applying the concept of "iconization" to the semiotics of youth language. In the following, the theoretical ideas will be applied to three empirical case studies.

3 Three concise scenarios

In the following subsections, three concise case studies (see Figure 14.1 for their geographic localization) will highlight divergent ideological angles and self-reflexive utterances by African youths. These young speakers do not conceptualize their own ways of speaking as anti-language, deviant speech nor necessarily as "youth language" in a narrow sense.

---

[4] The term multiethnolect was coined by Quist (2000) and by Clyne (2000). Clyne defines it as an "expression of a new kind of group identity". It is used collectively by several minority groups in order to express their minority status or to upgrade this status (Clyne 2000: 87).

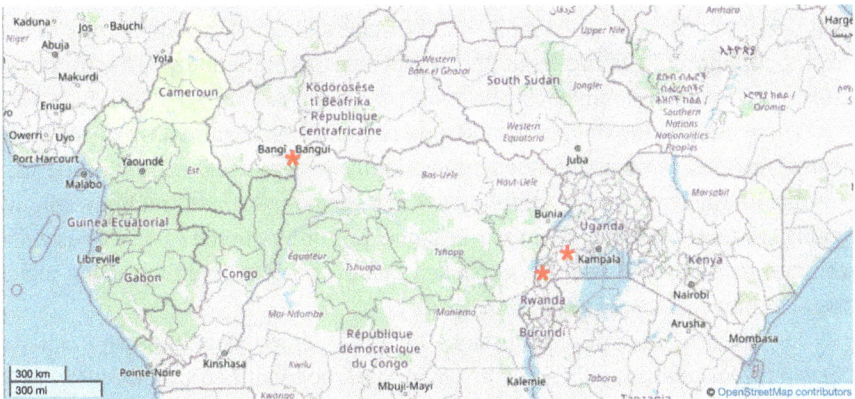

Figure 14.1: The studied communities in Bangui (CAR), Mbarara and Kisoro (Uganda) (openstreetmap).

3.1 "There is no such thing as slang!" – Rufumbira and rapping youth

"I have failed to get people who know slungs [sic]. They all say maybe English." We received this statement via WhatsApp from Capher N., a Mufumbira[5] and journalist of a local radio station, after several weeks of joint fieldwork. We had asked him to assist us in identifying different realizations of or ways of speaking Rufumbira, a Bantu language from southwestern Uganda and the most widespread language of Kisoro District, closely related to neighboring Kinyarwanda (spoken in Rwanda). We were specifically interested in young speakers' deviating speech styles that they would engage in when being among their peers, especially due to the fact that we had witnessed similar practices across the Rwandan and Congolese borders nearby.

In analogy with Bongo Fleva, the Tanzanian Swahili hip hop, the southwestern Ugandan town of Kisoro has witnessed the creation of Amahoro Fleva, a local hip hop style by local musicians. The lyrics are entirely in Rufumbira language, made up of rap lyrics and underlying hip hop beats. The term Amahoro Fleva (lit. 'peace flavor') was coined by Bafumbira artists Slenda MC and Echo MC (among others) in 2000. Over the years, Amahoro Flava has turned into an indexical representation of young Bafumbira's regional identity and is still gaining ground among the

---

5 *Rufumbira* is the glossonym, a speaker of the language is called *Mufumbira* (pl. *Bafumbira*), and the toponym of the region is *Bufumbira*.

young but increasingly also among older listeners. Beyond the community of rap lovers, Amahoro Fleva has begun to be perceived as Rufumbira music, different from music in neighboring districts.

When conducting fieldwork in Kisoro, southwestern Uganda, we interviewed young Rufumbira speakers about their linguistic practices, especially by discussing linguistic styles and different ways of speaking Rufumbira. Interestingly, young speakers stated that they would speak Rufumbira in the same way as elder community members, which was backed by our recordings (only proving regiolectal but no sociolectal variation).

In the focus of group discussions on the interconnectedness of Amahora Fleva and Rufumbira, only a few lexemes could be identified that were formerly ascribed to youth: *umudému* 'girl', *swaga* 'swagg, fashionable style', *bebi* 'girl, woman', *sawa* 'alright', *poa* 'fine, good', the latter ones borrowed from Kiswahili. However, all these terms were increasingly also employed by older speakers. But why would young Rufumbira speakers neither manipulate nor stylize their speech as is common practice in other Ugandan communities, e.g., among Baganda, Basoga, Acholi (Lorenz 2019, Rüsch and Nassenstein 2016)? Why do young Bafumbira apparently not seek linguistic differentiation from other Rufumbira speakers by creating a new stylect that transports and indexically refers to youth culture?

A few scholars have worked on youth language and the use of hip hop and its inherent globalized image, especially in the context of the sociolinguistics of globalization. The indexical value of Amahoro Fleva may be understood as "dusty foot philosophy" in the sense of Pennycook and Mitchell (2009: 25–26), who refer to the eponymous album of Somali-Canadian MC K'Naan. They (2009: 30) characterize locally emergent hip hop movements around the world as "local traditions being pulled toward global cultural forms while those traditions are simultaneously reinvented", regarding such process as instances of "the dusty feet that are grounded in local philosophical and poetic traditions" (ibid.: 34). Amahoro Fleva artists keep their "dusty feet" on Kisoro's soil, where they perform their songs, and in the more westernized and urban contexts of the Ugandan capital Kampala where these songs are produced. Local residents' voices characterize and describe Amahoro Fleva both as local practice and as "an imagination of localization that goes beyond appropriation of sounds, or references to local contexts" (ibid.: 26): The joint composition of global sounds and local language turns Rufumbira into a mainstream genre that is nourished by younger musicians and consumed by the entire community across different age groups, and rappers' extralinguistic hip hop features such as fancy gestures, clothing and hair styles are copied by the diversified audiences who listen to Amahoro Fleva. As indexical representation of local lifestyle and tradition, their music articulates local identity and simultaneously shapes it at the same time through metapragmatic comments on Rufumbira, which are contained in their rap lyrics.

Hip hop is per se perceived as a global genre but also as a globalizing engine for social and linguistic change. It is inextricably linked to the spread of (African) American culture (Pennycook and Mitchell 2009: 28) and is part of a global market. The local appropriation of hip hop as Amahoro Fleva among Bafumbira artists already marks a *meaningful difference*, which does not need to be enhanced at a linguistic level in youth's stylization of lexemes, their use of semantic manipulations or syllable reversal, just to name a few.

But why can the concept of differentiation be seen as essential in southwestern Uganda? Speaking with a difference (which we have studied more extensively in our own scholarly work) is of major importance to Bafumbira people, due to the historical burden of often having been politically categorized in different ways. First, they were classified as neighboring Rwandans but less than three decades ago Rufumbira was recognized as a language of Uganda.[6] There is no need for internal divisions or patterns of fractal recursivity (Irvine and Gal 2000), as the use of Rufumbira itself incorporates ideologies of resistance and anti-language – at least from a sociohistorical point of view. But what does this mean for the conceptualization of youth and youth language?

The fact that journalist Capher N. did not "find" any youth language practices or speakers shows the poetic value of Amahoro Fleva, which becomes tangible in lyrics such as Slenda MC's "Kiss my Town", a song that addresses the town of Kisoro and the beauty of nature around it and praises local culture. While in many parts of the world attitudes towards hip hop as a genre of resistance are commonly negative among older speakers or in mainstream society, in Rufumbira the hip hop style Amahoro Fleva has become an inverted emblem of local culture and pride. Instead of being associated with gangsterism, decaying language or bad-mannered youth, the language used in Amahoro Fleva lyrics is associated with positive prestige, as expressed by a research assistant:

> Those guys are seen as better, good . . . as good guys who promote Rufumbira. Their music is liked, their music is very liked by young talents, young guys, guys copy them. [. . .] And guys are like: "Wow, Rufumbira!" And people like them so so much. They are seen as good people because they love their language. When you feel proud of your language or land, people feel proud of you also. (S.A., interview excerpt, 2016)

The extrinsic and linguistic concept of young speakers' deviant speech styles as a clearly identifiable feature of "youth language" does not apply to Bafumbira

---

6 In the Ugandan constitution this was manifested in the 1990s.

youth in southwestern Uganda: Hip hop artists not only address contemporary topics in their lyrics but also include voices of old people, as explained by Amahoro Fleva artist Josh (interview excerpt, 2016):

> *Kisoro rwose, Slenda MC araza abajugunyira bantu amagambo mu rufumbira, harimo imigani ya kera hamwe n'ibiriho ubu* [in all of Kisoro, Slenda MC "throws" words to people in Rufumbira, there are old proverbs in it together with what is happening now]

Unlike their peers in the capital Kampala or other cities throughout the country, youth's language ideologies do not circle around linguistic differentiation between initiated in-group and excluded out-group on a meso-level but on a macro-level between Bafumbira and other ethnic communities.[7] The concept of "youth language" in Rufumbira-speaking communities thus does not express the same semiotic relationship between signs and their meaning as elsewhere.

Figure 14.2: Joint performances of artists as "Bufumbira All Stars" in traditional clothing.

---

7 This also becomes evident in joint musical performances of most Bafumbira artists under the band label „Bufumbira All Stars", integrating traditional dances and encompassing different music styles; see for instance Figure 14.2, a publicly accessible screenshot from YouTube [https://www.youtube.com/watch?v=Y2ddG-MGfPw] (accessed 20 November 2020).

3.2 Ruyaye: Imagined youth language in western Uganda

When we travelled to Mbarara in Western Uganda in March 2015 in order to record and document youths' linguistic practices,[8] we were directed to meet a popular dancehall musician, Nick Lee. He is said to be very knowledgeable with regard to the local youth language based on Runyankore, often labeled Ruyaye by young speakers, a name coined in relation to that of the youth language Luyaaye (based on Luganda) in the Ugandan capital Kampala (Namyalo 2015). Nick Lee ran a telephone shop in the city center of Mbarara, the third largest city in Uganda, where he also sold movies and mp3 music collections. His tiny salesroom, connected to the main road of Mbarara through a narrow path, was often frequented by teenagers from the entire city, who would exchange ideas about the latest linguistic innovations and also about upcoming artists from the entire area. When we met, he guided us to a small bar in another neighborhood of Mbarara and informed us that he himself – when performing – would not use the local youth language Ruyaye in his dancehall, in order to make the songs more accessible to a broader public, but he could give detailed background information about this linguistic practice.

The four largest linguistic communities in western Uganda are the Banyankore around Mbarara (speaking Nyankore language or Runyankore), the Bakiga (speaking Kiga or Rukiga), the Batooro (speaking Tooro or Rutooro) and the Banyoro (speaking Nyoro or Runyoro). All these neighboring languages are genetically closely-related with a high degree of mutual intelligibility, and the speakers share a historical and cultural heritage. Bernsten (2010) describes in detail the precolonial situation, and how the so-called Kitara Kingdom united four different ethnic groups of western Uganda in its realm, which lasted several centuries and the memory of which has survived in the name of the Bunyoro-Kitara kingdom. In this kingdom there was never one single language spoken. Only recently an artificial incentive to form one single out of the four individual regional languages was initiated by linguists at the biggest university of the country.

> In the 1990s the movement to amalgamate the western Ugandan languages inspired two conferences at Makerere University. At the first in 1990, supporters gathered to push for the teaching of the western Ugandan languages at the university level. One of the key decisions was what to call the unified language. [. . .] At the second conference in October 1994, the name Runyakitara was permanently adopted. [. . .] It is clear that over the first half of the

---

8 This trip was part of a larger project on youth language and hip hop in Uganda, focusing on youth language practices based on different languages from Uganda.

> century, the language known as Runyoro was involved in a four-way split, dividing into Runyoro, Rutooro, Runyankore and Rukiga. In the 1990s, the move has been to reconsolidate the four languages into one. (Bernsten 2010: 98–99)

While these academic efforts did not result in diffusing a new and common everyday language Runyakitara among the population, the youth language practice Ruyaye is claimed to have developed spontaneously in this area, albeit on a different level.

Nick Lee, in our conversations with a few other colleagues of his, stated that Ruyaye was perceived as one common youth language practice diffused all across western Uganda. We then got into contact with youth from other urban centers and compared linguistic manipulations, relexicalizations and emblematic terms as uttered by speakers from the urban centers of Mbarara, Masindi, Kabale and Fort Portal. While the manipulation strategies on phonological and morphological levels were very different – metathesis and epenthesis on the first level and specific patterns of affixation on the second – semantic manipulations showed significant similarities. Lexically, the recordings revealed diverse and numerous different synonyms.

We were also given a few shared metaphorical expressions. The first *nayoshe enjooka* is used in Rukiga-speaking areas, and *nyokeje enzoka* in Rutooro-speaking areas, both verbally translated as 'I burnt a snake', express that no financial profit could be taken out of a transaction. The second, a question *N'obaasa kumpeeka na mugongo gwawe?* used by Rukiga speakers and its equivalent *Osobola kumpeka ha mugongo?* by Rutooro speakers, means literally 'Can you carry me on your back?', but it expresses a man's interest in a sexual affair with a woman.

The recorded data from different settings do not confirm Nick Lee's statement that there is one common youth language. The given structural differences, however, do not outweigh semantic correspondences (in terms of used metaphorical expressions, euphemisms, dysphemisms, etc.), i.e. mutual intelligibility is not necessarily given among speakers from different areas.

> They are similar, the same, though spoken in different languages, but with the same meaning. Kabale [town in Rukiga-speaking area], their pronunciation is a bit little different from this one of Banyankore but mostly they are the same because we are Runyakitara, we are Banyankore, Bakiga . . . those from Fort Portal will also understand, of course, some words are a bit different [. . .] but whenever we are talking, we get each other because we are the same. (Nick Lee, interview excerpt, 2015)

The question arises how the actual apparent differences between the urban youth language practices can be explained away despite the linguistic differences that become evident. The artificial amalgam Runyakitara is mostly used in the media and in school education, and outside school youth share it as a *symbol* of regional identification. Runyakitara is, however, not used in daily life interaction on a local level, since phonological and morphosyntactic divergences in the four languages make mutual intelligibility difficult (Rubongoya 1999, Mpairwe and Kahangi 2013). Ruyaye may be understood as the expression of a regional shared language ideology, which is opposed to the dominance of Luganda, the language of the capital Kampala (center of Buganda Kingdom), and also to the national language policy. As a consequence, the implementation of Runyakitara on the macro-level has never been fully achieved, but amazingly it has become a common language on a micro-level. Ruyaye is thus a fluid set of youth language practices that are conceptualized by its speakers as one single language – mostly due to the youth's sense of belonging and the indexical value of a strong regional identity. Youth's communities of practice in different settings in western Uganda can be best categorized as an imagined community with one imagined language, in analogy with Anderson's (2006) idea of "imagined communities". He states that "[n]ot only communities but also languages must be imagined before their unity can be socially accomplished" and thus have to be imagined in order to exist, and Anderson (2006: 4) explains this as standing in opposition to the "anomaly of nationalism". In the Ugandan context, Ruyaye may be considered an instance, on a grassroots level, of the implementation of Runyakitara among young speakers, and it constitutes a regional register for young speakers, not uniquely street-based, nor stigmatized or defective. It is not even seen as an antilanguage, but rather as one that supports the governmental policy. Again, it reflects speakers' language ideologies as a local strategy of conceptualizing youth language – driven by a desire for unification and out of linguistic nostalgia (see also Figure 14.3 for a model of Ruyaye and its relation to the different local languages and Runyakitara).

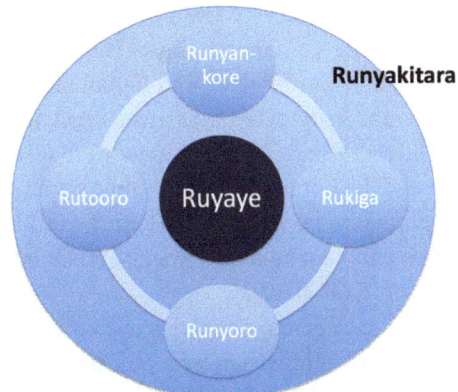

Figure 14.3: A model of Ruyaye and its relationship with Runyakitara and the four local languages.

3.3 Sango Godobé: Blurry boundaries between youth language and common speech

While most other youth languages, e.g., Sheng, were "discovered" as a result of other sociolinguistic or linguistic anthropological research, the emergence of Sango Godobé in scientific research is the result of a request for information by colleagues: Is there a youth language in Central African Republic? Prior to the investigations by Landi and Pasch (2015) and Pasch and Landi (2018), this youth language was basically unknown in linguistic and anthropological literature. Sélézilo's (1999) master's thesis, a description of Sango Godobé, was not published but is the first study to use this name.

In studies of the Ubangian language Sango and its development, the question whether the language underwent processes of pidginization and creolization (Diki-Kidiri 1986, Samarin 1984/1985, and many more) and how it could be developed as a national and official language for the use as written medium (Diki-Kidiri 1977, and many more) has attracted more interest among scholars than the question whether there is a specific youth language in CAR or not. Despite its high status and all language planning efforts (Bouquiaux 1978), many Central Africans consider the language defective because most technical terms have to be borrowed from French. After Sango was declared the official medium of CAR, a commission was established for the creation of a standard orthography and the compilation of a dictionary (Bouquiaux 1978: 243). Most members of the committee favored a so-called *resangolisation* of the language, and the dictionary contains a high number of technical terms that were coined according to the morphological rules of the language. Many of these terms are, however, not known by the broad public who rather use the equivalent French terms. Investigations of varieties of Sango focussed on interferences from ethnic languages and from French (Gerbault 1990, Wénézoui-Dechamps 1981).

The need for *resangolisation* was felt because only very few are able to speak "pure" Sango, i.e. Standard Sango, devoid of or containing only a few French loanwords. Among these are Catholic missionaries of French and Italian origin, the linguists at the University of Bangui and the *Institut de Linguistique Appliquée* who specialize in Sango, broadcasters in radio and TV and a few journalists (Landi and Pasch 2015: 215). The majority of the population use Common Sango for everyday communication, which contains many words from French. In his grammar, Samarin (1967) already observes people who do not speak French but who actually use French loanwords (Samarin 1967: 21–22).

The group who allegedly were the creators of Sango Godobé was mentioned for the first time in 1963 by Simha Arom, an Israeli musician who was invited by president Dacko to create a quality fanfare orchestra in Bangui. When he came across a group of homeless and jobless boys and girls of 17 to 20 years of age called Godobé (Arom 2009), he found in them the talented musicians he was looking for. The next mention of Bangui street children called Godobé (the Sango equivalent for 'crook') is an entry in the dictionary by Bouquiaux et al. (1978). The linguist Diki-Kidiri (1986) of Central African descent outlines the poor conditions of their life without labeling them gangsters or criminals. He does not refer to their way of speaking in a derogatory way, and he apparently did not consider it an argot incomprehensible to outsiders or a medium belonging to them alone.

When during the last decades of the 20th century economic conditions deteriorated and conditions of survival for street children worsened, they were obliged to carry out hard and unpleasant work, and they were often even forced into petty crime, which worsened their reputation, and until today they are usually considered to be criminals. Their language, if people really talk about it at all, is referred to as a language of gangsters or criminals. The educated elite criticizes the Godobé for their low standard way of speaking, saying "*ils parlent comme ils veulent*" [they speak as they want].

In 1991, when the second author heard the term "Double Sango", she was told that this was the name of a secret gangsters' language, but it was impossible to get further information. By accident, she came across a group of girls of around 10–12 years of age who were practicing a ludling of the pig-Latin type, which they called "Double Sango". The girls presented one after the other single sentences with all nouns and verbs being manipulated by syllable metathesis, which their friends were supposed to decipher and repeat in Common Sango. The presentation of the sentences was so difficult that the girls would have been unable to convey messages consisting of several sentences. They restricted themselves to simple sentences, regardless of the content – which was irrelevant. It was evident that this speech style was neither a gangster language nor really a secret language. In his paper "The morphological and phonological characteristics of Double Sango", presented at the colloquium on the status and use of Sango in CAR in September 1992, Erhard Voeltz (1992) provided recordings of entire stories recited in Double Sango by adult men as a performative task in competitive games. Here the same type of metathesis was given. When in 2011 Germain Landi carried out research on Sango Godobé, he observed again the same type of syllable metatheses, but now restricted to nouns, and also vowel conversions (Landi and Pasch 2015). He also learned that certain words and expressions were used in metaphorical ways, which make them difficult to be understood by outsiders, e.g., *súpù* (from French *soupe* 'soup') for 'big buttocks of a woman'.

Over time, many originally secret forms and expressions have been integrated into Common Sango, and most people can understand Sango Godobé at least to some degree. Comprehensibility is also possible due to the low frequency of manipulations in dialogues that may be applied only to the first or the most important noun of a sentence or an utterance. Nevertheless, many people of the middle class have the ideology that Sango Godobé is a language for the lower class, and they clearly distance themselves from Sango Godobé and do not use it themselves. People having university education even claim that they do not understand it at all, and that they have to ask their children for advice if they want to understand a given expression. At the same time, it is these middle class people who sometimes engage Godobé for jobs like digging graves or carrying heavy loads. For the negotiations with the Godobé, they use linguistic practices at the boundary of Common Sango and Sango Godobé, which they can do because they do have some competence of the latter way of speaking.

Musicians, rappers in particular, deliberately integrate Sango Godobé expressions into their lyrics, thereby making them accessible to practically everybody. They do so in order to express solidarity with the Godobé and to show that they are up to date with regard to the latest linguistic innovations. Their audiences of all social layers are expected to decipher the manipulated forms and to understand or learn the meanings of metaphors, e.g., in the expression *apendere mara* 'beautiful women' (< *mara* 'ethnic group; type of'). Rappers, however, not only use forms that they have learned from the Godobé, but they also create their own lexemes. A popular musician, Djou Gotto, who apparently grew up as a street child, works with the label *Goudoube* (/gúdúbè/), also embroidered on the cap that he wears in some of his video clips. Vowel conversion, replacing /o/ with /u/, which is the typical manipulation of bi- and trisyllabic words (*kodoro* > *kuduru* or *nyama* > *nyume*), make the name more salient since the vowel /u/ is relatively rare in Common and Standard Sango (Landi and Pasch 2015: 217).

Street children are part of the rappers' audience and their tragic fate (being marginalized and stigmatized) serves as a primary topic in many rap songs as a political statement. Song texts held in their way of speaking were used in June 2017 in the course of a jam session, which was part of a project to disarm youth fighting each other as members of the Seleka or Anti-Balaka (Baddorf 2017).

The blurry boundary between Common Sango and Sango Godobé indicates that, from a formal linguistic point of view, Sango Godobé is not a linguistic variety that can be clearly distinguished from Common Sango; furthermore the Godobé are not the only ones who speak and understand this variety. This raises the question of which factors contribute to the perception of Sango Godobé as a distinct medium of communication with ascriptions of non-conformity and (linguistic and social) deviation. Several factors play a key role based on attitudes and ideologies. First, Sango Godobé is the only language that Godobé usually master, while educated people have also access to French and to a form of Sango closer to the standard (see Figure 14.4 for the overlapping communities of practice who make use of Sango Godobé). Secondly, Godobé have the reputation of being creators and users of manipulated forms and complex metaphors, which establishes a close relation between their group and the linguistic practice Sango Godobé. It is true that rappers also create manipulated forms and metaphors, but while Godobé employ such forms in order to keep things secret, the rappers propagate them and demonstrate that they are up to date with regard to linguistic innovations and fashions. This clearly hints at a necessary redirection and redefinition of Sango Godobé – and a focus on the fuzzy division between speakers and non-speakers, preferably by taking (local) language ideologies of speakers into account (see Section 4).

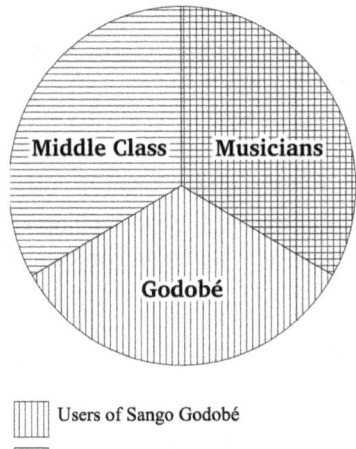

Users of Sango Godobé

People living in secure economic conditions

Figure 14.4: Musicians as blurry category using Sango Godobé and being part of the middle class.

4 Ideologies from the South: Local voices and alternative (youth) language concepts

Apart from mainstream ideological studies at the intersection of pragmatics, sociolinguistics and linguistic anthropology, a range of scholars such as Bauman and Briggs (2003) and Errington (2008) have focused on settings in the so-called Global South, where speakers' ideological choices are linked to postcolonial continuities and settings of inequality and injustice. In these contexts, speakers' ideologies may not correspond with dominant state ideologies, whose foundations are tied to colonial traditions. With regard to such situations, Hollington and Storch (2016: 2) state that "[t]here are multiple, sometimes contradictory ideological concepts of language, endangerment, ownership, experthood and speaker identity". The critical endeavor to study language ideologies against their postcolonial background can also be applied to youth language practices diffused in the Global South, even though this represents a new field (see Hollington and Akena, this volume, and also Hurst-Harosh 2019). Youth are often oriented toward more "global linguistic flows" (Alim, Ibrahim and Pennycook 2009) such as American hip hop. At the same time, mediatized forms of communication, fashionable language and matters of style, as well as critical notions of decoloniality, agency and ownership as opposed to prescriptive ideologies find their way into youth's speech and their artistic expressions. Especially African youth who are continuously facing systems of socioeconomic inequality in their access to education, communication and mobility, transform their reflections of marginalization and postcolonial experience into creative ways of speaking, mimetic forms of "speaking back" and poetic strategies (as becomes evident in the three case studies). Youth language practices that emerged in colonial times, such as Sheng in Kenya, Tsotsitaal in South Africa, Indoubil in the Congo, and so forth, may be remodeled and modified to such an extent that they no longer match established categories of "youth language" as expression of adolescent non-conformity, societal opposition or "resistance identity" but express their speakers' stance in contexts of postcolonial hardship:

> Another view on youth language practices, and the deviant in language is possible. Refocusing with a postcolonial perspective and historicizing such language practices within their context, we see that they often emerged in or toward the end of colonialism. We therefore suggest that youth language can often be seen as a kind of mimetic play in postcolonies. [...] Our aim is thus to understand youths' creative and manipulative means of language no longer as sociolectal deviations but as agency. Youth language can, when seen from a postcolonial angle and drawing upon what now is increasingly referred to as Southern Theory, be understood as power, magic and damnation.
> (Nassenstein, Hollington and Storch 2018: 19–20)

Given the seriousness of contexts where youth's linguistic strategies serve as a reaction to hegemonic continuities, their voices appear as less playful and hilarious than often attributed to youth language. At times, these artistic expressions may furthermore not be conceptualized by their users as "youth language" after all.

In agreement with Makoni and Pennycook (2007), Hollington and Storch (2016), in the preface to their special issue on language ideologies, address the intricate problem that scholars from the Global North (missionaries, colonial agents, language practitioners, etc.) have often tried to turn allegedly messy languages in the Global South into more linear and more esthetic forms. These ambitions necessarily reflect the role and impact of these scholars and their subjective evaluations and ascriptions of Otherness to specific speech styles:

> Language ideologies may help people to explain away the messy in communication, make it ownable, controllable, and turn untidy language as resulting from construction "out of messy variability" (Gal and Woolard 2001: 1) into order. Studying them, in turn, helps to uncover these processes by looking at the ways in which images and ideas about language(s) and communicative practices are constructed. This is an interesting process by itself, which has begun to be of interest in particular among critical sociolinguists: how do the ideologies of the linguists themselves contribute to the choices of their topics, shape their perspectives on order and disorder, methodologies and concepts of data?
>
> (Hollington and Storch 2016: 3)

Common views on and ideologies around youth language reflect in many cases *linguists'* ideologies, and the views of linguistic experts on processes of manipulation, identification and on the outputs of metacommunication. Hollington and Storch thus suggest that it is "of considerable import to change the perspective a bit and to focus on precisely those ways of conceptualizing language that [...] can also be seen as particularly meaningful where it hides meaning" (ibid.: 4). This goes along with a shift toward non-Northern perspectives on language ideologies, which require a turn toward delinking and decolonial approaches. Moreover, non-Northern language practices and the ideological sets of beliefs about them need to be de-exoticized, no longer classifying, inventorying and artefactualizing languages according to traditions and hegemonic standards from the Global North.[9] Instead, language practice needs to be studied from an emic perspective, without highlighting exoticized "Southerness". Southern knowledge systems need to be acknowledged as adequate ways of dealing with linguistic reality in the postcolony, as is said in the foundations of Southern Theory (de Sousa Santos 2015, Connell 2007, Comaroff and Comaroff 2012) – yet, one general problem hereby is that "[e]ven though Southern knowledges continue to exist, they are continuously turned, through their ongoing exclusion from authorized discourses and powerful institutions, into debris: they are nothing but colonial outfall" (Bongartz and Storch 2016: 156). In a paradigm shift within linguistics, speakers from the South no longer only provide data but are increasingly understood as theorists; speakers' self-reflexive judgments about their own multilingual and translingual language practices, their positionality and stance are therefore taken more seriously. Alim (2009) presents hip hop musicians as "cultural theorists", who not only participate in music production and performance but who also come up with theoretical reflections with regard to their translocal stylizations on a meta-level. In other terms, youth who take part in theory-building

---

9 Blommaert (2008) and Irvine (2008) have both elaborated upon these processes of turning specific African languages into artefactualized entities in analogy to European models of nation-states and national languages.

are not only "speakers", but they must be regarded as *auteurs* ('authors') and innovators who are conscious of their language use.

The three aforementioned Ugandan and Central African contexts reflect language users' agency and their stance, which diverge from what is usually considered youth's linguistic practices. Metalinguistic and metapragmatic exchanges on the meaning of specific expressions and their manipulations, on genres such as songs, poetic language, ritualized speech and speech acts such as greetings all need to be understood as being part of youth's language use seen from a more holistic perspective. Complexities in studying the ideological meta-level of youths' interactions lie in the historical depth of analysis (beginning with imperialism and coloniality), in the sociological dimension of analysis (of felt marginalization and exclusion, devalorization of specific practices and lifestyles, etc.) and in the fuzziness and subjectivity of the topic under scrutiny: language ideologies are hard to analyze.

Youth's everyday speech can moreover be understood as a kind of local languaging in Pennycook's (2010) sense, where the aforementioned "dusty feet" connect tradition and ritualized speech with global hip hop as glocalized bricolage. Local linguists and researchers who emerge from the contexts under study may incorporate another kind of authority and represent a different kind of agency than non-initiated and external researchers.

But what does a turn toward a more emic understanding of language ideology mean for the three studied contexts? Applying the aforementioned arguments of this section to Sango Godobé may clarify the change of direction. The ideology that Standard Sango is the most 'correct' and ideal variety of the language is widespread, although it is mastered only by linguists at the university and by those missionaries who are responsible for the production of written texts in Sango. This ideology, however, is not a topic in scholarly descriptions of the language like *A Grammar of Sango* by Samarin (1967) and the *Dictionnaire Sango-Français – Lexique Français-Sango* by Bouquiaux et al. (1978). Only studies by Wénézoui-Dechamps (1981, see also several subsequent publications) and Gerbaut (1990) consider the mixing of Sango and French a problematic development. As they are hardly accessible in CAR, we may therefore assume that prevalent language ideologies around Sango result from the introduction of French as a school subject, which was taught in a prescriptive way, i.e. the use of wrong forms and constructions was sanctioned. Sango Godobé reflects in the eyes of many people a low standard or a result of poor acquisition of the language. In analogy with Mignolo's (2012) framework, the schism between written European languages as media of knowledge and power from oral African languages was transferred to the differentiation of correct from non-correct forms of any written language, be it French or Sango. The missionary and colonial expectation was that Sango would eventually become a language of knowledge and power just like French. Sango, however, remained basically an oral medium but with three ways of speaking: Standard Sango, Common Sango and Sango Godobé (Pasch 2020). When musicians sing praise songs about the language, e.g., *Sango, yanga ti kodoro ti mbi* [Sango, language of my country] by Idylle, they raise the prestige of the language as an item of value and social and cultural identity, and when they sing in Sango Godobé, they raise the prestige of this way of speaking as being fashionable and attractive. They have sufficient influence on all layers of society to turn Sango Godobé into a language of modernity, of high artistic and social value, due to the fact that musical styles and performances were not affected by colonial policies as much as language.[10] They are not only saccadic leaders, i.e., opinion leaders in the sense of Labov (2001: 383), within the community of practice of speakers of Sango Godobé, but they spread knowledge of and about the language even beyond that community into the middle class: Due to the influence of rap music, speakers of Common Sango become acquainted with formerly low-standard and now fashionable linguistic forms and develop an interest in them, which should cause ideological dissonances. Musicians, rappers in particular, are not only efficient multipliers but to some extent also theorists, who analyze the linguistic market and innovate language according to the social network ties between Godobé and non-Godobé, blurring boundaries between formerly demarcated groups. Here, language ideology reflects quite well "how speakers' ways of thinking of language change" (Storch 2011: 47), and also the capacity of influential groups to raise the prestige of a language by focusing on the specific function of being fashionable and innovative.

5 Semiotic processes

Bucholtz and Hall (2004: 379) state that "the issue of power as a social phenomenon is central in the concept of ideology". With regard to the role and the prestige of Sango Godobé, "power" does not lie in the hands of academically or politically powerful individuals but in the hands of those who determine what is fashionable. Defining and claiming difference is therefore multi-facetted and may change according to the (local or non-local) perspective from which difference is perceived or enhanced. Irvine and Gal's (2000: 37) three semiotic processes, which they define as "the means by which people construct ideological

---

[10] Christian missionaries taught and introduced new European music styles but did not destroy the appreciation of local music.

representations of linguistic differences", may be of help when redirecting the focus on language ideologies from an emic perspective. Hollington (2016: 138, our emphasis) summarizes these three processes as follows:

> These three semiotic processes are *iconization*, a process turning the sign relationship between linguistic form and social image in a way that '[l]inguistic differences appear to be iconic representations of the social contrasts they index'; *[fractal] recursivity*, 'the projection of an opposition' within a group, thus creating subcategories or subvarieties, and *erasure*, a process in which certain aspects of sociolinguistic distinctiveness are eclipsed while focusing on others [. . .].

Iconization is frequent in numerous youth language contexts. However, in some of the studied contexts these differences are blurred and no longer clear. Being used by hip hop musicians and increasingly by non-Godobé, the linguistic forms that index Godobé identity do not stand out as being iconic in all aspects. With regard to the case of Ruyaye in western Uganda, for instance, iconic linguistic forms among youth from different parts of western Uganda do not index specific social images on the local level. Youth see themselves rather as one group across linguistic and cultural boundaries in western Uganda.

Fractal recursivity occurs when non-Godobé, who pretend not to understand Sango Godobé, turn the Godobé into the antagonistic "Others" by ascribing specific attributes to them. Stigmatization is a mutual endeavor here, and to be counted as a Godobé is favorable in certain situations, but disadvantageous in other situations. While from an outsider's perspective, internal fragmentations among Bafumbira in southwestern Uganda (e.g., between hip hop fans, street youth, students, etc.) are conceivable given the complex social stratification in Bafumbira communities, the local rap style Amahoro Fleva bridges differences rather than enhancing externally anticipated and projected linguistic fragmentations. In the neighboring city, Mbarara, Ruyaye-speaking youth do not perceive social or linguistic differences between different subgroups of youth, whereas formal linguists discern quite clearly differences between Kiga-based youth language in Kabale and Nyankore-based youth language in Mbarara, just to name an example.

Erasure is a recurrent phenomenon of linguistic differentiation in all three settings. Rufumbira-speaking youth do not distinguish themselves from other layers of society linguistically, since their music is consumed and diffused by Bafumbira of all age groups. In Central African Republic, there are only minor differences between Common Sango and Sango Godobé as the variety of the despised group of street children – to an extent that influential speakers wonder whether these are actually different varieties after all. Concerning Ruyaye, the alleged practice or the set of similar practices in western Uganda show only subtle and intricate differences. While linguists see differences between the practices of four communities of Tooro-, Nyoro-, Nyankore- and Kiga-speakers, these are not perceived by youth, as they hang on to the idea of one supraregional youth language practice in analogy with the artificial language Runyakitara (based on the idea of a precolonial kingdom).

6 Conclusion

The present chapter has outlined difficulties in approaching youth language from only one widespread perspective (of identifying and analyzing secret, fashionable and deviant speech) and it questions common categorizations and classifications of the concept of youth language in an African context. Language ideologies, i.e. speakers' beliefs and thoughts about their linguistic practices, their underlying motivations and incentives – and judgments about perceived conformity or non-conformity of their language – have to be taken into consideration in more detail, and the concept may require further adaptation.

Speakers' language ideologies with regard to their stylized practices and conceptualizations of "youth language" ask for a broader perspective beyond discourses around concealment, resistance identities and anti-language. A careful postcolonial and decolonial analysis in the study of ideologies is advisable in contexts where speakers' everyday speech is not distinguishable from other ways of speaking, or where communities of practice are made up of diverse subgroups or lump specific communities of speakers together on the basis of specific semiotic processes or recognized semiotic signs,

As shown in this chapter, most descriptions of and allegations around youth language do not provide satisfactory analyses: Youth's speech can be perceived as linguistic fashion or aesthetic practice with fuzzy divisions between speakers and non-speakers (as among users of Sango Godobé), as collective imagination and key to regional identity or regional affiliation (as is the case for Ruyaye), or as congruent with common or everyday language, while music styles fill the gap of youth culture and identification (as is the case with Amahoro Fleva). Rethinking the conceptualization of and approaches to youth language will inevitably make us rethink linguists' concepts of fluid language practice itself and their static ascriptions – and the wobbling fundament of descriptive and documentary linguistics when eyed against the background of speakers' many ways of speaking.

References

Ag, Astrid and J. Normann Jørgensen. 2012. Ideologies, norms, and practices in youth poly-languaging. *International Journal of Bilingualism* 17 (4). 525–539.
Alim, H. Samy. 2009. Translocal style communities: Hip hop youth as cultural theorists of style, language and globalization. *Pragmatics* 19 (1). 103–127.
Alim, H. Samy, Awad Ibrahim and Alastair Pennycook (eds.). 2009. *Global linguistic flows: Hip hop cultures, youth identities, and the politics of language*. New York: Routledge.
Anderson, Benedict. 2006. *Imagined communities: Reflections on the origin and spread of nationalism*. London/New York: Verso.
Arom, Simha. 2009. L'audience présidencielle. In *La fanfare de Bangui: Itinéraire enchanté d'un ethnomusicologue*. Paris: Editions de la découverte.
Baddorf, Zack. 2017. Hip hop in Central African Republic brings hope in crisis. *The Associated Press*, 1 July 2017. [https://apnews.com/article/ba2f1f7d2518425ea849231acf902ab5] (accessed 7 November 2020).
Bauman, Richard and Charles L. Briggs. 2003. *Voices of modernity. Language ideologies and the politics of inequality*. Cambridge: Cambridge University Press.
Bernsten, Jan. 2010. Runyakitara: Uganda's 'new' language. *Journal of Multilingual and Multicultural Development* 19 (2). 93–107.
Blommaert, Jan. 2008. Artefactual ideologies and the textual production of African languages. *Language & Communication* 28. 291–307.
Bongartz, Christiane and Anne Storch. 2016. Making sense of the noisy. *Critical Multilingualism Studies* 4 (2). 154–173.
Bouquiaux, Luc 1978. Un dictionnaire sango pour l'empire Centrafricain. *Recherche, Pédagogie et Culture* 34. 25–31.
Bouquiaux, Luc et al. 1978. *Dictionnaire sango-français et lexique français-sango*. Paris: SELAF.
Brookes, Heather and Roland Kouassi. 2018. The language of youth in Africa: A sociocultural linguistic analysis. In Augustin Agwuele and Adams Bodomo (eds.), *The Routledge handbook of African linguistics*, 391–408. London/New York: Routledge.
Bucholtz, Mary 2009. From stance to style: gender, interaction, and indexicality in Mexican immigrant youth slang. In Alexandra Jaffe (ed.), *Stance. Sociolinguistic perspectives*, 146–170. New York: Oxford University Press.
Bucholtz, Mary and Kira Hall. 2004. Language and identity. In Alessandro Duranti (ed.), *A companion to linguistic anthropology*, 369–394. Malden: Blackwell.
Clyne, Michael. 2000. Lingua franca and ethnolects in Europe and beyond. *Sociolinguistica* 14. 83–89.
Comaroff, Jean and John L. Comaroff. 2012. *Theory from the South. Or, how Euro-America is evolving toward Africa*. Boulder: Paradigm.
Connell, Raewyn. 2007. *Southern Theory. The global dynamics of knowledge in social science*. Cambridge & Malden: Polity Press.
Diki-Kidiri Marcel. 1977. Développement du sango pour l'expression du monde moderne, obstacles et possibilités. In *Les relations entre les langues négro-africaines et la langues française*. Colloquium, Dakar, 22–26 March 1976, 717–728. Paris: Conseil international de la langue française.
Diki-Kidiri. 1986. Le sango dans la formation de la nation centrafricaine. *Politique Africaine* 23. 83–99. Paris: Karthala.

Eckert, Penelope. 2012. Three waves of variation study. The emergence of meaning in the study of sociolinguistic variation. *Annual Review of Anthropology* 41 (1). 87–100.

Edwards, John. 1982. Language attitudes and their implications among English speakers. In Ellen B. Ryan and Howard Giles (eds.), *Attitudes towards language variation*, 20–33. London: Edward Arnold.

Errington, Joseph. 2008. *Linguistics in a colonial world. A story of language, meaning and power.* Malden: Blackwell.

Esposito, Elena. 2001. Kollektives Gedächtnis und soziales Gedächtnis: Erinnerung und Vergessen aus der Sicht der Systemtheorie. In Sonja Klein, Vivian Liska, Karl Solibakke and Bernd Witte (eds.), *Gedächtnisstrategien und Medien im interkulturellen Dialog*, 49–59. Würzburg: Verlag Königshausen & Neumann GmbH.

Fishman, Joshua A. 1965. Who speaks what language to whom and when? *La Linguistique* 1 (2). 67–88.

Gal, Susan and Kathryn A. Woolard. (eds.) 2001. *Languages and publics: The making of authority.* Manchester and London: St. Jerome/Routledge.

Gal, Susan and Judith T. Irvine. 2019. *Signs of difference: Language and ideology in social life.* Cambridge: Cambridge University Press.

Garrett, Peter. 2010. *Attitudes to language.* Cambridge: Cambridge University Press.

Garrett, Peter, Nikolas Coupland and Angie Williams. 2003. *Investigating language attitudes: Social meanings of dialect, ethnicity and performance.* Cardiff: University of Wales Press.

Gerbault, Janine. 1990. Modes d'appropriation langagière en Republique Centrafricaine. *Bulletin du Centre d'étude des plurilinguismes* 11. 35–70.

Halliday, Michael A.K. 1976. Anti-languages. *American Anthropologist* 78 (3). 570–584.

Hollington, Andrea. 2016. Reflections on Ethiopian youths and Yarada K'wank'wa: Language practices and ideologies. *Sociolinguistic Studies* 10 (1–2). 135–152.

Hollington, Andrea and Anne Storch. 2016. Tidying up: A CMS special issue on language ideologies. *Critical Multilingualism Studies* 4 (2). 1–9.

Honwana, Alcinda and Filip de Boeck (eds.). 2005. *Makers and breakers. Children and youth in postcolonial Africa.* London: James Currey.

Hurst-Harosh, Ellen. 2019. Tsotsitaal and decoloniality. *African Studies* 78 (1). 112–125.

Hurst-Harosh, Ellen. 2020 *Tsotsitaal in South Africa. Style and metaphor in youth language practices.* Cologne: Rüdiger Köppe.

Hymes, Dell. 1964. Introduction: Toward ethnographies of communication. *American Anthropologist* 66 (6). 1–34.

Hymes, Dell. 1989. Ways of speaking. In Richard Bauman and Joel Sherzer (eds.), *Explorations in the ethnography of speaking*, 433–452. Cambridge: Cambridge University Press.

Irvine, Judith T. 2008. Subjected words: African linguistics and the colonial encounter. *Language & Communication* 28. 323–343.

Irvine, Judith T. 2011/2012. Language ideology. In John L. Jackson, Jr. (ed.), *Oxford bibliographies: Anthropology.* Oxford: Oxford University Press. [http://www.oxfordbibliographies.com] (accessed 6 December 2020).

Irvine, Judith T. and Susan Gal. 2000. Language ideology and linguistic differentiation. In Paul V. Kroskrity (ed.), *Regimes of language: Ideologies, polities and identities*, 35–83. Santa Fe: School of American Research Press.

Kroskrity, Paul. 2004. Language ideology. In Alessandro Duranti (ed.), *Companion to linguistic anthropology*, 496–517. Oxford: Blackwell.

Kroskrity, Paul. 2016. Language ideologies and language attitudes. In John L. Jackson, Jr. (ed.), *Oxford bibliographies: Anthropology*. Oxford: Oxford University Press. [http://www.oxfordbibliographies.com] (accessed 4 November 2020).

Labov, William. 2001. *Principles of linguistic change. Social factors, vol. 2*. Oxford: Blackwell.

Landi, Germain and Helma Pasch. 2015. Sango Godobé: The urban youth language of Bangui (CAR). In Nico Nassenstein and Andrea Hollington (eds.), *Youth language practices in Africa and beyond*, 207–226. Berlin: De Gruyter Mouton.

Lorenz, Steffen. 2019. *Living with language. An exploration of linguistic practices and language attitudes in Gulu, Northern Uganda*. Cologne: University of Cologne dissertation. [https://kups.ub.uni-koeln.de/9855/1/Steffen%20Lorenz.%20Living%20with%20Language..pdf] (accessed 26 January 2021).

Lüpke, Friederike and Anne Storch. 2013. *Repertoires and choices in African languages*. Berlin: De Gruyter Mouton.

Lytra, Valli. 2015. Language practices and language ideologies among Turkish-speaking young people in Athens and London. In Jacomine Nortier and Bente Ailin Svendsen (eds.), *Language, youth and identity in the 21st century*, 183–204. Cambridge: Cambridge University Press.

Mignolo, Walter D. 2012. *Local histories/Global designs. Coloniality, subaltern knowledges, and border thinking*. Paperback reissue, with a new preface. Princeton and Oxford: Princeton University Press.

Morgan Marcyliena. 2004. Speech community. In Alessandro Duranti (ed.), *Companion to linguistic anthropology*, 3–22. Oxford: Basil Blackwell.

Mpairwe, Yusufu and G. K. Kahangi. 2013. *Runyankore-Rukiga grammar. A modern student's guide*. Kampala: Fountain Publishers.

Namyalo, Saudah. 2015. Linguistic strategies in Luyaaye: Word play and conscious language manipulation. In Nico Nassenstein and Andrea Hollington (eds.), *Youth language practices in Africa and beyond*, 313–344. Berlin: De Gruyter Mouton.

Nassenstein, Nico. 2016. *Speaking with a difference: Border thinking in Rufumbira*. Cologne: University of Cologne dissertation. [https://kups.ub.uni-koeln.de/10082/1/Nassenstein_Rufumbira_2019.pdf] (accessed 26 January 2021).

Nassenstein, Nico and Andrea Hollington. 2016. Global repertoires and urban fluidity: youth languages in Africa. *International Journal of the Sociology of Language* 242. 171–193.

Nassenstein, Nico, Andrea Hollington and Anne Storch. 2018. Disinventing and demystifying youth language: Critical perspectives. *The Mouth* 3: 9–28.

Pasch, Helma. 2020. Sango, a homogenous language with religiolectal and sociolectal varieties. *Sociolinguistic Studies* 14 (3). 277–298.

Pasch, Helma and Germain Landi. 2018. How do you get information about Sango Godobé and the Godobé of Bangui: A conversational interview between Helma Pasch and Germain Landi. *The Mouth* 3: 125–137.

Quist, Pia 2008. Sociolinguistic approaches to multiethnolect: Language variety and stylistic practice. *International Journal of Bilingualism* 12 (1–2). 43–61.

Pennycook, Alastair and Tony Mitchell. 2009. Hip Hop as dusty foot philosophy: Engaging locality. In Samy H. Alim, Ibrahim Awad and Alastair Pennycook (eds.), *Global linguistic flows. Hip Hop cultures, youth identities, and the politics of language*, 25–42. New York: Routledge.

Pennycook, Alastair. 2010. *Language as a local practice*. New York: Routledge.

Rüsch, Maren and Nico Nassenstein. 2016. Ethno-regional ideologies and linguistic manipulation in the creation of the youth language Leb pa Bulu. *Critical Multilingualism Studies* 4 (2). 174–208.
Rubongoya, L. T. 1999. *A modern Runyoro-Rutooro grammar*. Cologne: Rüdiger Köppe.
Samarin, William J. 1967. *A grammar of Sango*. The Hague: Mouton and Co.
Samarin, William J. 1984/1985. Communication by Ubangian water and word. *Sprache und Geschichte in Afrika* 6. 309–373.
Sélézilo, A. 1999. Description linguistique du sängö godobé en Centrafrique. Abidjan, Ivory Coast: University of Cocody Mémoire de DEA.
Silverstein, Michael. 1979. Language structure and linguistic ideology. In Paul Clyne, William Hanks and Carol Hofbauer (eds.), *The elements: A parasession on linguistic units and levels,* 193–247. Chicago: Chicago Linguistic Society.
de Sousa Santos, Boaventura. 2015. *Epistemologies of the South: Justice against epistemicide*. New York: Routledge.
Storch, Anne. 2011. *Secret manipulations. Language and context in Africa*. Oxford: Oxford University Press.
Verschueren, Jef. 2000. Notes on the role of metapragmatic awareness in language use. *Pragmatics* 10 (4). 439–456.
Voeltz, Erhard. 1992. The morphological and phonological characteristics of Double Sango. Unpublished manuscript.
Wénézoui-Dechamps, Martine 1981. *Le français, le sängö et les autres langues centrafricaines. Enquêtes sociolinguistiques au quartier Boy-Rabe (Bangui, Centrafrique)*. Paris: SELAF.

Electronic references

Bufumbira All Stars. 2017. Umubyeyi [parent]. [https://www.youtube.com/watch?v=Y2ddG-MGfPw] (last accessed 20 November 2020).
Slenda MC. 2011. Kiss my town [https://soundcloud.com/slenda-mc/kiss-my-town-slenda-mc] (last accessed 20 November 2020).
Idylle Mamba. 2012. Sango, yanga ti kodoro ti mbi [Sango, language of my country]. [https://www.youtube.com/watch?v=UjytN-AzK-E] (last accessed 20 November 2020).

Yusnita Febrianti and Nurenzia Yannuar
15 The youth linguistic index: Narrative persuasion and sense of belonging in a movie trailer

This study discusses the creation of persuasion in a movie trailer and how it may indicate indexicality about a sense of belonging to different sociolinguistic contexts. The selected trailer is *Yowis Ben* (Javanese for 'yes, let it be'), a movie released in 2018 that centers its storyline on the making of a band and the drama among the band members. Unlike most Indonesian movies that use Indonesian, the country's national language, the characters of *Yowis Ben* speak in a local language, Malangan Javanese. The findings show that the movie trailer's narrative persuasion is constructed by the local language, supplemented by the trailer's visual and sound elements. Furthermore, the use of a local language succeeds in making the movie characters' local linguistic practice appealing to a national audience. The study also touches on indexicality, in this case, how the use of Malangan Javanese reflects the youth culture in a particular sociolinguistic setting in Malang, East Java, and Indonesia in general.

1 Introduction

This chapter presents an investigation into the construction of persuasion through the narrative in a movie trailer. The selection of this specific movie trailer for the study's data is based on two important features, which constitute the primary focus of this study, namely the progression of the narrative structure using the combination of language, image, and sound and, regarding the linguistic choice, the use of the minor vernacular of Malangan Javanese that performs a specific appeal for the persuasion of the movie trailer.

A movie trailer is a unique exhibition that combines promotional discourse and narrative (Kernan 2004). It essentially functions as advertising for an upcoming movie. The narrative element employs a persuasive function to persuade people to watch the movie, hence the term narrative persuasion. A movie trailer not only relies on language to present the narration but also presents the interplay

Yusnita Febrianti, Universitas Negeri Malang, e-mail: yusnita.febrianti.fs@um.ac.id
Nurenzia Yannuar, Universitas Negeri Malang, e-mail: nurenzia.yannuar.fs@um.ac.id

https://doi.org/10.1515/9781501514685-018

of language, image, and sound elements. This study is motivated by the unusual use of a minor vernacular of Malangan Javanese, which outweighs the use of Colloquial Indonesian in the narrative of the selected trailer for the movie *Yowis Ben*.

Yowis Ben is a movie about a group of senior high school students trying to be cool by forming a pop music band. This theme is depicted in the movie title, as the Javanese word *ben* (loosely translated into 'let it be') is also a transliteration of the English word band (music group) when pronounced by a Javanese speaker. The main character, Bayu, is not a popular kid in his school. To impress a new girl from Jakarta, the capital city, Bayu recruits several unpopular boys to join his band. The movie has a high approval rating. Since it was released, the movie has attracted more than 1 million viewers and was cited as one of the most popular movies of 2018. At present, its first sequel, *Yowis Ben 2*, has been released. The second sequel, *Yowis Ben 3*, is being prepared. *Yowis Ben* is unique because it incorporates Malangan Javanese in its characters' spoken dialogues, which has not previously been used in other youth movies. Young students who struggle to be popular in school are shown to be speaking to each other in the Javanese dialect. Occasionally they include words from Walikan, a youth linguistic practice in the local area of Malang, East Java. Colloquial Indonesian is used when they speak to a new girl who just moved from the capital city, Jakarta.

The movie *Yowis Ben* was distributed nationally, but many cinemas showed their reluctance when it was released. They only gave limited space and time to play the movie because the primary language used was Malangan Javanese. They feared that it would only attract specific groups of people, such as those who understand Javanese. It was indeed the only national movie in a local dialect that was released that year. However, throughout the paper, we will argue that the trailer's persuasiveness, and perhaps the movie itself, partly lies in the use of Malangan Javanese. The viewers' comments on YouTube reveal that Javanese speaking audiences feel more connected to the movie, and they thought that the spoken dialogue is natural. They also feel more confident in speaking their own Javanese dialects. For non-speakers of Javanese, watching this movie is similar to watching a foreign movie. However, with the help of Colloquial Indonesian subtitles, they can follow the narration without any difficulty. Perhaps, they perceive the use of a local language as a reminder that they are part of a linguistically diverse nation.

Accordingly, this paper explores the role of a minor vernacular, Malangan Javanese, alongside image and sound, for building the structure of narrative persuasion in a movie trailer of a nationally distributed film, *Yowis Ben*. To some extent, the study will also touch on indexicality, in this case, how the use of Malangan Javanese reflects the youth culture in a particular sociolinguistic setting in Malang, East Java, and in Indonesia in general.

In order to explain the context, this paper first discusses the structure of narrative in general and describes the multilingual linguistic situation in Indonesia. The analysis of the findings later focuses on the multimodal narrative in the movie trailer, the persuasive role of Malangan Javanese, and indexicalities as reflected in the comment section of the movie trailer.

2 Narrative

Narration is considered the oldest form of storytelling structure. One of the essential requirements of a narrative is the unfolding of a story through a particular time sequence (Labov and Waletzky 1997). A specific characteristic that distinguishes the narrative from other storytelling genres features a world in which the protagonists face problematic experiences and must resolve them in some ways (Eggins and Slade 2006: 239). Understanding a narrative involves developing interpretive comprehension based on both the readers' background knowledge and the previewing of a sequence whereby the story unfolds gradually (Rose and Martin 2012). Therefore, the readers' challenge is to understand the sequence of events and the characters' actions in a narration.

The analysis of the structure of narrative texts utilized in this study was developed under the Systemic Functional Linguistics (SFL) tradition. This theory posits that every piece of language, termed text, performs social functions based on the immediate situational contexts and broader cultural contexts (Butt et al. 2012). Martin and Rose (2009) and Rose and Martin (2012) used SFL as a foregrounding theory to develop the narrative genre structure (see Table 15.1).

Table 15.1: Segmentation and function of narrative stages (adapted from Martin and Rose 2009, Rose and Martin 2012).

Stages	Function
Orientation	Setting the scene: characters, action, time, place
Complication	Presenting problems
Evaluation	Presenting evaluation in the narrative in two directions, i.e., backwards (to evaluate the preceding events as a Complication) and forward (to expect the following events as a Resolution).
Resolution	Presenting solution to the problems posed in the Complication.
Coda	Presenting the closure to the overall narrative.

A narrative is a genre, the social purpose of which is to tell a story. Table 15.1 presents the stages that make up a narrative text. Compulsory stages in a narrative text include complication, evaluation and resolution (Martin and Rose 2009, Rose and Martin 2012). In the complication stage, a problem is introduced. The evaluation stage contains a direction wherein preceding events and the following possible events are considered. A resolution stage, then, presents a solution to the problem in the complication stage. While the stages described in Table 15.1 are typically standard components of a narrative, Eggins and Slade (2006) argue that orientation at the beginning and closure, or coda, at the end are optional stages that are not always present.

Considering that the study's data is a movie trailer, the narrative structure is adapted to be applied to a text in a film. In this case, Martin and Rose (2009) suggest that genres are typically realized through more than one communication modality. While most narratives are realized in either spoken or written language, technology advancement has made it possible to transform them into other modalities by combining language, image, sound, action, and/or spatial design. Film data such as movie trailers are good examples of a narrative presented using various modalities, namely by co-deploying language, image, and sound.

In order to function as an advertisement for an upcoming movie, a trailer must perform a persuasive function (Kernan 2004). Different forms of rhetoric have been used to discuss persuasion in film advertising, for example, irony (Andersen 2013), argumentation (Rocci et al. 2013), and narrative (Hidalgo-Downing and Mujic 2015, Martinez et al. 2013). Relevant to these studies, Febrianti (2019) provides examples of the persuasive function in movie trailers using an incomplete narrative structure, whereby five Indonesian movie trailers are analyzed to reveal the structure of the narratives, and the results indicate the absence of the resolution stage as a way to augment the persuasiveness of the movie trailers. The result was in line with Wildfeuer and Pollaroli's (2017) study, which found that a movie trailer has a persuasive function in enticing movie-goers to satisfy their desire to fill in this lack of information by watching the movie. Persuasion in the narrative structure of a movie trailer is considered in this study. More importantly, due to the unique linguistic choices in the selected trailer, more focus is given to the use of Malangan Javanese as a persuasive appeal.

3 The linguistic situation in Indonesia

The movie advertised in the trailer uses two languages, colloquial Indonesian and Malangan Javanese, which is a reflection of the present-day linguistic choices of young people in Java. It represents how young people interact and deal with Indonesia's complex linguistic situation on a broader scale. Hence, it becomes necessary to situate the linguistic choices portrayed in the data against the multilingual Indonesian background. *Yowis Ben* is arguably the first Indonesian movie that breaks the norm. Despite the distribution of the movie nationally, the regional language Malangan Javanese is boldly used in the spoken dialogues of the trailer and movie. On the other hand, Colloquial Indonesian features in only a small portion of the spoken language and is used for subtitling throughout the trailer.

Standard Indonesian is the only national and official language in Indonesia, being introduced through formal education and used in formal contexts. In daily interaction, people typically resort to Colloquial Indonesian, the dialect of which may vary as influenced by local or regional languages. Local or regional languages are learned mostly outside of school, and their position is considered less prestigious than Standard and Colloquial Indonesian (Arka 2013). The daily Indonesian of Jakarta has become the most popular variety in the country because of the capital's strong influence in every aspect, and the term Colloquial Jakartan Indonesian has emerged (Englebretson 2003, Errington 1998, Sneddon 2006). Almost all nationally distributed youth films in Indonesia are in Colloquial Indonesian, a variety of Indonesian that is commonly used in everyday interaction. Sometimes the variety is associated with a specific register associated with upward mobility, termed Bahasa Gaul "social language" (Smith-Hefner 2007). This variety is widely spread across Java and other parts of Indonesia (see also Tropea, this volume). The present study uses the label Colloquial Indonesian to refer to this variety of Indonesian that is common among young people who want to identify themselves with trendiness (Bowden 2015, Djenar 2006, Djenar et al. 2018).

The dominance of Indonesian, in general, has put local languages, including Javanese, in challenging positions (Arka 2013, Mueller 2009, Nurani 2015, Ravindranath and Cohn 2014). Javanese is the largest local language in Indonesia, meaning that it has the highest number of speakers, namely 69 million in Indonesia (Simons and Fennig 2020). There are three main dialects of Javanese: Western Javanese, Central Javanese, and Eastern Javanese (Hatley 1984, Nothofer 1980, 2006, Ras 1985). Central Javanese is the basis for Standard Javanese, which is taught in primary levels of education (Poedjosoedarmo 1968, Wolff and Poedjosoedarmo 1982). Malangan Javanese is part of Eastern Javanese as it is spoken in Malang, a city in the Eastern part of Java island. Malang is well known in Indonesia as an educational city because it is home to a number of reputable universities and schools. However, its local dialect of Javanese is still considered peripheral and "funny" by Central or Western Javanese speakers.

Javanese has a specific way to show respect and politeness, in which speakers must select the appropriate speech level or register as they judge their hierarchical relationship with the addressee (Poedjosoedarmo 1968). The registers are marked by a selection of separate words and morphemes (Poedjosoedarmo 1968, Robson

2002). The highest level is Kromo, used in addressing someone older or of higher status than the speaker. Madyo is also used to show respect but is less polite than Kromo. Ngoko, on the other end, is the lowest level, used among friends or in addressing younger siblings (Errington 1998). The status of the Kromo register is vulnerable (Errington 1998, Poedjosoedarmo 2006, Vander Klok 2019), while the Ngoko of Javanese is also at risk but is still widely used (Vander Klok 2019). In Malangan Javanese, as shown in the *Yowis Ben* trailer and movie, the Ngoko register is used across social statuses and age groups. The politeness hierarchy is no longer strictly followed as the society is becoming more egalitarian. Malangan Javanese, similar to other East Javanese dialects such as Suroboyoan Javanese, has vast collections of profanities and vulgar swearwords (Hoogervorst 2014). They are also present in the trailer of *Yowis Ben*, highlighting the specific character of East Javanese.

The local language discussed in this study is Javanese and its local dialect, Malangan Javanese. Walikan words characterize this variety. Walikan, which originates from the Javanese word *walik* 'to reverse', is a popular youth linguistic practice in Malang. It uses a Malangan Javanese language structure but combines it with special lexical items that have undergone word-reversal processes (Yannuar 2019). For example, *apik* (Javanese for 'good') becomes *kipa*, and *mahal* (Indonesian for 'expensive') becomes *laham*. Walikan is one of many youth linguistic practices in Indonesia. As mentioned previously, Bahasa Gaul expresses a cosmopolitan culture and upward mobility (Smith-Hefner 2007). Bahasa Gado-gado 'mix language' presents a combination of Indonesian and English and is used to envision modernity (Martin-Anatias 2018). Walikan is used to represent commonality and in-group solidarity; thus, speaking Walikan enables the young people in Malang to verbalize their feeling of belonging to a particular culture (Yannuar 2019).

The study also observes indexicality in order to discuss the broader sociolinguistic contexts wherein the data is found. Eckert (2000) and Kiesling (2005) revealed that the repeated use of different variants of linguistic forms is semiotically associated with the formation of relevant local social groupings. According to Irvine (2001), linguistic characteristics or indexes carry social meaning and inform people's interpretations of their own social worlds and their position within them. The use of languages in the selected trailer represents two important issues. First, the use of Malangan Javanese reflects the pride of the locality of the specific area in East Java. The movie is made by Bayu Skak, formerly a university student in Malang, who uses YouTube to share comedic content in Malangan Javanese. Despite the featuring of a local dialect of East Javanese spoken only in Malang city and its vicinity, Bayu's videos became very popular, and the channel up to today has millions of subscribers. The appeal of Bayu's videos to his viewers is his authentic use of East Javanese, motivating him to speak in the dialect during most of his public appearances. In 2018, Bayu produced the movie comedy, *Yowis Ben*, which is set in Malang and spoken in Malangan Javanese, to be distributed nationally in Indonesia. Therefore, this leads to the second social issue, namely the indexicality towards the relative use of local language as opposed to the national language, Standard Indonesian. The relation may be measured by examining the abstraction level between the linguistic forms and social meanings that occur in a normative sociolinguistic context (Silverstein 2003). This social context will be used as a parameter for the appraisal of the indexicality in this study.

4 Methodology

This study's primary data (source) is the official trailer of the movie *Yowis Ben*.[1] The trailer was used as a promotional video and was uploaded on YouTube on 24 January 2018 by StarvisionPlus, the official YouTube account for the movie's production house. The duration of the video is two minutes and thirty seconds. For data analysis purposes, screen shots were made from the video. Relevant frames and language transcriptions are used in the paper to facilitate the analysis description.

The data analysis was conducted in three stages. First, the trailer was deconstructed based on the following narrative structure: orientation, complication, evaluation, and resolution (Martin and Rose 2009, Rose and Martin 2012), considering the language, image, and sound elements in the data. Second, the language use and the presentation of each language variety were analyzed in detail. This analysis includes the juxtaposition of Malangan Javanese in the spoken dialogues and Colloquial Indonesian in the written subtitles to understand the persuasive meaning in the context of their use in the trailer. The third analysis involved a content analysis of the comments from YouTube users. This is useful to draw upon indexical meanings as reflected by YouTube users regarding their perception of the use of Malangan Javanese. The parameter for indexicality is adopted from Johnstone and Kiesling (2008), which summarized Silverstein (2003) and Labov (1972), and formulates that indexicality presupposes the occurrence of language features that indicate community membership. Accordingly, indexical analysis in this study is directed towards showing the sense of belonging expressed by YouTube commenters to a particular social group.

---

[1] The trailer is available at [https://www.youtube.com/watch?v=PvjiH2U6G-Q] (accessed 30 January 2021).

5 Analysis and discussion

5.1 Multimodal narrative in the movie trailer

The analysis presented here shows that the selected trailer has a unique way of presenting a narration and can be considered a compressed full movie. Despite the limited duration, it is able to present the story in the precise sequential structure of a narrative. The narrative structure is identified by observing the language, image, and sound elements in the trailer using the narrative formulation in Table 15.1. Every stage of narrative storytelling performs a different textual function to guide the audience's comprehension (Martin and Rose 2009, Rose and Martin 2012).

The orientation of the narrative occurs with the introduction of the characters in the *Yowis Ben* movie. The male protagonist is shown visually from the beginning of the clip, standing out on the screen wearing a brightly-colored shirt. The character's name is revealed later in the clip via the supporting character's spoken language. The female character, later on, is introduced through an interaction with the male character. Her name is revealed when the male character calls her to have a conversation. Besides introducing the characters, the orientation stage also presents the movie's locative setting by showing the image of a colorful kampung (Javanese for a densely populated dwelling complex in an urban area). As shown in Frame 4 in Figure 15.1, this particular kampung is located in Jodipan, a well-known point of attraction in Malang, East Java. The locative setting also shows the high school explicitly. When these scenes are shown, a piece of non-diegetic[2] music plays, characterized by a fast tempo and bright tune. Figure 15.1 presents sample images in the orientation stage.

The plotline of *Yowis Ben* revolves around the formation of a music band. In this trailer, however, multiple complications are found. The first complication is indicated by a mockery made by a group of students who removed the band's member recruitment flyers from the wall (Figure 15.2).

The following sentence (1) is uttered by the antagonist in the movie in Malangan Javanese. Note that the subtitle is the translation of this utterance in Colloquial Indonesian. The language analysis is given in details below:

---

[2] Diegetic music is a type of music that is part of the story/narration. While non-diegetic music is a type of sound that is not part of the story but can be heard by the viewers.

(1) Antagonist   *Nggolek-nggolek personil, kate nggae ben   a?   Opo   iki!?*
    character: RDP~find   member   will make band DP what this
                'They're looking for band members? What the heck!?'
                (Malangan Javanese)

Figure 15.1: Character introduction in the orientation stage (up left: Frame 1, up right: Frame 2, down left: Frame 3, down right: Frame 4).

Figure 15.2: Mockery in the Complication stage.

While ripping out the flyer, he screams: *Opo iki!?* 'What the heck!?'. At this particular scene, the music pauses. Along the series of complications, the music keeps playing, characterized by a similarly bright music but on a more cheerful note. The volume seems to be adjusted to turn louder in the absence of dialogues and softer when dialogues occur. A piece of diegetic music can be heard when the competition issue between Yowis Ben and another band called Cholesterol is presented. The music is featured as proof that Cholesterol plays well. A discussion on youth identity and dilemma is also hinted as part of a complication when the main male character talks to his friends about their future aspirations:

(2) Bayu: *Wong-wong   iku   kudu   paham   suatu saat   kene   iso*
         RDP~person   DEM   must   understand   one   time   3PL   can
         dadi   keren.
         become   awesome
         'Everyone needs to know, that one day we will be awesome.'
    Doni: *He, yokopo   cara-ne,   Bay?*
          DP   how   way-DEF   NP
          'How do we do it, Bay?'
          (Malangan Javanese)

In a few scenes, a romance issue is highlighted as one of the complications. Figure 15.3 depicts the scene where the female character asks the male character to choose between the band and the relationship. The non-diegetic music pauses again at the scene where the male and female characters are arguing with each other.

Figure 15.3: Male and female protagonists' relationship featured in the Complication stage (left: Frame 1, right: Frame 2).

The impact of the relationship on the band is shown in the following dialogue between the supporting characters:

(3) Doni: *Sejak   arek   iku   melok   latihan   Bayu   gak   tahu*
          Since   kid   DEM   follow   practice   NP   NEG   EXP.PRF
          konsen   latihan-e.
          focus   practice-DEF
          'Ever since the kid (girl or Susan) came to the practice, Bayu has lost his focus.'
          (Malangan Javanese)

At the end of the complication scenes, the music turns softer, and a diegetic song from the band Yowis Ben is played. Along with the music, the scene then moves into the next stage, evaluation. Here, the main character, Bayu, threatens that he is going to quit the band. The verbal exchange is as follows:

(4) Spoken dialogue:
Aku   sing   metu   tekan   Yowis   Ben.
1SG   REL   exit   from   NP   band
'I quit *Yowis Ben*'
Guduk   koen   kabeh   sing   ngetok-no   aku!
NEG   2SG   all   REL   exit-BEN   1SG
'It was not all of you who kicked me out!'
(Malangan Javanese)

Written subtitle:
Aku   keluar dari   Yowis   Ben.
1SG   exit   from   NP   band
'I quit *Yowis Ben*.'
Bukan   kalian yang   ngeluarin   aku!
NEG   2PL   REL   exit-BEN   1SG
'It was not all of you who kicked me out!'
(Colloquial Indonesian)

The statement above is expressed with anger. However, the expected response to the anger is not shown, neither through image depiction in the scene nor through verbal responses. The evaluation stage, therefore, does not show whether there will be answers to the issues presented in the complication stage. As observed later on, the trailer's ending does not disclose any answer to the featured issues in the complication stage. According to Febrianti (2019), movie trailers do not include a resolution stage, but show features of a closure. The term closure is used in lieu of resolution due to the incompleteness of the trailers' final part. This characterizes the narrative in movie trailers in general. While the clips of the trailers observed in the study provided a closure, they do not characterize a resolution. Following Martinez et al. (2013), the term closure refers to the significant ending of a narrative (p. 100). The resolution stage should provide a clear answer to the problems posed in the complication stage of a narrative (Martin and Rose 2009, Rose and Martin 2012). Consequently, the *Yowis Ben* trailer is open for any possible answer to the featured complications. Arguably, this is a point of persuasion in the trailer.

While the narrative is constructed by a combination of language, image, and sound, the language presented in this particular trailer also plays an integral part in creating the persuasion. The use of Malangan Javanese as a local language has helped create a special appeal in promoting the film's persuasiveness. The presentation of different language varieties and their roles are described in the next section.

5.2 The persuasive role of Malangan Javanese

Throughout the trailer, most of the characters' dialogues are conducted in Malangan. For a general audience, including people who do not speak Javanese, the language may sound similar to standard Javanese. They might not be aware of the dialectal variation. The Malangan Javanese used in the trailer is in Ngoko, the lowest Javanese register based on the degree of politeness. The following discussion describes several key characteristics of Malangan Javanese that are present in the trailer.

The first instance takes place right after the opening at the orientation stage, where a Malangan Javanese spoken dialogue takes place between two male characters in the movie, as presented below:

(5) Doni: *Pokok-e nek arek iku noleh rene, njaluk*
main-DEF if kid DEM turn.around here ask
di-uber iku.
PASS-chase DEM
'The point is, if she turns her head around, that means she wants you to chase her.'

Bayu: *Nek gak noleh rene?*
If NEG turn.around here
'If she doesn't?'

Doni: *Gulu-ne loro paling.*
neck-DEF hurt maybe
'Maybe she hurts her neck'.

The word *arek* is a distinctive feature of the East Javanese dialect, literally meaning 'kid' or 'child'. In the Central Javanese dialect, the word for 'child' is *bocah*. As a result, the East Javanese dialect is also often referred to as Arek dialect (Hatley 1984, Nothofer 1980, Ras 1985). Example (5) also includes the negation *gak*, which can be considered an East Javanese lexical item. *Gak* and *nggak* are both negations that are put before verbal and adjectival predicates as well as prepositional phrases. The word *ora*, on the other hand, is more commonly used in the Central Javanese dialect.

Another Malangan Javanese feature is used in the orientation stage, namely the swearword *jancuk*, as presented in (6). Malangan Javanese, being part of the East Javanese dialect, is often regarded as more coarse than the other dialects of Javanese as it includes more profanities (Hoogervorst 2014).

(6) Spoken dialogue:
Oo jancuk lambe-ne Doni!
oh damn mouth-POSS Doni
'Oh damn Doni's mouth!'
(Malangan Javanese)

Written subtitle:
Dasar, mulut Doni!
DP mouth-POSS Doni
'Oh, Doni's mouth!'
(Colloquial Indonesian)

The scene shows Bayu being angry about something that was said by the supporting character, his friend named Doni. He condemned Doni for teasing him and vented his frustration by calling Doni's mouth *jancuk*. This particular swearword has an unknown origin and is regarded as the most impolite profanity in Malangan Javanese. It is also widely used in other East Javanese dialects but is still frowned upon in Central Javanese.

The word *jancuk* is a popular swearword in Malangan Javanese. Its equivalent in Indonesian, however, is difficult to find. Therefore, in the Colloquial Indonesian subtitle, the word *jancuk* is not translated, and a discourse particle *dasar* is added. The word *dasar* is often used to express annoyance, but it is not a profanity. While it is a close interpretation of the Javanese swearword, the Indonesian discourse particle cannot reflect all the original word's cultural associations.

In the evaluation stage, *jancuk* is also found in the contracted form, *cuk,* such as in *Cangkemmu cuk, iki wes pol!* 'Damn your mouth, this is already the maximum!' In this utterance, *cuk* functions as a vocative used by the main character to address a supporting character. Using this swearword as a vocative in daily exchanges is common in East Javanese, including in Malangan Javanese. While some people might find it still too harsh, it can produce a comedic tone in the utterance and then create a sense of friendliness in the dialog. In this trailer, it highlights the social context of the movie setting in East Java.

One special characteristic of Malangan Javanese is the use of Walikan words. As shown in (7), the word *tilis* (in bold) is used. The word is a total segment reversal of the Javanese word *silit*, which literally means 'bum' or 'asshole.' In this instance, the reversed word is judged less derogatory than the original word by native Malangan Javanese speakers. It is used to encourage Bayu to spank or slap his friends' ass if they do not trust him.

(7) Spoken dialogue:
Ceples-en ae **tilis**-e konco-konco-mu.
slap.IMP DP bum-POSS RDP~friend-POSS.2SG
'Just slap your friends in the ass.'
(Malangan Javanese)

Written subtitle:
Gebok aja pantat temen-temen-mu.
Slap just ass RDP~friend-POSS.2SG
'Just slap your friends in the ass.'
(Colloquial Indonesian)

As discussed previously, some spoken dialogues in the trailer use Indonesian, mainly due to the characterization of the female protagonist, Susan. Bayu, on the other hand, is shown to use Javanese most of the time instead of Indonesian. In fact, he only uses Indonesian when he addresses Susan. One of their dialogues is transcribed in (8):

(8) Bayu: San, Susan, leher kamu sakit ya?
NP NP neck 2SG hurt yes
'San, Susan, does your neck hurt?'
Susan: Enggak.
NEG
'No'.
(Colloquial Indonesian)

This exchange marks the introduction of the female character in the trailer. The use of Indonesian in the dialog informs the viewers that the female character does not have a Javanese background. Her accent also suggests that she is from the capital city, Jakarta. In addition, (9) shows another exchange between Susan and Bayu towards the end of the complication stage:

(9) Susan: Kamu lebih pilih Yowis Ben daripada aku?
2SG more choose NP band over 1SG
'Did you choose *Yowis Ben* over me?'

	Itu bukan masalah kecil buat aku.
	DEM NEG problem small for 1SG
	'This is not a trivial thing for me.'
Bayu:	Emang kamu masih mau kenal sama aku?
	really 2SG still want know with 1SG
	'(If I wasn't in a band) do you still want to hang out with me?'
Susan:	Mungkin.
	maybe
	'Maybe.'
	(Colloquial Indonesian)

Also conducted in Colloquial Indonesian, this exchange may predict the progress of the relationship between the male and female characters, i.e., Bayu and Susan. It is interesting to notice that Susan is the only character in the trailer who speaks in Indonesian, while Bayu only uses Indonesian when speaking to her.

Throughout the trailer, subtitles appear when dialogues are spoken in Malangan Javanese. The provision of the subtitle is intended to help the audience understand the dialogue, which happens to be a local language dialect. It is worth noting that the subtitle is in the colloquial form of Indonesian and is styled in a similar tone as the Javanese dialect. Both of them are in non-standard forms, which are typically used in youth social contexts. Table 15.2 below shows the way many of the Malangan Javanese vocabularies in the spoken dialogues are translated into written Colloquial Indonesian.

Table 15.2: Spoken Malangan Javanese and written Colloquial Indonesian compared to Standard Indonesian.

Malangan Javanese	Colloquial Indonesian	Standard Indonesian	Gloss
nek	kalo	kalau	'if'
opo iki	apaan sih	apakah yang mereka inginkan?	'What the heck?'
ae	aja	saja	'just'
yokopo	gimana	bagaimana	'how'
telat	telat	terlambat	'too late'
yo wis	ya udah	ya sudah	'be it'

As demonstrated above, the language choices in the trailer, namely spoken Malangan Javanese, Colloquial Indonesian, are presented in their informal forms. The language use in the trailer helps viewers to speculate about the advertised movie. First, it provides information about the general theme of the movie, which is casual and non-serious. Second, it indicates that this movie is created by local youth, featuring young actors and actresses and targeted for youth nationally. Although a local dialect is used, the language choice is presented in such a way that it is attractive to Indonesian youth groups in general.

5.3 Indexicality as reflected in YouTube comments

In a recent publication, Cornips and de Rooij (2018) noted that people develop feelings of belonging in social interaction by engaging with linguistic features as well as their reference to metapragmatic practices. In this study, two scopes are useful in examining the indexicality indicated in the sociolinguistic contexts wherein the trailer is situated, namely the context of Malang as a Javanese locality and Indonesia as the nation where the trailer is distributed. Both contexts are accounted for in the YouTube users' comments in relation to the *Yowis Ben* trailer. The comments were read manually. Due to time and space constraints, however, not all 1,411 comments were analyzed. The analysis is based on the categories of language used in the comments, namely those using Indonesian and Javanese in their written comments.

A majority of the comments indicate the public's appreciation for the upcoming movie. Many of the commenters express their relations to the city of Malang by repeating various forms of the Malangan Javanese spoken by the characters in the trailer. Their appreciation is also reflected in the use of various emoticons after the quotes to indicate how they relate to the comedic meanings carried by the linguistic forms of the spoken Malangan Javanese used in the trailer. The following is an example of the expression of pride from a commenter from Javanese background that a local dialect is used in a movie. The language use in the trailer has also motivated them to appreciate and learn more about their own culture (10).

(10) *Ini adalah suatu contoh memperkenalkan kembali bahasa daerah kita biar gak hilang... Ayok berkarya di mulai dari kita dari jawa dari bahasa jawa... Biar anak cucu kita nanti tidak lupa apa itu apa itu bahasa jawa sunda batak dll. Aku orang jawa dan aku bangga berbahasa jawa* ☺ *Bukan berarti aku tidak menghormati bhs lain. Karna keberagaman itu indah* ☺☺☺.

> [This (movie) sets an example to maintain our local language. If we are Javanese, let us create something in the Javanese language. Don't let our children and grandchildren forget their mother tongues, Javanese, Sundanese, Batak, etc. I am a Javanese and I am proud of the Javanese language. It does not mean that I do not respect other languages. It is because diversity is beautiful.]

The use of Javanese creates a natural tone in the movie. In this way, Malangan Javanese, as a local language, is able to give an impression to viewers that the scenes of the movie are part of a daily life reality (11). Other movies rendered in Indonesian sometimes sound unnatural, presumably because the variety of Indonesian used does not match the context.

(11) *Bagus loh... dialek Jawa tu bs kelihatan real. Kyk film2 Korea gitu kan Bahasanya bner2 sehari2 dialek desa jadi lebih real. Daripada film2/sinetron2 di Indonesia yg asal2an dialognya terkesan scripted bgt.*

[(The use of Javanese) is good. The Javanese dialect makes the movie look real. It is like Korean movies. They use local dialects, so the movies feel real (and natural). Unlike other soap dramas and movies in Indonesia that use sloppy dialogues, they sound very scripted.]

The use of spoken Malangan Javanese and written Colloquial Indonesian in the trailer is shown to be appealing and helpful. Several Internet users who are not of Javanese background commented that the written Colloquial Indonesian in the subtitles helped them understand the content of the trailer (12). According to them, had Indonesian been used throughout the spoken dialogues, the comic nature of the movie, which is built on Javanese culture, would be ruined.

(12) *Saya dari banjarmasin. Dan gk ngerti bahasa jawa. Tapi dibantu dengan tranlate subtitle jd ngerti kok malah bagusan pakai bahasa jawa. Kalau bahasa indo jadi kurang lucu menurut saya. Semangat terus mas bayu ini film komedi yg bagus dan layak di tonton. Gk rugi ngambil jam malam bela belain hahaha nice film.*

[I am from Banjarmasin. And I don't understand Javanese. But the subtitle has helped me understand, it is better to use Javanese in the dialogue. The use of Indonesian will make it less funny, I think. You go, brother Bayu, this is a good and a must watch comedy. I didn't waste my time doing night shift just to watch this movie. Nice movie!].

The examples above imply possible impacts of the use of a local language in a nationally distributed movie. For example, it may encourage the youth to learn local languages, whether Javanese or others, evoking their sense of belonging and pride in local languages. The fact that the movie had a good reception may also promote awareness for the importance of local languages as part of Indonesian cultural and linguistic diversity.

6 Conclusion

The *Yowis Ben* movie trailer, like all movie trailers, achieves its persuasion through its incomplete narrative due to the absence of the resolution stage. Additionally, the use of Malangan Javanese improves the movie's persuasive appeal and creates a bold statement to persuade national movie-goers. A combination of attractive visual and sound components that provide cues to the movie's locative setting and theme, a mix of a local dialect and Colloquial Indonesian in the spoken dialogues, and the use of Colloquial Indonesian in the written subtitles are also helpful for potential audiences.

In light of the analysis results in this study, it is expected that the national acceptance of the *Yowis Ben* trailer and movie may inspire the promotion of local languages. Although the use of Indonesian in media, schools, and other established institutions has threatened the vitality of local languages (Mueller 2009, Nurani 2015, Zentz 2014), more Indonesian movie production houses can promote pride and diversity within national identity through the use of local language varieties in their movies. This movie trailer also exemplifies that a local language that generally has a lower status in the Indonesian ecology (Arka 2013) can be presented nationally within the youth cultural context. The local language is slowly gaining more upward mobility as it is becoming more popular among young people. This is in line with the development of Malangan Javanese, containing features of reversed language, which has become more widely known as a marker of solidarity among the youth in the city (Yannuar 2018, 2019). As *Yowis Ben* also includes Walikan in their spoken dialogues, the variety is also exposed to national audiences. On a final note, our study only looked at one movie trailer as this is the only one found in the contexts. No other Indonesian movies have looked at the use of local language and distributed in theater and targeted specifically at young viewers. Future research can focus on other trailers or whole movies that feature local languages from different sociolinguistic contexts.

List of abbreviations

1	first person
2	second person
BEN	benefactive
DEF	definite marker
DEM	demonstrative
DP	discourse particle
EXP.PRF	experiential perfect aspect

NEG	negation
NP	proper noun
PASS	passive
PL	plural
POSS	possessive
RDP	reduplication
REL	relativizer
SG	singular

References

Andersen, Lars Pynt. 2013. Multimodal cueing of strategic irony. In Barry Pennock-Speck and María Milagros del Saz-Rubio (eds.), *The multimodal analysis of television commercials*, 43–60. Valencia: Universitat de València.

Arka, I Wayan. 2013. Language management and minority language maintenance in (eastern) Indonesia: Strategic issues. *Language Documentation & Conservation* 7. 74–105.

Butt, David, Rhondda Fahey, Susan Feez, Sue Spinks and Colin Yallop. 2012. *Using functional grammar: An explorer's guide*. South Yarra, Melbourne: Palgrave MacMillan.

Bowden, John. 2015. Towards a history, and an understanding of Indonesian slang. *NUSA* 58. 9–24.

Cornips, Leonie and Vincent de Rooij. 2018. *The sociolinguistics of place and belonging: Perspectives from the margins*. Amsterdam and Philadelphia: John Benjamins.

Djenar, Dwi Noverini. 2006. Patterns and variation of address terms in colloquial Indonesian. *Australian Review of Applied Linguistics* 29 (2). 22.1–22.16.

Djenar, Dwi Noverini, Michael Ewing and Howard Manns. 2018. *Style and intersubjectivity in youth interaction*. Berlin: De Gruyter Mouton.

Eckert, Penelope. 2000. *Linguistic variation as social practice: The linguistic construction of identity in Belten High*. Oxford: Blackwell.

Eggins, Suzanne and Diana Slade. 2006. *Analysing casual conversation*. London: Equinox.

Englebretson, Robert. 2003. *Searching for structure: The problem of complementation in colloquial Indonesian conversation*. Amsterdam and Philadelphia: John Benjamins.

Errington, J. Joseph. 1998. *Shifting languages: Interaction and identity in Javanese Indonesian*. Cambridge: Cambridge University Press.

Febrianti, Yusnita. 2019. Indonesian movie trailers: Persuading movie-goers through incomplete narratives. In Kumaran Rajandran and Shakila Manan (eds.), *Discourses of Southeast Asia: A social semiotic perspective*, 111–128. New Delhi: Springer.

Hatley, Ron. 1984. Mapping cultural regions of Java. In Ron Hatley, Jim Schiller, Anton Lucas and Barbara Martin-Schiller (eds.), *Other Javas away from the kraton*, 1–32. Clayton: Monash University.

Hidalgo-Downing, Laura and Blanca Kraljevic-Mujic. 2015. Recontextualizing social practices and globalization: Multimodal metaphor and fictional storytelling in printed and internet ads. *Revista Brasileira de Linguística Aplicada* 15 (2). 377–402.

Hoogervorst, Tom. 2014. Youth culture and urban pride: The sociolinguistics of East Javanese slang. *Wacana* 15 (1). 104–130.

Irvine, Judith T. 2001. "Style" as distinctiveness: The culture and ideology of linguistic differentiation. In Penelope Eckert and John R. Rickford (eds.), *Style and sociolinguistic variation*, 21–43. Cambridge: Cambridge University Press.

Johnstone, Barbara and Scott F. Kiesling. 2008. Indexicality and experience: Exploring the meanings of /aw/-monophthongization in Pittsburgh. *Journal of Sociolinguistics* 12 (1). 5–33.

Kernan, Lisa. 2004. *Coming attraction: Reading American movie trailers*. Austin: University of Texas Press.

Kiesling, Scott F. 2005. Variation, stance and style: Word-final -er, high rising tone, and ethnicity in Australian English. *English World-Wide* 26 (1). 1–42.

Labov, William. 1972. *Sociolinguistic patterns*. Philadelphia: University of Pennsylvania Press.

Labov, William and Joshua Waletzky. 1997 [1967]. Narrative analysis: Oral versions of personal experience. *Journal of Narrative and Life History* 7 (1–4). 3–38.

Martin, James Robert & David Rose. 2009. *Genre relations: Mapping culture*. London: Equinox.

Martinez, María Angeles Martínez, Blanca Kraljevich Mujic and Laura Hidalgo Downing. 2013. Multimodal narrativity in TV ads. In Barry Pennock-Speck and María Milagros del Saz-Rubio (eds.), *The multimodal analysis of television commercials*, 91–111. Valencia: Universitat de València.

Martin-Anatias, Nelly. 2018. Bahasa gado-gado: English in Indonesian popular texts. *World Englishes* 37 (2). 340–355.

Mueller, Franz. 2009. Language shift on Java. *LACUS Forum* 34. 179–185.

Nothofer, Bernd. 1980. *Dialektgeographische Untersuchungen in West-Java und im westlichen Zentral-Java*. Wiesbaden: Otto Harrassowitz.

Nothofer, Bernd. 2006. Javanese. In Keith Brown (ed.), *Encyclopedia of language and linguistics*, vol. 6, 113–115. Oxford: Elsevier Ltd.

Nurani, Lusia Marliana. 2015. *Changing language loyalty and identity: An ethnographic inquiry of societal transformation among the Javanese people in Yogyakarta, Indonesia*. Tempe: Arizona State University dissertation.

Poedjosoedarmo, Gloria. 2006. The effect of Bahasa Indonesia as a lingua franca on the Javanese system of speech levels and their functions. *International Journal of the Sociology of Language* 177. 111–121.

Poedjosoedarmo, Soepomo. 1968. Javanese speech levels. *Indonesia* 6. 54–81.

Ras, Johannes Jacobus. 1985. *Inleiding tot het modern Javaans*. Dordrecht: Foris Publications.

Ravindranath, Maya and Abigail C. Cohn. 2014. Can a language with millions of speakers be endangered? *Journal of the Southeast Asian Linguistics Society* 7. 64–75.

Robson, Stuart. 2002. *Javanese grammar for students*. Clayton: Monash University Press.

Rocci, Andrea, Sabrina Mazzali-Lurati and Chiara Pollaroli. 2013. Is this the Italy we like? Multimodal argumentation in a Fiat Panda TV commercial. In Barry Pennock-Speck and María Milagros del Saz-Rubio (eds.), *The multimodal analysis of television commercials*, 157–187. Valencia: Universitat de València.

Rose, David and J. R. Martin. 2012. *Learning to write, reading to learn: Genre, knowledge and pedagogy in the Sydney school*. Sheffield: Equinox.

Silverstein, Michael. 2003. Indexical order and the dialectics of sociolinguistic life. *Language & Communication* 23 (3–4). 193–229.

Simons, Gary F. and Charles D. Fennig. 2020. *Ethnologue: Languages of the world, twenty-third edition*. [https://www.ethnologue.com/country/ID] (accessed 31 January 2021).

Smith-Hefner, Nancy J. 2007. Youth language, Gaul sociability, and the new Indonesian middle class. *Journal of Linguistic Anthropology* 17 (2). 184–203.
Sneddon, James N. 2006. *Colloquial Jakartan Indonesian*. Canberra: Pacific Linguistics, Research School of Pacific and Asian Studies, The Australian National University.
Vander Klok, Jozina. 2019. The Javanese language at risk: Perspectives from an East Java village. *Language Documentation & Conservation* 13. 300–345.
Wildfeuer, Janina and Chiara Pollarolli. 2017. Seeing the untold: Multimodal argumentation in movie trailers. In Assimakis Tseronis and Charles Forceville (eds.), *Multimodal argumentation and rhetoric in media genres*, 190–216. Amsterdam and Philadelphia: John Benjamins.
Wolff, John U. & Poedjosoedarmo, Soepomo. 1982. *Communicative codes in Central Java*. Ithaca: Cornell University.
Yannuar, Nurenzia. 2018. Wòlak-waliké jaman; Exploring contemporary Walikan in public space. *Wacana* 19 (1). 100–121.
Yannuar, Nurenzia. 2019. *Bòsò Walikan Malangan: Structure and development of a Javanese reversed language*. Leiden: Leiden University dissertation.
Zentz, Lauren. 2014. "Love" the local, "use" the national, "study" the foreign: Shifting Javanese language ecologies in (post-)modernity, postcoloniality, and globalization. *Journal of Linguistic Anthropology* 24 (3). 339–359.

Jill Vaughan and Abigail Carter
16 "We mix it up": Indigenous youth language practices in Arnhem Land

On Australia's north-central coast, the regional hub of Maningrida is distinguished by a highly diverse language ecology, with local linguistic repertoires taking in elements of multiple traditional languages as well as localised Englishes, Kriol (an English-lexified creole), and a local alternate sign language system. Texts and talk in Maningrida are rarely monolingual. Youth culture in Maningrida is characterised by the interacting demands of traditional cultural life and an emergent urban subculture that increasingly connects to global phenomena. Young speakers are more, and differently, mobile compared to earlier generations, and their language practices are fundamentally implicated in community language change. While some elders are concerned that young people are connecting less deeply to their languages' traditional heartlands, young speakers themselves have different perspectives to offer. This chapter explores the language practices of Maningrida youth and centralises local Indigenous perspectives on this phenomenon. Drawing on data collected through collaborative community language research, we consider the emergence of a restructured urban variety of the Burarra language, a process of "linguistic urbanisation" in which youth are central. We further consider examples of the creative multilingual practices of young Maningrida speakers/signers, such as the recent success of an all-female band from the community who sing in five local languages. This chapter aims to illustrate how Maningrida youth create affordances within the diverse multilingual resources of their community, and the ways in which they draw on tradition and modernity to create new forms of meaning making.

Acknowledgements: This work has been funded by the Endangered Languages Documentation Project (C.I. Jill Vaughan, grant IPF0256), the ARC Centre of Excellence for the Dynamics of Language (C.I. Felicity Meakins, University of Queensland, grant CE140100041), the Linguistic Complexity in the Individual and Society project (C.I. Terje Lohndal) at the Norwegian University for Science and Technology, and a University of Melbourne Early Career Researcher Grant (C.I. Jill Vaughan).

Jill Vaughan, University of Melbourne, e-mail: j.vaughan@unimelb.edu.au
Abigail Carter, Maningrida College, e-mail: abigail.carter@ntschools.net

https://doi.org/10.1515/9781501514685-019

1 Introduction

Maningrida community on Australia's north-central coast serves as a regional hub for the Indigenous-owned region of Arnhem Land. The Arnhem region is distinguished by a highly diverse language ecology, with dozens of named languages belonging to several distinct language families and strongly oriented to in local language ideologies. Linguistic repertoires in Maningrida typically take in elements from various socially recognised codes: traditional languages as well as localised Englishes, often Kriol (an English-lexified creole spoken across northern Australia), and local alternate sign language systems. Texts and talk in Maningrida are rarely monolingual.

Youth culture in Maningrida is characterised by the interacting demands of traditional cultural life and an emergent urban subculture, which increasingly connects to global phenomena. Young speakers/signers are more, and differently, mobile compared to earlier generations, and their language practices are fundamentally implicated in community language change. Many Arnhem Land Elders are concerned that young people are spending less time on traditional country, and connecting less deeply to their languages' heartland: "when the young people step out from the town and go back to the homelands, they reconnect with their culture and get away from negative influences. A strengthening is present. A healing takes place" (Mayatili and Djanambi Marika, People Culture Environment 2014: 42). Young speakers/signers themselves, however, have different perspectives to offer.

This chapter explores the agentive and resistant language practices of Maningrida youth, and centralises local Indigenous perspectives on this phenomenon by drawing on collaborative, community-driven research (Section 1.1). We argue that although in some ways young people in Maningrida align with more general trends in northern Australia – i.e., through the emergence of a mixed urban variety – in other ways youth language use is exceptional within (and beyond) the Australian context in terms of how young people reproduce and reshape traditional ideologies and practices. We exemplify this argument by looking at various creative multilingual practices of young Maningrida speakers/signers.

In Section 2, we explore the contemporary life projects, new mobilities and linguistic repertoires of Maningrida youth. We present a personal linguistic biography from a young Burarra woman, the second author, and provide several examples of youth multilingualism in practice in the community, such as the recent success of an all-female band who sing in multiple local languages. Section 3 introduces a contemporary development in Maningrida's language ecology – the emergence of a mixed urban variety of the Burarra language. These changes reflect a process of 'linguistic urbanisation' in which youth are central (Section 3).

These sections, and the discussion that follows (Section 4) illustrate how Maningrida youth create affordances within the diverse multilingual resources of their community, and the ways in which they draw on tradition and modernity to create new forms of meaning making.

Our work in this chapter assumes certain theoretical orientations, which are briefly outlined here. Most importantly, language use is not understood to divide inherently into distinct "languages", but rather to draw on elements of speakers' diverse linguistic resources from across their repertoires. This approach in indebted to work by Jørgensen (e.g. 2008, 2010), Williams (1994), García (e.g. 2009, 2012, 2014) and others on "languaging" and "translanguaging", both of which rely on a fundamental scepticism of the psychological reality of discrete, named codes in the bi/multilingual speaker's linguistic system. This is not to say that labelled languages, ethnicities and other social formations have no reality. On the contrary, these categories are frequently presupposed by speakers and regimented through local language ideologies, and the indexicalities of socially recognised codes may fundamentally shape language practices, as we will see. Our adoption of this perspective is driven by a desire to normalise the kinds of diverse language practices observable in Maningrida (and elsewhere), which frequently transgress established linguistic boundaries – practices that have been unnecessarily treated as remarkable or even eccentric. Indeed, humanity has a long history (albeit not one well-documented) of non-polyglossic, "hybrid", translingual communicative practices, which draw on multiple named languages but which do not conform to monolingual or indeed established "orderly" multilingual ideologies (e.g. Dovchin and Lee 2019, Silverstein 2015, Vaughan 2020). Such an approach enables analyses to move beyond named language categories and to more readily reveal the emergent dynamics of situated communication.

1.1 Data collection and collaborative methods

The data relied upon in this chapter come largely from collaborative research across several language documentation projects conducted by the authors in Maningrida since 2015. The resulting corpus contains over 100 hours of language data that privileges naturalistic interactional language from a range of public and private domains, linguistic biography interviews and language drawings (e.g. Busch 2012), ethnographic notes and additional language data elicited using stimulus materials. Permission has been given by the relevant speakers for the use of all data included in this chapter. Supplementary data is drawn from earlier work in the region, in particular from linguist Vanessa Elwell's work on multilingualism in the community. This data will be discussed in more detail in Section 2.2.

The research featured here is fundamentally collaborative, reflecting established working partnerships between the chapter's authors and also with many members of the Maningrida community, including key community groups working in the language and culture space (Lúrra Language and Culture at Maningrida College, Bábbarra Women's Centre, and the Cultural Research Office at Maningrida Arts and Culture). The chapter's first author, Vaughan, is a non-Indigenous linguist who has conducted research and supported community language projects in Maningrida since 2014. The second author, Carter, is a Martay Burarra woman and a Language and Culture worker at Maningrida College. Carter has lived in Maningrida for most of her life, but also spends time at Wurdeja, a small outstation on her family's traditional country east of Arnhem Land's Blyth River, and in Darwin, northern Australia's major urban centre.

1.2 Indigenous Australian youth subcultures

Youth subculture in Indigenous Australia is a relatively new phenomenon. Its emergence has been facilitated by radical changes wrought by the colonial project since 1788, and is linked in particular to increasing urbanisation, movement away from traditional social categories, and the development of generational identities. The small, semi-nomadic, social groups that existed prior to colonisation are unlikely to have had large enough cohorts to support youth subculture (Hamilton 1981, Mansfield 2014a, Sutton 1978). Indexicality in language use was tied strongly to territory, with sociolinguistic variation dimensionalised into both the geographical and social cosmos (Evans 2013, Sutton 1991), and with overarching systems of linguistic differentiation sometimes going beyond the socially recognised boundaries of individual named languages (Evans 2003: 29). For example, systems of variation described for Arnhem Land languages index such distinctions as region and geographical oppositions (e.g. coastal vs. inland (McKay 2000)), moiety (e.g., Elliot 1991, Green 2003), and clan group (e.g., Garde 2008, Morphy 1977).

The past 200 years have seen a widespread shift to urban communities, comparable in some ways to 20th century urbanisation in other parts of the world (e.g., India, sub-Saharan Africa), but with settlement often occurring in much smaller urban communities of a few hundred to two or three thousand people. In much of remote Australia, Indigenous young people engage in "hyper-mobility essential to modern living" (Altman and Hinkson 2007: 199) and "orbiting diasporas" between "magnet communities" (Burke 2018). In the case of the focus region for this chapter, social orbits shifted significantly following the Second World War, with a general "drift into Darwin" (the major urban centre) (Bond-Sharpe

2013: 52) and the establishment of Maningrida as a welfare settlement in 1957. Earlier mobility was more localised and associated with seasonal food sources, ceremony and conflict (England et al. 2014). Contemporary trajectories for many community members follow a broadly triangular pattern taking in remote outstation communities on traditional country, larger regional hubs, and major urban centres. These shifts have engendered changing interactions with ancestral lands (Taylor and Bell 2004), dramatically altered social and sociolinguistic configurations, and prefaced the emergence of youth subcultures in communities across the region.

Contemporary Indigenous Australia has a young age structure, with 53.8% under 25 years of age in 2016 (compared to 31.3% of the non-Indigenous population) (ABS 2018), and many of this generation continue to suffer the effects of inter-generational trauma, prejudice, and socioeconomic disadvantage (AIHW 2018). Studies of Indigenous Australian youth subculture are few, but notable examples have focused on identity work around hip hop (e.g. Dawes 1998, Morgan and Warren 2011, Stavrias 2005) and heavy metal gangs (Mansfield 2013, 2014b).

The emergence of Indigenous youth subculture in Australia has had inevitable linguistic consequences, as these young speakers/signers seek to distinguish themselves and their language use from earlier generations. Understanding the linguistic practices of these groups is key to explaining the causes of changes within the broader language ecology of the region; Indigenous Australian languages are on the whole highly endangered or no longer in daily use (e.g., Simpson and Wigglesworth 2019), and younger people are frequently implicated in language change and shift. Mansfield (2014a) uses the term *linguistic urbanisation* to describe the explosion of new "ways of speaking" amid the shift to urban communities across northern Australia, and to highlight the rapid attendant language shifts and changes that characterise this shift. As urbanisation naturally reconfigures social structure, the social categories available for indexing in identity work are altered in the process (Stanford and Preston 2009). Furthermore, the changing life projects and social goals brought about by urbanisation necessitate new sociolinguistic solutions and, over time, linguistic innovations (Meyerhoff and Niedzielski 2003). Striking examples in the Australian context include the emergence of mixed languages like Light Warlpiri, which indexes membership in a "young Lajamanu Warlpiri" community of practice (O'Shannessy 2015), Murriny Kardu Kigay, a "slang" variety of Murrinh Patha spoken at Wadeye, which serves as an in-group language for young men in the community (Mansfield 2014a), and Areyonga Teenage Pitjantjatjara and its related secret "short-way" register (Langlois 2004, 2006), which are youth varieties of the Western Desert language Pitjantjatjara. All of these are distinguished at least in part by influence (especially in the lexicon) from English or the northern Australian creole, Kriol. Against a broader context of widespread traditional language loss and the rapid development of new varieties, the community of Maningrida stands out as a counter-example. Although the characteristics of linguistic urbanisation do apply here to an extent – some local languages are now highly endangered and a town-based variety of a traditional language is indeed emerging as we will see – Maningrida is distinguished by exceptionally intensive and resistant multilingualism and by strong ongoing connections to traditional clan estates.

1.3 Language and land in Maningrida community

On the northern coast of the Indigenous-owned region of Arnhem Land, Maningrida community serves as a regional hub for some 2,500 people from a diverse range of linguistic and cultural groups. Community members connect to traditional land further afield in Arnhem Land, and many regularly spend time on ancestral clan estates (e.g., Altman 2016) (Figure 16.1). A local multilingual "regional system" (e.g., Aikhenvald 2002) encompasses dozens of sociolinguistically distinct languages from several language families, with local individual repertoires taking in elements of several traditional languages, Aboriginal Englishes, often Kriol, and local alternate sign languages (see Figure 16.2).

The traditional languages of Indigenous Australia are ideologised by their speakers as inherently bounded. Each language connects to a specific territory, which is the primordial and perennial homeland of that variety and the people who own it (Merlan 1981). In Maningrida (and elsewhere to various extents), connections between language and land have genuine effects in lived experience. Individuals are understood to own a language by virtue of their clan membership, and they inherit language affiliations through kinship structures with the father's language (the patrilect) primary. Further languages are connected to through extended kinship. Actual language competence and use may not align exactly with ideologies around language ownership, and "appropriate" code use is sometimes socially monitored (e.g., a speaker may be chastised for using the "wrong" language or dialectal variant, even if it is within their linguistic repertoire). The community's linguistic diversity mirrors diversity in traditional social and cultural organisation: multiple distinct systems connect and overlap here, with reflexes in religious and ceremonial life, artistic practice, patterns of mobility, as well as language. Our recent work in the community has revealed that, while these social and cultural formations endure in Maningrida, their role in dictating the nature of social interaction is somewhat reduced as people engage in new kinds of social networks and changing life projects.

16 "We mix it up": Indigenous youth language practices in Arnhem Land — 321

Figure 16.1: The Maningrida (Manayingkarírra) region, showing local traditional language groups (in red) and associated territory (Map credit: Brenda Thornley[1]).

Such recent changes have had a significant impact on intergenerational language transmission, the emergence of new varieties, the make-up of linguistic repertoires and the deployment of linguistic variation across northern Australia (Simpson and Wigglesworth 2019). At Maningrida these effects are also evident, for example in the extreme endangerment of local languages like Yan-nhangu, Kunbarlang and Dalabon, yet almost uniquely in the region, Maningrida remains resolutely and intensely multilingual (e.g., Elwell 1977, 1982, Vaughan 2018a, 2020). Young people have played a key role in the evolution of the contemporary

---

[1] On behalf of the people of the Maningrida region, Batchelor Institute, Bawinanga Aboriginal Corporation and Maningrida College.

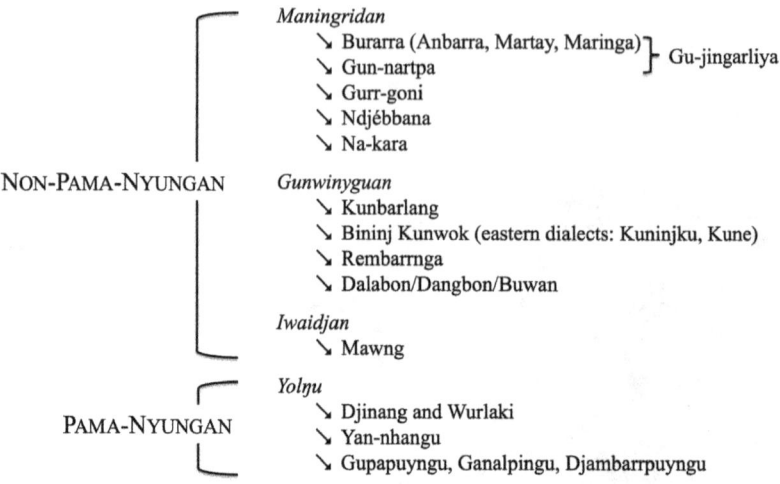

Figure 16.2: Genetic groupings of the traditional languages of the Maningrida region.

language ecology in recent decades, both in accelerating language shift and language change in local varieties (especially Burarra, as we will see), but also in sustaining engagement in the cultural systems that scaffold Maningrida's multilingualism.

2 Youth multilingualism in Maningrida

Many aspects of the contemporary life projects of young people in Maningrida would be unrecognisable to their grandparents' generation. Children in the region still grow up hearing one or more traditional languages at home, but English is since 2008 the predominant language of education at the local school (see, e.g., Simpson, Caffery and McConvell 2009). Contemporary Maningrida youth maintain complex identities off- and online. These identities centre around traditional ethno-linguistic categories (e.g., "An-barra Burarra man", "Kuninjku woman"), but also show allegiance to local communities of practice (e.g., around hip hop artists or the local football league) and connect to a globalised youth culture. The internet enables the pursuit of a wider range of life projects than was typically possible for earlier generations (Kral 2010). For many young traditional-language speakers, English is the primary language used in texting and social media, producing a kind of "digital diglossia" (Mansfield 2014a, Simpson and Wigglesworth 2019) in part necessitated by a lack of traditional-language literacy. Recent decades have seen increased population centralisation at Maningrida (although the trajectory has not been linear; see, e.g., Altman and Hinkson 2007, Bond-Sharp 2013). As a result, young people now engage in new kinds of mobilities, contributing to the "orbiting diasporas" that characterise much of remote Indigenous Australia. In this case, the diaspora orbits between small outstation communities located on traditional country, Maningrida as the central regional hub, and Darwin as the major urban centre in Australia's Top End.

For many young people in Maningrida, the "good life" incorporates both access to globalised culture and continued participation in traditional culture and knowledge (cf. Altman 2018, Langton 2013). Local life is punctuated by cultural milestones such as *japi* ('young men's initiation'), regional ceremonies and funerals. Yet these divided interests give rise to concerns among local Elders, who worry that young people are "floating away from our culture [. . . and their] first language" and are in need of "re-education" (George Gaymarrangi Pascoe, People Culture Environment 2014: 46). Still it is generally recognised among young people that their languages transport unique knowledge systems, connect them to kin and country, and serve as a major identity category. As we will see in the following sections, many young people proudly see themselves as "prime stakeholders" in maintaining the language practices of their forebears (Wyman, McCarty and Nicholas 2013: 1). Section 2.1 provides a personal account from second author Carter of how the languages she identifies with connect to kin, land and clan, while Section 2.2 explores examples of youth multilingualism in everyday practice around the community.

2.1 A young woman's reflection on language, land and kin

While high levels of youth multilingualism characterise the Maningrida community more generally, insight into the dynamics of this phenomenon is limited without considering its operation in the everyday lives of multilingual individuals (Pietikäinen et al. 2008). In this section, the second author, Carter, gives an account of her personal linguistic biography. The intention here is to provide an insight into ideological and embodied orientations to language use through the lenses of linguistic biography and language drawings.

Linguistic biography (e.g., Busch 2006) is a method of exploring an individual's linguistic repertoire that goes beyond merely listing languages to tap into the social regimes and ideologies that have shaped the role of languages and languaging in that person's life. Participants are asked to tell the interviewer about the languages they have used in their lives, and an open-ended, narrative interview follows in which they describe their own language use and that of others in their community, their social and linguistic identities, and their opinions about languages and language use. Participants are also invited to complete a language drawing, a multimodal task in which the linguistic repertoire is represented visually (often by colouring and annotating a black outline of a body – in that case a language "portrait") while they explain how each language is represented (e.g., Busch 2018, Singer and Harris 2016). The language drawing task was first introduced into our collaborative research by Indigenous staff at Maningrida College (including Carter), who saw a video of it being used in research elsewhere in Arnhem Land[2] and who suggested representing their own repertoires in this way. The drawing task is intended to provide an open-ended, subjective and personal window into the lived experience of languaging. These biographical methods have rarely been used in research on endangered languages or in linguistic research in Indigenous Australian communities (Singer forthcoming).

The following excerpts from Carter's linguistic biography and language drawings come from our ongoing collaborative work on multilingualism in Maningrida. In her own language, the Martay dialect of Burarra, she illustrates the lived connections between language, land and kinship:

> *Wurdeja rrawa wana ngu-ni with arr-ngaypa jaminya rrapa mununa. Wengga marn.gi nguninya galiyana rrapa ngu-wena Martay Burarra ngardawa gun-gata Wurdeja rrawa. Gun-gata Yirrchinga rrawa, rrapa Martay yerrcha Martay Burarra aburr-weya aburr-workiya. Martay minypa wengga wana gun-bapala gun-derta. Mix up nyiburr-weya nyiburr-workiya, mix nyiburr-negarra nyiburr-workiya minypa An-barra. Gapala yerrcha aburr-weya aburr-workiya arrburrwa, "ngika gurda wengga, gun-guna wengga! Gun-guna gun-burral, gun-derta gun-nginyipa." Ngayburrpa jechinawa arrburrwa wengga, minypa gun-derta. Jin-ngaypa mununa Martay Burarra jin-gata. Rrapa minypa Djinang ng-galiyarra ngu-workiya, ngardawa an-ngaypa jaminya gu-nika wengga. Rrapa an-ngaypa ninya rrapa bapapa, jungurda apula yerrcha gun-ngayburrpa wengga Yan-nhangu.*

> [I grew up at Wurdeja outstation with my grandfather and grandmother. I knew language because I listened and spoke Martay Burarra, and because Wurdeja is the country for that language. That's Yirrchinga[3] country, and Martay people always speak Martay Burarra. Martay language is really big and strong. We (young people) are always mixing up our speech, always mix it with like An-barra (dialect of Burarra). The old people always say to us, "don't speak that way, speak this way! This language is the true one, yours is the hard language."[4] In our way we talk straight, like hard way. My grandmother, she's Martay Burarra. And, like, I hear and understand Djinang, because that's my mother's father's language. And my father and auntie, all my grandfathers, our language is Yan-nhangu.]

---

2 Ruth Singer's collaborative work at Warruwi, as featured in the film *Language Matters with Bob Holman* (2014).
3 Yirrchinga is one of two moieties into which the Burarra social and natural world is divided. The other is Jowunga.
4 *Gun-derta* ('hard') and *gun-nyarlkuch* ('soft') are used as oppositional descriptors for named dialect groups within the Burarra language.

In the two images below, Carter represents these same connections through her language drawings (Figure 16.3). We discussed the option of using the standard language portrait template (the black outline of a body) to visualise her repertoire, but instead Carter chose to draw new images that were more meaningful to her and to her linguistic identity. In the first image, Carter's repertoire is represented by a tree, with her main language, Burarra, positioned closest to the land at the base of the trunk. Carter explained that this is to demonstrate its primary significance. Next along the trunk is Djinang, labelled with its connection to her matrilineal line. Yolngu Matha and Ndjébbana are placed next, reflecting their relative importance: Yolngu Matha is a language connected to through kin and which she speaks fairly well, while Ndjébbana is the language of the land where Carter lives (Maningrida). Kuninjku and Kune are located further out in the branches as community languages in which she has some limited competence but to which she has no central familial connection. Carter chose not to include English, which she speaks fluently, or Kriol, which she has some command of, as these were not seen to be part of her own linguistic biography. In the second image, Carter represents her own dialect of Burarra – Martay Burarra – with a branch of red eucalyptus blossoms. *Martay* is the Burarra name for these flowers, which appear in the dry season, and *Martay* also labels the Burarra-speaking clans from the eastern bank of the Blyth River for whom the flowers are an important emblem.

Figure 16.3: Carter's language portraits.

Such first-hand, holistic, biographical approaches to analysing the linguistic repertoire are valuable as they do not force a separation between language competence and personal perspectives on language, as other methods can do. Visual art can provide an appealing and revealing approach for language analysis, and one which has an important place in collaborative, participatory research. Visual art is an activity that is familiar and enjoyable to many Maningrida community members (as evidenced by the enthusiasm with which it was suggested and undertaken by language workers at the school) in a way that a traditional interview is not, and it has a long tradition as a means of knowledge production and learning in the region (Singer forthcoming).

Here, these multimodal accounts exemplify the nature of language ideologies in the region, in particular that languages belong to specific tracks of land, and that language is owned and inherent, and inherited through kinship links. Carter's linguistic repertoire is fairly typical of those of her peers and provides an insight into the multilingualism of Maningrida youth culture. Her spoken account highlights some tensions between ideologies of language ownership and the reality of the deployment of linguistic repertoires. Carter often draws on features perceived to belong to the neighbouring Burarra dialect, An-barra, and as a result is admonished by older Burarra speakers. As we have discussed, ideologically salient linguistic boundaries are frequently socially policed, and young people are viewed as particularly transgressive in this regard. However, a strong sense of language allegiance and continuity emerges from Carter's biography and drawings. She centralises the diversity of her linguistic repertoire, naming eight different varieties, but connects deeply to her ancestral language, Martay Burarra, through her grandparents and her clan estate at Wurdeja – it is "strong", "hard", "straight" and "true". In this way, Carter identifies herself as a "stakeholder" in the continuity of her ancestor's language practices.

2.2 Youth multilingualism in practice

Although the personal account given above illustrates ideological orientations to Maningrida's multilingualism, it is not immediately clear how daily language practices map onto these. In fact, Carter does use several languages on a daily basis: Burarra is used much of the time with family and friends, Djinang and Yolngu Matha with certain kin, Ndjébbana with friends and neighbours, and English in her work at the local school and with Balandas (non-Indigenous people).

Documentation of youth-specific language practices in Maningrida is scarce: most work in the region has either had a more general focus or featured predominantly older speakers. This is understandable given that most local languages are under-documented and the language practices of older generations have been somewhat less affected by post-colonial changes to the language ecology. A small body of work, however, does provide a window into how young people communicate, including some work by the first author (Vaughan). Work by Green (2003), Hamilton (1981) and Auld (2005) illuminates the continuing transmission of Gurr-goni, Burarra and Ndjébbana (respectively) to children, and the preference of members of each group to use their own language in everyday communication. Yet these studies also note increasing pressure from English and larger traditional languages among the younger generation (e.g., Auld 2005: 9, Green 2003: 133). Hamilton (1981) and Green (2003) focus on language socialisation practices, and provide rich illustrations of common interactional routines that scaffold ideologies of patrilineal language inheritance. Green observed very young babies of Gurr-goni fathers (whose mothers spoke another language) being held and told "*Ngarrpu Gurr-goni nji-wekiya ya!*" ('You speak Gurr-goni, don't you!'). When the question was posed to older children, they were prompted with the response, "*Yita ngaw!*" ('Say yes!').

Perhaps the most targeted account of youth multilingualism in the region is now several decades old: Elwell (1977, 1982) explored the interactional deployment of Maningrida's highly multilingual repertoires across different community settings, including at the local school. We present Elwell's data here as it was originally published – that is, as a basic count of named languages recognised within the recordings, and with some brief notes about the type of interaction (e.g., "intermixture", "2-way conversation", and notes about the first languages of the students)[5]. The nature of the reported data does not allow for any additional interpretation, such as of the nature of the mixing or whether "single language" is an accurate account of the interactions. Nevertheless, it does demonstrate the diversity of language resources drawn upon by local students during interactions at the school. Table 16.1 shows language choices among students (aged 8 to 12) with a range of primary languages during several "reading periods" at the library.

Table 16.1: Code choice across 29 dyadic and multiadic interactions at the school library (Elwell 1977: 93–98 and Appendix F).

Mode of interaction	Languages used	Number of interactions
Single language	Burarra (with < 5 English words)	11
	Ndjébbana	4
	Gupapuyngu	4
	Gumatj	1
	English	4

---

5 Unfortunately, Elwell's original recordings are not currently readily available to be re-analysed.

Table 16.1 (continued)

Mode of interaction	Languages used	Number of interactions
Code-mixing	Burarra and Gupapuyngu	1
	Ndjébbana, Na-kara and English	1
	Ndjébbana and Na-kara	1
Receptive multilingualism[6]	Ndjébbana and Na-kara	1
	Wangurri and Gumatj	1

Although the language choices in Elwell's data often appear to reflect the primary language affiliations of one or more of the interlocutors, she found that knowing the composition of individual linguistic repertoires was not sufficient to predict which language would be used in any given interaction. Burarra was the choice for a third of the interactions, reflecting its status as a common L1 and L2 in the community, but several other communicative strategies were employed, including two forms of language mixing distinguished by Elwell. Evidently, language use here is strategic, sensitive to complex socio-indexical pressures, often unpredictable, and not always restricted by socially recognised linguistic boundaries.

Interactions like these are still a daily occurrence in Maningrida, although the increased presence of English and the declining use of language resources associated with certain local languages, such as Na-kara, are evident. Recent data collected by the first author exemplifies the persistence of this diversity in public community settings featuring communication amongst multiple generations. At a church gathering in 2015, features from six named languages were used amongst a group of some fifty people from across all generations (Table 16.2). This was a loosely ritualised interaction to mark Good Friday, whereby church members paraded across the community, performing the roles of Jesus and the crowd accompanying him to his crucifixion. Communication was broadcast to the community more generally, rather than targeted towards individual interlocutors. In this case, the linguistic resources used in about half of the utterances aligned fairly straightforwardly with the primary language affiliation of the speaker, a fifth were in English (an important code in the church domain), and the remainder consisted of resources from more than one named language (see also Section 3, and Vaughan 2018b, 2020).

---

[6] Receptive multilingualism or 'two-way' conversation refers to bilingual conversations where each interlocutor uses a different code (e.g., Singer and Harris 2016).

Table 16.2: Code choice across 135 clauses/short utterances[7] at a Good Friday church event.

Mode of interaction	Linguistic resources used	Number of clauses
Single language	English	28
	Kuninjku	26
	Burarra/Gun-nartpa	21
	Djinang	11
	Ndjébbana	3
	Rembarrnga	1
	Shared regional features	1
Code-mixing	Burarra and English	33
	Kuninjku and English	7
	Burarra/Gun-nartpa and Kuninjku	1
	Kuninjku and shared	1
	Burarra, Kuninjku and English	1
	Burarra, Djinang and English	1

Another example of youth multilingualism currently in the public eye is the recent success of Maningrida's Ripple Effect Band, a young, all-female rock band who have been playing together since high school. The women sing in five languages: Ndjébbana, Burarra, Na-kara, Kune and English, and their lyrics touch on connection to country, bush food, local animals and mythological beings. Indigenous ceremonial music is a traditionally male domain, and Maningrida has produced a number of successful male bands like Letterstick Band and Sunrize Band. Ripple Effect have broken significant new ground in bringing female voices into this arena, and have attracted a good deal of success and positive attention at festivals and solo gigs around Australia. Their song *Ngúddja* ('language') explicitly celebrates Maningrida's linguistic diversity. Written by Patricia Gibson and Jodie Kell in Patricia's first language, Ndjébbana, *Ngúddja* connects the community's multilingualism with its landscape and ancestor spirits. The song, included in full in example (1), lists the different languages in daily use in Maningrida, but emphasises that their use does not reflect divisions within the community. Indeed, the performance of "difference" is key to the semiotics of cultural life in Arnhem Land. Brown (2016: 9), for example, describes a "conscious differentiation" in local Arnhem Land musical practice whereby differences in song rep-

---

[7] The utterances transcribed reflect those that were in clear hearing distance of the first author's recording gear. As the communicative context was highly dynamic, a number of utterances were omitted from the count as they were unclear.

ertoires and performance occur "'together' in a shared ceremonial social space and within a unified musical framework" – characterised as "different together". Evans (2010: 14) describes the "constructive fostering of variegation" for the same phenomenon in language variation in the region, and reflexes can be observed in other domains such as ceremony, kin classification and artistic practice. This cultural priority is expected to be displayed in certain contexts in various prescribed ways, and continues to have reflexes in youth language practices: "we all call out in our own different languages [but] we sit down on this land here together".

(1) **Ngúddja**
Balawúrrwurr wédda nganda-mangkayana
Balawúrrwurr ngúddja ngarra-kaláya
Balawúrrwurr barrómaya ka-bala-ddjórrkka
Ngarra-karráwanga karrakárriba
Ngarra-ngúddjeya ngúrra-mala
Ngarra-ngúddjeya ngúrra-mala
Ngarra-ngúddjeya ngúrra-mala
Djibba wíba ngabayuka-na
Nga-kalaya Ndjébbana, Na-kara, Kun-barlang
Burarra, Gun-nartpa, Gurr-goni, Kuninjku
Rembarrnga, Kune, Djinang, Dalabon
Ngarra-karráwanga karrakarríba

[The wind comes across the land
Bringing the words and the language
Carrying the spirits of our ancestors
As we look out over the land
Even though you, me, we all call out in our own different languages
We sit down on this land here together
We can hear Ndjébbana, Na-kara, Kun-barlang, Burarra, Gun-nartpa, Gurr-goni, Kuninjku, Rembarrnga, Kune, Djinang, Dalabon
As we look out over the land]

3 Maningrida Burarra style

Against this backdrop of persistent, intensive multilingualism, a mixed urban variety has emerged in Maningrida, which draws on elements of the local Burarra language and English. This newer code has been referred to by linguists as "Maningrida Burarra" but is not so much a stable variety as a kind of multilingual "style" (in the sense of e.g. Eckert 2008) – in that it is not currently the primary code of any speaker but rather associated with particular domains, interactions types and indexical values – or a "multilingua franca" (Makoni and Pennycook 2012: 447) – in that it draws on a "multilayered chain" of mixed features that is not fixed but adapts or "relocalises" to situations as they arise (Vaughan 2018b).

In Maningrida itself, the variety is not quite socially salient enough to have attracted a distinct, commonly used name. It is understood to be a type of Burarra, but many of its features are associated by Burarra people, usually negatively, with the practices of local young people. It is widely used among the younger generations of several local language groups (especially Burarra youth) alongside other codes in their repertoires, but it has been fundamentally shaped by the linguistic repertoires, language practices and mobilities of older generations. It occupies an important niche in the contemporary language ecology of the community.

Maningrida Burarra is distinguished from "traditional" Burarra in a number of ways. The most striking is the significant presence of English lexical stock. As can be seen in example (2) below, features from Burarra, English and, to a lesser extent, Kriol are freely mixed within the clause (albeit with some limited emerging grammatical patterns[8]) in a way that is almost never seen in mixing between traditional languages, which is more constrained, more socially motivated, and less widely attested (Vaughan 2018b, 2020). The mixing that characterises the Maningrida Burarra style is much less socially and grammatically restricted, and is comparable to what McConvell (2002) suggests to be a "standardized style of unmarked codeswitching" among traditional languages mixed with English in northern Australia. Maningrida Burarra also displays evidence of levelling processes that have occurred within the contributing Burarra dialects, especially Martay and An-barra, as referred to in Carter's personal account in 2.1. A short example of Maningrida Burarra in use at a school event is given in example (2), with Burarra lexical stock underlined[9]. In this interaction a language and culture teacher from the Djinang language group (eastern Arnhem Land) is addressing a large group of school children.

(2)   *Yaw, good afternoon gu-ngarda yerrcha! Mun-guna book launching nguburr-ni barra* – it's the most powerful dreamtime creation story. Wisdom *arrbu-wuna* from our old people. And we're very lucky, recording *burr-negarra* our old

---

8 For example, the frequent use of English verbal particles or adverbs followed by an inflected 'light verb', such as in the case of *launching nguburr-ni barra* (launching 1PL-be FUT) 'we will be launching' in the example given (see also Mansfield 2016).
9 This is not to imply a strict separation of codes on the part of speaker, but rather to facilitate the reader's navigation of the example.

people, <u>aburr-ngayburrpa</u> Gun-nartpa clan group, <u>aburr-ngayburrpa</u> family. [. . .] <u>Gun-ngarda yerrcha</u>, gun-ngayburrpa culture is very, very important and it is the oldest ancient culture around the world! <u>Gu-gurda ngacha bunggul rrapa manakay gala barra nyiburr-bamapa</u>.

[Yes, good afternoon all the kids! This book we will be launching, it's the most powerful dreamtime creation story. Wisdom they gave us from our old people. And we're very lucky that she recorded our old people, our Gun-nartpa clan group, our family. [. . .] Kids, our culture is very, very important and it is the oldest ancient culture around the world! Indeed you must never forget that dancing and those songs.] (SR: 20150325-GN_launch)

Maningrida Burarra is frequently drawn on in the community's "hybrid" spaces – spaces like the school, church and football matches – which are shaped by the interaction of diverse groups, institutions, and ways of speaking (Vaughan 2018b). Although it is a style that is particularly prevalent among younger community members, for most Burarra speakers Maningrida Burarra sits alongside a more "traditional" Burarra style (with less influence from English) that is drawn on more often at home and in smaller group communication. Amongst the exceptional linguistic diversity of north-central Arnhem Land, the emergence of Maningrida Burarra style provides a local reflex of the linguistic urbanisation phenomena observable across northern Australia (Mansfield 2014a).

4 Discussion and conclusion

Youth language practices in northern Australia have in recent times been characterised by an explosion of new ways of speaking brought about by a general shift to urban communities. In one sense, the young people of Maningrida are no exception. Maningrida Burarra style has emerged in response to increased centralisation at Maningrida and in service to changing life projects and new social goals, especially among its youth. As a common L2, this mixed variety enables the temporary crossing of linguistic boundaries that are otherwise socially policed. Similarly to Australian sociolects such as Murriny Kardu Kigay and Areyonga Teenage Pitjantjatjara, Maningrida Burarra style is frequently recruited in indexing youth subculture due largely to the prominence of English features. But it is also a key feature of the wider community ecology, drawn upon in "hybrid" public settings.

In other ways, however, the communicative practices of Maningrida youth are exceptional within the Australian context. Youth identity here is drawn in part from the continuation of longstanding multilingual practices and an enduring orientation to traditional language ideologies around language inheritance and ownership. A shared ethos of "conscious differentiation", which has long characterised cultural semiotics in the region, is reshaped as a shared feature of Maningrida community identity, with multilingualism both a practical solution and an ideological orientation to communication.

In this chapter, we have briefly summarised some linguistic outcomes of emerging youth identities in Maningrida, Arnhem Land, and we have endeavoured to demonstrate the value of centralising local perspectives on linguistic variation and change. We have seen evidence of how young people in the community are creating new affordances within the rich multilingual resources they have at hand to develop linguistic solutions to new social challenges. Contrary to dominant discourses in circulation which position youth practices as a threat to traditional language maintenance, these young people play an active role as "prime stakeholders" (Wyman, McCarty and Nicholas 2013: 1) in the cultural continuity of their languages and language ecologies, while also engaging in the creative manipulation of modern linguistic resources to meet the needs of their rapidly evolving social worlds.

References

Aikhenvald, Alexandra Y. 2002. *Language contact in Amazonia*. Oxford: Oxford University Press.
Altman, Jon. 2016. Imagining Mumeka: Bureaucratic and Kuninjku perspectives. In Nicholas Peterson and Fred Myers (eds.), *Experiments in self-determination: Histories of the outstation movement in Australia*, 279–299. Canberra: Australian National University Press.
Altman, Jon. 2018. 'The main thing is to have enough food': Kuninjku precarity and neoliberal reason. In Chris Gregory and Jon Altman (eds.), *The quest for the good life in precarious times: Ethnographic perspectives on the domestic moral economy*, 163–196. Canberra: Australian National University Press.
Altman, Jon and Melinda Hinkson. 2007. Mobility and modernity in Arnhem Land: the social universe of Kuninjku trucks. *Journal of Material Culture* 12 (2). 181–203.
Auld, Glenn. 2005. *The literacy practices of Kunibídji children: Text, technology and transformation*. Ballarat: University of Ballarat dissertation.
Australian Bureau of Statistics. 2018. *Estimates of Aboriginal and Torres Strait Islander Australians, June 2016*. ABS cat. no. 3238.0.55.001. Canberra: ABS.
Australian Institute of Health and Welfare. 2018. *Aboriginal and Torres Strait Islander adolescent and youth health and wellbeing 2018*. Canberra: AIHW.
Bond-Sharp, Helen. 2013. *Maningrida: A history of the Aboriginal township in Arnhem Land*. Howard Springs: Helen Bond-Sharp.
Burke, Paul. 2018. *An Australian Indigenous diaspora: Warlpiri matriarchs and the refashioning of tradition*. New York: Berghahn.

Busch, Brigitta. 2006. Language biographies for multilingual learning: Linguistic and educational considerations. In Brigitta Busch, Aziza Jardine and Angelika Tjoutuku (eds.), *Language biographies for multilingual learning*, 5–17. Cape Town: Project for the Study of Alternative Education in South Africa (PRAESA).

Busch, Brigitta. 2018. The language portrait in multilingualism research: Theoretical and methodological considerations. *Working Papers in Urban Language & Literacies* 236. 1–13.

Dawes, Graham. 1998. The art of the body: Aboriginal and Torres Strait Islander youth subcultural practices. *Journal of Intercultural Studies* 19 (1). 21–35.

Dovchin, Sender and Jerry Won Lee. 2019. Introduction to special issue: 'The ordinariness of translinguistics.' *International Journal of Multilingualism* 16 (2). 105–111.

Eckert, Penelope. 2008. Variation and the indexical field. *Journal of Sociolinguistics* 12 (4). 453–476.

Elliott, Craig. 1991. 'Mewal is Merri's name': Form and ambiguity in Marrangu cosmology, North Central Arnhem Land. Canberra: Australian National University MA thesis.

Elwell, Vanessa. 1977. *Multilingualism and lingua francas among Australian Aborigines: A case study of Maningrida*. Canberra: Australian National University Honours dissertation.

Elwell, Vanessa. 1982. Some social factors affecting multilingualism among Aboriginal Australians: A case study of Maningrida. *International Journal of the Sociology of Language* 36. 83–104.

Evans, Nicholas. 2003. Context, culture, and structuration in the languages of Australia. *Annual Review of Anthropology* 32 (1). 13–40.

Evans, Nicholas. 2013. *Multilingualism as the primal human condition: What we have to learn from small-scale speech communities*. Keynote lecture presented at the International Symposium on Bilingualism, Singapore, 10–12 June.

García, Ofelia. 2009. *Bilingual education in the 21st century: A global perspective*. Malden: Wiley-Blackwell.

García, Ofelia. 2012. Theorizing translanguaging for educators. In Christina Celic and Kate Seltzer (eds.), *Translanguaging: A CUNY-NYSIEB guide for educators*, 1–6. New York: CUNY-NYSIEB.

García, Ofelia. 2014. Countering the dual: Transglossia, dynamic bilingualism and translanguaging in education. In Rani S. Rubdy & Lubna Alsagoff (eds.), *The global-local interface and hybridity: Exploring language and identity*, 100–118. Bristol: Multilingual Matters.

Garde, Murray. 2008. Kun-dangwok: "Clan lects" and Ausbau in western Arnhem land. *International Journal of the Sociology of Language* 191. 141–169.

Green, Rebecca. 2003. Gurr-goni, a minority language in a multilingual community: Surviving into the 21st century. In Joe Blythe and R. McKenna Brown (eds.), *Maintaining the links: Language, identity and the land*, 127–134. Bath: Foundation for Endangered Languages.

Hamilton, Annette. 1981. *Nature and nurture: Aboriginal child-rearing in north-central Arnhem Land*. Canberra: Australian Institute of Aboriginal Studies.

Jørgensen, Jens Normann. 2008. Poly-lingual languaging around and among children and adolescents. *International Journal of Multilingualism* 5 (3). 161–176.

Jørgensen, Jens Normann. 2010. *Languaging. Nine years of poly-lingual development of young Turkish-Danish grade school students*, vol. I–II. Copenhagen: University of Copenhagen.

Kral, Inge. 2010. *Plugged in: Remote Australian Indigenous youth and digital culture*. Centre for Aboriginal Economic Policy Research Wording Paper 69. Canberra: CAEPR.

Langlois, Annie. 2004. *Alive and kicking: Areyonga teenage Pitjantjatjara*. Canberra: Pacific Linguistics.

Langlois, Annie. 2006. Wordplay in teenage Pitjantjatjara. *Australian Journal of Linguistics* 26 (2). 181–192.

Langton, Marcia. 2013. *The right to the good life: Improving educational outcomes for Aboriginal and Torres Strait Islander children*. Sydney: The Centre for Independent Studies Limited.

Mansfield, John. 2013. The social organisation of Wadeye's heavy metal mobs. *The Australian Journal of Anthropology* 24 (2). 148–165.

Mansfield, John. 2014a. *Polysynthetic sociolinguistics*. Canberra: Australian National University dissertation.

Mansfield, John. 2014b. Listening to heavy metal in Wadeye. In Amanda Harris (ed.), *Circulating cultures: Exchanges of Australian Indigenous music, dance and media*, 239–262. Canberra: Australian National University Press.

Mansfield, John. 2016. Borrowed verbs and the expansion of light verb phrases in Murrinhpatha. In Felicity Meakins and Carmel O'Shannessy (eds.), *Loss and renewal: Australian languages since colonisation*, 397–424. Berlin: De Gruyter Mouton.

McConvell, Patrick. 2002. Mix-Im-up speech and emergent mixed languages in Indigenous Australia. *Proceedings of SALSA 2001 (Symposium on Language and Society), Texas Linguistic Forum* 44 (1). 328–349.

McKay, Graham. 2000. Ndjébbana. In R. M. W Dixon and Barry J Blake (eds.), *Handbook of Australian languages*, vol. 5. Melbourne: Oxford University Press.

Merlan, Francesca. 1981. Land, language and social identity in Aboriginal Australia. *Mankind* 13. 133–148.

Meyerhoff, Miriam and Nancy Niedzielski. 2003. The globalisation of vernacular variation. *Journal of Sociolinguistics* 7 (4). 534–555.

Morgan, George and Andrew Warren. 2011. Aboriginal youth, hip hop and the politics of identification. *Ethnic and Racial Studies* 34 (6). 925–947.

Morphy, Frances. 1977. Language and moiety: Sociolectal variation in a Yu:lngu language of North-East Arnhem Land. *Canberra Anthropology* 1 (1). 51–60.

O'Shannessy, Carmel. 2015. Multilingual children increase language differentiation by indexing communities of practice. *First Language* 35 (4–5). 305–326.

Pietikäinen, Sari, Riika Alanen, Hannele Dufva, Paula Kalaja, Sirpa Leppänen and Anne Pitkänen-Huhta. 2008. Languaging in Ultima Thule: Multilingualism in the life of a Sami Boy. *International Journal of Multilingualism* 5 (2). 79–99.

People Culture Environment. 2014. *The elders' report into preventing Indigenous self-harm and youth suicide*. [https://bepartofthehealing.org/EldersReport.pdf] (accessed 7 January 2021).

Simpson, Jane, Josephine Caffery and Patrick McConvell. 2009. *Gaps in Australia's Indigenous language policy: Dismantling bilingual education in the Northern Territory* (AIATSIS discussion paper 24). Canberra: AIATSIS.

Simpson, Jane and Gillian Wigglesworth. 2019. Language diversity in Indigenous Australia in the 21st century. *Current Issues in Language Planning* 20 (1). 67–80.

Singer, Ruth. forthcoming. Language portraits as a tool for generating shared understandings of multilingualism in an Indigenous Australian community. In Judith Purkarthofer and Mi-Cha Flubacher (eds.), *Speaking subjects – biographical methods in multilingualism research*. Clevedon: Multilingual Matters.

Singer, Ruth, and Salome Harris. 2016. What practices and ideologies support small-scale multilingualism? A case study of Warruwi Community, northern Australia. *International Journal of the Sociology of Language* 241. 163–208.

Stanford, James N. and Dennis R. Preston. 2009. The lure of a distant horizon: Variation in indigenous minority languages. In James N. Stanford and Dennis R. Preston (eds.), *Variation in Indigenous minority languages*, 1–22. Amsterdam: John Benjamins.

Stavrias, George. 2005. Dropping conscious beats and flows: Aboriginal hip hop and youth identity. *Australian Aboriginal Studies* 2. 44–54.

Sutton, Peter. 1978. *Wik: Aboriginal society, territory and language at Cape Keerweer, Cape York Peninsula, Australia*. St. Lucia: University of Queensland dissertation.

Sutton, Peter. 1991. Language in Aboriginal Australia: Social dialects in a geographical idiom. In Suzanne Romaine (ed.), *Language in Australia*, 49–66. Cambridge: Cambridge University Press.

Taylor, John, and Martin Bell. 2004. Continuity and change in Indigenous Australian population mobility. In Martin Bell and John Taylor (eds.), *Population mobility and Indigenous peoples in Australasia and North America*, 13–43. London and New York: Routledge.

Vaughan, Jill. 2018a. "We talk in saltwater words": Dimensionalisation of dialectal variation in multilingual Arnhem Land. *Language & Communication* 62. 119–132.

Vaughan, Jill. 2018b. Translanguaging and hybrid spaces: Boundaries and beyond in North Central Arnhem Land. In Gerardo Mazzaferro (ed.), *Translanguaging as everyday practice*. Cham: Springer.

Vaughan, Jill. 2020. The ordinariness of translinguistics in Indigenous Australia. In Jerry Won Lee and Sender Dovchin (eds.), *Translinguistics: Negotiating innovation and ordinariness*, 90–103. London and New York: Routledge.

Wyman, Leisy T., Teresa L. McCarty and Sheila E. Nicholas. 2013. Beyond endangerment: Indigenous youth and multilingualism. In Leisy T. Wyman, Teresa L. McCarty and Sheila E. Nicholas (eds), *Indigenous youth and multilingualism: Language identity, ideology, and practice in dynamic cultural worlds*, 1–25. New York: Routledge.

Anne Storch
17 Youth language before youth language

Much of the colonial cultural production that dealt with the exotic and Other was directed at young audiences. In the late 19th and during the first decades of the 20th century, a large body of novels, travelogues, adventure tales, feature films and documentaries were produced that were intended to convey a particular idea about Africa, the Americas and Oceania to the youth. Clad as education and entertainment, these texts conveyed ideologies whose scope lay well beyond what young audiences were able to experience in their daily lives: the lives of Others in the colonialized parts of the world. Youth language closely connected to literacy and to state fetishism in the decisive early twentieth century, this contribution argues, stands in a close relationship with fascism. It further argues that it remains a crucial task to linguists to remind themselves of the historical context of their constructions of "youth language", 'anti-language', and so on, and to ask for the political and social contexts of the emergence of these constructions. This contribution attempts to look at youthful language practices pertaining to Africa, but gets stuck in provincial Germany in Hesse.

1 Retrospective

When Max Weber's *Economy and society* was first published, my grandfather was nineteen. He had grown up as the third son of a dentist and a housewife, who were considered upper middle class in the small town where they lived. This was in a remote and rural region north of the city of Frankfurt am Main (Germany), situated amidst low hills, Protestant and modest. He had been born with a cleft palate and underwent surgery when he was still an infant, but his speech remained affected by his birth defect. As a boy, he was protected by a melancholic mother and disciplined by an authoritarian father. His whole life as an adult he was afraid that certain schedules could not be met, lunch at twelve for example.

Acknowledgments: I am deeply grateful to Nico Nassenstein for encouraging me to write about youth and language, as well as for many stimulating conversations. I thank two reviewers for their many helpful comments on an earlier version of this contribution, and Katrin Storch for faithfully keeping all these books.

Anne Storch, University of Cologne, e-mail: astorch@uni-koeln.de

https://doi.org/10.1515/9781501514685-020

I have two pictures of him as a youth. One shows him as a student, wearing the cap and ribbon of the fraternity he belonged to from then on. The back of the photograph bears the dedication "*meinen lb. Eltern zum Andenken an meine Studentenzeit.* Ludwig." '[to] my dear parents, as a souvenir of my student days'. The English translation 'student days' fails to express the complex connotations of the German *Studentenzeit*, which elicits contradictory notions of youth movements and state authority, independence and nationalism, disciplining and revolution. The other photograph must have been taken a few years later and shows my grandfather wearing the clothes of a hunter, and binoculars around his neck. He stands amidst a forest of beech, next to two hunting companions who remain unbeknownst to me now. The picture is meaningful though; he had wanted to be a forest warden but was expected to live up to higher expectations.

Economy and society is about the structure of power and the difference between community and society. Max Weber distinguishes between dominance and power, and defines the latter as "the probability that a command with a given specific content will be obeyed by a given group of persons" (Weber 1978: 53), while the former is "the probability that one actor within a social relationship will be in a position to carry out his own will despite resistance, regardless of the basis on which this probability rests" (ibid.). Discipline, Weber adds, is "the probability that by virtue of habituation a command will receive prompt and automatic obedience in stereotyped forms, on the part of a given group of persons" (ibid.). Power, dominance and discipline are based on the creation, and maintenance, of the potential of a relationship between volition and subordination. This relationship is made an enduring one through the implementation of bureaucracy, which, Weber observes, can manifest its own agency and dominance. The bureaucratic state thereby possesses efficiency and rationality – resting upon technical innovation, enhanced organization and accelerated communication – which are perceived as being inescapable in their adaptability and dynamicity.

Instead of becoming a forest warden, my grandfather studied political economy. Max Weber's work formed part of the curriculum, together with other seminal texts on sociology and political science in the 1920s. I do not know whether, just over a hundred years ago today, he was able to relate Weber's anatomy of the power of the state and patriarchy to his own situation. He completed his studies and obtained a doctoral degree, then became a member of the NSDAP in the early thirties and a civil servant in 1933. It was once said he went to the war front more or less voluntarily because he couldn't stand it any longer and wanted to disappear. Shortly after they said this, he disappeared finally and spent the last years of his life forgetting almost everything but his youth. Retaining memories of his early life included the persistent use of a language he spoke as a schoolboy and student.

While reflecting on my grandfather's youth, which fell into an era in which the foundations of modern sociology were laid, and during which the media and technologies of communication on which later practices of pop culture and youth language were to be based became available to large audiences (Burke 2012), I wonder why the intellectual contributions by its important thinkers remain fairly unrecognized in sociolinguistic youth language studies. Weber claimed that the time around the year 1910 with its new electrification, skyscrapers and accelerated traffic was a pivotal moment in history, which created a new type of modernity and man. I wonder why one should, after all, discuss such constructions as youth language, anti-language, and so on, without asking for the political and social contexts of their emergence (Hollington and Nassenstein 2015, Thurlow 2005). In this contribution, I attempt to look at that which lies at the base of youth language at the beginning of a time that we now consider "modernity". Data used in this contribution stem from my grandmother's attic and from my childhood memories.

2 Repertoire

Nothing indicates that my grandfather thought of himself as someone who ever spoke in unusual ways, and neither would he ever have seen himself as a member of any subculture. Even though, during his childhood, his lifestyle and that of his family must have differed from that of other people in his environment, who were mostly farmers, craftsmen and workers, it was a lifestyle that represented the dominant social class, its norms and ideologies. Yet, this life was lived in an environment of considerable complexity, with structures and ideologies of feudal order still present in spite of the implementation of the new democratic system, and with different, often contradictory, concepts of the home and the world, the village and the town, the past, the future, charismatic and rationalist leadership, modernity, mobility, contemporaneity and the Self at play.

> Populism and the figure of the leader who expresses the will of the people are one of the fourteen features that determine Ur-fascism in Eco's (2020) posthumously published book.

Sociologists of his time, for example Weber, believed that increasingly complex processes of social differentiation resulted in increased individual agency, which at the same time required disciplining. Weber suggested that "the concept of discipline includes the habituation characteristic of uncritical and unresisting mass obedience" (Weber 1978: 53). Weber's famous differentiation of community (*Gemeinschaft*) and society (*Gesellschaft*) also resonated in his thinking about language. While community is based on a feeling or understanding of belonging together, society is based on a rational calculation of the benefits of communality. Language to him had the social function of making *difference* between people conceivable, upon which practices of inclusion and exclusion could be based:

> A common language, which arises from a similarity of tradition through the family and the surrounding social environment, facilitates mutual understanding, and thus the formation of all types of social relationships, in the highest degree. But taken by itself it is not sufficient to constitute a communal relationship, rather, it facilitates intercourse within the groups concerned, hence the development of associate relationships. This takes place between individuals, not because they speak the same language, but because they have other types of interests. Orientation to the rules of a common language is thus primarily important as a means of communication, not as the content of a social relationship. It is only with the emergence of a consciousness of difference from third persons who speak a different language that the fact that two persons speak the same language, and in that respect share a common situation, can lead them to a feeling of community and to modes of social organization consciously based on the sharing of the common language.
> (Weber 1978: 42–43)

Hence, the relatively large communicative repertoires shared by students during the early twentieth century did not automatically signify diversity, or even openness, or language ideologies that positively rationalized multilingualism, but were part of a number of features that simply marked social class (Block 2014) across different metropoles and regions in Europe by that time. The mainstream, aspiring middle class, of which my grandfather's family was a part, strove to provide their offspring with an education that enabled them to partake to a certain extent in canonic literacies beyond German (French, English). While discourse shared among members of European elites (and increasingly among other people as well) extended across their linguistic repertoires (which among elites oftentimes included some knowledge in four or five of the European colonial languages), Otherness was constructed through the exclusion of other (Indigenous) languages from any critical consideration and through the construction of Othered speakers, whose communicative practices were presented as being deficient (Derrida 1998, Fanon 1986, among others).

> *Appeal to the middle class and the rejection of lower classes and immigrants is a feature of Ur-fascism in Umberto Eco's posthumously published work.*

In my memory, my grandfather's English was rudimentary, and he made use of phonological similarities to his (regional) German. He would say things like *open the deer!*, meaning 'open the door!', mixing English with the German word *Tür*, which in the Hessian dialect he spoke was realized as /diːr/. He had also learned French and Latin, which he was a bit more fluent in (although not very). It formed a significant part of a fraternity student jargon (*Burschensprache*) that he continued to use, which by the time he lived had lost its transgressive connotations and rather had become part of mainstream elitist practices. Objartel's (2016) description and analysis of German fraternity language mainly of the 18th and 19th centuries provides insights into language practices that still were very much in place in the early decades of the 20th century at small and traditional German universities such as Gießen and Marburg. These practices included the extensive use of Latin and French phrases within German speech, and of obsolescent words (*jerum* 'alas'). Compound nouns consisting of French, Latin and German components were common (*Couleurbruder* 'fellow member of a dueling fraternity', *Obersekunda* 'eleventh year at school').

> Umberto Eco's study of Ur-fascism lists the cult of traditions, focusing on national or racial origin, as one of its fourteen characteristic features.

Youth language here has much to do with class performance, but also with the theater of disciplining. Latin or French were not simply languages of higher education and international intellectual debate (which to a considerable degree took place in various European colonial languages by then), but – especially in the ways they were used in *Burschensprache* – languages that referred to old practice, to nineteenth century formations in society and to such practice as part of canonic repertoires. Being clad with cap and ribbon of the fraternity and speaking a particular jargon, taking part in ritual drinking and dueling expressed not transgression and social critique but showed one's inclusion in a "tradition" that was constructed as being ancient and inherited from one's father and forefathers (Hobsbawm and Ranger 1983). Other practices shared by young privileged men were the use of the equally traditionalist practice of hunters' jargon and the inclusion of large repertoires of memorized 19th century verse into everyday speech.

> Eco, in his text on Ur-fascism, considers action for action's sake, connected with anti-intellectualism, as one of its fourteen defining features.

There seems to have been little space for any performance of intergenerational critique or subversion in my grandfather's environment, which makes Weber's contemporary observations of the relationship between socialization, discipline and language interesting. There is no trace in his early life of the new revolutionary movements that were considered to be the beginnings of a new, modernist society by literati and artists elsewhere in Germany – no expressionism, *Jugendstil*, naturalism, reform school, or sexual liberation.

> In Eco's analysis of Ur-fascism, the rejection of diversity, and subordination of knowledge to war and the state, is one of its fourteen characterist features.

3 Rhetoric

How, then, were male youth in small-town middle-class contexts addressed through the arts? Which literature and leisurely pleasure were they permitted or encouraged to enjoy? In her analysis of books for young people, Heidrun Kämper (2001) emphasizes the importance of popular student literature. There, in books that are largely forgotten today, the emotional turmoil of adolescents and the problems faced by young people who tried to liberate themselves from parental duress are addressed in a way that reflects the *zeitgeist* and offers insights into the ways in which critical replies to disciplining and subjugation could be uttered. Kämper states:

> Hesse und Musil, Heinrich und Thomas Mann sind die Meister. Einfühlsam gestalten sie das jugendliche Seelenleben, dessen sprachlich authentische Ausformung hingegen oftmals auf Andeutungen beschränkt bleibt. Torberg und Ebermayer, Süskind und Thieß aber, die weniger hohe, zu ihrer Zeit viel gelesene und heute weitgehend vergessene Gebrauchsliteratur, unter dem Namen 'deutscher Schülerroman' auf ihre Weise beinahe Literaturgeschichte, ist das eigentliche Archiv der historischen deutschen Jugendsprache. Die Dichter erkennen die Missstände vor allem auf den Gymnasien und (Ober-)Realschulen, sie setzen das Zeitempfinden [. . .] literarisch um und machen sich dabei zum Anwalt der Jugendlichen. (Kämper 2001: 48)

> [Hesse and Musil, Heinrich and Thomas Mann are the masters. They empathically write about the youths' psyche, whereby authentic youth language is only presented as a trace. Torberg and Ebermayer, Süskind and Thieß, however, less elevated, but at the time widely read, and now largely forgotten, wrote trivial literature of a type that has been called 'German school novel'. Even though they did not become part of [canonic] history of literature, they form an important archive of historical German youth language. The writers are interested in the grievances at high schools and secondary schools, they find a literary language that represents the zeitgeist [. . .] and they act as advocates of young people.][1]

The material studied by Kämper provides an interesting glimpse at the contradictions that characterized youth literature around 1900 and during the first decades of the 20th century. Reform and historicism, nationalism and psychoanalysis, bureaucracy and nudism were the points of orientation from which authors wrote or developed the characters about whom they wrote. One recurrent motif was the dilemma of youth being trapped in authoritarian relationships (with teachers, parents, etc.) and envisioning liberation, which elicited, both in novels and in real life, suicidal phantasies and practices. Many books written for young audiences might have had a hidden agenda of addressing suicide among students at the authoritarian secondary schools and offering alternatives.

> *To Eco, disagreement conceived as treason is one of the fourteen defining features of Ur-fascism.*

---

[1] All translations my own unless indicated otherwise.

The surviving library from my grandfather's student days does not offer any books that deal with the problems of school life or adolescence. The sexually most liberating book in the collection of a dozen volumes is a book about life in a forester's lodge in a German forest, *Im Forsthause Falkenhorst* by Albert Kleinschmidt (1910). It tells about the adventures of the forester, his companions and family in the surrounding nature in the course of the year – spring, summer, fall and winter. The spring chapter begins with a dialogue about hares. The hares had been (sexually) active too early, and now their offspring (creatively referred to using hunting terminology as *Setzhasen* 'doe', *Löffelmännchen* 'spoon-boy', *Meister Lampe* 'Master Hare', etc.) would perish in the cold. Animal life and death, family and nature, as well as jokes and games, are the topics of the book, in which nobody ever leaves the forest. Only the occasional play with honorific address terms reveals the book's sociohistorical context:

> "Ich habe meine Spielkameraden organisiert!" sagte Otto gewichtig. "Organisiert – tausend noch einmal!" rief der Oberförster verwundert, während Kurt und Bruno herzhaft lachten. "Wie haben den Durchlaucht das gemacht?" [. . .] "Da werden Durchlaucht der Führer der Forstleute sein", warf Kühn ein. (Kleinschmidt 1910: 22)
>
> ["I organized my playmates!" Otto said seriously. "Organized – astonishing!" exclaimed the forester, while Kurt and Bruno laughed heartily. "How did Your Highness do it?" [. . .] "Your Highness will be the leader of the forestry folks," said Kühn.]

Clad in a naïve and joking tone, the honorific terms used in feudal and militaristic contexts, as well as words referring to the subtleties of hierarchy and discipline are transmitted to the youth. One gets oriented, in terms of the year's seasons, the forest, and social deixis.

> *Elitism is another of the fourteen defining features of Ur-fascism in Eco's essay.*

Another book in my grandfather's collection, which he must have received from his senior brother to whom it bears a dedication, is also about a forester, but this time the forester has left his forest lodge and gone to war. In Wilhelm Arminius' *Der Kraftsucher* ('The searcher for power', 1914), young male audiences are taught about *Deutschlands Darniederliegen* 'Germany's defeat', referring to the Prussian war in the 19th century. On the first pages of the book, the forester is characterized through a scene in which he has a conflict with a Polish man:

> "Hab' ich's nicht immer gesagt, das Preußische, was das Militär ist – *Psia krew* – Hundeblut! In Osterburg haben wir's nahe gehabt: *messieurs* – als Kürassiere! [. . .]" [. . .] "Da lieg, Polacke, und friß Staub, bis du von den Preußen besser sprechen lernst!" ruft der Förster noch, dann faßt er seinen Knaben still bei der Hand und schreitet mit ihm heimwärts.
> (Arminius 1914: 9–11)

["Haven't I always said that anything Prussian, concerning military issues, is – *Psia krew* – dog blood! In Osterburg we had it close: *messieurs* – as cuirassiers! [...]" [...] "There, Polish [derogatory], bite the dust until you learn to speak better of the Prussians!" the forester shouted, then took his boy by the hand and walked home with him.]

Prussian, and therefore German, supremacy and the necessity of war to restore an inevitable order of power are the topics of the book throughout.

> *The cultivation of social resentment is one of the fourteen features that characterise Ur-fascism according to Umberto Eco.*

An editorial note at the end of the book informs readers and their parents and reads as follows:

> Die Frage der Jugenderziehung rückt wieder in den Blickpunkt des ganzen Volkes. Welcher Art das Geschlecht sein wird, das nach uns die Geschicke des Vaterlandes lenken soll, die Sorge darum bleibt in jedem ernsten Volksgenossen. Dass ein großer, reiner Wille das heranwachsende Geschlecht belebt, opferfreudige Liebe zum Vaterland, Lust am eigenen Volkstum, scheint uns vor allem erstrebenswert. (Kotzde, in Arminius 1914: n.p.)

> [The issue of youth education again is in the focus of the whole nation. Of what type the generation might be who will be responsible for the fate of the native country after us remains a concern of every reputable fellow German. We consider it desirable that strong and pure willpower should inspire the coming generation, as well as sacrificial love for the fatherland, and love for our national culture.]

The purpose of these books is to implement ideologies of traditionalism, irrationalism, heroism, nationalism and elitism into young readers' intellectual and emotional lives, whereby ideology comes across clad in the cloak of a forester. The figure of the forester and the motif of the forest, nature, and play, in other words, all turn into the instruments with which young audiences would be disciplined into becoming young adults ready to be "sacrificed" in the coming war. There always also is, of course, the notion of "Prussian values", masculine toughness that has never been eradicated.

> *Eco mentions that the cult of heroes and death forms part of the fourteen defining features of Ur-fascism.*

A third book of the surviving collection from my grandmother's attic is *Die Goldgräber von Angra Pequena* 'The gold diggers of Angra Pequena' by Otto Elster (1893). Before my grandfather owned the volume, it belonged to Hermann Duchardt, who was killed in the First World War. Like the other two books, it contains illustrations. It differs in this respect from the remaining part of the library, as the images in this book resemble images that form part of the colonial ethnographic library.

There are tables that illustrate different "Hottentot" and "Bushman"[2] "characters", and depict oxen carts, oxen drivers, village heads, horses, and gunfights. Namibia had become a German colony in 1884, and the book intends to prepare 'the matured youth' (*die reifere Jugend*) for the new regimes of power they were expected to participate in. Colonialism, an aspect that Kämper's analysis of youth language in literary works of the period ignores, was a salient topic in much of the literature offered to male audiences, besides militarism and nationalism. Elster's book not only fits into the genre of the adventure tale by providing a very detailed picture of its main characters' interiorities, their actions and history, but also links its adventurous story to contemporary figures and events, which makes it a prime example of propaganda literature. While the European protagonists of the book encounter various dangers, the matured reader is informed about the correlations of these dangers:

> Dass jetzt der König der Hereros, Maherero, mit den Deutschen einen Schutzvertrag abgeschlossen hatte, kam ihm [Jan Jonker] sehr ungelegen und er suchte nun eine größere Macht zusammenzubringen, um die Hereros mit einem Schlage zu vernichten. Der Tanzberg sollte der Sammelpunkt all jener kriegerisch gesinnten Stämme sein, welche sich dem Kriegszug gegen die Hereros anschließen wollten. Hendrik Witbooi mit seiner aus Bastards und Namas zusammengesetzten Bande war der erste, welcher den Tanzberg erreichte. [. . .] Während Hendrik Witbooi mit Abraham und den anderen Leuten auf Kundschaft und Viehdiebstahl ausgezogen war, hatte der größere Teil der ganzen Bande sich im Lager in der Schlucht am Tanzberge vereinigt. (Elster 1893: 56–57)
>
> [The fact that the king of Hereros, Maherero, had now concluded a protection contract with the Germans was very inconvenient to him [Jan Jonker] and he now sought to bring together a greater power in order to destroy the Hereros with one blow. The Tanzberg mountain was to be the gathering point for all those warlike tribes who wanted to join the war against the Hereros. Hendrik Witbooi with his gang composed of Bastards and Namas was the first to reach Tanzberg mountain. [. . .] While Hendrik Witbooi had moved out with Abraham and the other people in order to explore the area and steal cattle, the greater part of the whole gang gathered in the gorge on the Tanzberg mountain.]

Disguised as education and entertainment, these texts convey ideologies whose scope lay well beyond what young audiences were able to experience in their

---

[2] These terms are usually explained as the respective colonial labels for the Khoi and San groups of southern Africa, as colonial Others due to language (featuring clicks) and lifestyle. Anette Hoffmann (p.c., 2020), however, argues that the historical sources in the colonial archives tell a different story. The early colonial use of "Hottentot" refers to those Indigenous people who adopted certain practices of the Europeans, while "Bushman" refers to those communities who did not. In other words, this is a terminology of conquest rather than of linguistics, and only later – ignoring its historical semiotics – was adopted by anthropologists (and, of course, linguists).

daily lives, namely the lives of Others in the colonialized parts of the world. Adolescents here were encouraged to identify with norm-breaking heroes, who in the end would return to their homes or would be saved and taken back to from where they had been lost.

> Permanent war against permanent (left, socialist) revolution is one of Eco's fourteen characteristics of Ur-fascism.

Language in tales of adventure, as well as in stories about forest, home and nation was indeed creative, as argued by Kämper (and others), often making use of mimetic and transgressive strategies, very much like youth language after its construction as language-against-establishment. But in the late 19th and early-to-mid-20th century, it served a different rhetoric, as part of strategies of disciplining and of implementing colonial and imperial regimes of power. The use of a language that resembles registers used in the home or among fellow students (in everyday settings), and of a lexicon that emblematically indexicalizes class, dominance and power, is a means of the colonization of youth in early popular culture, disciplining young males into existences that were presented as resembling those of their forebears, but differed.

> Eco's study on Ur-fascism mentions appeal to precarious people and the exploitation of their resentment as one of its characteristic features.

This also holds true for the newly emerging cinema and other forms of popular culture, such as the radio play, for example. Outside the educational institutions such as school and university, and away from the paternal home with its reading suggestions, young audiences would have been offered something more modern. Yet, this often enough was similar fare. Many of the silent movies and early talkies on adventure and romance resemble the books from the attic in terms of tropes and motifs, language and attitude.

> Newspeak and propaganda which hinder critical thinking, something already noticed by Orwell [1949], are among the fourteen features that characterize Ur-fascism in Eco's book.

My grandfather would most likely have preferred a movie about nature above those on romance. In 1929, the German production *Pori* (von Dungern 1929) was introduced and advertised by a popular journal, the *Film-Magazin*, where an article on how the movie was made was published. Like in the books on nationalist topics and colonialism, the text introducing the film uses snippets of different (Indigenous) language in order to characterize the Other as being deficient and subaltern. The producer, Paul Curt von Gontard of the *Ostafrikanische Filmsyndikat* in Berlin, writes:

Wenn man nach Afrika kommt, wird man, gleichgültig wie man heißt oder welche Religion man hat, zunächst einmal wieder getauft, und zwar deshalb, weil sich die Eingeborenen unsere für sie unaussprechlichen Namen nicht merken können. [. . .] Meistens erhält man sogar zwei Namen: einen, mit dem man angeredet wird und einen, unter dem man von den Eingeborenen, wenn sie unter sich sind, besprochen wird. Der letzte ist meistens der treffendere, wenn auch nicht immer der schmeichelhaftere. Z. B. hieß ich wegen meines großen Texashutes, der in Afrika etwas Neues war, offiziell "Bwana Cofia" (Herr Hut). [. . .] Wenn aber meine guten, schwarzen Jungen um ihr Feuer saßen, den Maispamps mit ihren schwarzen Händen in kleine Kugeln rollten, in den Mund steckten, dazu, wie allabendlich, über die Weißen diskutierten und meistens kein gutes Haar an ihnen ließen, dann hieß es nicht mehr Bwana Cofia, sondern etwas ironisch "Bwana Piga Nayaga" (der Herr, der dauernd schießen muß). (von Gontard 1929: n.p.)

[When you come to Africa, regardless of what your name or religion is, you are baptized once more because the natives cannot remember our names, which are impossible to pronounce for them. [. . .] Most of the time you even get two names: one with which you are addressed, and one with which the natives talk about you when they are among themselves. The latter is usually the more appropriate, though not always the more flattering. For example, because of my large Texan hat, which was something new in Africa, I was officially called "Bwana Cofia" (Mr. Hat). [. . .] But when my good, black boys were sitting around their fire, rolling the corn mush into small balls with their black hands, sticking them in their mouths, and spoke about the Whites as usual, without saying much positive about them, then it was no longer called Bwana Cofia, but somewhat ironically referred to as "Bwana Piga Nayaga" (the man who has to shoot constantly).]

The Other names and teases, but as we have learned from Arminius' book, remains inferior. Class now translates into racist categories, and the Black skin replaces the poor appearance of the Polish menial or the poacher in the other, slightly earlier, texts. The narrator has grown up and talks about his "good black boys". Age, too, now translates into a racist category, and the colonized turn into children, perhaps youths. Their games with names are playful and never seem to end, like the provocative word play of the schoolboys in the books on schoolboys analysed in Kämper's text. Criticism and provocative practice get racialized, as well. The good Black boys, we are told, sit around the fire and criticize the Whites whom they cannot understand, like adolescents who cannot understand their patriarchal father but soon will, once they have grown up. There were blueprints for all this. Once the youthful reader Hermann Duchardt had matured and grown up, he went to war and died.

Fear of difference, such as racism, is one of the fourteen features that help to define Ur-fascism in Eco's posthumously published book.

4 Recollection

A confusing picture. The youth who were given youth literature to read, were asked to watch educative films, were made members of student fraternities, were told that their habitus and ways of speaking were perceived as elite practice, were basically socialized into fascism and led their lives as young adults in national-socialist Germany (cf. Haneke 2009). In his foreword to the German edition of Umberto Eco's *Il fascismo eterno* (2020), Roberto Saviano writes:

> Der Faschismus war keine Doktrin, sondern eine Rhetorik. Und dieser Erkenntnis liegt nicht nur seine [Eco's] scharfe Ablehnung der faschistischen Programme zugrunde, sondern auch sein genauer Blick auf die faschistische Rhetorik, die eher eine Rhetorik des Verlusts als eine des Gewinns ist – wenn man alles verliert, jedwede Art von Identität, die auf Kultur beruht, auf Arbeit, auf Träumen, dann bleibt einem nur die Gemeinsamkeit der Geburt, der Abstammung oder Zugehörigkeit, und man fragt sich: Bin ich in der Nachbarschaft geboren? In derselben Gegend? Mit der gleichen Hautfarbe? Mit den gleichen Gebeten? Wenn ja, dann kann es sein, dass sich ein gemeinsamer Boden auftut und dass dieser als Mittel zur Abwehr benutzt wird, um alle anderen auszuschließen.
>
> (Saviano 2020: 8)

> [Fascism was not a doctrine but a rhetoric. And this realization is based not only on his [Eco's] sharp rejection of the fascist programs, but also his close look at the fascist rhetoric, which is a rhetoric of loss rather than profit – if you lose everything, any kind of identity that is based on culture, on work, on dreams, then all that remains is the common ground of birth, descent or belonging, and one wonders: Was I born in the neighborhood? In the same area? With the same skin color? With the same prayers? If so, common ground may open up and be used as a means of defense to exclude everyone else.]

Saviano's comment helps to turn the gaze away from the Eurocentric images of colonial Others and from racialized Otherness, which had been so closely connected with the rhetoric of deficiency – the colonized body and the language that belonged to it, the cultural practices of the colonized constructed as deficient, lacking, allochronic (e.g., Fabian 1983). Saviano is interested in what Eco's dissection of fascism helps to demonstrate when we change the perspective a bit and look at the effects of fascism among those who lead its rhetoric. The deficiency he refers to is the lack of almost all aspects of humanity, which finally includes the loss of the ability to be hospitable, as the Other is not given access any longer.

> *Nationalism and conspiracy theory are among the fourteen features of Ur-fascism in Eco's study.*

This void must be impossible to fill, even though that might be easy to conceal. I suppose that Freud's (1920) observation about desire having an intense relationship with the dynamics of completion is important to consider here, also intensity and its potential of the experience of death (Deleuze and Guattari 1974). After the end of historical fascism (which is not, Eco cautions us not to forget, the end of fascism itself) the consequence of this experience was not grief but the performance of completion. Collecting things and images was an important activity. In the attic, there was an album of collectible picture cards (featuring historical personalities such as Körner, Blücher and the Queen of Württemberg). The younger family members established collections of postcards, beer mats, bottle caps, stamps – as long as they were already used – coins, and butterflies. Some of these collections remained unfinished projects, such as the postcard collection, whereas others have been completed. Specific series of stamps were completed, series of beer mats, coins of a particular period of time, butterflies from a given place. The completion of a collection creates an illusion of agency and sovereignty, I suppose. Albums with photographs piled up, completing memories of picknicks and sightseeing trips.

In the 1950s and 1960s, two of my grand aunts and my great-grandmother became "informants" for linguists. They were asked for lexical items in their dialect, which by then had begun to fall out of use. A collection of words was remembered. Many of them had not been written before but had been used in everyday, informal speech, mostly when these women had still been young. I remember some examples, which conclude this contribution. In terms of their expressivity, playful use of humor, irony and ambiguity, as well as in their orality, they resemble characteristic examples of youth languages other than those that surface in the books from the attic:

Table 17.1: A collection of words.

Deichselhersch	'horse'	< towing bar deer
Gemiesraup	'gardener (fem.)'	< vegetable caterpillar
Rückschwätzapparat	'telephone'	< speaking-back machine
Blechboggel	'plumber'	< tin tooler
Breggelcher lache	'vomit'	< laugh nuggets
Ejeujeuche	'whiny child'	(onomatopoeic)
Fuijaggel	'untidy child/lad'	< ugh-jacket
Aal Groggel	'old woman'	< old + (onomatopoeic pejorative term)
Gollevielchen	'marybird'	< golden bird

References

Arminius, Wilhelm. 1914. *Der Kraftsucher*. Mainz: Scholz.
Block, David. 2014. *Social class in applied linguistics*. Oxon and New York: Routledge.
Burke, Peter. 2012. *A social history of knowledge, II*. Cambridge: Polity.
Deleuze, Gilles and Félix Guattari. 1974. *Anti-Ödipus. Kapitalismus und Schizophrenie I*. Frankfurt am Main: Suhrkamp.
Derrida, Jacques. 1998. *Monolingualism of the other*. Redwood City: Stanford University Press.
von Dungern, Adolph. 1929. *Pori*. Berlin: Ostafrikanisches Filmsyndikat.
Eco, Umberto. 2020. *Der ewige Faschismus*. Munich: Hanser.
Elster, Otto. 1893. *Die Goldgräber von Angra Pequena*. Leipzig: Brockhaus.
Fabian, Johannes. 1983. *Time and the other*. New York: Columbia University Press.
Fanon, Frantz. 1986 [1952]. *Black skin, white masks*. With an introductions by Homi Bhabha and Ziauddin Sardar. Translated by Charles L. Markmann. London: Pluto Press.
Freud, Sigmund. 1920. *Jenseits des Lustprinzips*. Leipzig, Vienna and Zurich: Internationaler Psychoanalytischer Verlag.
Gandert, Gero (ed.). 1993. *Der Film der Weimarer Republik. 1929*. Berlin and New York: De Gruyter.
von Gontard, Paul Curt. 1929. Der Bwana Yoka. *Film Magazin* 37. n.p.
Haneke, Michael. 2009. *Das weiße Band*. Burbank: Warner Home Video.
Hobsbawm, Eric and Terence O. Ranger (eds.). 1983. *The invention of tradition*. Cambridge: Cambridge University Press.
Hollington, Andrea and Nico Nassenstein. 2015. Conclusion and outlook: Taking new directions in the study of youth language practices. In Nico Nassenstein and Andrea Hollington (eds.), *Youth language practices in Africa and beyond*, 345–356. Berlin: De Gruyter Mouton.
Kämper, Heidrun. 2001. Jugendsprache um 1900 und die schöne Literatur. *Der Deutschunterricht* 1 (2001). 47–58.
Kleinschmidt, Albert. 1910. *Im Forsthause Falkenhorst*. Gießen: Emil Roth.
Kotzde, Wilhelm. 2014. Editor's note. In Wilhelm Arminius, *Der Kraftsucher*, n.p. Mainz: Scholz.
Objartel, Georg. 2016. *Sprache und Lebensform deutscher Studenten im 18. und 19. Jahrhundert*. Berlin: De Gruyter.
Orwell, George. 1984 [1949]. *1984*. Frankfurt am Main: Ullstein.
Saviano, Roberto. 2020. Vorwort. In Umberto Eco, *Der ewige Faschismus*, 7–14. Munich: Hanser.
Thurlow, Crispin. 2005. Deconstructing adolescent communication. In Angie Williams and Crispin Thurlow (eds), *Talking adolescence: Perspectives on communication in the teenage years*, 53–72. New York: Peter Lang.
Weber, Max. 1978 [1921]. *Economy and society*. Berkeley, Los Angeles and London: University of California Press.

Subject Index

abbreviations 34, 35, 37, 39, 40, 43–45, 47, 68–74, 79, 98–100, 225
acronym 42, 44, 45, 68, 69, 71, 72, 79, 86
address terms 19, 89–92, 194, 234, 237, 343
agency 20, 177, 179, 181, 183, 190, 196, 198, 267, 282, 284, 338, 339, 349
Amazon 17, 121, 122, 123
anticipatory change 121, 125, 126
applicative 16, 49, 51–56, 60–62
Argentina, Argentinian 141, 225, 226, 228, 230, 231, 233, 235
Arnhem Land 21, 315–333
Australia 21, 124, 315–333

Bahasa Gaul 7, 8, 16, 31–47, 297, 298
belonging 2, 16, 19, 33, 34, 38, 39, 43, 64, 180, 181, 183, 184, 196, 197, 243, 268, 277, 279, 293–310, 348
borrow, borrowing 13, 31, 34, 35, 44, 49, 56–63, 101, 107, 146, 150, 160, 194, 272, 278
boundary, -ies. See social boundary, -ies and linguistic boundary, -ies
Buenos Aires 11, 19, 225, 226, 233, 234, 237

causative 16, 49, 51–53, 55, 56, 58, 60–62
Central African Republic 5, 11, 20, 265, 267, 268, 278, 286
Chile, Chilean 140, 225, 226, 228, 230, 231, 233, 234, 235
cigar(-ette), see tobacco
clippings 98, 99
CMC 15, 16, 67, 68, 71, 74, 75, 79, 85–87
code-switching, code-mixing 10, 32, 34, 38, 39, 43, 46, 131, 150, 159, 205, 247, 254, 255, 261, 328, 329
collaborative research 317, 324
Colloquial Indonesian 294, 296, 297, 299, 300, 303, 305–307, 309, 310
Colloquial Jakartan Indonesian 2, 297
colonial Others 345, 348
colonial/colonialism 7, 13, 18, 106, 165, 166, 167, 169, 170, 174, 175, 176, 177, 281, 282, 283, 284, 285, 289, 290, 318, 337, 340, 341, 344, 345, 346, 348
colonization of youth 346,
computer-mediated communication, see CMC
criminals, gangsters 33, 36, 52, 87, 98, 100, 110, 191, 193, 268, 273, 279
critical youth language 144

decolonial 8, 13, 18, 23, 139, 144, 163, 165, 166, 167, 172, 176, 177, 178, 267, 268, 270, 282, 283, 287, 289
derivation 16, 36, 49–63, 216
Diaspora v, 118, 243, 267, 270, 323
digital 2, 9, 15, 16, 19, 29, 30, 86, 98, 102, 144, 243, 245, 246, 247, 248, 249, 250, 251, 256, 261, 262, 322
discourse 7, 13, 14, 69, 74, 87, 89, 121, 124, 131, 132, 142, 149, 152, 166, 176, 179, 181, 183, 185, 188, 225, 231, 235, 236, 237, 261, 267, 283, 293, 305, 310, 333
DR Congo 5, 7, 9–14, 16, 18, 49, 50, 51, 62, 63, 107, 139, 141, 145, 153, 282

East Tucanoan languages 121, 123, 134
education 8, 12, 13, 16, 18, 20, 36, 51, 82, 109, 121, 165–173, 175–177, 183, 190, 191, 192, 243, 251, 260, 277, 280, 282, 297, 322, 323, 337, 340, 344–346
Efik 183, 192–195
emoticons 101, 308
ethnography 4, 142, 266, 268,
euphemism 17, 42, 67, 68, 71, 72, 74, 76, 78, 79, 276

face (negative face, positive face) 71, 75, 79
fascism 337, 339, 348–349
female, girls -- see gender
focus group 179, 183–185
fractal recursivity 270, 273, 286
fraternity (*Burschenschaft*) 340–341

gender vii, 11–12, 112–115, 117, 151, 154, 179–182, 187–189, 204, 208, 221, 231–235, 300, 302, 307, 315–316, 329, 342–346
generational differences 5–6, 32–33, 46, 86, 97, 106, 117, 121–135, 166, 208, 246, 315–333
Germany 5, 197, 337–349
Godobé 5, 7, 11, 16, 243, 278–281, 284–287

hangout culture 34–35
Hausa 192
hip hop 7, 96–97, 106, 197, 243, 268, 271–275, 282–286, 319, 322
humour/humor 14, 141–162, 255, 349
hybridization, hybrid 29, 67–72, 86, 317, 332

icon, iconization 86, 270, 286
ICT, see technology
identity/ies 1–8, 11–12, 15, 29, 31–47, 49–52, 71, 106, 114, 122–123, 139, 143, 146, 161, 166, 174–177, 179–198, 205, 208, 221, 228, 243, 270–273, 277, 282, 285–287, 302, 310, 318–325, 332–333, 348
ideology/ies 1–2, 6–9, 12–14, 29–30, 51, 139, 166, 170, 176–177, 179–184, 196–198, 243–244, 245–262, 265–287, 316–317, 320–327, 333, 337–346
Igbo 188, 192, 194
index/indexicality/ies 6, 11, 18–19, 139, 143–146, 162, 181, 183, 197, 250, 260, 271–272, 286, 293–299, 308–310, 317–319, 328–332, 346
Indonesia/n 7–8, 11–12, 31–47, 208, 293–311
intensifier/intensification 71, 89, 94–95
Internet 15–16, 86–87, 122, 133–135, 197, 246, 309, 322
inverted language 31, 33, 37, 159

Jamaica/n 87, 95–96
Javanese 7, 31–47, 208, 293–311

Kinshasa 14, 50–52, 63, 153–160

language ecologies 310, 316–333
language game 10, 19, 42–44, 203–224, 279
languaging vi, 10, 270, 284, 317, 323–324

Lingala/Lingala ya Bayankee/Yanké 9, 13–14, 49–63, 141, 153–161, 269
linguistic biography 316–317, 323–326
linguistic boundary, -ies 106, 126, 213, 214, 216, 220, 232, 266, 278, 280, 286, 317, 318, 326, 328, 332
linguistic exogamy 121, 123
linguistic styling 146, 150–153, 160–161

Malangan Javanese 7, 11, 293–310
male, boys, see gender
Maningrida 20, 316–333
media vi, 14, 74, 79, 108–109, 190–192, 277, 310
media ideology/ies 19
metapragmatics 245–262, 265
mode-switching 15, 245–262
morphology, morphological pattern(s) 9, 31–47, 49–64, 67–82, 121, 153, 220–221, 276, 278–279
movie trailer 19, 20, 293–300, 303–305, 307–310
Multicultural London English 17, 85, 86, 88
multilingualism 18, 106, 121, 123, 220, 316, 317, 320, 322–324, 326–330, 333
multimodality 101
music VI, 12, 18, 35, 80, 93, 96, 100, 106, 146, 165, 173, 177, 181, 182, 194, 197, 246, 265, 271–275, 278–281, 283, 285–287, 294, 300–303, 329, 330

narrative 18, 20, 131, 135, 142, 146–153, 155, 157, 160–162, 179, 184, 197, 266, 293–296, 299, 300, 303, 310, 323
nation/national 3, 7, 18, 20, 32, 46, 107, 109, 121, 153, 165, 245, 277, 278, 283, 293, 294, 297, 299, 308–310, 338, 341, 342, 344–346, 348
negation 42, 47, 64, 94, 129, 135, 198, 304, 311
neutral meaning (of bad words) 231
New Ireland 19, 140, 203, 205–209, 214, 216–221
new words 42, 204
Nigeria 7, 13, 18, 89, 140, 169, 179, 180, 182, 183, 188, 192, 197, 198
Nigerian Pidgin 183, 192, 193, 195
norm-breaking heroes 346

Subject Index

orthography 53, 101, 123, 128, 133, 217, 278
Othering 20
Otherness 183, 269, 282, 340, 348

participant observation 15, 18, 123, 179, 183, 184
periphrastic constructions 17, 49, 50, 53, 55, 60–64
persuasion 19, 20, 293, 294, 296, 303, 304, 310
phonological change 125, 127, 129–131
politics/policy 16, 18, 165, 167, 170, 171, 175, 180, 277
pragmatic function 72, 74, 75, 78, 87, 92
pragmatic(s) 10, 18, 29, 30, 67, 68, 70, 71, 73, 74, 75, 77, 78, 79, 92, 93, 139, 141–144, 160, 162, 231, 232, 236, 281
proud sense (of local rootedness) 34

rap/rapper 17, 85, 86, 88–90, 92, 96, 98, 101, 102, 188, 265, 271–273, 280, 281, 285, 286
reciprocal 16, 49, 51–54, 57, 58, 60–62, 64, 194, 253
reflexive 49, 51–53, 56–58, 60–62, 64
repertoire(s) 10, 29, 102, 130, 153, 166, 183, 194, 198, 253, 315–317, 320, 321, 323–328, 331, 339–341
resistance/resistant 12, 18, 20, 139, 165, 167, 168, 170, 172–176, 180, 270, 273, 282, 287, 316, 320, 338
ritual 18, 71, 161, 165, 174, 179, 181, 182, 188, 189, 195, 204, 205, 284, 328, 341
Rufumbira 243, 168, 271–274, 286
rural, rurality VI, 2, 18, 19, 51, 106, 111, 114, 170, 179–183, 185, 186, 189, 191, 197, 198, 337
Ruyaye 243, 268, 275–277, 286, 287

Sango 5, 7, 11, 13, 14, 16, 243, 268, 278–281, 284–287
Santiago de Chile 225, 226, 234
school novel (*Schulroman*) 20, 342
secret language 19, 203–205, 208, 211, 219, 221, 279
semantic change 10, 96, 236

semiotic(s) 19, 29, 143, 198, 245–252, 256, 257, 260, 266, 268, 270, 274, 285–287, 329, 333, 345
Sepitori 17, 105, 108–117
social boundary, -ies 20, 232, 183, 243, 244, 265, 268, 278, 280, 285, 286
social language 31, 33, 297
social media 14–15, 18, 35, 37, 85–88, 122, 133, 135, 190, 197, 243, 245–262, 322
social network(-s), (-ing) 85–102, 246
song(-s)/sing(-ing) 5, 88, 96, 97, 98, 100, 139, 167, 168, 172–175, 205, 272, 273, 275, 280, 284, 285, 303, 315, 316, 329, 332
Sotho/Sesotho 105–117
South Africa 8, 11–13, 17, 18, 105–117, 141, 145, 148, 149
Spain/Spanish 70, 86, 100, 140, 177, 225–237
sports/sports education 18, 139, 165–177, 181
street kids 36
student jargon (*Burschensprache*) 7, 20, 243, 340, 341
stylect 106, 146, 150, 152, 152, 272
stylize, stylization, 18, 154, 265, 270, 272, 273, 283, 287
subtitle(-s) 300, 303, 305–307, 309
syllable/syllable structure 10, 36, 37, 125, 127, 140, 204, 208–221

taboo (words) 11, 35, 42, 43, 67, 68, 71, 72, 76–78, 97, 144, 145, 154, 205, 225, 226
Tariana 5, 17, 18, 121–135
technology 15–16, 85–102, 194–195, 245–262, 296
Tiang 205–220
tobacco 140, 179–198
Tok Pisin 19, 203, 205–209, 215–221
translanguaging VI, 10, 317
Tsotsitaal 7, 11, 14, 17, 105–117, 141, 146, 150, 151, 196, 282
Tswana/Setswana 106–108, 111, 112, 114, 116
Twitter 15, 17, 85–102, 109, 115

Uganda 5, 8, 18, 20, 107, 139, 165–178, 243, 265–292
urban vernacular, see vernacular

Vaupés River Basin 121–123, 129
verbal derivation, see derivation
vernacular/urban vernacular 13, 17, 88, 94, 105–107, 293, 294
vocative use of bad words 233–235, 305

word formation 17, 29, 44, 67, 68, 72, 89

Yanké/Lingala ya Bayankee 16, 18, 49–64, 141, 153, 160, 166, 269
Yogyakarta VII, 16, 31–46
Yoruba 192, 195

www.ingramcontent.com/pod-product-compliance
Lightning Source LLC
Chambersburg PA
CBHW050512170426
43201CB00013B/1935